MANAGING WITH
MICROSOFT® PROJECT

How to Order:

For information on quantity discounts, contact the publisher: Prima Publishing, P.O. Box 1260BK, Rocklin, CA 95677-1260; (916) 632-4400. On your letterhead include information concerning the intended use of the books and the number of books you wish to purchase. For individual orders, turn to the back of this book for more information.

MANAGING WITH MICROSOFT® PROJECT

Lisa A. Bucki

Prima Publishing

PRIMA is a registered trademark of Prima Publishing, a division of Prima Communications, Inc.

Prima Publishing is a registered trademark of Prima Communications, Inc.

Prima Publishing, Rocklin, California 95677.

Project Editor: Chris Haidri

Copy Editor: Kathy Simpson

Technical Reviewer: Marty Wyatt

Indexer: Sharon Hilgenberg

Windows, Project, and Microsoft are registered trademarks of Microsoft Corporation. Screen shots are reprinted with permission from Microsoft Corporation.

Important: If you are having serious problems installing or running Microsoft Project (for example, the program no longer starts and you get an error message) and are a registered user, call Microsoft technical support at 206-635-7155 or check the online help system for technical support information. Prima Publishing cannot provide software support.

Prima Publishing and the author have attempted throughout this book to distinguish proprietary trademarks from descriptive terms by following the capitalization style used by the manufacturer.

Information contained in this book has been obtained by Prima Publishing from sources believed to be reliable. However, because of the possibility of human or mechanical error by our sources, Prima Publishing, or others, the Publisher does not guarantee the accuracy, adequacy, or completeness of any information and is not responsible for any errors or omissions or the results obtained from use of such information.

ISBN: 0-7615-0688-8

Library of Congress Catalog Card Number: 96-68064

Printed in the United States of America

96 97 98 99 BB 10 9 8 7 6 5 4 3 2 1

To Steve and Bo, who always know how to help me get the job done.

CONTENTS AT A GLANCE

TABLE OF CONTENTS

Chapter 5: Resolving Overallocations and Overbooked Resources

Chapter 6: Optimizing the Schedule

Chapter 7: Comparing Progress versus Your Baseline Plan

Acknowledgments

The team members at Prima Computer Books deserve my thanks and
congratulations for bringing this project together. I valued the support
of Don Roche, Alan Harris, and Heather Urschel, as well as their virtual
team members Jenny Watson, Chris Haidri, and Kathy Simpson. Finally,
thanks to all of those who made this book look and handle like a dream—
the folks in production, proofreading, and manufacturing at Prima.

Introduction

Over the past few decades, thousands of software tools have emerged to help computer users tackle a variety of tasks. Some of these tools are ubiquitous, like word processing and spreadsheet programs. Others address specialized needs, performing tasks such as scanning your system for viruses or organizing graphic images stored on your hard disk.

It wasn't surprising, then, that Microsoft and other companies developed software tools to automate the process of project management. Early efforts were clunky, and weren't much of an improvement over the time-honored tradition of drawing project flowcharts on a whiteboard in an office or conference room. Many programs lacked the ability to handle key components of project management, such as cost analysis and communication. Thus, there wasn't much payoff for learning how to use some of these early products.

In the last few years, however, the developers of the leading project management program, Microsoft Project, have taken great steps in honing this software tool into an effective management weapon. Project 4.1 for Windows 95 (as well as the most recent version for Windows 3.1x, version 4.0) covers all the bases, enabling you to review and control many facets of a project from start to finish.

With Project, there's a significant payoff for your time investment in learning how to use the software. Not only will you be more organized, but your team will be more effective, you'll be able to anticipate problems, and your ability to make resource estimates will improve, so that over time you'll become a stronger manager.

This book is designed to help you make the most of your company's financial investment in Project, as well as your professional investment—the time you'll spend learning to work with Project, and the impact Project will have on your performance.

Who Should Read This Book

This book assumes that you or your company have already purchased and installed the Project software, and all the supporting tools needed to work effectively with Project. As such, you won't find information here designed to help you justify using Project in business. Instead, this book is for anyone who suddenly needs to work with Project, such as:

- Managers and assistants whose company has adopted Project
- Managers beginning to use Project as a method to standardize the planning process
- Project or team leaders who need to use Project to create graphical printouts of task assignments, or to allocate resources between several projects
- Professional project managers who have purchased Project to implement an organized planning system for their companies or clients

Where to Find Information Inside

Whether you review the chapters here from start to finish, or browse around to review specific subjects when you need information about them, Managing Microsoft Project is structured for easy use. Here's a brief review of what you'll find in each part of the book:

Part 1, "Project Management Basics," focuses on the minimum you need to know to set up a project. You'll learn how to create a file in Project, set the overall project parameters, define the tasks that must be completed, and indicate the resources that will be used to complete each task.

Part 2, "Making Adjustments to Projects," helps you learn to work out project kinks, and more. Here, you look at identifying and resolving resource overcommitments, adjusting tasks, and tracking how successfully a project is progressing.

Part 3, "Viewing, Formatting, and Printing Projects," discusses using the information you've so diligently captured in Project. Here, you'll look at how to choose different graphic formats for a project, as well as how to print, work with forms and reports, review costs, use outlining features, and control other formatting.

Part 4, "Handling Multiple Projects," builds on the skills you've previously mastered, showing you how to move and copy information between projects, create and use project templates, combine projects and resources, and use master projects and subprojects.

Part 5, "Working with Advanced Features," covers how to share information using Microsoft Exchange, customize the way you work with Project, and create macros to make your work in Project even more efficient.

Conventions Used Inside

To make it easier for you to use this book, Prima uses "shorthand," or conventions for consistently presenting different kinds of information. You should review these conventions before moving on in the book:

- **Key combinations**—Pressing and holding one key, then pressing another key is called a *key combination*. In this book, key combinations are indicated by a plus sign (+) separating the keys you have to press. For example, Ctrl+O is a key combination that requires you to press and hold the Ctrl key, then press the O key.

- **Menu names, commands, and dialog box options**—In virtually all Windows programs, each menu name, command name, and dialog box option name contains an underlined letter called a *selection letter*. The selection letter is used to make that particular selection via the keyboard, sometimes as part of a key combination. In this book, all selection letters are indicated as an underlined letter, as in <u>V</u>iew.

- **Text you type**—When you need to type some text to complete a procedure, or when I'm providing an example of text you can type in, the text you need to type appears in bold, as in the following:

Type the name for the task, such as **Request Price Quotes**.

Special Elements

At times, I'll provide you with information that supplements the discussion at hand. This special information is set off in easy-to-identify sidebars, so you can review or skip these extras as you see fit. You'll find the following types of special elements in this book:

Tips provide shortcuts to make your job easier, or better ways to accomplish tasks.

Notes provide supplemental information that are a bit more technical or that describe special situations you might encounter.

Cautions protect you from what can be your worst computing enemy—yourself. When particular operations are risky and might cause you to lose some of your work, I'll forewarn you in these boxes.

Contacting Prima Publishing

We welcome your feedback, and would like to hear more about the kind of help you need, other computing topics you'd like to read about, or any other questions you have. Please use the reader response card in the back of this book to get in touch with us.

For a catalog, call 1-800-632-8676, or visit our World Wide Web site at **http://www.primapublishing.com**.

PART I

PROJECT MANAGEMENT BASICS

CHAPTER 1

GETTING STARTED WITH PROJECT

So, you've broken Microsoft Project out of the box and installed it (or your MIS person has). You're all set up, but where do you go? With many applications, how to get started is obvious. To begin working in Microsoft Word, for example, you just start typing. In Microsoft Excel, you just click and type numbers and formulas.

With Project, the starting point is not so obvious, but don't worry. This chapter and the next one introduce the steps you should take to begin your work and set up a project.

This chapter covers the following topics:

- The benefits of project management
- Key tools provided in Project
- How to start Project
- Online help resources
- How to exit Project

Understanding Why You Need to Manage Projects

"Project management" used to be primarily a catch phrase used to flesh out a résumé. At best, in many cases, it referred to being the keeper of a long to-do list, and dealing with problems once someone else had pointed them out. In its broadest sense, *project management* was an individual's ability to complete most of his or her own work assignments.

In today's business climate, project management has emerged into a serious discipline that's being incorporated into programs at technical schools and universities worldwide. For example, certain MBA programs include project management courses. Some international organizations, such as the Project Management Institute, train project management professionals, certify them with designations such as Project Management Professional, and provide accreditation for project management courses. Finally, some consulting firms now specialize in providing project management services, and some businesses have developed formalized project manager positions.

Even if you don't have specific training in project management, you—like millions of others—might be discovering that project management skills are essential to career success. You need to have a precise handle on the steps involved in a project, how many resources you'll need, how long each portion of the project will last, and how much all of it will cost.

Business trends from the past decade are making those with project management skills increasingly valuable as managers or team leaders. Here are just a few examples:

- The dreaded corporate downsizing compels us all to accomplish more with fewer resources. As resources become more scarce, you have to plan further in advance, and have to become more skilled at identifying and eliminating conflicts.
- In today's smaller workgroup or team environment, each team member's role becomes less specialized. Thus, you must be prepared to carefully define each person's role in the context of a particular project.

- To bring products to market more quickly, most companies distribute tasks across several departments so that different project phases can be handled concurrently. In such cross-departmental situations, tracking performance and communicating expectations becomes more challenging and necessary.
- Companies that are under headcount restrictions—or that are unwilling to invest in specialized technology—increasingly rely on outside contractors for a variety of functions. Project management techniques and tools can help in keeping these outside resources on track.

Management Techniques Offered in Project

Keeping your arms around far-flung details and resources used to require several tools. You would outline the project in a word processor, budget with a spreadsheet, and so on. Project handles all the key facets of project planning, blending traditional project management models such as Gantt charts and critical path analysis with more contemporary techniques such as printing custom calendars and importing information from other programs. With Project, you can track the completion of various tasks, manage costs, reallocate resources, and more.

Overall, the process you follow when you use Project is to create a schedule by defining the tasks that need to be completed, determining the probable cost for each task, and determining what people, supplies, contractors, and other resources are needed to complete the task. Once the schedule is established, you can fine-tune it to decrease the total timeframe, deal with resource conflicts, and so on. Finally, you can track the team's progress toward completing the project, and communicate the schedule to others from start to finish by printing an overall chart, printing charts about individual resources, generating reports for your manager, and e-mailing information to other team members.

Thus, Project offers a variety of techniques for establishing, modifying, and managing the parameters for each project plan you pull together.

Key Benefits of Using Project

As with many other new types of software, users often wonder whether it's worth the time investment to learn the Project program and enter all the necessary information about a project. Why not simply stick with a word processor and spreadsheet to get the job done? Well, because you don't want to have a regular hammer when the job calls for a sledgehammer or jackhammer. Project not only makes the basic job of managing projects easier, but also offers features and capabilities that give you more control over the scope of the project.

You'll realize the following benefits if you use Project as a planning and management tool:

- **Get your arms around more information.**—Project can track 9,999 tasks per project, 9,999 resources per project, and more.
- **Automatically create project diagrams.**—Project automatically generates Gantt and PERT charts, as well as calendars, to provide a look at how project tasks relate, and a method to relay information to others.
- **Track specific aspects of the project and anticipate problems.**—You can take a look at costs, the commitments of a particular resource, and more.
- **Track overall progress.**—As you enter task completion dates, you can compare progress with the original plan.
- **Generate forms and reports to share information.**—Use a variety of predefined forms and reports, or create custom forms for particular situations.
- **Communicate via e-mail.**—Project is optimized to enable you to share project information via existing e-mail tools, such as Microsoft Mail and Microsoft Exchange.

Starting Project

As with most other Windows 95 programs, the easiest way to start Project is via the Windows Taskbar:

1. Click the Start menu button, then click Programs.
2. Click Microsoft Project.

If Project doesn't appear as a choice on the Start menu, follow these steps to start the program:

1. Double-click the My Computer icon on your desktop to open the My Computer window.

2. Double-click the icon for the drive where Project is installed.

3. By default, Project installs to a subfolder in the Msoffice folder, along with other Microsoft Office applications. Thus, first double-click the icon for the Msoffice folder to open it and display the Project subfolder, named Winproj. If you chose not to install Project in a subfolder of the Msoffice folder, or gave the folder another name, you should open that folder instead. Double-click the icon for your Project folder to display its contents (see Fig. 1.1, in which my Project folder—named Project—is shown).

Figure 1.1
The Project folder, or whatever it's called on your system, contains all the icons for the Project program.

Project icon   Project shortcut

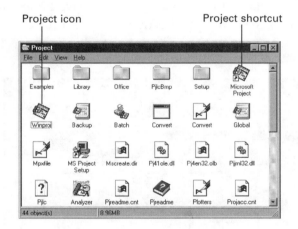

4. Double-click the Winproj icon (or the Microsoft Project shortcut) to start Project.

TIP: If you want faster access to Project, move the shortcut icon from the Project window to the desktop. To do so, place the mouse pointer on the Microsoft Project shortcut icon, press the right mouse button, and drag the icon to the desktop. Release the mouse button, then click <u>M</u>ove here on the shortcut menu that appears.

No matter what method you use to start Project, by default you'll see the Welcome! startup screen shown in Figure 1.2. This screen offers four choices for how to proceed, as well as a check box:

- Create Your First Project—Click this button to use the Up and Running tutorial, which walks you through the process of creating a project schedule.

- Take a Short Guided Tour—Click this button to view an on-screen presentation about Project and its tools.

- Open Your Last File—Click this button to open the project file you were working with when you last exited Project (unless, of course, this is your first time using Project).

- Work On Your Own—Click this button to go directly to a new, blank project file.

- Don't display this startup screen again—Select this box before clicking any of the other buttons to have Project skip the Welcome! screen and go directly to a blank project file during subsequent startups.

Figure 1.2
The Welcome! screen enables you to start working with Project in a variety of ways.

Understanding the Project Screen

When Project displays a new, blank project, the screen looks like Figure 1.3. By default, you'll see the Gantt Chart view for the new project. This screen enables you to enter tasks for your project. In the left pane of the screen, you enter the name of the task, its duration, and more. (Chapter 2, "Setting Up a Project," covers creating tasks in more detail.) The right pane displays each task you create as a graphical bar in a weekly schedule, so you can see at a glance how long a task lasts, or where tasks overlap in time.

Figure 1.3
This Gantt Chart view is the default view for a new project.

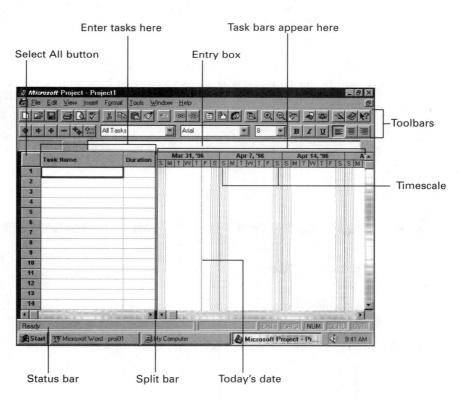

The top of the screen displays a title bar and menu bar with commands, as in other Windows applications. Below the menu bar, two toolbars are displayed by default; each toolbar button is a shortcut for executing a particular command. A text entry box appears between the toolbars and the panes where you enter data; you'll use this box to enter and edit task entries. The box changes in appearance when you use it, as you'll learn in the next chapter.

Looking at the Toolbars

As noted in the preceding section, Project by default displays two toolbars, Standard (top) and Formatting. To discover what a particular
toolbar button does, simply place the mouse pointer on it to display a
yellow tooltip describing the button (see Fig. 1.4).

Figure 1.4
Point to a toolbar
button to learn
what it does.

Project enables you to control toolbar display to select the shortcuts
you prefer to work with, and to control how much of your screen is
taken up by toolbars. As shown in Figure 1.5, you can drag a toolbar to
another location on-screen, which automatically places the toolbar in a
floating window that you can resize by dragging any of its borders.

A check means that a toolbar is being displayed.

Right-click a toolbar for a toolbar shortcut menu.

Figure 1.5
In Project, you can
make your toolbars
more convenient by
converting them to
floating windows.

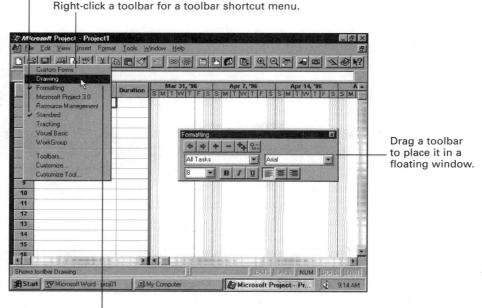

Drag a toolbar
to place it in a
floating window.

Click to check or uncheck a toolbar.

The fastest way to choose which toolbars appear on-screen is to right-click a toolbar to display the toolbars shortcut menu. A check beside a toolbar name in the list indicates that the toolbar is presently displayed (toggled on). To select or deselect a toolbar, click its name on this shortcut menu. To close the shortcut menu without changing a toolbar selection, click outside the menu (or press Esc).

Getting Help When You Need It

Project offers several different "flavors" of help, via the Help menu as well as two tools on the Standard toolbar. The most common way to start working with the help system is to access the list of available help topics. You can do this in either of the following ways:

- Open the <u>H</u>elp menu and click Microsoft Project <u>H</u>elp Topics.
- Click the Help Topics button on the Standard toolbar, which by default is the second-from-last button at the right end of the toolbar.

TIP: For more information about Project and other Microsoft products, visit the Microsoft home page on the Web at `http://www.microsoft.com`.

Displaying the help topics (see Fig. 1.6) enables you to choose from among four tabs, each offering a different kind of help:

- **Contents**—The Contents tab lists several "books" or topic areas within the help system. To view the topics within a book, double-click the book so that its icon changes to an open book and its contents (additional books and topics) are displayed. Specific topics are indicated by a page icon with a question mark. Double-click any topic to view it. To close a book, if needed, also double-click it. This tab is ideal for browsing through the available help.
- **Index**—If you have a rough idea of the topic you're searching for and how it might be referenced in Help, click the Index tab. The top text box prompts you to type all or part of the

topic you want information about. The list at the bottom scrolls to display the topics that most closely match your entry. Whenever you see an entry you want to view in the bottom list, double-click it (or click it and then click <u>D</u>isplay).

Figure 1.6
Once you access the Help Topics dialog box, you can click a tab to select the kind of help you need.

- **Find**—The Find tab allows you to search to find terms used within help topics, enabling you to zero in on pertinent details. The first time you choose the Find tab, the Find Setup Wizard dialog box appears. This dialog box lets you control how many terms appear in the Find database; follow the on-screen prompts to build the database. Once the Find tab becomes active, type the word(s) to be searched for in the top text box. To further narrow the search, make a selection from the second box, which presents a scrolling list of terms similar to those you've typed. If the term you want to view appears in the bottom scrolling list, double-click it. Otherwise, click the Find Si<u>m</u>ilar (which, when available, finds topics related to the selected topic, not necessarily direct matches) or <u>F</u>ind Now button to display a list of possible matches in the bottom box.

- **Answer Wizard**—This feature enables you to ask for help in plain English. You can access this feature (see Fig. 1.7) by clicking the Answer Wizard tab (or by opening the <u>H</u>elp menu and clicking Answer <u>W</u>izard). Type your question in the upper text box, and then click <u>S</u>earch. A list of topics that might answer your question appears in the lower box. To view a topic from this list, double-click it (or click it and then click <u>D</u>isplay).

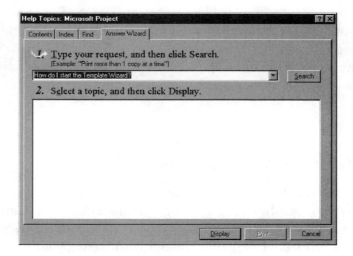

One last toolbar tool can provide instant help for the task at hand. Click the Help icon on the Standard toolbar (the last button on the right). The mouse pointer turns into a question mark pointer. Click the on-screen item that you're curious about, and Project displays a description of it.

TIP: Most dialog boxes have a Help button you can click to view the help topic for that dialog box. For a description of a particular dialog box option, click the question mark button in the upper-right corner, and then click the option you're wondering about.

Once you've displayed a help topic in its own window, you can click the <u>O</u>ptions button in that window to display a menu with options for working with the help topic information. Choosing <u>A</u>nnotate from the menu, for example, displays a window where you can add your own comments to the help topic. Choose C<u>o</u>py to copy the help topic contents to the Windows Clipboard, so you can paste that information into another document; if you select part of the Help topic by dragging over it before you choose Copy, then only the selection is copied. Print Topic enables you to print the help topic for easy reference. Font enables you to adjust the text size in the help topic display. Keep Help on Top enables you to control whether or not the help window remains in the foreground as you continue working in Project and other applications. Finally, Use System Colors lets you toggle between the default help colors (when this menu choice is unchecked) and the currently-selected Windows 95 colors (when this menu choice is checked).

Working with Files

As in all other applications, in Project you must store your work by saving it to a file on your computer's hard disk. You won't be able to track your project's progress if you can't use your file over and over, so it's essential not only to be careful when saving your files but also to choose filenames that are specific and descriptive—this makes it easy to find the file you need. This section takes a look at preserving and organizing your work.

Starting a New File

As you learned earlier in this chapter, you can open a new, blank file when you launch the Project application. There might be occasions, however, when you finish working with one file and then want to create a new file without exiting Project. Doing so is easy. Either click the New icon on the Standard toolbar (it's at the far left and looks like a piece of paper), or open the File menu and click New. Project displays the Project Info dialog box for the new file, and gives the file the temporary name Project X, where X is a number sequentially assigned to each new file you open in a Project work session. This dialog box enables you to enter facts such as the starting and ending dates for the project. (You'll learn in detail how to work with this dialog box in Chapter 2, "Setting Up a Project.")

Once you click OK to accept the information you've entered for the new file, Project displays the empty file on-screen. It displays the file's temporary name in the title bar, until you save the file and assign a unique name for it (see the section "Saving a File," later in this chapter).

Opening an Existing File

If you've ever opened files that have been previously created and saved in other Windows 95 applications, then you'll be relatively comfortable with Project's File Open dialog box. This dialog box enables you to open Project files you've previously saved, so you can enter new information, change the view, print, and more.

To open a file, follow these steps:

1. Open the File menu and click Open. Alternatively, you can press Ctrl+0, or click the Open icon on the Standard toolbar (it's second from the left, and looks like an open file folder). The File Open dialog box appears (see Fig. 1.8).

Use these to navigate to the folder holding the file to open.

Click here to move up one folder level.

Click here to view details about listed files.

Figure 1.8
This dialog box enables you open an existing file to work with it again.

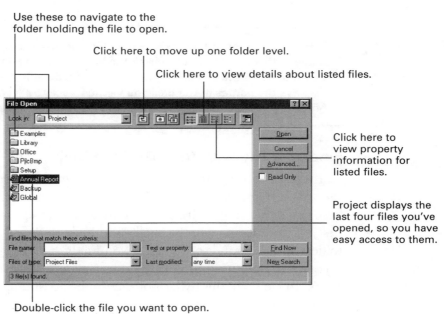

Click here to view property information for listed files.

Project displays the last four files you've opened, so you have easy access to them.

Double-click the file you want to open.

2. Click the drop-down arrow beside the Look in list, and select the disk drive where your Project file is stored.

TIP: Select the Network Neighborhood icon from the Look in list if the file is on a drive connected to another network.

3. Double-click a folder in the list of folders that appears; this displays the contents of that folder in the dialog box list. You might need to double-click subfolder icons to reach the file you want to open.

4. (Optional) If you want to view or print the file, but don't want to edit it, select the <u>R</u>ead Only check box. This option prevents you from making unwanted changes to the file.

5. When the file you want to open appears in the list, double-click its name (or click its name and then click <u>O</u>pen) to load the file into Project.

Once you select the file to open, Project displays it on-screen, ready for you to alter it, print, or whatever.

TIP: If you've recently worked with a file and want to open it again, there's a shortcut—check the bottom of the <u>F</u>ile menu to see if the filename is listed there. By default, Project displays the names of the files you've most recently worked on. If you see the name you want, click it to open the file.

Finding a File with the File Open Dialog Box

As the sizes of hard disks on individual computer systems—and the sizes of networked drives—increase to one gigabyte or more, it becomes increasingly difficult for users to keep track of files. Even the best human memory can be challenged by hard disks with dozens of folders and thousands of files. Or, you might have many files that are very similar, and need to use a Find feature to distinguish between them. To facilitate this, Microsoft has built file-finding help into the File Open dialog box in most of its applications.

NOTE: Try to use a consistent strategy when organizing your folders and files on a hard disk. For example, at any given time, I'm involved in up to a dozen book projects. For each project, I create a master folder with the project name, then I create a subfolder for each key element of the project: text files, figures, memos, and so on.

When you perform a find, you can use *wild-card characters* if you remember part of a filename. Project will list files with names similar to the name you specified using wild cards. The asterisk (*) wild card stands in for any group of characters in the location where you use it within a filename. For example, entering **a*** in the File name text box results in a list of all filenames that begin with the letter a, such as Annual Report and Accidents. The question mark (?) wild card stands in for any single character in the location where you use it. For example, entering **anders?n** in the File name text box finds files named Anderson and Andersen.

If you're working in the File Open dialog box and can't remember the exact location of the file you want to open, follow these steps to perform a basic find:

1. Open the File menu and click Open to display the File Open dialog box.

2. Navigate to the drive and folder where you think the file is located.

3. Use any one or a combination of the following entries (see Fig. 1.9) to specify how Project should look for the file:

    • In the File name text box, enter the name of the file you're searching for (or use an approximation with wild cards).

    • In the Text or property text box, enter any text that might appear in the project file or in the file's Properties dialog box. Be sure to enclose your entry in quotes. For example, enter **"1996"** for files that might include that year.

    • Make a selection from the Last modified list to search for a file depending on when you last saved changes to it. For example, if you know you've made changes to the file recently, you can select the this month choice.

4. Click the Find Now button. Project searches the current folder for matching file(s). When the search is finished, Project displays a message in the lower-left portion of the dialog box to tell you how many files match the search criteria you specified. If only one file matches the criteria, that file is highlighted in the dialog box.

5. Double-click the name of the file you want to open (or click to select its name and then click Open).

Figure 1.9
Use the text boxes
at the bottom of
this dialog box to
narrow the search
to files that meet
specific criteria.

Advanced Finds

To perform a basic find, you need to be fairly familiar with a file, remembering where you saved it, its approximate name, and perhaps text that it contains. In some instances, though, you might not have that much information about the file. For example, if you have no idea where you saved the file, you need to use some more powerful searching capabilities to find the file. The advanced find features in the File Open dialog box will expand the search, enabling you to search more than one folder, more than one disk, and so on. Use the following steps to take advantage of the advanced search features:

1. Open the File Open dialog box as described in step 1 of the preceding procedure.

2. Specify any basic search criteria that apply, such as an approximate filename, as described in step 2 of the preceding procedure.

3. Click the Advanced button to display the Advanced Find dialog box (see Fig. 1.10). Notice that the Find files that match these criteria list displays any criteria you specified before clicking the Advanced button as well as additional criteria you add in the Advanced Find dialog box.

TIP: If you want to remove one of the criteria you've defined, click it in the list of criteria, and then click the Delete button. To remove all the criteria, click the New Search button.

List of all criteria

Figure 1.10
Creating a list of
criteria increases
the power of a
find operation.

Figure 1.10
Creating a list of
criteria increases
the power of a
find operation.

4. To add a new criterion to the list of criteria, start by selecting either the A<u>n</u>d or O<u>r</u> option button. A<u>n</u>d means that Find must match the original criteria (if any) *and* the new criterion you're specifying. In contrast, O<u>r</u> means that the file can match any one (or more) of the criteria you've specified.

5. For the criterion you're creating, use the <u>P</u>roperty drop-down list to select the file property that will be used in the find operation, and use the <u>C</u>ondition list to indicate how the <u>P</u>roperty and Val<u>u</u>e entries should correspond.

6. Finally, enter the Val<u>u</u>e that the Find operation should look for in that criterion. For example, if you have selected the Keyword <u>P</u>roperty, you might enter **report** as the value. If the Val<u>u</u>e entry contains more than one word, surround the entry with quotation marks, as in **"1995 report"**.

7. Click the <u>A</u>dd to List button to finish defining the criterion.

8. Repeat steps 4–7 to add more criteria based on file properties.

9. To further fine-tune a single text criterion, select it by clicking it in the list of criteria, then select either the Match all word forms check box (when you want to match multiple tenses such as "run" and "ran") or the <u>M</u>atch case check box (when you want to match the exact capitalization you've used).

10. Use the Look in drop-down list to specify a disk or folder to be searched. (If you want to search the current drive, but search all folders on the drive, make sure that the root directory is specified in the Look in list, rather than the current folder on that disk. To do so, double-click the Look in text box, and then edit the entry to specify the root of the disk, as in C:\. Select the Search subfolders check box if you want to search subfolders within the selected disk or folder.

11. (Optional) To save the search (that is, all the criteria you've specified), click the Save Search button, enter a name for this search in the Name text box, and click OK.

> **NOTE:** To reuse a search you've saved, click the Open Search button, select the named search in the Open Search dialog box, and click Open. You also can use Delete or Rename in the Open Search dialog box to delete or rename saved searches.

12. Click the Find Now button to execute the search. Project searches the specified folder(s) for the file(s). When the search is finished, Project displays a message in the lower-left portion of the Open File dialog box telling you how many files match the search criteria you specified. If only one file matches the specification, that file is highlighted in the dialog box.

13. Double-click the name of the file you want to open (or click to select its name and then click Open).

Saving a File

Saving a file on disk preserves it (as permanently as possible, given the imperfections of electronic storage media) so that you can work with it again. The first time you save a file, you also have the opportunity to give the file a unique name. Project 4.1 for Windows 95 enables you to take advantage of Windows 95 long filenames. Previously, filenames had to conform to the old DOS limitation of eight characters plus a three-character extension. Under Windows 95, you can enter up to 255 characters, including spaces; however, keep in mind that the 255 characters must include the path, slashes, and so on, so the real limitation for the filename is closer to 230 characters. This enables you to create filenames that are substantially more descriptive and useful.

To save a file for the first time and give it the name of your choice, perform the following steps:

1. Open the File menu and click Save. Alternatively, you can press Ctrl+S, or click the Save button on the Standard toolbar (it's the third button from the left and looks like a floppy disk). The File Save dialog box appears (see Fig. 1.11).

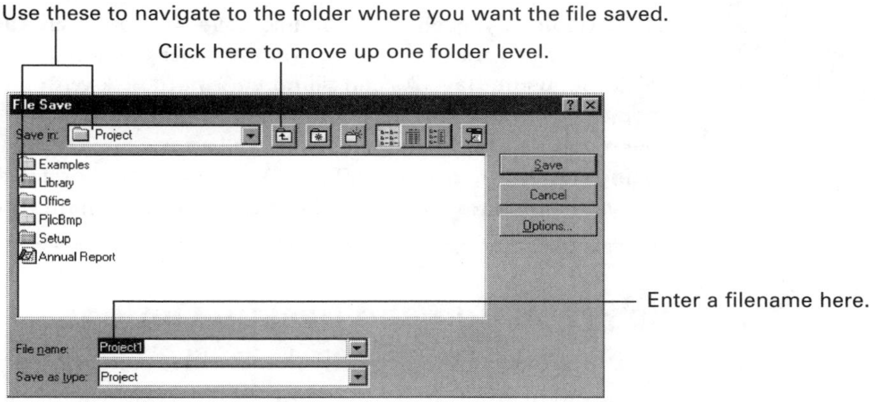

Use these to navigate to the folder where you want the file saved.

Click here to move up one folder level.

Figure 1.11
Use this dialog box to save and name a file.

Enter a filename here.

2. Navigate to the drive and folder where you'd like to save the file, using the Save in drop-down list and the folders that appear below (double-clicking a folder icon opens that folder so you can store the file there).

3. Type a name for the file in the File name text box. Try to use something descriptive, even if it's lengthy, like **Rider Bike Product Introduction**.

4. Click the Save button to save the file.

After you've saved a file for the first time, you can save changes you make to it anytime in the future by pressing Ctrl+S (or clicking the Save button on the Standard toolbar).

There might be occasions, however, when you want to save a file with a new name. For example, if you have a lengthy project, you might want to save a version of the main project file at the end of each month, to keep a record of your progress and create a series of progressive "backup" copies of your file. In such a case, you must first save your file to ensure that the existing version reflects your most current changes. Next, redisplay the File Save dialog box by opening the File menu and clicking Save As. In the File Save dialog box, you can (but don't have to) change the selected folder to specify a new location for the renamed file. Then, type the new name—such as **March 96 Rider Bike Product Introduction**—and click Save to finish creating the new version of the file.

> **TIP:** Obviously, each time you use Save As, you're creating a new copy of your file, and leaving the older version intact on disk. So, using Save As can fill up your hard disk with file copies. Use Save As sparingly. You wouldn't want to use it every day to create a new copy of a file, for example, but using it monthly to save different versions of a file might provide adequate records without clogging your hard disk.

File Protection and Backup Options

Part of the beauty of Project is that its files can be used easily in a networked environment. At any time, other team members can open the master plan for a project and review where things stand, or update information about tasks as they're completed. The downside to this, of course, is the difficulty in controlling who can view the file and how changes are made.

Fortunately, the File Save dialog box provides a method for applying some protection to files; you can do so either the first time you save them or after the fact. Display the File Save dialog box by opening the File menu and clicking Save the first time you save the file, or by opening the File menu and clicking Save As for existing files. If necessary, specify the directory where the file should be saved, and then enter the filename. Next, click the Options button to display the Save Options dialog box (see Fig. 1.12).

If you want Project to automatically create a backup copy of the file each time you save it, select the Always Create Backup check box.

Create a <u>P</u>rotection Password if you want users to enter a password to be able to open the file. Enter a <u>W</u>rite Reservation Password if you want users to be able to view a read-only version of the file without a password, but want to require a password for a user to be able to edit the file and save the edited version.

Figure 1.12
Protect your files, especially when they're on a network, by specifying a password and backup protection.

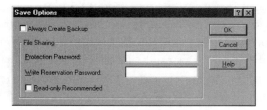

> **CAUTION:** Passwords in Project are case-sensitive, so if happY is the password you create, it will not match user entries such as Happy, happy, or HAPPY. Be sure to carefully record the correct password and its capitalization in a secure location where it won't be seen by unauthorized eyes.
>
> Also, though you've probably heard this before, your passwords need to be as unique as possible to prevent others from infiltrating your system or the network. Steer clear of using passwords that others might be able to guess or discover, such as your birthdate, your Social Security number, names (your spouse's, pet's, or child's), and the like.

Select the <u>R</u>ead-only Recommended check box if you want Project to display a dialog box giving the user the option of opening a read-only version of the file each time it's opened.

After you've specified any desired save options, click OK. If you've specified a new password (or have changed a password), Project asks you to enter the password again to verify it. Do so, then click OK. Click <u>S</u>ave to close the File Save dialog box and put your protection options in place.

If you ever want to make changes to the specified protection options—for example, change a password—just open the file, redisplay the Save Options dialog box, and make whatever changes you want. To remove a password, for instance, double-click to select the whole password, and then press Backspace or Delete. Click OK and then <u>S</u>ave to finalize the changes and return to your Project file.

Saving and Opening a Workspace

You might encounter situations where you regularly need to work with several Project files. For example, if you frequently copy information between two project files (such as one for all tasks in your group and one for a specific project), it might be more convenient to have them open automatically and appear side-by-side on-screen. You might even want to have each file appear in a particular view.

Luckily, you can save such an on-screen configuration of multiple files and settings as a *workspace*. To reopen multiple files, position them precisely on-screen, and specify the appropriate views and settings, all you have to do is open a single workspace file.

NOTE: Workspace files have the MPW file extension; however, file extensions aren't as important under Windows 95 as they were with other operating systems.

To create a workspace file:

1. Open all the project files that you want to include in the workspace.

2. Arrange the files on-screen (covered in the next section), and specify the appropriate view for each file (views are covered where they apply throughout the book, and also are covered in detail in Chapter 9, "Working with the Different Project Views").

3. Open the <u>F</u>ile menu and click Save <u>W</u>orkspace. The Save Workspace as dialog box appears (see Fig. 1.13).

4. Select the folder where you'd like to save the workspace file by using the Save <u>i</u>n list and double-clicking the folders below the list.

Figure 1.13
Create a
workspace so
you can easily
open multiple
files.

5. Type a name for the workspace in the File name text box.

6. Click Save to finish saving the workspace.

Opening a workspace is virtually identical to opening a file. Use any of three methods: open the File menu and click Open; press Ctrl+O; or click the Open button on the Standard toolbar. In the File Open dialog box, navigate to the directory where the workspace file is saved. Click the down arrow to open the Files of type drop-down list, and select Workspaces from the list. When you see the name of the workspace file you want opened, double-click the name.

TIP: You can use the find feature described earlier in this chapter to find a workspace file if you can't recall where you've saved it or exactly what its name is. Simply make sure that you've selected Workspaces from the Files of type list.

Selecting, Arranging, and Closing Files

Each time you open a file in Project, it remains open until you specifically close it after you've finished working with it (and presumably after you've saved it). If you're viewing each open file at full-screen size (maximized), the easiest way to switch between open files is to use the Window menu. To choose which file to display, open the Window menu and click the name of the file you want to select (see Fig. 1.14).

A dot indicates the current file.

Figure 1.14
Select the file you want to work with from the Window menu.

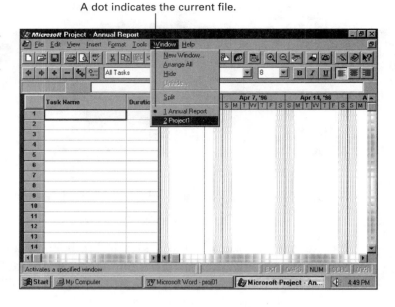

Notice that the Window menu offers some other useful options:

- New Window opens a new window of an open file. Doing so enables you, for example, to show two different views of the same file on-screen.

- Arrange All arranges all the open files and windows so that they fill the screen, with each file at least partially visible.

- Hide hides the currently-selected file or window; this is handy if you want a file out of view during your lunch break, for example.

- Unhide displays a list of hidden windows so that you can select one to be redisplayed.

- Split breaks the current file into two panes so that you can display different areas of a file simultaneously.

After you've finished working with a particular file and have saved it, you should close the file so that it's no longer consuming system memory. To close the current file, open the File menu and click Close.

Exiting Project

When you're finished with your work in Project, you can close the program in any of several ways:

- Press Alt+F4.
- Double-click the close box (with the X in it) in the upper-right corner of the Project application window.
- Open the File menu and click Exit.

> **NOTE:** If you haven't saved your work before you try to close Project, Project asks whether or not you want to save your changes. Choose Yes to do so, or No to exit without saving.

CHAPTER 2

SETTING UP A PROJECT

Traditionally, when you were assigned a new activity on the job, one of the first things you did was sit down with a yellow notepad and compile a "To Do" list. You made notes about your deadline for the whole project, and perhaps sketched out timeframes for individual assignments. As you completed each step, you simply scratched the item off your list.

The first step of the planning process in Project is somewhat similar to the yellow pad method. You begin by mapping out your timeframe and the tasks to be completed.

This chapter covers that process, including the following:

- Establishing an overall schedule for your project

- Setting daily working hours for the schedule

- Defining each task in the schedule

- Working with the order of the tasks

- Setting up milestones

- Understanding file properties

- Controlling the base calendar schedule for the project

Managing Project Start and End Dates

As discussed in Chapter 1, "Getting Started with Project," the Project Info dialog box appears (see Fig. 2.1) each time you start a new project file by opening the File menu and clicking New. You use this dialog box to work with the overall time schedule for your project.

Figure 2.1
The Project Info dialog box is where you establish some overall timing issues for your project.

The first two text boxes in the dialog box are Start Date and Finish Date. Initially, the Start Date entry displays the current date, and the Finish Date entry is grayed out (disabled). That's because you enter only one of these dates; Project calculates the other one for you, based on the tasks you enter for the project and how long each task lasts. So, to determine how the duration of your schedule is calculated, you can use one of the following two methods:

- **Have Project calculate the Finish Date.** Leave Project Start Date as the Schedule From selection, and edit the Start Date text box entry, if needed.

- **Have Project calculate the Start Date.** Click the arrow beside the Schedule From drop-down list, and select Project Finish Date. Then, edit the Finish Date text box entry.

NOTE: There might be instances where you want new tasks to be scheduled based on the current date rather than the project start or finish date. To override the Schedule From drop-down list choice in the Project Info dialog box, open the Tools menu and click Options. Click to select the Schedule tab. Select Current Date from the New Tasks Start On drop-down list, then click OK.

When you enter or edit either Start Date or Finish Date, enter the date in m/dd/yy or mm/dd/yy format. You don't need to enter the abbreviation for the day of the week; Project specifies it after you finish making changes to the Project Info settings.

The Current Date text box enables you to calibrate your project schedule with the actual calendar. By default, however, the starting date used for all new tasks you add to the project will be the Start Date or Finish Date you've specified (depending on which of those entries Project is calculating for you). For example, if you've chosen Project Finish Date for the Schedule From entry and have entered **6/14/96** as the Finish Date, the tasks you enter will be scheduled with a finish date of 6/14/96, regardless of the Current Date entry.

The last setting to adjust when you set up your new project is the Calendar setting. This setting determines the *base calendar*, or the working hours and days for the project. This calendar determines the number of hours per week available in the project schedule. (You can change the working schedule for any particular resource, however, as explained in Chapter 4, "Managing Resources"). You can select one of the following choices from the Calendar drop-down list:

- **Standard**—This choice, the default, assigns corporate America's standard work week to the project. The project schedule is based on a Monday through Friday work week, with daily working hours of 8 a.m. to noon and 1 p.m. to 5 p.m.—thus, each workday is eight hours and each work week is 40 hours.

- **24 Hours**—If you make this selection, the schedule is continuous. Each workday is 24 hours long, and work is scheduled seven days a week.

- **Night Shift**—This option provides a schedule based on a 40-hour night shift week as scheduled in many companies, from Monday evening through Saturday morning:

Days	Scheduled working hours
Mondays	11 p.m. to 12 a.m.
Tuesday through Friday	12 a.m. to 3 a.m. 4 a.m. to 8 a.m. 11 p.m. to 12 a.m.
Saturdays	12 a.m. to 3 a.m. 4 a.m. to 8 a.m.

> **CAUTION:** The number of working hours per day is important because it affects how Project calculates the schedule for a task. For example, let's say that you estimate a certain task will take 24 working hours. Under the Standard calendar, that task is assigned to three workdays. Under a 24-hour calendar, the task gets a single day. Unless your resources truly will be working 24 hours a day, selecting 24 Hours as the Calendar setting can cause Project to drastically underestimate the schedule.

After you make your choice for the Calendar setting, click OK to close the Project Info dialog box.

Changing Project Information

After you've created project information, it's by no means set in stone. You can redisplay the Project Info dialog box at any time to make changes to the options there. In addition, you might want to check the calculated Start Date or Finish Date for the schedule. To view or change schedule information, click to open the File menu, and then click Project Info. When the Project Info dialog box appears, make any changes that you want, then click OK to close the dialog box.

Be careful when making changes to this setting after you've added tasks to the schedule. For example, changes to the Calendar option can have a drastic effect on your project's timeline. Also, if you make a change to the project Start Date or Finish Date, and have tasks falling outside the new overall schedule, Project will warn you after you click OK in the Project Info dialog box (see Fig. 2.2). You can either click OK and then reschedule individual tasks to fit within the new schedule, or click Cancel and choose a new start or finish date.

Figure 2.2
Project warns you if any tasks are scheduled outside the new dates you've entered for the project.

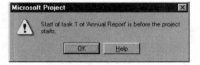

Viewing Project Statistics

Project provides numerous ways to review the information you've entered for a project. In fact, it automatically tracks particular project statistics for you, so you can review the overall status at a glance. These statistics are displayed in the Project Statistics dialog box (see Fig. 2.3).

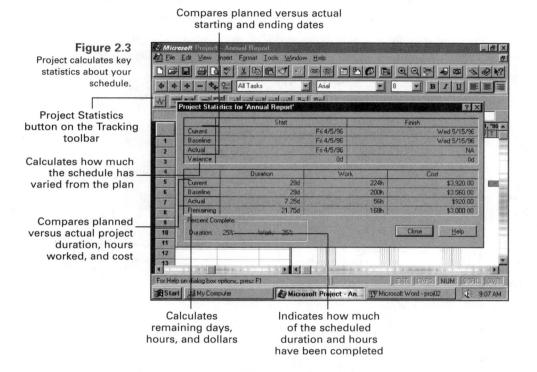

Compares planned versus actual starting and ending dates

Figure 2.3
Project calculates key statistics about your schedule.

Project Statistics button on the Tracking toolbar

Calculates how much the schedule has varied from the plan

Compares planned versus actual project duration, hours worked, and cost

Calculates remaining days, hours, and dollars

Indicates how much of the scheduled duration and hours have been completed

You can display the Project Statistics dialog box using either of two methods:

- Display the Tracking toolbar by right-clicking any on-screen toolbar and then clicking Tracking. Click the Project Statistics button at the far left on the Tracking toolbar.

- Click the File menu and click Project Info. Click the Statistics button in the Project Info dialog box.

Project does not allow you to edit or print the information in the Project Statistics dialog box. When you finish viewing the information, click the Close button to exit the dialog box.

Adding and Deleting Tasks

After you've set up the overall parameters for the schedule, you're ready to begin entering the individual "jobs" that need to be done. This phase of building the project blueprint is most analogous to jotting down a to-do list, with each task roughly equating to a "to-do." Generally, you add tasks to the schedule in the default view, *Gantt Chart view*. In this view, the left pane (the *Task Sheet*) is where you enter basic information about each task.

As shown in Figure 2.4, the Task Sheet resembles a spreadsheet grid. You enter information about each task in a single row in the Task Sheet. You can use the scroll bar at the bottom of the Task Sheet to display more columns; each column holds a particular type of information.

Figure 2.4
Enter tasks in the Task Sheet.

Click to select the whole Task Sheet

Row number; click to select the whole row

Use to view additional columns

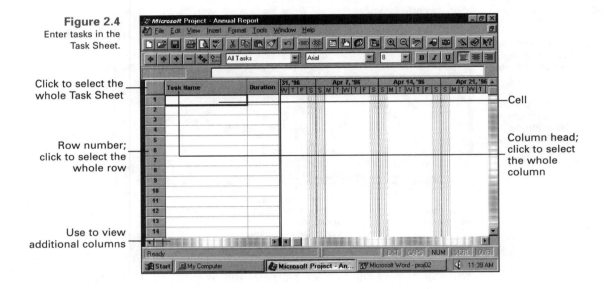

Cell

Column head; click to select the whole column

- **Task Name**—This column holds the descriptive label you want to identify each task. These names should be unique enough to differentiate individual tasks. The name can include spaces as well as upper- and lowercase characters. And, although the name can include more than 100 characters, as a rule you should stick with names that are as brief and descriptive as possible.

- **Duration**—This column holds the time you're allowing for the completion of each task. If you enter no duration, Project assumes a default duration of one day (d). Other durations are assumed to be in days unless you specify otherwise (see "Using Differing Durations" later in this chapter).

- **Start**—This column holds the date when work is scheduled to begin on a particular task. Normally, this date is assumed to be the project Start Date or End Date specified in the Project Info dialog box. You can edit this date as needed to adjust the start date for the project.

- **Finish**—This column holds the date when work on each task is to be completed. If you've specified that Project should schedule tasks from the starting date in the Project Info dialog box, then the date in this column is automatically calculated based on the entries in the Duration and Start columns. On the other hand, if Project is scheduling tasks from the ending date, then the date in the Start column is calculated.

TIP: When you change the date that Project is calculating (the date in either the Start or Finish column for the task in the Task Sheet, depending on whether the project is set up to calculate from the project start date or finish date, as specified in the Project Info dialog box), Project automatically changes the Task Sheet Duration field for the task to reflect your change. For example, let's say that you've entered a Duration of one day (1d) for a task that's being calculated from a Start of 4/10/96. If you change the date in the Finish column from 4/10/96 to 4/12/96, Project changes the Duration to 3d.

- **Predecessors**—This column indicates when a task is linked to one or more preceding tasks. Project can fill in this column for you, or you can use this column to establish links. Chapter 3, "Fine-Tuning Tasks," covers linking tasks.

- **Resource Names**—This column enables you to enter one or more resources (team member, outside contractor, and so on) responsible for completing a task. Chapter 4, "Managing Resources," explains how to create resources for use in your schedule.

Entering tasks in the Task Sheet works much like making spreadsheet entries. Although later chapters cover some of the entries for a task in more detail, here's an overview of the steps for creating a task:

1. Click the cell in the Task Name column of the first available row in the Task Sheet. Clicking selects the cell and prepares it for your entry (see Fig. 2.5).

2. Type the name of the task. For example, you might type a name like **Develop Theme Proposal**. As you type, the text appears in the entry box above the Task Sheet. To complete the entry, press Tab, or click the Enter button and then click the next cell to the right in the Duration column. Clicking the Cancel button stops the entry altogether.

Figure 2.5
You can accept or cancel the entry you're making into any cell.

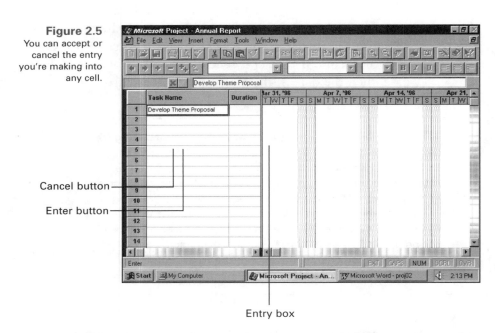

Cancel button

Enter button

Entry box

 TIP: To quickly enter a list of tasks, press Enter after each task name you create. Project assigns each task a 1d duration and the default start date. You then can go back and adjust the duration and other entries.

3. Type a number such as **3** for the new duration entry. The new entry appears in the Entry box as you type. Unless you include more duration information (described later in the section "Using Differing Durations"), Project assumes the duration to be days. To finish the entry, press Tab; alternatively, you can

click the Enter button, scroll to the right, and then click the Start cell for that task.

4. The Start cell is selected. If Project is set to automatically calculate the Finish date, type the desired starting date in mm/dd/yy format and click the Enter button. This finishes the basic task creation, and creates a bar for the task in the *Gantt Chart pane* on the right side of the screen (see Fig. 2.6). If Project is set to automatically calculate backward (based on the ending date, which by default is the Project Finish Date in the Project Info dialog box), do not change the Start column entry; go to step 5.

Figure 2.6
Project creates a Gantt chart bar to graphically represent your task on the schedule.

This three-day task...

...is charted here

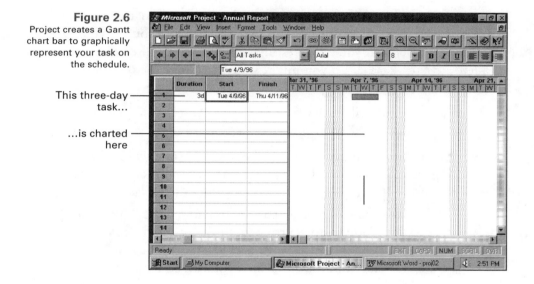

5. Press Tab (or scroll and then click the Finish cell for that task). Type the desired ending date in mm/dd/yy format and click the Enter button to complete it.

6. (Optional) Make entries in the Predecessors and Resources cells, as described in Chapters 3 and 4. Press Tab or click the Resources cell after your Predecessors entry; go to step 7 after you make the Resources entry.

7. To create the next task, you need to move to the next row of the Task Sheet. To do so, scroll and click to select the first cell (the Task Name cell) in the next row; alternatively, you can press Enter and then press Ctrl+Left Arrow to select that cell.

8. Repeat steps 2 through 7 as many times as needed to enter all the tasks for your project.

Based on all the tasks you create and the durations you enter for them, Project calculates the total schedule for the project. To check the total schedule, click the File menu and then click Project Info.

Editing a Task

No matter how well-formulated a business plan is, you can count on it to change. For example, you might start out using somewhat generic names for your tasks—or even code names. Later, after the project is announced, you might want to replace the temporary names with the real project names. Or, after consulting a particular resource, you might discover that you've overestimated the time required to complete a particular task, so you might want to change the duration you've specified for that task.

To edit any of the cell entries for a task, click to select the cell you want to edit. Use one of the following two methods to make your changes:

- To completely replace the cell entry, just start typing. Whatever you type completely replaces the previous entry. Click the Enter button when you're done making the replacement entry.

- To make changes to only part of an entry, click to position the insertion point in the entry box, or drag to highlight the text you want to replace. Type your changes. Once the insertion point is placed in the entry box, you can edit text as you would in most word processors, using the arrow keys, Backspace, and more. When you've finished making your changes, click the Enter button.

Using Differing Durations

As you've seen, when you assign a duration for a particular task, Project by default interprets that duration in terms of *days*. Each day consists of a full day's worth of working hours, depending on the base calendar you've set for the schedule using the Calendar drop-down list in the Project Info dialog box. So, if your project is based on the 24 Hours calendar, each day of duration consists of 24 working hours; on the Standard calendar, each day of duration consists of eight working hours.

For the Night Shift base calendar, each "day" of duration is eight hours. Under this calendar, each *working day* spans two *calendar days*. For example, a task that begins on a Friday and is scheduled to last 1d starts Friday at 11 p.m., when the working day starts, and spans to 3 a.m. on Saturday; after a 1-hour lunch break, the workday and task continue from 4 a.m. to 8 a.m., which is the end of the shift.

> **NOTE:** Under the Night Shift calendar, keep in mind that when you enter a start date for a task, Project schedules the task for the workday that begins at 11 p.m. of that start date and runs over to the next day. Thus, if you want work to be completed on a task during the early morning hours of a given day (12 a.m. to 3 a.m. and 4 a.m. to 8 a.m.), specify the preceding date as the start date for the task.

Obviously, not every task requires eight to 24 hours. Likewise, not every task is completed within the bounds of the workday hours (as much as we wish they all would be). For example, if you want to include a key meeting on your schedule, it's likely you only need to block out a few hours for it, not an entire day. At the other extreme, if you expect a supplier to work during the weekend to deliver a product, or you know something will be shipped to you during a weekend, you need to schedule a task outside of normal working hours.

Project enables you to control the exact amount of time a task will take to finish, based on the abbreviation you include with the entry in the Duration column of the Task Sheet. Some duration abbreviations are for *elapsed durations*, where you specify work according to a 24-hour, seven-day-per-week calendar even though that isn't the base calendar for the project. To specify the new duration, simply enter the correct abbreviation along with your numeric entry. Table 2.1 lists the available abbreviations.

When you enter an elapsed time, the Gantt chart bars at the right reflect how the task falls in terms of real time. For example, Figure 2.7

compares the actual scheduled time for a task entered as three working days (3d) and a task entered as 24 elapsed hours (24eh). When scheduled as standard workdays, a 24-hour period covers three days; as elapsed hours, however, a 24-hour period occupies a single day on the Gantt chart.

Table 2-1. Duration Abbreviations

Time Unit	Abbreviation	Example
Minutes	m	30m means 30 working minutes
Hours	h	30h means 30 working hours
Days	d	30d means 30 working days
Weeks	w	30w means 30 working weeks
Elapsed minutes	em	30em means 30 consecutive, elapsed minutes
Elapsed hours	eh	30eh means 30 consecutive, elapsed hours
Elapsed days	ed	30ed means 30 consecutive, elapsed days
Elapsed weeks	ew	30ew means 30 consecutive, elapsed weeks

Figure 2.7
Elapsed times are scheduled consecutively.

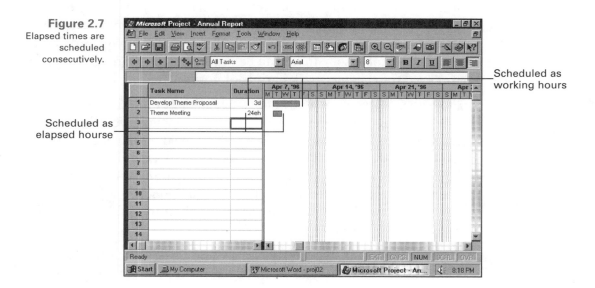

Scheduled as working hours

Scheduled as elapsed hourse

Selecting, Inserting, and Deleting Tasks

When you're creating any kind of business plan, you start with the overall framework and refine it as you go along, adding details as you flesh out some ideas and discard others. You might discover the need to adjust the framework for your project, adding new tasks into the Task Sheet as you discover that they're necessary, or dropping them as you determine that they're extraneous or already included within the scope of other items. Project gives you total flexibility in determining which tasks appear on the Task Sheet.

Use the following steps to add a task to your Task Sheet:

1. Select any cell in the row above which you want to insert a new task. To select the cell, use the scroll bars at the far right and bottom of the screen to display the cell, and then click it. Alternatively, you can use the arrow keys to reach a cell in the appropriate row.

2. Press the Insert key (or open the Insert menu and then click Insert Task) to insert a new, blank row.

3. Enter information for the new task, as discussed previously in this chapter.

Use the following steps to delete a particular task:

1. Select the row in the Task Sheet that holds the task. To select the row, use the vertical scroll bar or the arrow keys to bring the row into view, and then click the row number. A highlight appears on the task row that's selected. To select additional consecutive rows after you select the first row, press Shift and click the row number for the last row in the group you want to delete. To select additional rows that are noncontiguous, press and hold down the Ctrl key while you click additional row numbers.

TIP: You can click the Select All button in the upper-left corner of the Task Sheet to select the entire Task Sheet.

2. Use one of the following methods to remove selected tasks:

- Press the Delete key.
- Open the <u>E</u>dit menu and click <u>D</u>elete Task.
- Right-click the selected task to display a shortcut menu, then click Delete Task (see Fig. 2.8).

Figure 2.8
This shortcut menu speeds up the job of deleting or inserting tasks.

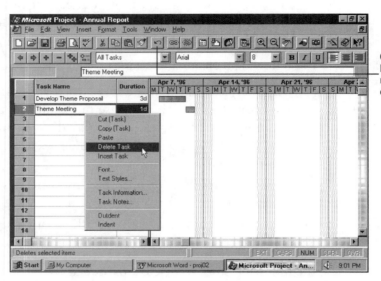

Click the Undo button if you mistakenly delete a task.

CAUTION: Project doesn't warn you about lost information when you choose to delete a task, even if other tasks are linked to the task you're deleting. If you mistakenly delete a task, immediately do any of the following: open the <u>E</u>dit menu and click <u>U</u>ndo; press Ctrl+Z; or click the Undo button on the Standard toolbar.

NOTE: Notice that the task shortcut menu also offers an Insert Task command. You can choose that command to insert a new task row above the currently selected task row.

Moving and Copying Tasks

One of the many features that makes Project more efficient than a yellow pad for process planning is that you can easily change the order of the tasks on your list. There's no more endless renumbering or trying to figure out which arrow points where to indicate the final order of tasks.

The easiest way to move a task on the Task Sheet is by dragging the task information (see Fig. 2.9). Click the row number for the task you want to move; this selects the whole task. Point to one of the selection borders until the mouse pointer turns into an arrow, then click and drag the row into its new position. As you drag, a gray insertion bar indicates exactly where the task row will be inserted if you release the mouse button.

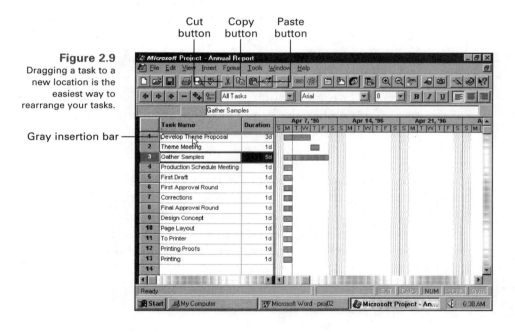

Cut button   Copy button   Paste button

Figure 2.9
Dragging a task to a new location is the easiest way to rearrange your tasks.

Gray insertion bar

TIP: You also can drag-and-drop cells to move their contents.

Dragging is convenient when the task you want to move is relatively close to the new location you'd like for it. It's a bit more difficult to drag a task into place, however, if you have to scroll other tasks to do so. Likewise, when you want to copy a task from one location to another, you need a different process to do the job. For example, if you have two tasks that will run on the same schedule and be completed by the same resource, it's much easier to copy the original task, and then edit the task name on the copy. In such cases, use the following steps to move or copy the task:

1. Click the row number for the task you want to move or copy to select the whole row.

2. If you want to move the task, open the Edit menu and click Cut (Task). Alternatively, you can press Ctrl+X, click the Cut button on the Standard toolbar, or right-click the selection to display a shortcut menu and then click Cut (Task).

   If you want to copy the task, open the Edit menu and click Copy (Task). Alternatively, you can press Ctrl+C, click the Copy button on the Standard toolbar, or right-click the selection to display a shortcut menu and then click Copy (Task).

3. Click any cell in the row above which you want to insert the task you've cut or copied.

4. Open the Edit menu and click Paste. Alternatively, you can press Ctrl+V, click the Paste button on the Standard toolbar, or right-click to display a shortcut menu and then click Paste. Project pastes the task as a new row.

Cut-and-paste (or copy-and-paste) operations also can be used to move or copy information in individual cells. When you select a cell, the Edit and shortcut menu commands change to Cut (Cell) and Copy (Cell). After copying or cutting the selected cell as just described for rows, select a destination cell and then paste the cut or copied information.

NOTE: When you paste a cut or copied cell, the pasted information replaces any existing information in the selected destination cell. (It's not inserted above the cell you've selected.)

TIP: You can select more than one row or cell to cut or copy by clicking and dragging over multiple row numbers or multiple cells.

Clearing Task Information

Cutting a task removes the task altogether from the Task Sheet. The remaining rows close the space vacated by the cut task. There might be instances, however, when you want to remove the information from a task, but want to keep the row that was occupied by that task in place. For example, you might know that you want to replace the old task with information about a new task; if you simply change the entries for the old task, however, you might neglect to edit one, resulting in a schedule error.

An alternative to cutting information in a task or cell is to clear the information. *Clearing* removes cell contents, but leaves all cells in place. Unlike cut information, however, cleared information can't be pasted, so you should clear material only when it's no longer needed.

Use these steps to clear information from your Task Sheet:

1. Select the task row or cell you'd like to clear.

2. Open the Edit menu and click Clear. A submenu appears (see Fig. 2.10), offering you a choice of the kind of information to clear.

Figure 2.10
This is where you choose the kind of information to clear.

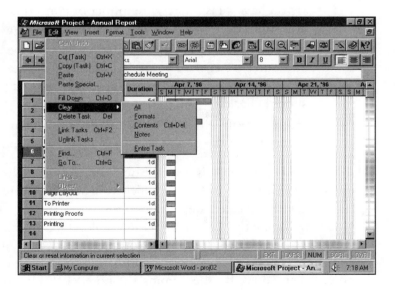

3. Choose the kind of information to clear by clicking the appropriate submenu item, as follows:

A̲ll—Choosing this item removes the task contents, formatting, and any note you've added for the task (the next section explains how to add a note).

F̲ormats—Choosing this item returns the selected task or cell contents to the default formatting, removing any formatting you've added (such as a new font or color).

C̲ontents—Choosing this item is equivalent to pressing Ctrl+ Delete. It removes the contents of the selected task or cell.

N̲otes—Choosing this item clears any note you've added for the task (as described in the next section).

E̲ntire Task—Choosing this item clears the contents of the entire task when you haven't selected the entire task row.

Adding a Task Note

A *task note* enables you to capture information that doesn't need to appear within the Task Sheet, but does need to be recorded with the schedule. For example, you might create notes like these:

- If you have a task that's a reminder of a meeting, you can create a note listing who should be invited to attend the meeting.

- If a task relates to research gathering that will be completed by a resource other than yourself, you can include a note mentioning information sources that the designated researcher should check.

- If a task deals with proofreading or fact-checking, you can use a note to list the details that need to be reviewed.

Adding a note to a task is a straightforward process. Select the task row—or a cell in the task—for which you want to create a note. Right-click the selected area, or open the I̲nsert menu. Choose Task N̲otes to display the Task Information dialog box, which appears with the Notes tab selected. Click the No̲tes text entry area, and then type your note (see Fig. 2.11). Press Enter to start each new line in the note. When you've finished typing the note, click OK to close the Task Information dialog box. Project inserts an icon beside the task row number to remind you that you've added a note for that task.

Figure 2.11
Recording
more detailed
information
about a task.

Project tells you
when there's a
note for a task.

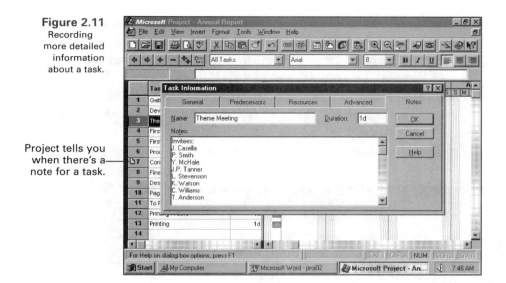

Adjusting the Task Sheet

By default, the Task Sheet occupies roughly the left third of the screen in Gantt Chart view, and offers six columns with preset names and sizes. The narrow screen area allocated for the Task Sheet means that you might spend more time than you prefer scrolling or tabbing back and forth to display particular cells or columns. Or, if you have a column where the entries become rather lengthy, the column might be too narrow to display the column contents. Finally, the columns provided by default might not capture all the information you'd like to have available on the Task Sheet. As you'll see next, Project enables you to control the appearance of the Task Sheet to customize it for your project creation needs.

Sizing the Sheet and Columns

One of the first changes you might want to make is to display more of the Task Sheet to make editing easier. This change isn't permanent, so while you're entering information about various tasks in your schedule, for example, you can fill most of the Project application window with the Task Sheet. After you've entered the task information, you can return the Task Sheet to its previous size so that the Gantt Chart pane of the window becomes visible again.

You can resize the screen area occupied by the Task Sheet with simple dragging. A split bar separates the Task Sheet pane on the left from the Gantt Chart pane on the right. Move the mouse pointer onto that split bar, and the pointer changes to a split pointer with a double-vertical line and left and right arrows. Press and hold the mouse button, then drag the split bar to move it. A gray, shaded line (see Fig. 2.12) indicates where the bar will be repositioned; when this line reaches the location you want, release the mouse button.

Figure 2.12
With a single drag operation, you can view more of the Task Sheet for easier task entry.

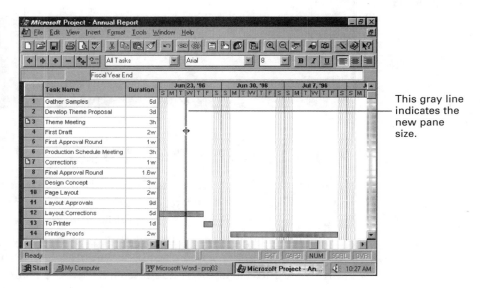

This gray line indicates the new pane size.

Just as you can drag to resize the whole Task Sheet area, you can drag to resize the width of any column or the height of any row. To change a column width, point to the right border of the column, beside the column name. To change a row height, point to the bottom border of the row, below the row number. The mouse pointer changes to a resizing pointer with a line and a double-headed arrow (see Fig. 2.13). Press and hold the mouse button, then drag the border to change the size of the column or row. A dotted line indicates what the new size of the column or row will be; when the column or row reaches the new width or height you want, release the mouse button.

Figure 2.13
Drag a column's
border to
resize the
column.

This dotted line
indicates the new
column width.

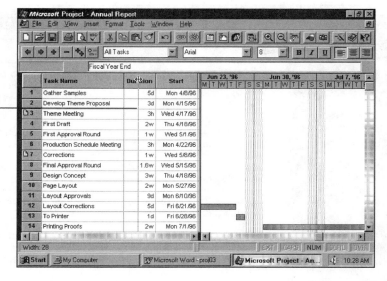

Adding Columns (Fields)

When there are many pieces of data to capture about a particular process, six measly columns cannot do the job effectively. Also, you might want to display some information that Project normally calculates for you. For example, if a given task is being completed by a particular resource at a certain hourly rate and you've entered the actual hours the resource spent to complete the task, you might want to see the resulting actual cost on-screen. You might even want the Task Sheet to display certain information that you can print and distribute to others. Table 2.2 lists several *predefined columns* (also called *fields*), many of which are self-calculating, that you can add to the Task Sheet. Project offers more than 70 of these column formats, so Table 2.2 only describes the most significant ones.

NOTE: Project's online help system contains a listing of all the Task Sheet column types, including a detailed description of each one. To view the list, open the Help menu and click Microsoft Project Help Topics. Click the Index tab, then type *task fields* in the upper text box. Double-click task fields **in the scrolling list box below, then click** Task Fields **in the Overview of Fields help topic window. For more information on a particular field, click its name.**

Table 2-2. New Information You Can Display in the Task Sheet

Key	Key
Actual Cost	Calculates the actual cost for the hours required to complete a project, or lets you enter an actual cost if the project was completed for a fee
Actual Duration	Calculates the actual time that has elapsed since the scheduled start of the task, based on your entry in a Remaining Duration or Percent Complete field if displayed
Actual Finish	Lets you enter the actual task completion date if it differs from the scheduled date
Actual Start	Lets you enter the actual task starting date if it differs from the scheduled date
Actual Work	Calculates or lets you enter the work completed for the task
Baseline (various fields)	Displays the total planned cost, duration, finish, start, and work for the task
BCWP	Baseline Cost of Work Performed—Displays the projected actual cost, calculated from the budgeted baseline cost and the percentage of work actually completed
BCWS	Budgeted Cost of Work Scheduled—Lets you compare the cost of what has actually been accomplished (BCWP) versus the cost of what you had planned to accomplish by a particular date
Contact	Lets you enter an e-mail address for the resource assigned to complete the task, for easier messaging
Cost Variance	Calculates the difference between the baseline cost and scheduled work cost for tasks in progress, and between the baseline and actual cost for finished tasks—negative values indicate that a cost came in under budget
Critical	Indicates whether a project is critical or noncritical, via calculations based on the Total Slack field entry and some other dialog box entries for the task
Duration Variance	Displays the difference between the planned duration for the task and the currently scheduled duration
Finish Variance	Calculates the difference between the planned (baseline) finishing date for the task and the currently scheduled finishing date—negative values indicate that the task is now scheduled to finish earlier than initially planned
ID	Calculates a task's current position in the schedule, even if two tasks have the same name
Marked	Used however you want; for example, you might assign each task a number indicating its original entry order, so that you later can re-sort the tasks to the original order
Notes	Lets you display or enter the notes created about the task

Key	Key
Percent (%) Complete	Calculates or lets you enter the percentage of a task's duration that has passed
Percent (%) Work Complete	Calculates or lets you enter the percentage of a task's work that has been completed
Remaining (various fields)	Calculates or lets you enter the cost, duration, or work still available to complete a task
Resource (various fields)	Displays the group, initials, or names for the resources assigned to a task
Start Variance	Calculates the difference between the scheduled (baseline) starting date and the actual starting date
Successors	Lists later tasks that depend on (are linked to) the current task
Total Slack	Indicates, when the value is positive, that there's time in the schedule to delay the task
Update Needed	Specifies when schedule changes need to communicated to a resource via the Send Task Updates command
Work	Calculates the total work that all resources are scheduled to dedicate to the task
Work Variance	Calculates the difference between the baseline amount of work scheduled for the task and the work currently sc

The process for adding a new column resembles adding a new task to the schedule. Here are the steps:

1. Click any cell in the column next to wherever you want to insert the new column. The inserted column will appear to the left of the column where you've selected a cell.

2. Open the Insert menu and click Insert Column. (As an alternative to steps 1 and 2, you can select an entire column, right-click it, and then click Insert Column). The Column Definition dialog box appears (see Fig. 2.14).

3. Click the down arrow to display the Field Name drop-down list. Use the scroll bar to display the name of the field you want to add, and then click the name to select it.

4. (Optional) If you want the inserted column to be identified with a name other than the built-in field name (say you want "Actual $" rather than "Actual Cost"), click to place the cursor in the Title text box, and then type the name you want.

Figure 2.14
This dialog box enables you to create or edit the columns in the Task Sheet

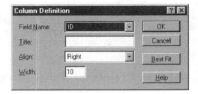

5. (Optional) If you want the entries you make in the new column to be left-aligned or centered automatically, rather than right-aligned, click the down arrow to display the <u>A</u>lign drop-down list, and then click to select the alignment you want.

6. (Optional) If you know that the entries in the new column will require many characters (for example, a note) or very few characters (for example, a one- or two-character ID), double-click the value shown in the <u>W</u>idth text box, then type the new number of characters you want the column to display.

7. Click OK to finish creating the column. The column you've specified appears in the Task Sheet, as shown in the example in Figure 2.15.

Figure 2.15
A new column, % Complete, has been inserted before the Duration column.

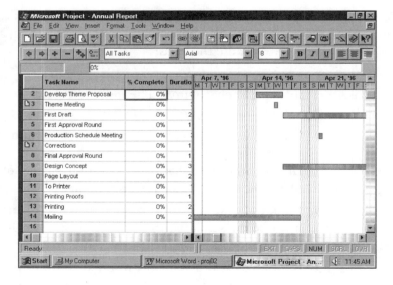

Deleting and Editing Columns

In some instances, you might realize that you no longer need a Task Sheet column, or that you need to make changes to it so that it's more useful and relevant to everyone using the project schedule you've created.

In cases where a column is no longer needed, you can delete it by right-clicking it, then clicking Delete Column from the shortcut menu. Alternatively, you can select the column, then press the Delete key (or open the Edit menu and click Delete Column).

> **CAUTION:** When you delete a column, Project doesn't require you to confirm the deletion. If you mistakenly delete a column, you can immediately click the Undo button on the Standard toolbar to reinstate the column.

To edit an existing column, you need to display the Column Definition dialog box containing information about that particular column. To do so, double-click the column name. Make the changes you want in the Column Definition dialog box, then click OK to accept them. When you edit a column (as opposed to when you first create it), you might find it useful to click the Best Fit button in the Column Definition dialog box. Clicking this button resizes the column so that it's wide enough to fully display every entry already made in that column.

Dealing with the Planning Wizard

As you start entering information about tasks, you might discover that a Planning Wizard dialog box appears from time to time. The Planning Wizard pops up to point out situations where you might need to make a decision about the information you're entering; the dialog box prompts you with specific, easy choices (see Fig. 2.16). For example, the Planning Wizard might ask whether you want to establish a link between tasks, or it might point out that you're about to create an error in your schedule.

Figure 2.16
The Planning
Wizard helps you
make decisions
about the task
information you're
entering

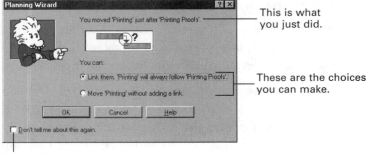

This is what
you just did.

These are the choices
you can make.

Check this box if you
no longer want this
kind of message from
the Planning Wizard.

To continue working after the Planning Wizard appears, click to select an option button to respond to the Planning Wizard's question. If the Planning Wizard has asked you this particular question previously and you no longer want to be reminded of the issue, click to select the Don't tell me about this again check box. Click OK to finish working in the Planning Wizard.

> **TIP:** Clicking Cancel closes the Planning Wizard and also cancels the task entry or edit you were making.

You can turn off all the Planning Wizard suggestions. Chapter 20, "Customizing Microsoft Project," explains how to use the Options dialog box to control certain Project features, including the Project Wizard.

Creating Milestones

Milestones were once stone markers used to identify one's relative position along a road—the particular distance to a certain city on that road. Figurative milestones enable you to gauge your progress through your life, through a particular phase of your career, or through a particular process. *Milestones* in your Project files enable you to mark a particular point of progress or a particular event during the course of a project.

For example, suppose that the project you're managing is the creation and production of your company's annual report, and the company's fiscal year ends June 30. Producing the annual report is tricky, because you want to release it as soon as possible after the close of the fiscal year, yet you have to wait for the final, audited financial information for the year in order to compile the report. In this case, you might mark the end of the fiscal year with a milestone, to help you keep that key, approaching date in mind. In other cases, you might want to mark particular dates, such as the date when you're 25% or 50% through your total allotted schedule.

Creating a milestone isn't very different from creating a task. You insert a task into the Task Sheet, if needed, and then enter information about the task. To specify the task as a milestone, give it a duration of 0 by entering **0d** in the Duration column. Project then identifies the new task as a milestone, and displays a milestone marker for it in your schedule's Gantt chart (see Fig. 2.17).

Figure 2.17
This project contains a milestone, which is visible in the Gantt Chart view.

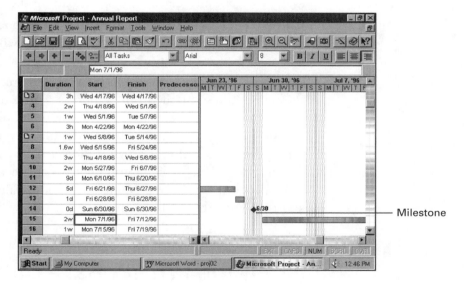

Looking at Project Properties

As with the files you create in other Microsoft applications, Project tracks certain *properties*, or details, to better be able to search for files, and more. Some of the properties tracked for your Project files include statistics about the task scheduling and tracking information you enter in the file.

You can review the properties for a particular file by opening the Properties dialog box (see Fig. 2.18). To do so, open the File menu and click Properties. This dialog box offers five tabs, some that simply calculate and display information, and others that enable you to add details about the file:

- **General**—This tab displays the file type, creation date, date the file was last modified, DOS file name, and more.

- **Summary**—This tab is selected by default. It enables you to enter or edit information about your name, your company, your manager, a title for the file or project, a category to identify the file, keywords to uniquely identify the file if you're trying to find it from a Windows 95 file window, and more.

- **Statistics**—This tab displays when the file was created and last modified, and also indicates when the file was last printed, who last saved it, how many times it's been revised, and how many total minutes have been spent editing the file.

- **Contents**—This tab displays some key facts about the scheduling information you've entered, including the scheduled dates and total projected cost.

- **Custom**—This tab enables you to create a custom property to facilitate finding the file from Windows. For example, you can create a custom property to assign a unique number—such as the job number for the project—to the file. If you create a custom job number field for all your Project files, you can search for any project file by its job number. To create a custom property, specify values for the Name, Type, and Value text boxes, and then click the Add button.

Adjusting the Project Base Calendar

As you learned earlier in this chapter, when you create a new project file, you assign a base calendar for the schedule using the Calendar drop-down list in the Project Info dialog box. Thus, unless you select the 24 Hours base calendar, each workday in the schedule is eight hours long, and it takes three working days to complete a task that's 24 hours in duration.

Figure 2.18
You can view
schedule
information via the
Properties
dialog box.

There might be instances, however, when you want to change the working calendar slightly. For example, if the project you're tracking is a plan for some kind of special event, and the event takes place on a Saturday, you need to make that Saturday a working day. Or, if you want certain workdays to be ten hours long, you can make that change. This section explains how to alter the base calendar for your project schedule.

> **CAUTION:** Make sure that you specify base calendar changes before you begin building your project schedule, to ensure that a calendar change doesn't cause unpredictable results. Also, under the default method of resource-driven scheduling, if you've assigned a special calendar to a resource, that calendar overrides your base calendar. Thus, you need to be sure that you make the same changes to custom resource calendars, when needed, to keep them in synch with the base calendar.

Changing Working Hours or Adding a Day Off

Project gives you the flexibility to change the working hours for any day in any base calendar, or to specify any day as a nonworking day.

To do so, follow these steps:

1. In Gantt Chart view, click to open the <u>T</u>ools menu, then click C<u>h</u>ange Working Time. The Change Working Time dialog box appears, as shown in Figure 2.19.

Figure 2.19
Use this dialog box to adjust the base calendar for your project.

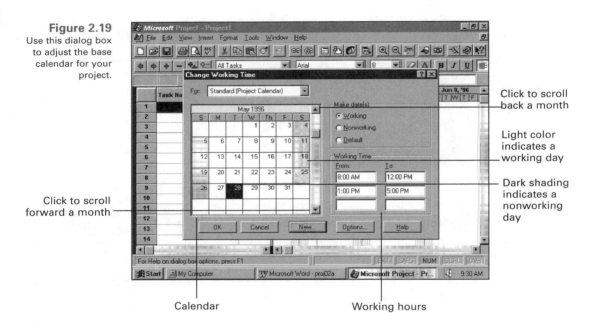

Click to scroll back a month

Light color indicates a working day

Dark shading indicates a nonworking day

Click to scroll forward a month

Calendar

Working hours

2. Use the scroll bar beside the calendar to display the month containing the date you want to adjust.

3. To specify a date as a nonworking day, click that date on the calendar. Then, in the Make date(s) area of the dialog box, click <u>N</u>onworking. Dates you specify as <u>N</u>onworking should include holidays, vacation days, and other scheduled unavailabilities.

TIP: The Default choice returns a date to its default base calendar scheduling. This includes rescheduling the task as a working or nonworking day, as well as returning the Working Time entries to their defaults for the selected date.

4. To change the Working Time (daily working hours) for a date, select that date and make sure that it's specified as a <u>W</u>orking day or has the <u>D</u>efault setting under Make date(s). In the Working Time area, edit or delete the desired <u>T</u>o and <u>F</u>rom entries.

5. Continue editing the calendar view as needed, repeating steps 2 through 4 to change the schedule for additional dates. As you change the schedule for each date, Project marks the edited date in the calendar with light-blue shading.

6. Click OK to close the Change Working Time dialog box and implement the scheduling changes you've made.

Creating a Custom Calendar

For clarity, you might not want to make changes to the actual base calendar you've selected for a project file. Instead, you might want to save your changes in a custom calendar for the project. (The resources you assign to the project also can use the custom calendar.) To create a custom calendar, follow these steps:

1. In Gantt Chart view, click to open the <u>T</u>ools menu, then click Change Working Time. The Change Working Time dialog box appears.

2. Click the <u>Ne</u>w button. The Create New Base Calendar dialog box appears, as shown in Figure 2.20.

3. Because the <u>Na</u>me text is highlighted, you can simply type a new name for the custom schedule.

4. Below the <u>Na</u>me text box, click an option button to select whether you want to Create (a) <u>n</u>ew base calendar or <u>M</u>ake (a) copy of an existing base calendar. If you opt to copy a calendar, select one from the <u>c</u>alendar drop-down list.

5. Click OK. Project returns to the Change Working Time dialog box, where the custom calendar you've created appears as the <u>Fo</u>r drop-down list selection.

6. Make any schedule changes you want for your custom calendar, as described in the preceding set of steps.

Figure 2.20
To create a new, custom base calendar for your project, use this dialog box.

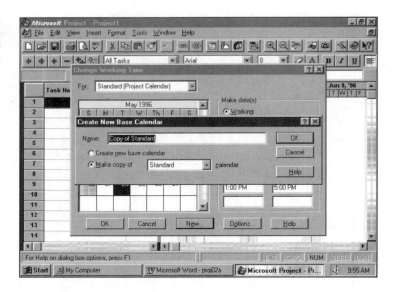

7. Click OK to close the Change Working Time dialog box and implement the new schedule.

CHAPTER 3

FINE-TUNING TASKS

Most designers and artists who create masterpieces don't start by creating subtle shading and fine lines, just as architects don't start a building design by selecting a brick color. In putting the whole picture together, most of us—professionals and amateurs alike—start by sketching out a rough idea of what we want. Then, we go back and draw in the details.

In Chapter 2, "Setting Up a Project," you learned how to sketch out the schedule for your project in the default Gantt Chart view. This chapter helps you to continue working in the Gantt Chart view to begin the refinement process, making changes here and there, and starting to draw in some details to make your plan clear. This chapter explores the following key topics:

- Graphically managing task schedules
- Identifying and creating tasks that you know will repeat
- Working with links that show relationships between tasks
- Understanding how lead times and lag times affect your schedule
- Applying constraints that further specify when the task should be performed
- Reviewing and changing other information stored about a task

Creating and Editing Tasks with the Mouse

The last chapter focused on becoming comfortable working in the Task Sheet to create and edit task information. You learned to change the schedule for a task by editing the duration, start date, and finish date. In many cases, to change the schedule for a task, you simply have to change an entry in one of the columns in the Task Sheet.

There are, however, a few limitations when you use the Task Sheet to schedule your tasks:

- By default, the start or finish date is assumed to be the project's Start Date or Finish Date, depending on the settings you selected in the Project Info dialog box. Thus, you have to change the start or finish date for virtually every task you enter.

- Typing might not be your strong suit. If you're not an ace typist, entering information cell by cell can be tedious.

- You might be more comfortable working on an actual calendar, rather than trying to count dates in your mind and visualize where weekends fall.

If any of the preceding points applies to you, then you might prefer to create and edit tasks directly on the Gantt Chart pane of the Gantt Chart view. Project enables you to define the schedule for a new task—or change the schedule for an existing task—by using the mouse directly on the Gantt chart.

Dragging to Create a New Task

When you create a new task by dragging, you place it on the schedule exactly where you want it to appear. Creating tasks in this way is akin to using a marker to draw a line through successive dates on a calendar to block them out for a particular purpose. To use the mouse to add a task to your schedule, do the following:

1. Scroll the Gantt Chart pane to display the approximate dates where you want to schedule the new task. (Use the scroll bar at the bottom of the pane.)

2. If needed, scroll down to display the task row where you'd like to place the new task.

3. Point to the location that's roughly where the row for the task and your desired start date for the task intersect.

4. Press and hold down the mouse button—the mouse pointer changes to a crosshair. Drag to the right to begin defining the task. As you drag (see Fig. 3.1), the outline for the Gantt chart bar appears, and an informational Create Task box shows you the dates you're establishing for the task.

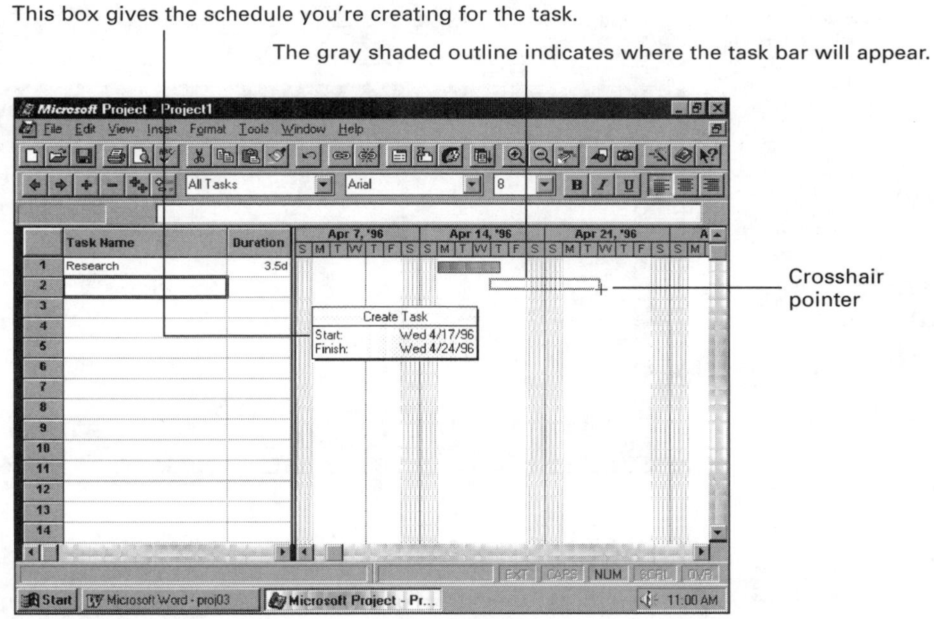

This box gives the schedule you're creating for the task.

The gray shaded outline indicates where the task bar will appear.

Figure 3.1
Dragging directly on
the Gantt chart is an
easy way to add a new
task to your schedule.

Crosshair
pointer

5. When the bar for the task is the length you want it, and the Create Task box displays the dates you want to schedule for the task, release the mouse button. The new task bar appears on the Gantt chart, and the new start date, finish date, and duration appear in the appropriate columns in the corresponding row of the Task Sheet.

6. Click to select the Task Name cell for the new task, and enter a name (see Fig. 3.2).

7. Enter any other information that's needed for the task on the Task Sheet.

> **NOTE:** You can drag from left to right (start to finish) or from right to left (finish to start) when you're dragging to create a task.

Figure 3.2
After you add the new task, give it a meaningful name.

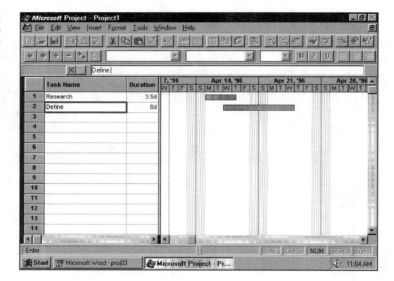

Dragging to Move or Reschedule a Task

If you're inclined to work with the schedule via the Gantt chart, you can also use the mouse to move and change the schedule for a task.

When you move a task using the mouse, the duration for the task never changes; in effect, dragging the task simply changes the start and finish dates. To move a task on the Gantt chart, point to the task bar until the mouse pointer changes to a four-headed arrow. Press and hold down the mouse button; Project displays a Task box containing information about the task (see Fig. 3.3). Drag the task to its new location; when you drag, the mouse pointer changes to a two-headed arrow, a gray outline appears to indicate the bar's position, and the changing task dates are reflected in the Task box. You can drag the task to the left to schedule it earlier, or to the right to schedule it later. Release the mouse button when the dates you want appear in the Task box.

This pointer indicates that you can move the task.

Figure 3.3
While you're moving a
task bar, information
about the task
appears on-screen.

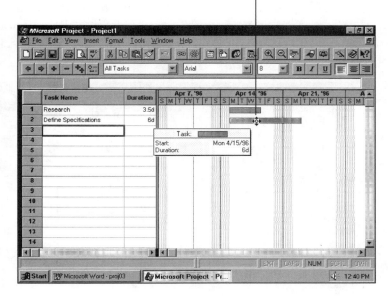

CAUTION: If you've selected `Project Start Date` for the Schedule From option in the Project Info dialog box, you need to reset Start Date in that dialog box if you ever drag a task earlier than the present start date. If you're scheduling the project from the Finish Date, you need to reset that date if you ever drag a task later than the present finish date.

You can change the finish date, thus altering the task's duration, by dragging the right end of the task bar. (You can't resize the task bar from its left end.) Simply point to the right end of the bar on the Gantt chart so that the mouse pointer changes to a right-pointing arrow. Press and hold down the mouse button; the Task box appears as shown in Figure 3.4. Drag to the left to make the task shorter or to the right to make the task longer. When the Duration value in the

Task box is the duration you want, release the mouse button to complete the change. When you drag to change the duration, the control you have might not be as precise as it would be if you made the change in the Duration column of the Task Sheet. For example, in the Task Sheet you can enter small increments of duration, such as 7.25d. When you drag, however, you can only reset the duration in increments of .5d, so you can choose 7.0d or 7.5d, but not 7.1d or 7.25d.

Figure 3.4
Dragging on the Gantt chart is a quick way to change the task's scheduled completion date.

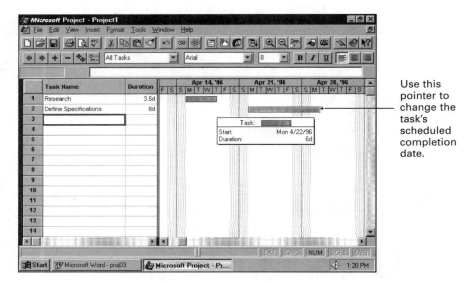

Use this pointer to change the task's scheduled completion date.

> **CAUTION:** If you try to drag the completion date to a time that's before the starting date, Project resets the task duration to 0d and converts the task to a milestone. See Chapter 2, "Setting Up a Project," to learn more about milestones.

It's possible to use the mouse to change both the start date and duration for a task, but it requires two separate operations. First, drag the task's Gantt chart bar to reposition it at the correct start date. Second, resize the duration by clicking and dragging the right end of the bar.

Creating Recurring Tasks

In previous versions of Project, if you had a task that would occur repeatedly during a project, such as a weekly review meeting to discuss the project's process, you had to enter a separate task for each meeting. In this version of Project (version 4.1 for Windows 95), however, you can automatically schedule tasks that will occur at set intervals; these are called *recurring tasks*.

For example, you can schedule monthly team meetings, a weekly conference call, or a daily status report. You can even set tasks to occur more than once each week—for example, every Monday and Wednesday.

TIP: Although you can create recurring tasks from a few different views in Project, adding these tasks from the Gantt Chart view often works best, because there you get a clear picture of where the recurring tasks fit in.

To add a recurring task to your schedule, perform the following steps:

1. In the Task Sheet, click to select the row that the first instance of the recurring task should precede. You do this because the recurring task will be inserted as a summary task on a single row of the Task Sheet, with the subtasks representing each recurrence hidden from view. (See Chapter 13, "Working with Outlining," to learn more about viewing subtasks.) Because the recurring tasks aren't dispersed throughout the task list by default, you need to place the summary recurring task early in the schedule, where it will be noticed by users of the file.

2. Open the Insert menu and click Insert Recurring Task. The Recurring Task Information dialog box appears, as shown in Figure 3.5.

3. Enter the desired Name and Duration for the task by clicking in each text box and typing the desired entry. Remember that you can use abbreviations to specify the exact timing you want to assign, such as 2h for a two-hour task.

4. Click to select one of the choices in the This Occurs area of the dialog box: Weekly, Monthly, and so on.

...controls the options that appear here.

Name your
recurring task
and set its
length.

Figure 3.5
You can specify that
a task recurs
several times.

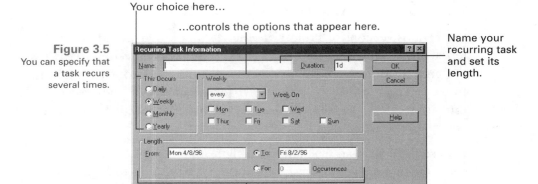

Project calculates or lets you specify how many times the task should recur.

5. Specify the interval between recurrences in the area to the right of This Occurs. The available choices vary depending on the This Occurs option you've selected. Basically, you can choose from the following:

- Dai_ly—Use the drop-down list to specify whether the task appears every day, every second day, every third day, and so on—up to every twelfth day. The D_ay choice includes all days in the schedule, and the Wor_kday choice only schedules the recurring task on days included in the calendar for the project.

- W_eekly—Use the Wee_k On drop-down list to specify whether the task appears every week, every second week, and so on—up to every twelfth week. Next, select each day of the week on which you want the task to recur. Change the entry in the From text box only if you want to schedule recurrences starting before—or a specified interval after—the project start date. Use the _To option to specify an ending date for the recurrence; otherwise, click the For O_ccurrences option and specify the number of times that the task should be scheduled after the start date.

- _Monthly—Use the D_ay option button to specify the day of the month (by date number, such as the 25th of every month), and the corresponding drop-down list to specify whether or not to schedule the task in every month of the project timeframe. If you want to schedule the recurring task by a day of the week rather than a date within each month, click the The option button, and use its drop-down lists to specify particular weekdays when the task should be scheduled, and whether or not to schedule the task every month. The Length options work exactly like the ones described under Weekly above.

TIP: Whenever possible, schedule tasks by selecting a day of the week rather than entering a date. This helps you to avoid scheduling any instances of the recurring task on a nonworking date.

- Yearly—Click the option button beside the upper text box, and enter a single schedule date for the recurring task. Or, click the The button and use the drop-down lists to choose a month, weekday, and particular weekday in that month (first, second, and so on) for the task. Again, the Length options work as described above.

6. Click OK to accept your choices. If, by chance, one or more of the recurrences you've scheduled appears on a day that's not a working day according to the project calendar, Project asks if you want to reschedule the task (see Fig. 3.6). To reschedule the task and continue, click OK.

Figure 3.6
If a recurring task doesn't fit into the working schedule, Project offers to reschedule it.

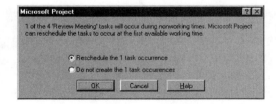

The recurring task appears in the Task Sheet in boldface to indicate that it's a summary task. If you look at the row numbers to the right, you'll notice that some numbers no longer appear. For example, if the summary task appears in row 2, but the next row in the sheet is row 7, it's because rows 3–6 are hidden rows that each contain an individual recurrence. The duration, start date, and finish date for this summary task will span all the recurrences of the task.

To make adjustments to the schedule for the recurring task, click any cell in the summary task row. Press Shift+F2; alternatively, open the Insert menu and click Recurring Task Information (or right-click the task and click Recurring Task Information). Make the changes you want, and then click OK to complete your changes.

To delete the recurring task, select the summary task by clicking its row number, then press the Delete key (or open the Edit menu and click Delete Task); alternatively, right-click the selected row and click Delete Task. This deletes the summary line and all the hidden rows that represent recurrences of the task.

Linking and Unlinking Tasks

One major drawback to the yellow pad method of project planning is that it almost forces you into a simple type of thinking: because each task is on a separate line, it is separate and distinct from all other tasks on the list. That's perception, not reality.

Most projects don't progress in so neat a fashion. Many tasks *are* completely independent of one another, but sometimes tasks need to occur simultaneously. Other times, one task cannot start until another finishes. Some tasks need to start or finish simultaneously. Such a connection between the "destinies" of two tasks is called a *task relationship*. In Project, you define task relationships by creating *links*.

Links in your schedule define how tasks should proceed. The first task in a link, which usually must be completed before the other linked tasks can start, is called the *predecessor*. Tasks that follow and depend on predecessors are called *successors*. A predecessor can have more than one successor, and successors can serve as predecessors for other tasks, creating a "chain" of linked events. A successor task can even have multiple predecessors—for example, in a situation where three tasks must finish before one successor task can start.

One detail that might be difficult to get your arms around is that a predecessor task is identified by its ID number. The task ID is based on the task's current position (what row it's in) on the Task Sheet, *not* its individual schedule. It's perfectly okay to specify the task in row 20 as the predecessor to the task in row 12 in a Finish-to-Start link (described next), as long as the finish date for the row 20 task precedes the start date for the row 12 task. Task ID numbers change automatically if you move tasks to a new row, or sort the tasks in the Task Sheet.

Link Types

Project offers four types of links. Links are visually represented by lines and arrows between tasks in Gantt charts, calendars, and PERT charts that are based on your schedule. Each link is identified with a particular abbreviation:

- The most common kind of link is a *Finish-to-Start (FS) relationship*, where the first task must be finished before the next task can begin (see Fig. 3.7). For example, a product prototype might need to be approved before prototype testing can begin. An FS relationship is the simplest type of link to create. It's the default link type, and Project creates an FS relationship if you don't specify a different link type.

The task in row 10 must be completed before work can begin on the task in row 12.

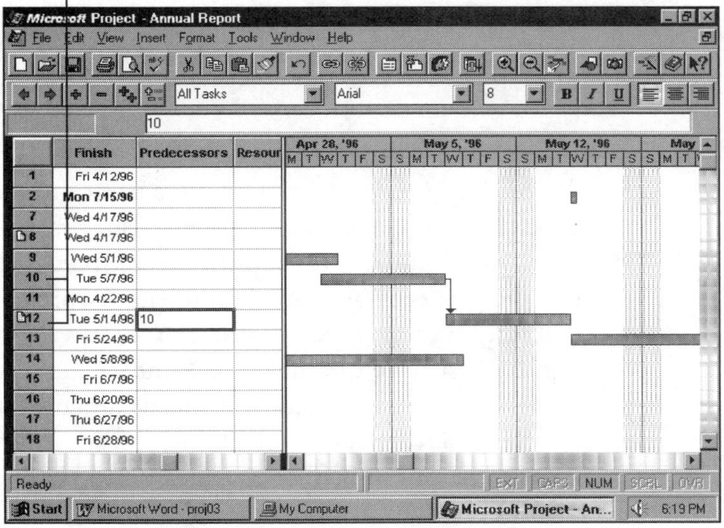

Figure 3.7
A Finish-to-Start (FS) link means that the predecessor task must finish so the successor task can start.

- A *Start-to-Start (SS) relationship* specifies that two tasks must start at the same time (see Fig. 3.8). Use this type of relationship in situations where you want resources to work closely together, such as when an internal engineering department is working in concert with freelance resources. In this case, you're specifying that there can be no delay in the start of the successor task once the predecessor task starts; as soon as your engineering department's ready to go, the freelancer also must be ready to go.

The tasks in rows 9 and 14 must start simultaneously.

Figure 3.8
A Start-to-Start (SS) link indicates when tasks must begin at the same time.

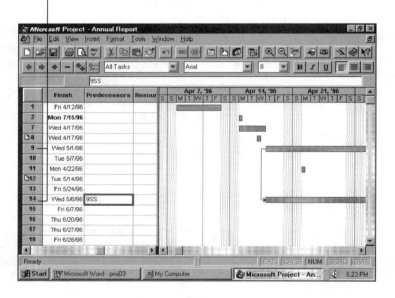

- A *Finish-to-Finish (FF) relationship* means that two tasks must end at the same time (see Fig. 3.9). Such a situation might arise when multiple tasks must be completed simultaneously, but the predecessor task is more lengthy or resource intensive than any successor task. For example, let's say that you're creating the first issue of a new magazine. When the page layout task (the predecessor) ends, it means an automatic end to the ad sales task (the successor), because at that point the magazine's page design is finalized, and no more time is available to incorporate new advertisements.

The tasks in rows 7 and 8 must end simultaneously.

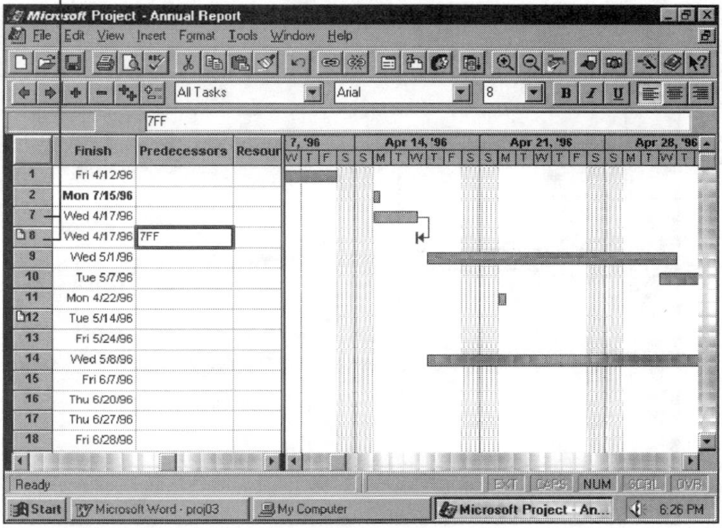

Figure 3.9
A Finish-to-Finish (FF)
relationship identifies
tasks timed to end
together.

- *A Start-to-Finish (SF) relationship* is a bit more complex than the other relationships, and therefore is used less often. In such a relationship, the predecessor task cannot finish until the successor task begins (see Fig. 3.10). Consider this accounting example: A company's quarterly or annual books have to remain "open" until the period-end closing procedures begin, no matter when that actually occurs.

CAUTION: Before you begin linking with abandon, here's a word of caution. At times, when you create a particular relationship that requires it, Project might change the schedule for a successor task so that its schedule is consistent with a linked task. For example, if you create an FF relationship and the successor task's finish date is earlier than the predecessor's finish date, Project shifts the successor task's schedule so that it has the correct finish date yet retains its original duration. Project might also shift successor tasks that are attached to any predecessor task you move, so don't be too surprised.

The task in row 10 must get underway before the task in row 9 can end.

Figure 3.10
A Start-to-Finish (SF) relationship identifies when the successor task must start before the predecessor can end, such as when a publication design cycle must begin before the copy can be finalized.

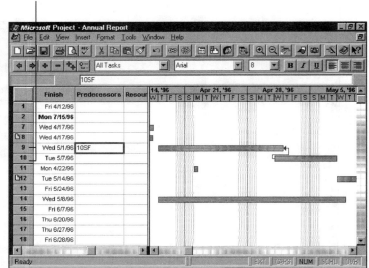

Linking Tasks on the Task Sheet

Recall from the description of the Task Sheet in Chapter 2, "Setting Up a Project," that one of the columns in the default Task Sheet is the Predecessors column. You can use this column to create links simply by typing; to do so, follow these steps:

1. Click to select the cell in the Predecessors column in the row holding the task that will be the successor task. For example, if you want the task in row 12 to start when the task in row 10 finishes, click the Predecessors cell in row 12.

2. Type the row number for the predecessor task.

3. If you want to designate a Start-to-Start, Finish-to-Finish, or Start-to-Finish link rather than the default Finish-to-Start link type, type its abbreviation using upper- or lowercase characters. You don't need a space between the predecessor's row number and the abbreviation. Your entry might resemble any of the ones shown in Figures 3.8, 3.9, and 3.10.

4. (Optional) To specify an additional predecessor, click any cell in the row holding the predecessor task, and then type the link type abbreviation; or, in the Predecessors cell of the successor

task, continue the entry by typing a comma followed by the task number and link type abbreviation (without any spaces).

5. (Optional) Repeat step 4 if you want to add other predecessors.

6. After you've created all the links you want in the successor task's Predecessors cell, press Enter to finalize the link(s).

If you decide to make a change to a link, simply edit the link information by clicking the appropriate Predecessors cell and making your changes.

Linking Tasks with the Mouse

Using the mouse along with the Task Sheet can make even faster work of creating links between tasks—but only if you want to create the default type of link, an FS relationship. Also, links created with the method described next always assume that the task that's lower in the task list (with the higher row number) is the successor task; therefore, Project adjusts that successor task's schedule, if needed, to ensure that it follows the predecessor.

TIP: You can create links between tasks shown in Calendar view or in PERT Chart view by dragging between the tasks. You'll learn more about these views in Chapter 9, "Working with the Different Project Views."

One of the advantages to using the mouse to create your links is that you don't have to scroll right to the Predecessors column (which, at the default Task Sheet pane size, scrolls the Task Name column out of view), so you can see the task's name as well as the Gantt bar representing its schedule. The following steps also make it easy to link several tasks in a single operation:

1. Drag to select cells in two or more adjacent tasks. If you want to select noncontiguous tasks, click a cell in the predecessor task row, press and hold down the Ctrl key, and click a cell in the successor task row—both cells will be selected (see Fig. 3.11). If you want to select additional noncontiguous tasks, continue to hold down Ctrl and click the other rows.

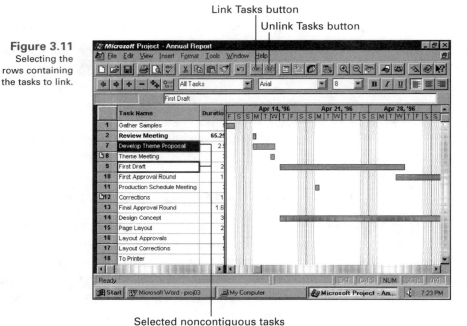

Link Tasks button

Unlink Tasks button

Figure 3.11
Selecting the
rows containing
the tasks to link.

Selected noncontiguous tasks

2. Press Ctrl+F2, click the Link Tasks button on the Standard toolbar, or open the Edit menu and click Link Tasks. Project creates the link(s) between the rows you've selected.

Linking via Task Information

The Task Information dialog box lets you view and alter numerous crucial details about a task. This dialog box offers five tabs of information, including the Notes tab that you learned about when creating task notes in Chapter 2, "Setting Up a Project," and the Predecessors tab, which enables you to create and edit links to predecessors for the selected task. The obvious disadvantage to this method is that you have to be familiar with details about the predecessor task you want to choose, or the schedule for the predecessor, because you might not be able to view that information while the dialog box is displayed.

To display the Predecessors tab in the Task Information dialog box, click a cell in the task for which you want to create or work with predecessors (that is, click a cell in the successor task row). Press Shift+F2; alternatively, click the Information button on the Standard toolbar,

or if you prefer, open the Insert menu and click Task Information
(or right-click the task and then click Task Information). As another
method, you can simply double-click a cell in the successor task row in
the Task Sheet. When the Task Information dialog box appears, click
the Predecessors tab so that the dialog box resembles Figure 3.12.

Type the predecessor task's ID (row) number.

Information button

Figure 3.12
You can use the
Predecessors tab in the
Task Information dialog
box to create or edit
links to predecessor
tasks.

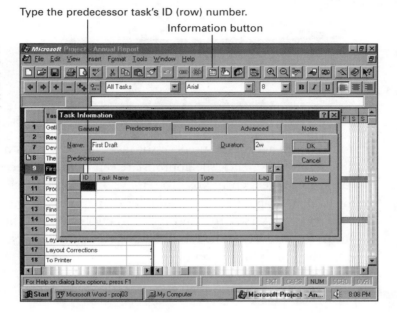

To add a predecessor, type the ID (row) number for the predecessor
task in the first cell of the ID column below the Predecessors choice.
Press Enter or Tab, or click the Enter button (it looks like a checkmark) beside the text entry box above the column heads. (The text
entry area here operates just like the one above the Task Sheet.) Project
enters the predecessor's task name, and by default enters Finish-to-
Start (FS) in the Type column.

To specify a different type, click the Type cell for this predecessor, and
do one of the following:

- Select the type that currently appears in the text entry box,
  type the abbreviation for the preferred type of link, and click
  the Enter button (which looks like a checkmark).

• Click the down arrow at the right end of the text entry box to display a drop-down list of link types (see Fig. 3.13), and click the preferred type of link.

Figure 3.13
Select another link
type.

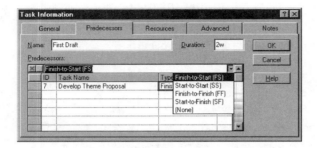

You can add additional predecessor tasks in lower rows of the tab. To edit any link, click the appropriate cell in the predecessor line, then edit it in the text entry box. To remove a predecessor, click the ID cell for it, then drag over the ID number that appears in the text entry box, press Backspace to remove it, and click the Enter button. When you're finished using the tab to add or edit predecessors, click OK to close the task information dialog box.

NOTE: For information about the Lag column for predecessor tasks, see the "Working with Lead Times or Lag Times" section later in this chapter.

Unlinking Tasks

To remove a link between tasks, you have to work from the successor task, not the predecessor task. Removing a link does not change the schedule for the successor task, unless that schedule was changed by Project when the link was created. If Project did automatically adjust the successor task schedule based on a link you added, then when you remove the link, Project returns the successor task to its original schedule.

Use any of the following methods to break the link:

- Click to select any cell in the successor task row, then click the Unlink Tasks button.
- Click to select the Predecessors cell in the successor task row. Right-click the cell, then choose Clear Cell.

> **CAUTION:** Do not press Delete to clear the contents of the Predecessors cell! Doing so deletes the entire task rather than the task link.

- Click the Information button on the Standard toolbar (or use the method of your choice) to display the Task Information dialog box, then click the Predecessors tab. Delete the ID number for the predecessor to remove the link.
- Double-click the appropriate link line between two tasks in the Gantt chart. Choose Delete in the Task Dependency dialog box that appears.

Working with Lead Times and Lag Times

Reality dictates the way your schedule must progress, and also dictates how Project enables you to define task relationships. Time is analog, or continuous. Even though it can be expressed in discrete units such as minutes and seconds, it flows and blends together. Moreover, events blend together in time—even though tasks might seem to follow one after another, they in fact might flow together more loosely, overlapping or occurring after a delay.

Project accounts for this flexibility of time by enabling you to schedule *lead time* and *lag time* for linked tasks. Adding lead time causes the successor task to overlap with the predecessor task; this means that even though the task link is, for example, Finish-to-Start, the successor task can start before the predecessor task is finished. Adding lag time on a Finish-to-Start relationship enables you to insert a delay between the finish of the predecessor task and the start of the successor task. For example, if a predecessor task is scheduled to end on a Wednesday, you can schedule the successor task to begin the following Wednesday, without breaking the link between the two tasks.

You can schedule lead or lag time by entering the proper code for it in the Predecessor column entry (by appending it to the predecessor task number and task type specification), or by entering the code in the Lag column of the Predecessors tab of the Task Information dialog box, or in the Lag text box of the Task Dependency dialog box. You specify lead time using a minus sign (-) and lag time using a plus sign (+). You can specify the timing in terms of duration intervals (2h for two hours, 2d for two days, and so on) or as a percentage of the predecessor task's duration.

For example, if you want to create a Finish-to-Start link to task 7 with a two-day lead time, enter **7FS-2d** on the Task Sheet in the Predecessors cell for the successor task (see Fig. 3.14). If you're entering the lead time in the Lag column (Task Information dialog box) or Lag text box (Task Dependency dialog box), you only have to enter **-2d**. A Lag entry using percentages might be **7FS-50%** (on the Task Sheet) or **-27%** (in either of the dialog boxes), which respectively would insert lead time equivalent to 50% or 27% of the predecessor task's duration before the start date of the successor task. To specify lag time (a pause) rather than lead time, you simply use a plus sign rather than a minus sign in your entries.

However, there's a glitch when you're creating lead time. Project might not automatically reschedule the successor task to an earlier start date when you create lead time, just as it won't let you drag the left end of a Gantt chart bar to adjust the start date of a task. In such a case (which occurs when Project is not set to automatically recalculate schedule changes), you have to adjust the start date for the successor task in the Start column of the Task Sheet, or press F9 if you see Calculate in the status bar to tell Project to move the successor task's Gantt chart bar to the left to show the lead time.

By contrast, you can create lag time by dragging the Gantt chart bar for an existing successor task to the right. As soon as you release the mouse button, Project adds the lag time.

Lag time   Lead time

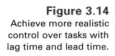
Figure 3.14
Achieve more realistic
control over tasks with
lag time and lead time.

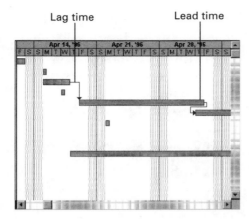

NOTE: In real life, problems arise, resources are detained, and other delays gum up the works. You should always include a bit of "cushion time" in your schedule to allow for such problems.

You have two choices of how to build this cushion into your project schedule. The first is to schedule extra time for some tasks, especially those for which you're less confident estimating a duration. The second is to assign the anticipated duration for a task, but to build in some lag time after the task. I prefer the latter method, especially when dealing with a resource outside my company. I give the outside resource a task deadline (finish date) that's at least a couple of days before the real (internal) date when I require the task to be completed. This technique not only provides cushion time, but allows you, as manager of the project, some time to review the work from the outside resource, which is especially prudent if you haven't previously dealt with that resource.

Setting Task Constraints

As you've learned elsewhere in this book, Project will calculate a project <u>f</u>inish date or start <u>d</u>ate for you depending on the duration and nature of the tasks you create. This book has focused quite a bit already on the flexibility you have in moving or rescheduling parts of tasks.

That flexibility is great if you're the only person able to edit the schedule. If, however, you want to make the schedule a bit more solid in most cases, you can establish *constraints* for tasks, just to make tasks a bit more difficult to move, and to control how the schedule progresses. Table 3.1 reviews the constraints.

Table 3.1 Constraints for Controlling Individual Task Schedule		
Constraint	**Abbreviation**	**Description**
As Soon As Possible	ASAP	Ensures that the task starts as soon as possible, based on the completion of any predecessors, and is the default constraint if you enter only the Duration for the task
As Late As Possible	ALAP	Ensures that the task starts as late as possible when the project is being scheduled from its finish date, and is the default constraint if you enter only the Duration for the task in this type of schedule
Finish No Earlier Than	FNET	Prevents a task from finishing prematurely, and is the default if you edit or enter the task's finish date
Start No Earlier Than	SNET	Prevents a task from starting before the specified date, and is the default if you edit or enter the task's start date
Finish No Later Than	FNLT	Sets the drop-dead deadline for the task, but enables the task to start earlier if needed
Start No Later Than	SNLT	Sets the absolute latest date when the task can commence, but enables the task to start earlier if needed
Must Finish On	MFO	Specifies that a task must finish no sooner or later than a specified date
Must Start On	MSO	Specifies that a task must start no sooner or later than a specified date

To create constraints for a task, perform the following steps:

1. Click a cell in the Task Sheet row of the task you want to create constraints for.

2. Right-click the task or open the Insert menu and click Task Information. Alternatively, press Shift+F2 or click the Information button on the Standard toolbar. The Task Information dialog box appears.

3. Click the Advanced tab to display the advanced options (see Fig. 3.15).

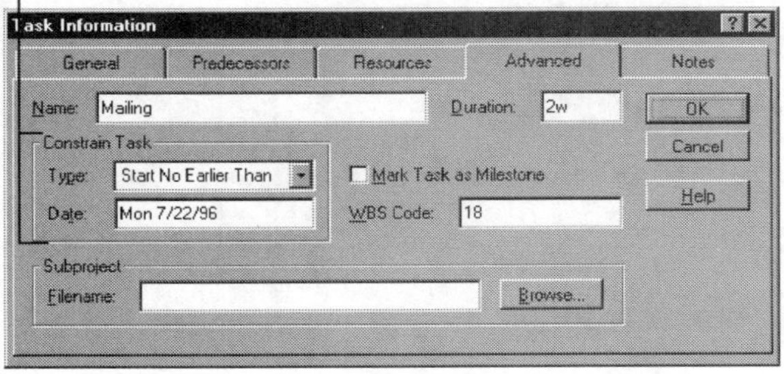

Set the constraints

Figure 3.15
Use this tab of the Task Information dialog box to create constraints.

4. Click the down arrow beside the Type drop-down list to display a list of constraint types. Select the type of constraint you want for the selected task.

5. Double-click the date in the Date text box, and type the new date to define the constraint.

6. Click OK to close the dialog box and finalize the constraint.

Editing Other Task Information

So far, you've worked in the Predecessors, Advanced, and Notes tabs of the Task Information dialog box. The fastest way to display this dialog box is to click a cell in the task that you want to learn more about or change information for, and then click the Information button on the Standard toolbar. You can click any tab in the Task Information dialog box to display its options, edit them as needed, and then click OK to close the dialog box. This section takes a brief look at the options not examined thus far.

The first tab in the Task Information dialog box is the General tab (see Fig. 3.16). It lets you work with general parameters for the task, like its start and finish date, which you've also learned to adjust via other methods.

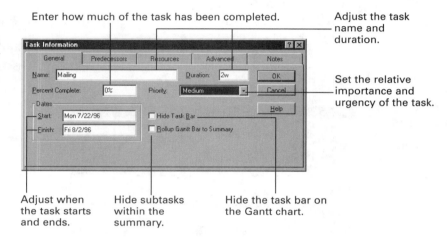

Enter how much of the task has been completed.

Adjust the task name and duration.

Figure 3.16
Here's another opportunity to revise task basics.

Set the relative importance and urgency of the task.

Adjust when the task starts and ends.

Hide subtasks within the summary.

Hide the task bar on the Gantt chart.

The Predecessors tab was described earlier in this chapter. It enables you to alter the task name and duration, as well as specify predecessors for the selected task to create links. The Resources tab, shown in Figure 3.17, is covered in Chapter 4, "Managing Resources." This tab enables you to assign one or more resources (coworkers, vendors, and so on) who will complete the specified task.

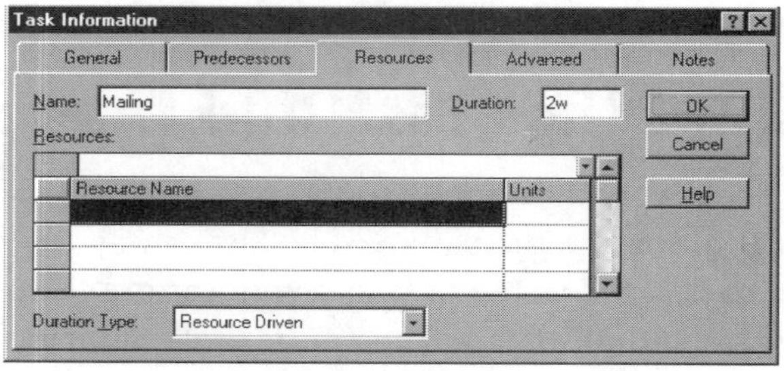

Figure 3.17
This tab enables you to specify the means to ensure that a task is completed.

In addition to the Constrain Task options you learned about in the preceding section, the Advanced tab (refer to Fig. 3.15) offers a few more options of interest. The Mark Task As Milestone check box converts the task to a milestone. If you want to use a specialized coding system, enter the code to use for the task in the WBS Code text box. If you want to use a subproject in a separate file that defines the steps for a task, specify a Filename or Browse for it. The final tab is where you enter and edit notes about the selected task.

NOTE: As an example, you might want to use WBS codes starting with 1000 (1001, 1002, and so on), or you might want to use the year as a code prefix (9601, 9602, and so on). The latter method can be useful if your project schedule falls into more than one calendar year.

CHAPTER 4

MANAGING RESOURCES

If you're a person who lives by your lists, then the first few chapters of this book might already have introduced you to the key concepts you need to be familiar with when using Project. In those chapters, you learned the steps for building and scheduling the tasks associated with your plan. All the information you've compiled so far, however, doesn't answer the most critical question of all: How in the world is everything on the list going to be done? This chapter explores the following:

- ■ **What resources are in Project**
- ■ **How the resources you select affect the schedule**
- ■ **Adding resources for your project**
- ■ **Controlling how a resource's time is scheduled**
- ■ **Evaluating how much each task will cost**

What Is Resource-Driven Scheduling?

Resources complete the tasks you've specified in a plan or schedule, and can consist of more than simply the name of a coworker or team member. For example, a resource can be an outside freelancer or consulting firm; it can be a vendor that provides printing or manufacturing; it can be raw materials or supplies needed for a project, such as paper that needs to be purchased for a printing job; or, a resource can be a piece of equipment you might need to use during a project, whether that equipment exists in your company and is shared by others, or is leased from an outside firm. In a nutshell, resources include all the people and equipment used to complete tasks in a project.

You face several challenges when you try to assign resources to a project:

- You're generally limited in the number of resources available to you. That is, you can't just ask anyone in your company to handle a task for you. You have to work with the resources made available to you, and figure out how to maximize the contribution made by each one.

- You're generally competing with others for each resource's time. For example, a resource from your company's marketing department might be handling items for you and five other colleagues in a given week.

- Even if money is no object, you generally can't just hand an entire project off to outside resources. It takes an insider—you or someone else—to coordinate with and manage contracted outside resources, and to ensure that your tasks don't suffer because of an external resource's commitments to other clients.

- Even in the most extreme circumstances, certain tasks require at least a minimum amount of a resource's time. For example, if a task requires that a resource fly from Los Angeles to your city with an approval mock-up of a new product, and the flight plus the commute from the airport always requires eight hours, you simply can't ask the resource to do it in six. People like to deliver excellent, timely work, but most haven't perfected the ability to warp time.

If you've had any education in economics, you'll recognize that the preceding points sound a lot like the concept of *scarcity*. When resources in a marketplace are scarce, competition for the resources increase, so that people pay more for them and also have to use them more wisely.

With scarcity of resources or anything else, what you can accomplish is limited by your access to the resources to do it. You can't make steel, for example, if scarcity makes coal so expensive that you can't afford to buy it for the furnace.

Project takes resource scarcity into account by using *resource-driven scheduling* by default. Under resource-driven scheduling, Project may adjust a task's duration to take into account both the amount of work the task requires and the amount of resources assigned to it. For example, suppose that you have a task with a duration of three days, and the default calendar for the project calls for eight-hour workdays. This means that the project's duration in hours is 24. Suppose, however, that you assign a resource to the project, and the resource only works six hours per day. It'll take that resource four working days (6 hours times 4 days equals 24 hours) rather than three to finish the project, so Project adjusts the start or finish date for the task accordingly.

NOTE: You can override the resource-driven duration for any task. To learn how to do so, see the "Overriding a Resource-Driven Duration" section later in this chapter.

So, resource-driven scheduling results in the resources you select having a critical impact on your plan. As you create resources and make the related choices described in the remainder of this chapter, keep in mind how those choices might affect the overall schedule. If you encounter difficulties or conflicts as you create and work with resources, read Chapters 5, "Resolving Overallocations and Overbooked Resources," and 6, "Optimizing the Schedule," which provide techniques for addressing those difficulties.

Viewing and Using the Project Resource Sheet

The Task Sheet, which you learned to work with in earlier chapters, specifies *what* needs to happen in a project and *when* it needs to happen. (I'll assume that someone in your company also knows *why* it needs to happen.) The Resource Sheet for your schedule enables you to specify *who* will make it happen, and *how*.

Use the Resource Sheet to build the list of resources you'll need to complete all the tasks you've listed on the Task Sheet for the schedule. To view the Resource Sheet, shown in Figure 4.1, open the View menu and click Resource Sheet. Just as each row in the Task Sheet holds information about a single task, each row in the Resource Sheet holds all the details about a single resource. Each column represents a particular *field*, or type of information. You can add columns that show information Project calculates, such as cost variances.

Figure 4.1
You can use the Resource Sheet to add resources to your project file.

Click a cell to select it

Click a column heading to select a whole column

Click a row number to select a whole row

Each row holds information about a single resource

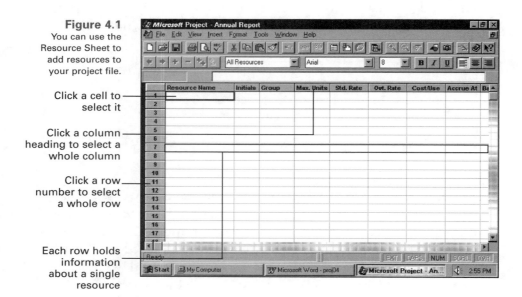

To select a cell in the Resource Sheet, click it, or drag to select (highlight) groups of cells. Alternatively, use the arrow keys to move the cell selector around. To select an entire column or row, click the column name or row number. Right-clicking any selection displays a shortcut menu with commands that you can perform on the selection. For example, you can click Insert Resource on the shortcut menu to insert a new, blank resource at the selected location in the Resource Sheet.

> **NOTE:** You can make adjustments to the size and position of columns—or add columns—in the Resource Sheet just as you did in the Task Sheet. The steps are virtually the same in the Resource Sheet as they were in the Task Sheet. To learn more, see "Adjusting the Task Sheet" in Chapter 2, "Setting Up a Project." One important column you might want to add is for resources' e-mail addresses.

Setting Up a New Resource

By default, the resource sheet has 10 columns that enable you to track information that might be crucial to your plan. This section takes a look at the basic method for making entries in these columns, as well as the five columns that are most essential to use in defining the resource. Because the remaining columns deal with the resource calendars and costs, each of which requires a detailed discussion, I'll cover those columns in the next two sections of this chapter, after you get your feet wet here.

To start a new resource, click the first cell of a new, blank row in the Resource Sheet, and type the resource name. As you type, the Enter button and Cancel button appear beside the text entry box above the column headings (see Fig. 4.2). To finish entering the name, click the Enter button. Project fills in some default information about the resource, such as entering a 1 in the Max. Units column. Then, you can press Tab to move to the next column to the right, or press Enter to move down to the next row and list all resources by name only.

> **CAUTION:** To remove the contents of a cell in the Resource Sheet, do not simply click the cell and press Delete. Doing so removes the entire resource, not just the contents of the selected cell. Instead, right-click the cell and then click Clear Cell to remove its contents.

Figure 4.2
Navigate in the
Resource Sheet as
you do in the Task

Cancel button—
click to cancel the
entry

Enter button—
click to finish
the entry

Text entry box—

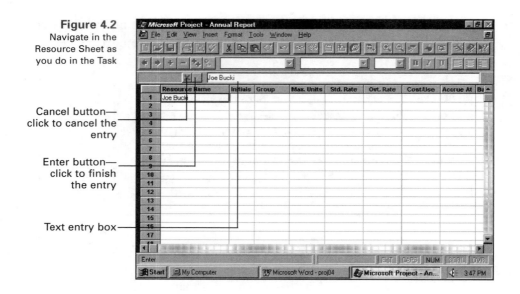

The style you use to create resources is up to you. You can use the Tab key after each entry to move across the row and complete each field entry for that resource. Or, you can simply enter all the resource names, then come back to each row and fill in the details. As noted at the start of this section, five of the columns or fields are basic, yet essential in identifying each resource as you assign it to tasks in your plan:

- **Resource Name**—Enter the full name for the resource, such as the name of a team member, supply vendor, or independent contractor.

- **Initials**—Don't be afraid to use long resource names. Project also enables you to identify a resource by its initials, entered in this column. By default, Project will use the first initial of the Resource Name entry for the Initials column. You should, however, select the Initials entry and type another that's more specific. I recommend making them more specific than a person's first and last initials, because it's pretty common to encounter people with the same initials. One approach is to use all or part of the first name, along with the last initial, as in JoeB, short for Joe Bucki.

- **Group**—When your resource belongs to a group and it might be significant to identify that group for the purposes of your project, enter the group name in the Group column. For example, if your team members come from several departments in your company, and you want to track each department's contribution, enter the department name. Or, if you're working with several different contractors for a project, each of which needs to be entered as a separate resource, you can enter **Contract** in the Group column for each of them to be able to track their collective performance.

- **Max. Units**—The default entry for this column, 1, means that for each scheduled workday, the resource offers one person (or machine, or so on) for the full duration of the workday. Entries of less than one indicate part-time work (more on that in Chapter 5), but entries of more than one don't assign overtime (more on overtime in Chapter 6). Entries of more than one mean that the resource might be offering additional people (or machines) for assignments. So, for example, if a resource offers four people to handle each task, you would change the Max. Units entry for the resource to **4**. The maximum entry for this column is 100.

- **Code**—This column at the far right side of the Resource Sheet enables you to enter an alphanumeric code to identify the resource. This code might be a department number that corresponds to your entry in the Group column, or might be a unique number such as a Purchase Order number that you've obtained for payment of the resource.

Once you've entered this basic information about several resources, your Resource Sheet might resemble the one shown in Figure 4.3.

Assigning Resource Costs

There's a cost associated with every resource, even when the resource is seemingly free because it comes from within your company. In fact, tracking your use of internal resources during the year can be useful during year-end budgeting, when your company determines how costs from administrative or service departments are allocated to (charged to) departments that are profit centers. For example, you don't want your department to be charged for a third of the marketing department's time, if your department only used about 10% of that time, while two other profit centers each used 45%.

Figure 4.3
Here's what the
Resource Sheet
looks like after you
sketch out
resources.

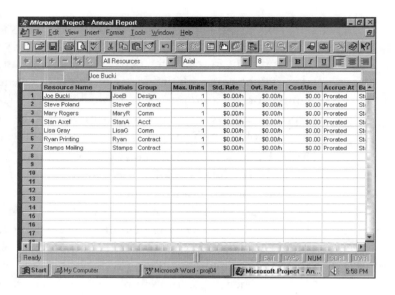

Similarly, you want to be smart about using resources with the correct responsibility level for projects, and resource cost can help you make such decisions. For example, let's say that one task in a project is calling various companies for examples of annual reports to use as idea-starters for the project. A designer in your company is paid about $15 per hour, and an administrative assistant is paid $10 per hour, and both resources are capable of and have the time to make the calls. In this case, it's much more efficient to have the less-expensive resource, the administrative assistant, handle the calls. Such a strategy frees up more of the designer's time for true creative work, yielding better results on your project and more time for other projects.

CAUTION: If your company doesn't require you to track internal resource costs, then don't enter any cost information for the resource. This will simplify tracking for costs that you do have to report.

Three columns on the Resource Sheet enable you to assign costs to the work performed by a resource. For most of these entries, you can simply select the cell and make your entry. Here are the fields that control costs on the Resource Sheet:

- **Std. Rate**—Enter the cost for work performed by the resource during normal working hours. To indicate an hourly rate, simply enter the hourly cost, such as **20** for $20 per hour. However, if the resource charges—or will be paid—by the minute (*m*), day (*d*), or week (*w*), enter the appropriate abbreviation along with your cost, such as **2000/w** for $2,000 per week. You also can enter yearly salary amounts using the *y* abbreviation, and Project will calculate the appropriate compensation for the actual length of the task.

- **Ovt. Rate**—If there's a possibility the resource will be working overtime on your project and your company is willing (or required by law, as for hourly, non-exempt workers) to pay a premium for the overtime, enter the overtime rate for the resource in this column, using the same method and abbreviations described above for the Std. Rate column.

- **Cost/Use**—A resource might have a set cost every time you use it; this cost might be the total cost for using the resource, or might supplement the hourly rate. For example, a courier service might charge you a set fee per delivery rather than an hourly rate. Or, a resource might charge you a set travel fee to your office in addition to an hourly rate. Enter an amount in this column (such as **15** for $15) to charge that fee to your project each time you assign the resource to a task and the task is completed.

TIP: If you're a consultant and need to provide both schedules and cost estimates for clients, then assigning costs to every resource can help you build a reasonably accurate cost estimate. Build some cushion into the cost estimate you provide to your client, however, unless the client is willing to pay for budget overruns.

Setting How Costs are Calculated

As you just learned, the costs for a resource can be calculated based on units of work completed, a per use fee, or both. Most of us, however, aren't foolish enough to pay for work before it's completed—and doing so isn't a standard accounting practice. On the other hand, it's not reasonable to expect that all task costs for any given task will hit your project's bottom line after the work on the task is completed, especially if the task lasts more than a week or so.

To have a realistic picture of the real costs incurred for your project at any given date, you need to specify the correct option for the resource's costs using the Accrue At column in the Resource Sheet. After you click a cell in this column, you can type the name for one of the available options. After you click a cell in this column, however, a drop-down list arrow appears at the right end of the text entry box. Click this arrow to display the Accrue At choices (see Fig. 4.4), and then click the method you'd like to select for the current resource:

- **Start**—Specifies that a resource's total cost for a task is expended as soon as work on the task starts. Use this method if you need to pay for contract work when the work begins. This choice also applies when a resource only has a per use cost that's due in advance, such as having to pay for a supply when you order it.

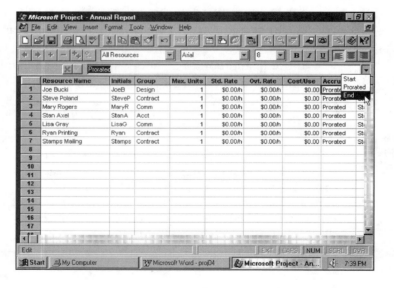

Figure 4.4
Use the drop-down list of the text entry box to select an Accrue At method.

- **Prorated**—Under this method (the default), costs hit your project's bottom line as the work progresses. For example, if a resource charges $10 per hour and has completed 10 hours of work on a task, under this Accrue At method, the project will show $100 in expenses to date for the task. Use this method when tracking expenses for resources within your company, or for resources that you need to pay on a regular monthly basis.

> **CAUTION:** Using the Prorated Accrue At method for resources that you work with only on a Per Use fee structure can lead to misleading reporting, because you might owe the full fee even if you need the resource for less time. For example, if you rent certain equipment, there might be a per-week minimum fee, due in advance. Make sure that you change the Accrue At method to Start or End for such Resources.

- **End**—This method specifies that the expense will officially be charged to the project when the task is completed. Use this choice when you need to approve work before payment or when payment isn't due until work on a task is completed.

Working with Fixed Costs

Some tasks have a particular cost no matter what resource handles the work. For example, you might know from experience that the freight for a particular shipment of products costs approximately $1,000 if you use either of two shippers. Or, you might know what a particular type of material costs, or might have an accurate estimate of what it costs to complete the task.

In such a case, if the cost won't vary and you don't plan to assign a specific resource to the task, assign a fixed cost for the task rather than creating a resource entry with a per use or other cost assignment. You have to go back to Gantt Chart view to start this process, as indicated in the following steps:

1. Open the View menu and click Gantt Chart, if you're not already at the Gantt Chart view.
2. Open the View menu, point to Table, and click Cost. Although it might not be immediately visible, the Task Sheet

pane at the left side of the view changes to display columns specific to tracking costs for the tasks.

3. Use the scroll bar to display the Fixed Cost column (see Fig. 4.5), or drag the vertical split bar to the right to display that column.

Figure 4.5
This is an example of working with the cost information for tasks instead of resources.

Enter fixed costs in this column

Drag to adjust the size of the left pane

Scroll

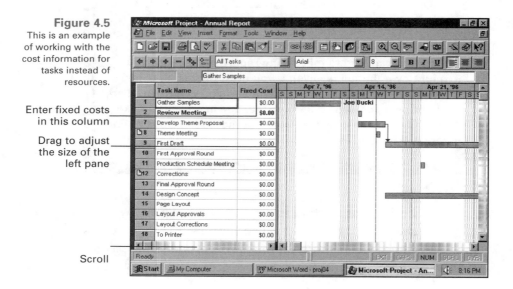

4. Click to select the Fixed Cost cell for the task to which you want to assign a fixed cost.

5. Type the amount (in dollars) of the fixed cost; for example, type **500** for $500. Press Enter or click the Enter button next to the text entry box to complete entering the fixed cost.

6. (Optional) Return to the view you were working in by using a choice on the <u>V</u>iew menu; for example, open the <u>V</u>iew menu and click Resource <u>S</u>heet. Or, to simply change the Task Sheet pane of Gantt Chart view back to its normal entry mode, open the <u>V</u>iew menu, point to <u>T</u>able, and click <u>E</u>ntry.

Working with Resource Calendars (Work Schedules)

By default, when you assign a resource to a task, Project assumes that the resource will follow the base calendar you've established for the schedule (using the Calendar drop-down list in the Project Info dialog box, as discussed in Chapter 2, "Setting Up a Project"). Thus, if the normal workday is eight hours, the resource's typical workday is eight hours; under this scenario, it takes the resource three working days to complete a project that's 24 hours in duration. Sometimes, however, a resource's real working schedule differs from that of the project.

Under Project's resource-driven default scheduling method, you need to ensure that you specify the real working schedule for each resource to develop an accurate schedule. For example, if the base calendar for the project is set to 24 hours, but the resource works only eight hours per day, the durations for the tasks you assign to that resource need to be three times longer than you had anticipated.

Choosing a Calendar

Use the Base Calendar column of the Resource Sheet to select the appropriate working schedule for a resource. The base calendars available for resources are the same as those available for projects. The 24 Hour calendar runs round the clock, seven days a week. The Standard calendar provides 40 hours per week, scheduled 8 a.m. to noon and 1 p.m. to 5 p.m., Monday through Friday. The Night Shift schedule also offers 40 hours per week, scheduled from Monday evening through early Saturday morning.

To change the Base Calendar entry for a resource, click the Base Calendar cell for the resource. When you do so, a drop-down list arrow appears at the right end of the text entry box. Click this arrow to display the three choices (see Fig. 4.6), click the calendar you want, and then press Enter or click the Enter button next to the text entry box.

Customizing a Resource Calendar

Sometimes you need to adjust the base calendar for a resource. For example, a resource might work two shifts per day, four days per week. Or, a resource might have upcoming dates when it's unavailable for use in your project. To ensure that the resource-driven scheduling properly adjusts the durations of tasks to which you assign this resource, and to prevent you from scheduling the resource for times when its unavailable, make sure that you adjust the selected base calendar for any resource that has special scheduling requirements.

Figure 4.6
It's easy to adjust
when a resource
works.

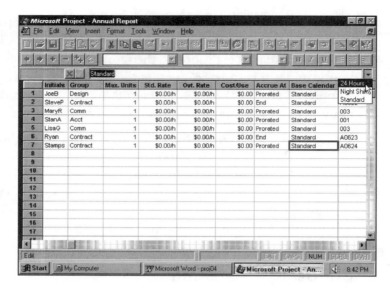

Figure 4.6
It's easy to adjust
when a resource
works.

To do so, follow these steps:

1. In the Resource Sheet, you'll use the Base Calendar column to select the working schedule that most closely approximates the actual availability of the resource.

2. Click to select the Base Calendar cell for the resource whose calendar you want to adjust.

3. Choose Tools, Change Working Time. The Change Working Time dialog box appears, as shown in Figure 4.7.

Figure 4.7
You can customize
the base calendar
for a resource.

Light shading
indicates a
working day

Calendar

Dark shading
indicates
nonworking day

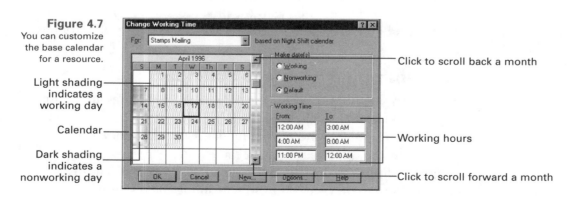

Click to scroll back a month

Working hours

Click to scroll forward a month

4. To specify whether or not the resource works on a particular day, click the date you want to change on the calendar. Then, in the Make date(s) area of the dialog box, click Working or Nonworking as needed. Dates to specify as Nonworking include holidays, vacation days, and other scheduled unavailability.

TIP: The Default selection returns a date to its default scheduling according to the selected base calendar. This includes both rescheduling the task as a working or nonworking day, and returning the Working Time entries to the defaults for the selected date.

5. To change the Working Time (daily working hours) for a date, select the date and make sure that's it's specified as a Working day or with the Default setting under Make date(s). In the Working Time area, edit or delete the desired To and From entries.

6. Continue scrolling the calendar view as needed, repeating steps 4 and 5 to change the schedule for additional dates. As you change the schedule for each date, Project indicates the edited date in the calendar, by marking the date with a light-blue shading (see Fig. 4.8).

Figure 4.8
The shading on April 9th indicates that it has custom scheduling.

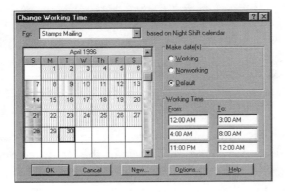

7. Click OK to close the Change Working Time dialog box and implement the scheduling changes you've specified.

Displaying Resource Information

If you're not comfortable working in the spreadsheet-like cells of the Resource Sheet, and would prefer a more convenient format in which to enter and edit the information about a resource, you can use the Resource Information dialog box shown in Figure 4.9. The Resource Information dialog box displays an entry for each column that appears in the Resource Sheet, with the same options available for each entry.

TIP: You also can display information about a resource by double-clicking any cell in that resource's row in the Resource Sheet.

Figure 4.9
Once you've displayed this dialog box from the Resource Sheet, you can use it to enter or edit information about a resource.

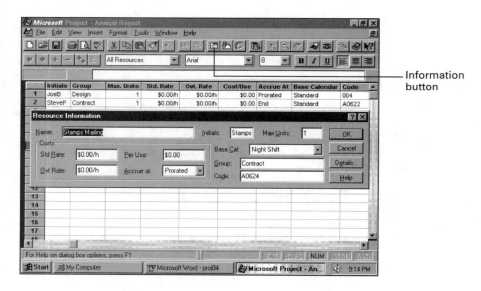

Information button

To display the Resource Information dialog box for a resource in any view in Project that shows all or part of the Resource Sheet, start by clicking a cell in the row for the desired resource. Then, open the Insert menu and click Resource Information (or right-click and then click Resource Information). Alternatively, press Shift+F2 or click the Information button on the Standard toolbar. Enter or edit information about the resource in the dialog box, then click OK to close the dialog box and accept the entries you've made. Your changes appear in the appropriate columns for the selected task in the Resource Sheet.

> **TIP:** You can create a new resource by clicking a blank row of the Resource Sheet, displaying the Resource Information dialog box, entering information about the new resource, and clicking OK.

Adding a Resource Note

Just as you can add more detailed notes about a particular task you've created, you can use a note to capture information about a particular resource. This feature can be particularly important when you're working with outside resources, or when a resource is handling particularly complex tasks. For example, you can use a note to record the name, title, and phone number for your contact at an external vendor. Or, you can add a note to a resource explaining why the resource has a per use fee in addition to an hourly rate. You can remind yourself of the names of key clients the resource has served in the past, in case someone working with your project file is interested in knowing more about the project resources.

The Notes for Resource dialog box is extremely flexible, to accommodate these kinds of information, and more. It offers a large, scrolling box where you can enter your note text, as shown in Figure 4.10.

To display and use the Notes for Resource dialog box to enter or edit information about a resource in the Resource Sheet, do the following:

1. Click a cell in the row holding the resource for which you want a note.

2. Click to open the Insert menu or right-click to display the resource shortcut menu. Click Resource Notes. Alternatively, click the Attach Note button on the Standard toolbar. The Notes for Resource dialog box appears.

3. Click the Notes box, and then type or edit the text of your note. If you highlight and delete all this text, Project removes the note altogether from the resource.

4. Click OK to close the Notes for Resource dialog box.

Figure 4.10
The Notes text entry box offers scrolling for longer notes.

Attach Note button

Click here and begin typing.

This marker indicates that you've entered a note about a resource.

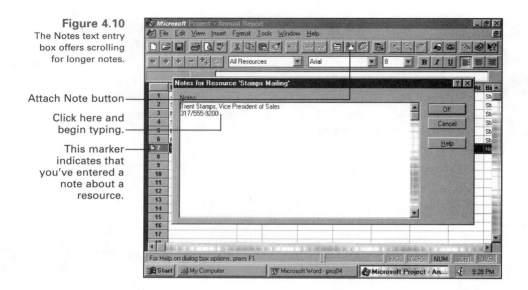

Assigning a Resource to a Task

Until now, this book has described tasks and resources as somewhat separate, discrete entities. You enter information about tasks in one part of Project and information about resources in another. In this section, you'll learn to mesh these two forms of information in your schedule. Keep in mind that the resources you assign to a particular task might cause Project to adjust the start or finish date for the task, depending on the availability of the resource. If a resource assignment causes a schedule change you don't want, use one of the methods described later in this section to choose a different resource for the task.

To assign resources to a particular task, you need to return to the location where you list the tasks for your schedule, the Task Sheet, or (in most cases) another view, the Task Entry view. To speed your work with resources, you might also want to display the Resource Management toolbar shown in Figure 4.11. To do so, right-click any toolbar on-screen and click Resource Management.

Figure 4.11
On this toolbar, you'll find tools for adding resources to tasks.

Resource Management toolbar

Task Entry View button

Resource Assignment button

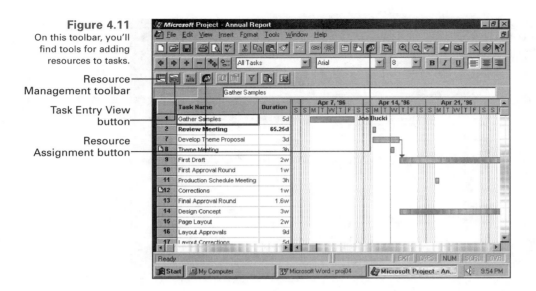

NOTE: You can work with task and resource information in other views, also. Chapter 9, "Working with the Different Project Views," introduces more of the views that are available, and helps you work with task and resource information. Most of the options in other views, however, work like the ones described here, so once you learn to display the other views in that later chapter, you can apply the techniques you learn here to those views, as well.

If you're most comfortable working in the Task Sheet, you might prefer to assign resources there by using the Resource Names column, along with the text entry box, or simply by typing. Switch to the Task Sheet, if necessary, by opening the View menu and clicking Gantt Chart. Scroll the Task Sheet pane so that it shows the Resource Names column. Click the cell for the task to which you want to assign a resource. If you remember the full resource name, type it in the selected cell and press Enter. Otherwise, click to display the drop-down list that appears at the right end of the text entry box, click the name of the resource you want (see Fig. 4.12), then press Enter or click the Enter button.

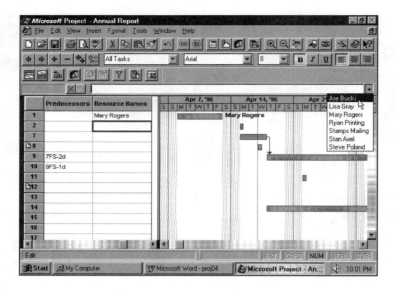

> **TIP:** If you type the name of a resource in the Resource
> Names column of the Task Sheet in Gantt Chart view, and
> the name is for a brand-new resource, Project adds a new
> row for that resource in the Resource Sheet. You then can
> open the <u>V</u>iew menu and click Resource <u>S</u>heet to switch to
> the Resource Sheet, where you can enter the remaining
> information about the resource.

If you're not comfortable with a lot of typing, or plan to enter multiple resources and want a faster method, you can display and use the Resource Assignment dialog box. (You can't use this method to assign a resource to a summary task; you can only use this method to assign resources to the tasks being summarized, if they're displayed.) To display this dialog box, click a cell in the Resource Names column. Open the <u>I</u>nsert menu and click Resource <u>A</u>ssignment. Alternatively, click the Resource Assignment button on the Standard or Resource Management toolbar, or press Alt+F8. The Resource Assignment dialog box appears, as shown in Figure 4.13.

To assign a resource to the cell you've selected, click the desired resource name in the Re<u>s</u>ources From list, then choose <u>A</u>ssign. You can continue using this dialog box to assign resources to other tasks. Simply select the

Resource Names cell for another task, then use the Resource Assignment dialog box to select and assign the resource. When you've finished assigning resources, click Close to close the Resource Assignment dialog box.

Figure 4.13
The Resource Assignment dialog box might be faster when you need to work with many resource assignments.

The resource assignment you make appears here.

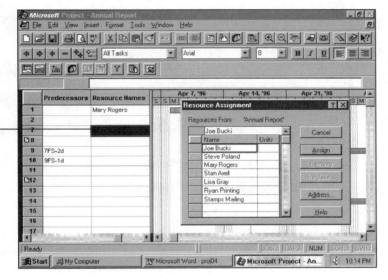

A final way to assign a resource to a single task from the Task Sheet is to right-click the task, then click the Task Information command (or click the Information button on the Standard toolbar). In the Task Information dialog box, click the Resources tab. Click the drop-down list arrow beside the text entry area, click a resource name, and click the Enter button. Click OK to close the Task Information dialog box.

The biggest drawback to a couple of the resource assignment techniques just described is that unless you've displayed the whole Task Sheet, you might not be able to see the name of the task to which you're assigning a resource. As such, you can use another view, *Task Entry view*, to enable you to be clear about which task you're entering a resource for. This view is sometimes referred to as the *Task Form*. To use this view to assign resources to tasks, do the following:

1. To switch to Task Entry view, click the Task Entry View button on the Resource Management toolbar. Alternatively, open the View menu and click More Views; then, in the Views list, scroll down to display Task Entry, click it, and click Apply. Task Entry view appears as shown in Figure 4.14.

Figure 4.14
You can use this view to enter and edit resource assignments.

Task Sheet

Use these buttons to select a task, if you prefer.

Specify a resource here.

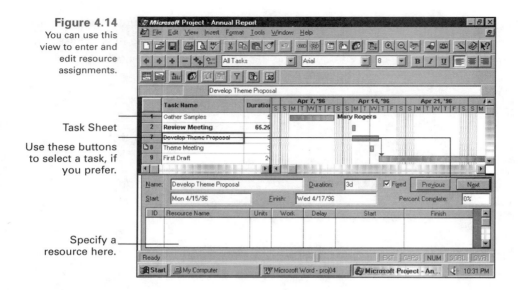

2. Select a task by choosing it from the Task Name column of the visible portion of the Task Sheet, or by using the Pre<u>v</u>ious and N<u>e</u>xt buttons in the lower area of the view.

3. Click the first blank row of the Resource Names column of the lower portion of the view. A highlight appears on the name of the selected task in the Task Sheet.

4. Click the drop-down list arrow at the right end of the text entry box, then click the name of the resource you want to select. Press Enter or click OK (which appears in place of the Pre<u>v</u>ious button) to complete your entry. After you do so, information about the selected resource appears in the lower pane of the display, as shown in Figure 4.15.

5. Repeat steps 2–5 to assign resources to other tasks.

When you're done working in Task Entry view, open the <u>V</u>iew menu and click the appropriate menu command to return to another view, such as <u>G</u>antt Chart. If the window remains divided into upper and lower panes, remove the split by opening the <u>W</u>indow menu and clicking Remove <u>S</u>plit.

Figure 4.15
Here's how a resource
assignment appears
when displayed in Task
Entry view (Task Form).

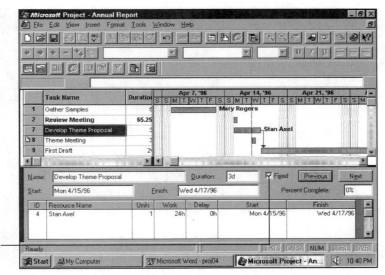

Specifying that a
resource schedule —
can't move

Start Dates and Delays

As you can see in the lower pane of the Text Entry view in Figure 4.15, the view shows the project and resource names, task duration, number of work hours the resource will require to finish the project, and start and finish dates. Beside the Work column, however, you'll find the Delay column. You can use this column to specify that you don't want a resource to begin exactly when the start of the working day begins, or that you have more than one resource assigned to the task (see the next two chapters for more details) and want one to start a certain length of time after the first resource, perhaps to check the first resource's work.

To enter a delay for a resource, switch to Task Entry view, and display the task information by clicking the task in the Task Name column of the Task Sheet (or by using the Previous and Next buttons). Click the Delay column and enter the delay time period, along with a time unit specification such as **h** for hours or **d** for days. Figure 4.16 shows an example.

Click OK in the lower pane of the view to complete specifying the delay. If necessary—such as when you're creating a delay for the sole resource assigned to the task—Project adjusts the start and finish dates for the task. Keep in mind that such changes can introduce scheduling conflicts, particularly if other linked tasks depend on the scheduled completion of the task you're working with.

Figure 4.16
You can create a
delay to adjust the
start of a resource's
work.

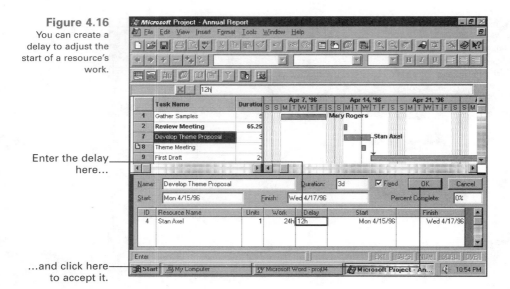

Enter the delay
here...

...and click here
to accept it.

Overriding a Resource-Driven Duration

This chapter has noted repeatedly that under Project's default resource-driven method of scheduling tasks, the resource(s) you assign to a task might cause Project to adjust the schedule for the task depending on the resource's availability. You can stop this happening for selected tasks, if you want, to prevent them from moving. For example, if your project requires filing accounting information by a particular federal filing deadline, you'll want the duration and schedule for the task to remain fixed.

You can specify a fixed duration for a task in the Task Entry view by selecting the task, then clicking to select the Fixed check box. You also can specify a fixed duration for a task from any view that shows the Task Sheet. Right-click the task you want to fix, and then click Task Information; alternatively, click the task and then click the Information button on the Standard toolbar. The Task Information dialog box appears. Click the Resources tab. Click to display the Duration Type drop-down list (see Fig. 4.17), and then click Fixed Duration. Click OK to close the dialog box.

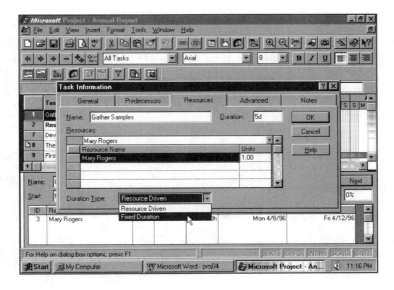

Figure 4.17
Use the drop-down list
shown in this dialog
box to prevent Project
from adjusting the
task's schedule.

NOTE: If you want all your tasks to be scheduled
with the fixed duration you enter, and Project to be
prohibited from adjusting task schedules based on
assigned resources, you can do so using the Default
Duration Type drop-down list on the Schedule tab of
the Options dialog box. Chapter 20, "Setting Up and
Customizing Microsoft Project," explains how to change
this and other default settings.

Deleting Resources

There are instances when a resource is no longer needed, either within
a task assignment or within the Resource Sheet. At that point, you'll
want to delete it.

From a Task

To delete a resource from a task, you can use any of a number of
methods, depending on the current view. From the Task Sheet view,
click to select any cell in the task for which you want to remove the
resource. Display the Resource Assignment dialog box by clicking
the Resource Assignment button on the Standard or Resource

Management toolbar (or pressing Alt+F8). In the Resource Assignment dialog box (see Fig. 4.18), click the resource to delete, which has a checkmark beside it to indicate that it's assigned to the current task. Click Remove to remove the resource. From here, you can use the dialog box to add and remove resources for other tasks, or can simply click Close to close the dialog box.

Figure 4.18
You can use the Resource Assignment dialog box to remove task resources.

Here's a selected resource.

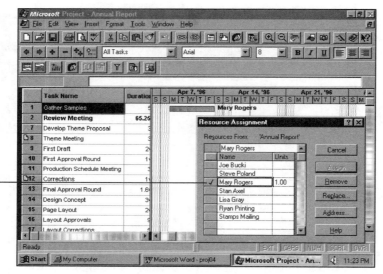

CAUTION: Selecting a cell in the Resource Names column and pressing the Delete key deletes the whole task entry, not just the resource. To delete the Resource Names entry only, right-click the appropriate cell and click Clear Cell.

You can use Task Entry view to make removing a resource from a task even easier. Simply click the name of the resource to delete in the Resource Names column of the bottom pane, and then press Delete.

From the Project

Just as you can use the Resource Sheet to add new resources to a project, you can use the Resource Sheet to remove entries for resources you no longer use. For example, let's say that you've added the name of a person from another department to the resource list, but that person has been transferred to another city and is no longer available to work on the project. After you open the View menu and click Resource Sheet, use either of the following methods to remove the resource:

- Select any cell in the resource you want deleted, then press Delete.
- Click the row number for the resource you want deleted; this selects the whole row. Open the Edit menu and click Delete Resource (or right-click to access the shortcut menu, then click Delete Resource).

PART II

MAKING ADJUSTMENTS TO PROJECTS

CHAPTER 5

RESOLVING OVERALLOCATIONS AND OVERBOOKED RESOURCES

I'm sure you've heard colleagues moan, "I wish there were more than 24 hours in a day, because I can't seem to get enough done." It might be a cliché, but only because it reflects our common tendency to cram too many activities into each and every day. As a leader under pressure, you'll need to fight this natural tendency when creating your project plans.

Project provides features designed to help you make your schedule realistic and attainable. Some of the best of these features quietly point out to you when you've made a mistake such as assigning a resource 16 hours' worth of work on an eight-hour workday.

Read this chapter to learn the following:

- What it means to overallocate a resource
- How to find overallocation problems in your plan
- How to use automatic leveling to eliminate overbooked schedules
- Your best bets for addressing overallocations on your own

Discovering Overallocation

Early in the book, you learned to sketch out your schedule by simply listing the tasks to accomplish. Chapter 3 helped you make adjustments to the tasks you listed to help them flow together more cohesively. Chapter 4 focused on giving you the information you need to determine who handles what for your project, and now you need to go back and look at whether the resources you assigned to projects make sense.

Because Project uses resource-driven scheduling by default, you generally don't have to worry about having too few or too many resources assigned to a particular task. If the resource's working hours enable the resource to handle the task more quickly, Project shortens the task duration. Conversely, Project automatically lengthens the task if needed. For example, suppose that your schedule is based on a 24 Hour base calendar, but the resource you want to use follows the Standard calendar with eight-hour days. A task scheduled for one 24-hour day will be rescheduled to take three days if you assign the eight-hours-per-day resource to it.

Instead, what you need to be concerned about is assigning a resource to separate tasks that occur simultaneously. If your list includes 25 different tasks, then in theory any number of them could partially occur during the same week. Let's say that the task in row 5 begins on the Monday of the third week of your project. The task in row 7 begins the same week, but on Thursday. You've assigned the same resource to both tasks. Each of the tasks needs to be handled as quickly as possible, so it requires that the assigned resource give it full-time attention during the eight-hour workday defined for the project schedule. The problem is obvious—during Thursday and Friday, the resource needs to handle two full-time tasks. Thus, for Thursday and Friday, you've *overallocated* (overbooked) the selected resource.

You might be able to quickly spot overallocations in Gantt Chart view when tasks are close together in your list. Generally, though, you'll only be able to see 14 task rows on-screen at any time, so you can't visually compare the tasks in, let's say, rows 1 and 25 without scrolling back and forth. For that reason, Project provides a couple of other methods, described next, for quickly finding overallocations.

Checking the Status Bar

After you've assigned resources to various tasks and have saved your file, you can look at the status bar at the bottom of the Project screen. The middle portion of the status bar, a messaging area, will indicate if there's an overallocated resource, as shown in Figure 5.1. The message that tells you an overallocation exists is the Level: message. The message basically suggests that you use the leveling feature, which automatically removes overallocations by rescheduling some tasks, as you'll learn later in the section "Using Automatic Leveling to Fix Overallocations."

Figure 5.1
Check the status bar for the Level: message, which means that a resource has been overallocated.

Name of the resource assigned to the task

Indicates there's an overallocated resource

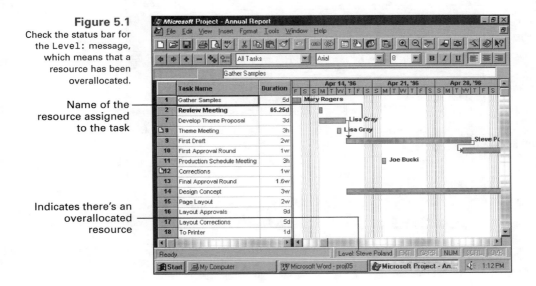

Because the Level: message appears in the status bar, it's available no matter which view of Project you're in, offering you a great deal of convenience. While checking the status bar is fast, the information you receive is limited, as the status bar can only identify one overallocated resource at a time. Moreover, it doesn't tell you which day(s) the overallocation occurs on.

Another quick way to identify an overallocation in the default Gantt Chart view is to use the Resource Management toolbar. To display the Resource Management toolbar, right-click any toolbar on-screen, then select Resource Management. To go to a task in the Task Sheet that's assigned to an overallocated resource, click the Goto Overallocation button on the Resource Management toolbar. Project selects the Task Name cell of the task with the overallocated resource, as shown in Figure 5.2. Clicking the Goto Overallocation button again takes you to the next task in the list with an overallocation. If you click the Goto Overallocation button when there are no more overallocated tasks in the list, you'll see a message telling you that there are no further overallocations. Click OK to close the message box and continue.

Figure 5.2
The Resource Management toolbar offers a fast way to find a task with an

Click here...

...to select the name of the next task in the list with an overallocated resource.

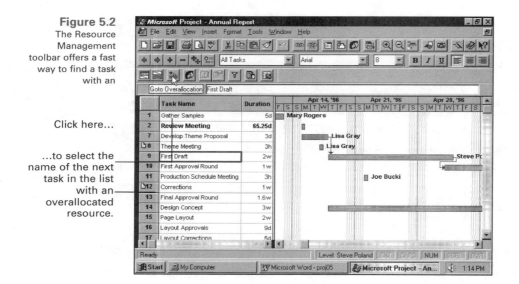

Looking at Resource Usage

To make a good decision about how to fix an overallocation, you have to know the date(s) on which the overallocation occurs, and how extensive the overallocation is. Have you assigned 24 hours worth of work for an eight-hour day, or have you assigned only an extra hour or two? For more extensive schedules, you might have multiple overallocations, and might even have overallocated more than one resource on the same date.

Project offers a couple of options for getting a clearer overall picture of the overallocations in your schedule. (These are views, which you'll learn more about in Chapter 9, "Working with the Different Project Views.")

First, you can display the resource usage in a tabular format. To do so, open the View menu and click Resource Usage. The Resource Usage view appears on-screen, as shown in Figure 5.3. The Resource Name column in this view lists each resource you've added to the schedule. The Work column shows you the total amount of work (in hours) that you've scheduled for the resource. The scrolling pane on the right side of the screen shows you the amount of work you've assigned to each resource on each date. You can see which resources are overallocated at a glance, because Project displays the Resource Name and Work entries in bold, red text. Figure 5.3 shows overallocations for both the Steve Poland and Lisa Gray resources. If you look to the right along the row of an overallocated resource, you'll see that Project also highlights the particular dates when you've overbooked the resource according to the resource's work calendar. For example, on Thursday during the week of April 14, I've scheduled Steve Poland for 16 hours of work, much more than most mere mortals are willing to handle.

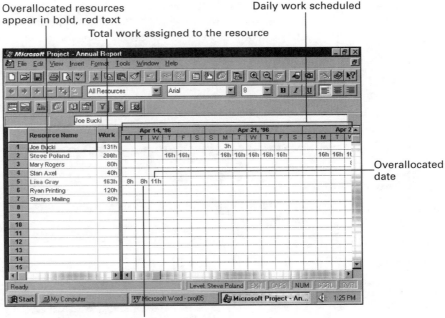

Figure 5.3
The Resource Usage view summarizes how much work you've assigned.

The Resource Allocation view combines the tabular layout for the Resource Usage view with a lower pane where you can see the assignments for the selected resource as a Gantt chart. To display the Resource Allocation view, you can click the Resource Allocation View button on the Resource Management toolbar. If you haven't displayed that toolbar, open the <u>V</u>iew menu and click <u>M</u>ore Views, then double-click Resource Allocation in the <u>V</u>iews list of the resulting dialog box. Project displays your schedule in the Resource Allocation view, as shown in Figure 5.4. When you select a resource from the Resource Usage view in the upper pane, a Gantt chart in the lower pane shows you the tasks for the resource, so you can see which ones overlap (are scheduled for the same dates). This view is ideal for changing the schedule for overallocated resources, as you'll see later in the "Manually Cutting Back the Resource's Commitments" section; refer to that section for more information about working in this view.

> **NOTE:** If you switch back to the Resource Sheet (by opening the <u>V</u>iew menu and clicking Resource <u>S</u>heet), overallocated resources are also indicated in bold, red text. You won't get any information, however, about where in the schedule the overallocation occurs.

Resource Allocation View button   Overallocated resources appear in bold, red text

Figure 5.4
The Resource Allocation view shows the work summary and a Gantt chart for the selected resource.

Resource usage information

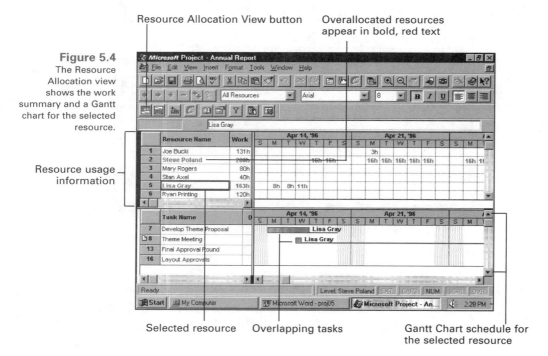

Selected resource   Overlapping tasks   Gantt Chart schedule for the selected resource

> **CAUTION:** When you display another view from the Resource Allocation view, the screen may remain split into upper and lower panes. Open the <u>W</u>indow menu and click Remove <u>S</u>plit to restore the view to normal.

Project can automatically create and print a report that lists each over-allocated resource and the tasks assigned to that resource. Reports don't let you edit the information entered in your schedule, but they serve as a convenient tool for looking at particular types of information when decision-making. Although Chapter 12, "Creating and Printing a Report," provides more details about generating and printing the various types of reports in Project, here's a brief rundown of how to have Project compile an Overallocated Resources report:

1. Open the <u>V</u>iew menu and click <u>R</u>eports to access the Reports dialog box.
2. Double-click <u>A</u>ssignments, or click it once and then click <u>S</u>elect. Project displays the Assignment Reports dialog box (see Fig. 5.5).

Figure 5.5
Project offers reporting about resource assignments.

Double-click to compile your overallocations report

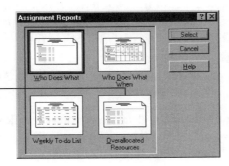

3. Double-click <u>O</u>verallocated Resources, or click it once and then click <u>S</u>elect. Project creates a list of overallocated resources for you, and displays it on-screen.
4. To take a closer look at the information, as in Figure 5.6, click the report with the zoom pointer, which looks like a magnifying glass.

Click to print the Overallocated
Resources report as is

Click to leave
the report
without
printing

Figure 5.6
You can take a closer
look at the reporting
about your resource
assignments.

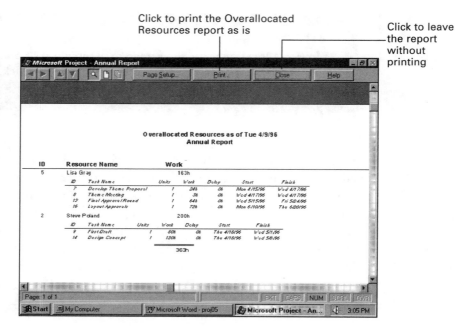

Using Automatic Leveling to Fix Overallocations

When you've overbooked a resource, something has to give. You want to eliminate huge peaks in a resource's workload to achieve an even, realistic workload. The process of smoothing out the workloads for resources is called *resource leveling*. Project can level resource schedules automatically, when you specify, for any schedule where Project calculates the finish date automatically.

To level resources, Project basically delays a conflicting task to a later time when the resource has available working hours. (You'll learn how to manually specify delay time later in this chapter, in the "Creating a Delay" section.) Project decides which tasks to delay by examining the information you've entered about tasks, in particular looking for *slack*. Slack occurs when a task can be moved to a later date without delaying another task.

When tasks are linked, Project takes the links into consideration before delaying a particular task. This is important because linked tasks may be handled by different resources, and you don't want to create a problem for another resource as a result of the leveling. For example, if two tasks are linked using the default Finish-to-Start (FS) link type and there's no lag time between the two tasks, the first task can't be moved without the second task being moved as well—unless you change the nature of the link.

> **NOTE:** The next chapter provides more detail about working with slack, but here's a quick example. Suppose that a resource is scheduled to handle a task that begins on Monday, 4/15/96, and has a duration of four days. The next task assigned to the resource begins on Monday, 4/22/96, and has the Start No Later Than (SNLT) constraint, meaning that it cannot move beyond its scheduled start date. Thus, there's one day of slack between the two tasks. The 4/15/96–4/18/96 task can only be delayed one day to a 4/16/96–4/19/96 schedule, because the resource must start working on the second task on the following Monday.

Here are a few more important issues to keep in mind before you level:

- Schedules built backwards from the finish date have no slack, so there's nowhere to move any tasks. You'll have to work manually to level resources for this type of schedule.

- By default, it's conceivable that Project may move a task that's listed earlier in the schedule, say in row 2, rather than the later conflicting one that's, say, in row 5. Project moves whichever task is easier to move based on links and other factors, regardless of its ID number or order in the Task Sheet. For example, compare the tasks for Steve Poland before and after leveling in Figure 5.7. In some cases, such moves do not make sense, so double-check automatic leveling results carefully.

- Project can't change history. If a task has already started, Project can't move it when leveling a resource schedule.

- Automatic leveling can have a massive impact on the flow of your schedule. If your schedule is very complex or you want to limit the scope of the changes made but still take advantage of automatic leveling, use automatic leveling for one resource at a time (see the following steps that explain how to use automatic leveling) and check the results after leveling each resource.

Figure 5.7
Leveling decisions aren't based on a task's order in the Task Sheet, as shown in this example of the same set of tasks before and after leveling.

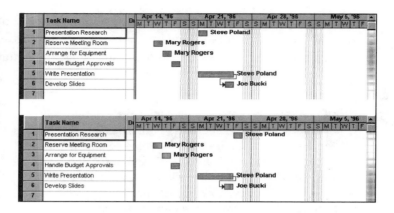

Setting Options and Leveling

Project enables you to level resources with the Resource Leveling command on the Tools menu. As you proceed through the leveling process, Project gives you the opportunity to set numerous leveling options. To use automatic leveling, follow these steps:

1. Open the file with the resources you want to level, and make any desired adjustments to tasks, such as changing link types and priorities (see the "Reprioritizing Tasks Before Leveling" section later in this chapter).

> **TIP:** If you want to level a schedule but also be able to see the original dates, create a copy of the schedule file (by opening the File menu and clicking Save As, and then giving the file a new name). Then apply leveling to the copied file. Reopen the original file if you want to compare the two.

2. (Optional) If you want to level a single resource, change to Resource Sheet, Resource Usage, or Resource Allocation view, then click the resource name for the resource you want to level. (Press Ctrl and click other resource names if you also want to select those resources for leveling.)

3. Open the Tools menu and click Resource Leveling. The Resource Leveling dialog box appears (see Fig. 5.8).

> **CAUTION:** If you don't select a resource from one of the resource views, Project levels the whole schedule, and does not warn you before doing so.

Figure 5.8
Select leveling options in this dialog box.

4. If you want Project to automatically level the schedule each time you make a change in a task or resource assignment, select the Automatic option button in the Leveling area of the dialog box. Otherwise, you have to redisplay the Resource Leveling dialog box to level the schedule again after you make any changes.

5. By default, the Delay Only Within Slack option is not selected, meaning that Project can adjust the finish date of your schedule as needed when it moves tasks. However, this could lead to a delay of weeks or even months in your schedule, depending on the scope of your project. If you don't want the leveling operation to change the finish date, check this option so that Project moves tasks only within available slack time.

6. By default, the Automatically Remove Delay check box is selected, which means that leveling removes any existing delays that you've scheduled in tasks before leveling. Deselect this option to have Project add the new leveling delays to any delays you've manually added.

7. Use the Order drop-down list to tell Project how to choose which tasks to delay. This drop-down list offers three choices. The default is Standard, in which Project considers links, slack, dates, and priorities to determine which task to delay. If you select ID Only, Project delays the task that appears latest in the Task Sheet and thus has the highest ID number. If you select

the final choice, Priority, Standard, the priority you've assigned to tasks takes precedence over other factors in determining which tasks to delay.

8. Click the Level Now button. If you've selected a particular resource to level as described in step 2, or are displaying your schedule in one of the resource views, Project displays the Level Now dialog box (see Fig. 5.9).

Figure 5.9
Specify whether to level all resources in your project.

9. Leave the Entire Pool option selected to level all resources, or select Selected Resources to tell Project to level only the resource(s) you selected in step 2.

10. Click OK to complete the leveling operation. When a resource has been leveled, it no longer appears in bold, red type.

11. (Optional) If you're not happy with the leveling changes, immediately click the Undo button on the Standard toolbar, press Ctrl+Z, or open the Edit menu and click Undo Level.

Clearing Leveling

While you work with *resources* to add leveling, you work with *tasks* to remove leveling. Thus, you need to be in a view where you can select tasks, such as Gantt Chart view where the Task Sheet appears in the left pane, or Resource allocation view where you can select tasks for a particular resource in the lower pane of the view.

CAUTION: You can't select a resource name from any resource list and clear leveling. You have to be working from a task-oriented view or pane. You'll know you're in an incorrect place if the Clear Leveling button isn't available in the Resource Leveling dialog box.

Removing leveling removes any delay that Project inserted for a task or tasks during leveling. To remove leveling, perform the following steps:

1. Select a task-oriented view. (If you select the Resource Allocation view, you'll also have to select a resource that has been leveled in the upper pane, then click where the tasks assigned to the selected resource appear in the lower pane.)

2. (Optional) If you only want to remove leveling from a particular task, click that task name. To select more than one task, press and hold down the Ctrl key and click additional task names.

3. Open the Tools menu and click Resource Leveling. The Resource Leveling dialog box appears.

4. Click the Clear Leveling button. Project displays the Clear Leveling dialog box (see Fig. 5.10).

Figure 5.10
Choose whether to remove the delay from all or selected tasks.

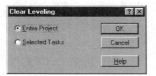

5. If you chose one or more particular tasks to have leveling removed in step 2, click the Selected Tasks option button.

6. Click OK to remove the leveling.

Reprioritizing Tasks Before Leveling

The last section of Chapter 3 provided an overview of the settings in the Task Information dialog box. The first tab in that dialog box, the General tab, enables you to enter and edit the basic information that defines the task, such as its name and duration. One of the settings in that dialog box is the Priority drop-down list, shown in Figure 5.11.

By default, all tasks are assigned Medium priority, meaning that each task is equally important in the schedule. You can specify which tasks are more important by changing the Priority setting to any of the choices from Lowest through Highest, or to Do Not Level. (You can prevent Project from leveling a task at all by choosing Do Not Level.)

Figure 5.11
The Priority drop-
down list enables
you to define the
relative importance
of tasks.

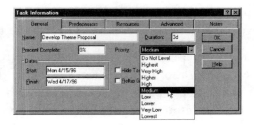

Project uses the priority settings as a factor in automatic leveling, and the priority is given even more precedence if you select the Priority, Standard Order choice in the Resource Leveling dialog box. Project moves tasks with lower priority settings before moving those with higher priority settings.

TIP: You can sort your list of tasks by priority. See Chapter 9, "Working with the Different Project Views," for details.

You should change task priorities before leveling, when necessary. Assuming that you'll be doing much of your leveling work in the Resource Allocation view, here's how to change a task's priority from that view (refer to Chapter 3 for a refresher on displaying the Task Information dialog box from the Task Sheet):

1. In the upper pane of the Resource Allocation view, select the resource scheduled to handle the task for which you want to set the priority (usually an overallocated resource) by clicking it.

2. In the lower pane, right-click the task for which you want to set the priority—this displays the shortcut menu shown in Figure 5.12—and click Task Information. Alternatively, do any of the following: open the Insert menu and click Task Information; click the Information button on the Standard toolbar; or press Shift+F2.

3. On the General tab of the Task Information dialog box, click the drop-down list arrow for the Priority option, then click the setting you want.

4. Click OK to close the Task Information dialog box.

Click this button for task information...

Figure 5.12
Click the Task
Information choice
from this shortcut
menu on your way to
changing the selected
task's priority.

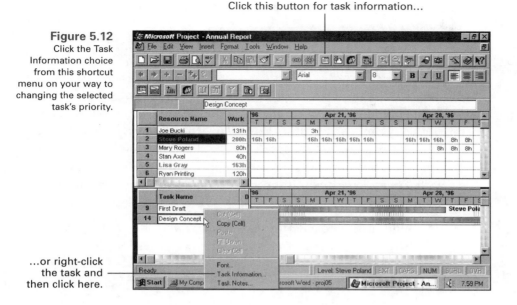

...or right-click
the task and
then click here.

Use a similar approach to make such changes from other views that
show a list of tasks.

Manually Cutting Back the Resource's Commitments

While automatic leveling offers a no-brainer way to ensure that your
resources can handle the work you've assigned, some resource adjustment chores require some thought. For example, as noted earlier in
this chapter, if you've set up your schedule file to have Project calculate
its start date based on a finish date you've entered, you can't use automatic leveling to deal with overallocations. Other instances where you
might not want to use automatic leveling are if the tasks involved are
high in priority, or if you need a solution that is more creative than
simply delaying some tasks.

The methods described next enable you to resolve overallocations with
precision and flexibility. To perform most of these adjustments, you
work in Resource Allocation view. In the next chapter, you'll learn to

adjust the schedule and make some resource adjustments from the Task Entry view.

Creating a Delay

Automatic leveling creates a delay for a task, so that tasks for a resource no longer overlap in the schedule. Without considering task linking, lead time, or lag time, this delay generally means that the second task starts after the first task ends, so the work flows in a continuous stream. If you instead enter a delay manually, you can create a delay that's any length you want. For example, you might want to do the following:

- Build in extra delay time of a day or two (or more) between the tasks, in case the resource's first task takes longer than planned

- Enter a smaller delay that still lets the two tasks overlap by, let's say, one day; then you can use another method—such as adding another resource or specifying overtime—to take care of the smaller overallocation

To enter a delay of the length you prefer, do the following:

1. In Resource Allocation view, click the resource name for the overallocated resource in the upper pane.

2. In the lower pane, click the task name for the task you want to delay. Remember that entering the delay will move the task's start date; this technique doesn't work for schedules calculated backward from the project's finish date.

3. Press right arrow or Tab key to scroll one column to the right (to the Delay column). You also can use the scroll bar below the Task Name column to scroll over, then click the desired cell in the Delay column.

4. Enter the delay that you desire (see Fig. 5.13) and press Enter.

When you press Enter, Project pushes out the task. It adjusts the task's Start column entry, and moves the task to the right on the Gantt chart. For example, compare Figure 5.14 with Figure 5.13.

Figure 5.13
It's possible to manually enter a delay.

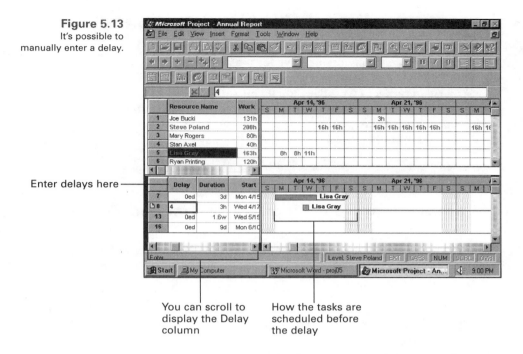

Enter delays here —

You can scroll to display the Delay column

How the tasks are scheduled before the delay

Figure 5.14
After you specify a delay value, Project moves the task based on that value.

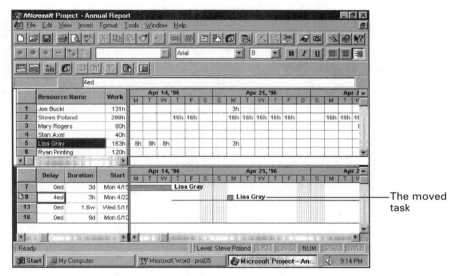

The moved task

> **CAUTION:** Delays are scheduled in elapsed days (ed), meaning that nonworking days for the resource are included in the delay timeframe. You cannot schedule a delay in terms of workdays (d). If you enter a delay of 1w (one week), Project converts that entry to 7ed. Thus, after you enter a delay, make sure that it delays the task far enough based on the schedule's working days.

Removing or Replacing an Overbooked Resource

There will be times when delaying a task is not an option. For example, you might be required to finish a product by a particular date or else lose a customer's order. Or, certain tasks might need to be completed before the end of a financial period. Finally, a task might be so pivotal in your schedule, and linked to so many successor tasks down the line (see the next chapter to learn more), that delaying it will ruin your entire schedule.

In situations like this, you need to look closely at the resource you've assigned, rather than the schedule. You might be forced to remove a resource from a task (especially if you've assigned more than one task to the resource) or to replace the resource with another one that's available to complete the task. Here's how to do so:

1. In Resource Allocation view, click the resource name for the overallocated resource in the upper pane.

2. In the lower pane, click the task name for the task you want to remove or replace the resource for.

3. Open the Insert menu and click Resource Assignment (or press Alt+F8). Alternatively, click the Resource Assignment button on the Standard toolbar or the Resource Management toolbar. The Resource Assignment dialog box appears (see Fig. 5.15).

4. Click to select the assigned resource, which should have a check mark beside it.

Figure 5.15
Take a look at your
options for the resource
you've chosen.

The assigned
resource

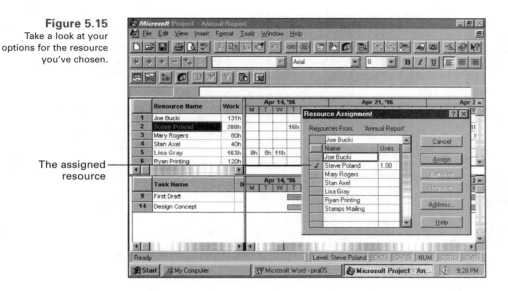

5. To take the resource off the task, click the Remove button.
Project immediately removes the resource from the task, and
removes the task from the list corresponding to that resource
in the lower pane. To replace the resource, click the Replace
button. Project displays the Replace Resource dialog box (see
Fig. 5.16).

Figure 5.16
This is where you can
select another resource
for your task.

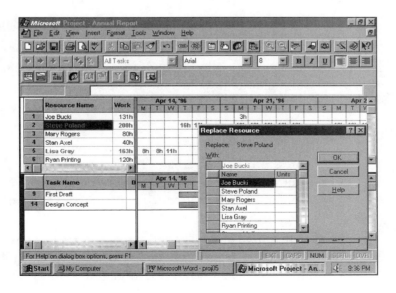

6. Click a new resource for the task in the <u>W</u>ith list, then click OK. Project reassigns the task, removing it from the task list for the original resource and adding it to the task list for the newly selected resource.

Changing resource assignments in this way can fix one overallocation but create another; the new Resource Name entry changes to bold, red text to indicate a new overallocation. Pay careful attention to the results of your resource reassignment.

TIP: Click the Close button to put away the Resource Assignment dialog box when you're finished with it.

Part-Time Work

There might be times when you're not in a position to delay one task or another altogether, perhaps because a third successor task is unable to start until its predecessor starts, as in an SS relationship. Or, there might be an instance where you don't want to remove a resource from a task altogether, but do want to scale back its commitment to the task and add another resource (as described in Chapter 6, "Optimizing the Schedule") to help finish the task in a timely fashion.

In such cases, you have the option of cutting back a resource to a part-time commitment to a task. Here's how:

1. In Resource Allocation view, click the resource name for the overallocated resource in the upper pane.

2. In the lower pane, click the task name for the task for which you want to reduce the resource assignment.

3. Open the <u>I</u>nsert menu and click Resource <u>A</u>ssignment (or press Alt+F8). Alternatively, click the Resource Assignment button on the Standard toolbar or the Resource Management toolbar. The Resource Assignment dialog box appears (refer to Fig. 5.15).

4. Click the Units cell for the assigned resource, which should have a check mark beside it. Begin typing to replace the existing Units entry, as shown in Figure 5.17. Type a number that's

a decimal portion of 1.00, to indicate how much of each workday you want the resource to spend on the selected task. For example, if you want the resource to work on the task for half the day, type **.5**.

Click here to finish your edit

Figure 5.17
You might want to change the resource's time commitment during the duration of the task.

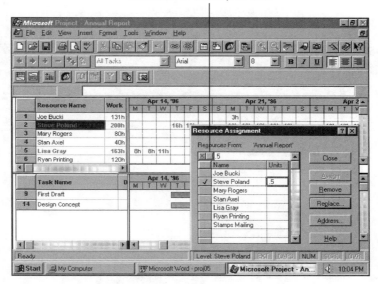

CAUTION: If you enter a number that's greater than 1.00, Project does not assume that you want the resource to work overtime. It instead assumes that the resource has that proportion of extra time available within the bounds of the workday. For example, if the resource is a consulting firm you're working with, and you change the Units entry to 2.00, Project assumes that two members of the firm will work on your task each day. To learn how to specify overtime for a task, see "Authorizing Overtime Work for a Task" in Chapter 6, "Optimizing the Schedule."

5. Click the Enter button beside the text entry box to finish your entry. On the Gantt chart for the task, an indication beside the Resource label tells you what portion of the workday the

resource will spend on the assignment (see Fig. 5.18). If the task uses a resource-driven duration type, Project adjusts the task's duration (lengthening the Gantt chart bar) so that the resource works the same total hours on the task. For example, if a task originally has a one-week duration and you reduce the resource's commitment to half-time, the duration is extended to two weeks.

Figure 5.18
Check the Gantt chart for part-time resources.

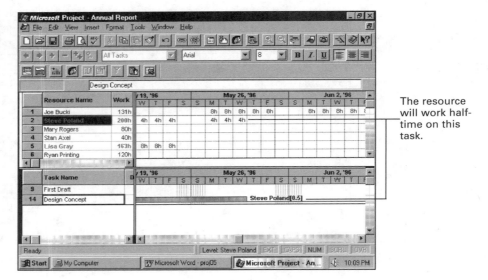

The resource will work half-time on this task.

Avoiding Underallocations

If you remove a resource from a task altogether in Resource Allocation view, that task no longer appears on the task list for any resource. Therefore, you should make a note of the task name and ID (row) number before you remove its resource. Make sure that you go back to Gantt Chart view or any other view where you can assign resources to tasks, and add a resource for the task. Otherwise, the task is completely underallocated—there's no resource at all scheduled to handle it.

An even trickier situation occurs if you change a resource from a full-time to a part-time commitment to a task. If the task has a fixed duration, Project will not increase the task's duration when you cut back the resource to a part-time commitment. In reality, the task still requires the same number of hours it initially did, but on the schedule there are fewer hours of work scheduled to get the task done. For example, suppose that you have a task with a 3d duration, which equates to 24 hours of work by the project's eight-hours-per-day base calendar. The duration type is Fixed, which means that the task's start and finish date don't change. If you cut back a resource assigned to this task to half-time work for the task, Project assumes that only 12 hours of work are now required on the task. In such a case, you need to add one or more additional part-time resources to the task to replace the 12 hours of work that the first resource no longer provides. (The "Adding More Resources" section in Chapter 6, "Optimizing the Schedule," covers how to do this.)

If you cut back a resource assignment to part-time but the task duration doesn't change, you should check the duration type. If it's Fixed, make sure that you add more resources for the task as needed.

> **NOTE:** Remember that you can quickly check a task's duration type by clicking the task name in any task list, then clicking the Information button on the Standard toolbar. Click the Resources tab, then check the Duration Type drop-down list. Click OK to close the dialog box.

Changing the Resource's Work Schedule

The "Working with Resource Calendars (Work Schedules)" section in Chapter 4, "Managing Resources," explains how to assign a calendar for a resource to determine how many hours per week the resource works, and to set days the resource has off. Rather than cutting back a resource's commitment to a project, you can change a resource's schedule, adding more hours or days to remove the overallocations. While you might not have much leeway to do this for resources within your company (you can't make certain people work extra hours without paying overtime, for example), there are instances when adjusting a resource's calendar—or selecting a new calendar—can resolve an overallocation. Consider the following examples:

- If a salaried employee is willing to give up a holiday or week-end day to complete a task, you can make that day a working day in the calendar. For example, if an employee has to attend a trade show on a weekend, you can specify those weekend days as working days.
- On a day that requires an evening or morning meeting, you can adjust the working hours for the resource.
- If you're working with a vendor that normally has a standard eight-hour workday, but can work around the clock when you request it, make the request and change that resource's schedule.

Although you can refer to Chapter 4, "Managing Resources," to review the details of making changes to the working days and hours for a resource, here's a quick way to select a different calendar for a resource:

1. Double-click the resource name in any view or resource list, or in the Resources From list in the Resource Assignment dialog box. The Resource Information dialog box appears.

2. Use the Base Cal drop-down list to select another calendar, as shown in Figure 5.19.

Figure 5.19
You can quickly change the base calendar for a resource.

3. Click OK to complete the change.

CHAPTER 6

OPTIMIZING THE SCHEDULE

When you lead a project, you have to use a lot of creativity to bring everything together on time and on budget. You need to look at different ways to apply the resources you have, check for every place where you can trim back time, and do everything you can to ensure that as many tasks are moving along simultaneously as possible.

In the last chapter, you looked at how to make your schedule attainable by ensuring that you haven't assigned too much work to any particular resource. Now, you can apply your managerial creativity to tighten up your schedule to ensure that it gets the job done as quickly as possible. You'll explore the following topics in this chapter:

- Understanding which tasks are critical and how they affect your schedule

- Looking for ways to finish critical tasks more quickly

- Finding "dead" time in the schedule and taking it out

- Giving yourself more room by adjusting the project base calendar

Identifying and Tightening the Critical Path

In the Midwest and northern regions of the United States, the building industry is seasonal, because certain building tasks can't be completed under certain weather conditions. For example, if the weather isn't right, the foundation can't be constructed; if the foundation isn't constructed, the framing for the walls and roof can't be erected; without the framework, other key systems can't be installed. Once the most important features of the building are in place, however, the schedules for many tasks are a bit more flexible; for example, work on finishing the exterior can proceed at the same time as work to complete the interior.

In the building example, the tasks that can't be delayed without drastically affecting the overall schedule—the foundation and framing work, for example—are called *critical tasks*.

Your schedule will have critical tasks, as well. If any of these tasks slip (either begin late or take more time than you allowed), the finish date for your project will move further out. Together, the critical tasks form the *critical path* for your schedule, the sequence of tasks that must happen on time for the project to finish on time. While moving tasks that aren't on the critical path might even out resource assignments or help you improve milestones, such changes won't really affect the full schedule for your project.

Thus, if you want to reduce the overall timeframe for your project, you need to reduce the length of time it takes to complete the critical path. You need to be able to identify which tasks comprise the critical path, and make adjustments to compress the schedules for those tasks.

> **CAUTION:** The techniques covered in this chapter can introduce resource overallocations. After you make any of the changes you'll learn about in this chapter, check for resource overallocations as described in Chapter 5.

You can use a formatting technique to identify critical tasks in the Task Sheet in Gantt Chart or Task Entry view (you'll learn about the latter shortly). You also can format critical tasks in the lower pane of

Resource Allocation view, but that formatting won't appear if you switch back to Gantt Chart or Task Entry view. To highlight the critical tasks in your schedule, follow these steps:

1. Click the visible portion of the Task Sheet in whichever view you're presently using. For example, in Gantt Chart view, click the left pane of the screen, or in Task Entry View, click the upper pane.

2. Open the Format menu and click Text Styles. Project displays the Text Styles dialog box.

3. Click the drop-down list arrow to display the Item to Change choices, and click Critical Tasks (see Fig. 6.1). This choice means that the formatting choices you make next will apply to any task that's part of the critical path.

Figure 6.1
Use this dialog box to specify how you'd like to identify critical tasks in the Task Sheet.

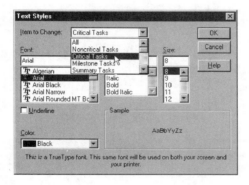

4. In the scrolling Font list, display and click the name of a font to use for the critical task text.

5. Use the Font Style list to apply attributes such as bold or italic to the text. Depending on the font you've chosen, italic often is a better choice than bold, because it more clearly differentiates the text.

6. Use the Size list to select a size for the critical task names in the list. This further emphasizes the critical task names and makes them easier to read.

7. Click to select the Underline check box if you want to apply underlining to the critical path tasks.

8. Finally, click to open the Color drop-down list (see Fig. 6.2), and click the color you want to apply to the critical task text in the Task Sheet.

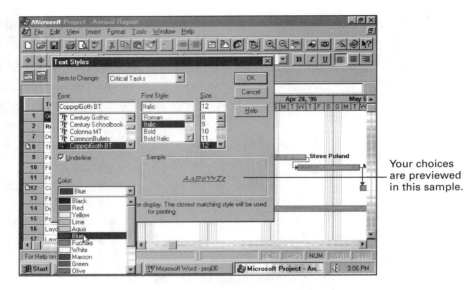

Your choices
are previewed
in this sample.

9. Click OK to apply your changes and close the Text Styles dialog box. The text formatting changes you specified now apply to all the tasks that are critical to your schedule. Figure 6.3 shows an example.

Figure 6.3
Critical path tasks
now appear as
you've specified in
the Task Sheet.

Project now
identifies these
tasks as critical.

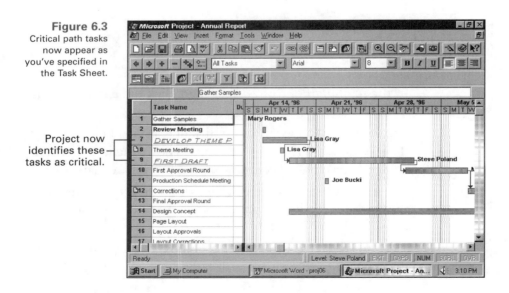

CAUTION: Your changes might cause a column in the Task Sheet to be filled with asterisks so that you can't see the data the column contains. If this happens, try repeating the preceding steps with different settings (especially the font size) until you find settings that work.

TIP: You can use *filtering* to limit the displayed lists of tasks to critical tasks only. To learn how to filter the Task Sheet, see "Filtering the Resource and Task Sheet" in Chapter 9.

If you use the preceding steps and the only task that changes formatting in the list is the last one, Project isn't making an error. It simply means that you haven't built enough details into your schedule to define a true critical path. You can go back, however, and take the time to define task relationships (links) and add constraints to tasks (such as defining that a task should start no later than a particular date) using the Advanced tab of the Task Information dialog box. When you make alterations to task information that identify some tasks as critical, Project will apply the critical path formatting.

NOTE: To ensure that you can tighten up the schedule for critical tasks, make sure that the tasks have the `Resource-Driven` **duration type. Double-click the task in a Task Sheet, click the Resources tab, and check the specified Duration <u>T</u>ype; change it if necessary.**

Using Task Entry View

After you've identified which tasks are critical in your schedule, you can begin examining them one-by-one to look for areas where you can make adjustments to decrease the duration of each critical task. You could simply double-click each task in the Task Sheet to display the Task Information dialog box to make your changes, but that would be time-consuming, and wouldn't let you immediately see the effects of your changes on other tasks that were linked. It's better to use another view you haven't yet seen, *Task Entry view*, which displays Gantt Chart view in the upper pane, and an area for entering and changing task and resource information in the bottom pane. Switch to Task Entry view by one of the following ways:

- Click the Task Entry View button on the Resource Management toolbar, if that toolbar is displayed.
- Open the <u>V</u>iew menu and click <u>M</u>ore Views. In the <u>V</u>iews list of the resulting dialog box, double-click Task Entry.

No matter which method you use to reach it, Task Entry view appears on-screen as shown in Figure 6.4.

Figure 6.4
Task Entry view combines the Gantt chart with a lower pane for working with different types of information.

Select a task here...

...then work with its schedule and resource information here.

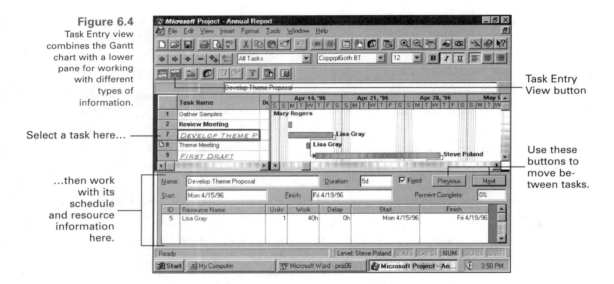

Task Entry View button

Use these buttons to move between tasks.

You can vary the details that appear in the lower pane of Task Entry view. In fact, some of the details you can modify here aren't available in other areas like the Task Information dialog box. To change the information displayed in the lower pane of Task Entry view, right-click the pane to display its shortcut menu (see Fig. 6.5), then click one of the choices to change the pane. The top choice on the shortcut menu, Hide Form View, closes the bottom pane of Task Entry view, essentially returning to Gantt Chart view.

Figure 6.5
It's possible to adjust the lower pane of Task Entry view.

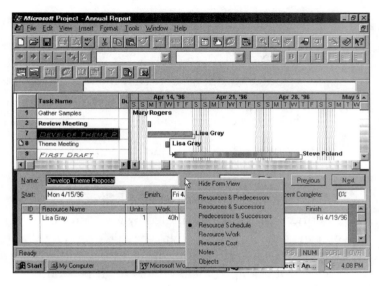

When you're working in Task Entry view, you can jump back and forth between panes, selecting a task in the upper pane, making changes in the lower pane, and then selecting a different task in the upper pane, changing its settings in the bottom pane, and so on.

Understanding Driving Resources

So far, for simplicity's sake, we've been looking at tasks with a single resource assigned to them. Imagine how restricted your options would be, though, if each task your team handles could only be assigned to one resource! Teams, by definition, mean that people work together to accomplish a goal. You can think of a goal in terms of the overall project, or in terms of any individual task. This means that you can use more than one resource (a mini-team, if you will) to accomplish each task in your schedule.

Before I explain how to assign additional resources to a task, you need to understand that Project doesn't treat all resources assigned to a task the same. Rather, Project looks at the resource that's assigned to do the most work for the task, called the *driving resource*.

The time that the driving resource has available to work on the task determines the task's duration. If you want to shorten the task's duration, then, you must do one or more of the following things:

- Add more hours to the resource calendar, which you learned to work with in Chapter 4
- Make more units available for the resource, indicating that the resource is adding more staff members to handle the task
- Add another resource so that you can reduce the number of hours the driving resource needs to spend working on the task

The latter two techniques are described next.

Adding Resources for a Task

If a critical task is being handled by a resource outside your company, you can start optimizing your schedule by asking that resource to assign more workers or equipment to the task to finish it more quickly. For example, the resource might be willing to assign three people or three pieces of equipment to your task to get it done in a third of the time originally planned.

CAUTION: Adding more resource units to a critical task can be tricky. Project always decreases the task duration directly in proportion to the number of additional resource units. Thus, if you increase the units from one to two, Project automatically cuts the task duration in half; however, the two resource units might not get the task done if half the time. It might take a little longer, because the resource units need to communicate among themselves. To allow for this possibility, consider building in lag time between the critical task and any successor tasks that depend on its completion.

To increase the number of units for a resource assigned to a critical task, follow these steps from Task Entry view:

1. Click the task name of the critical task in the top pane, or use the Pre**v**ious and N**e**xt buttons in the bottom pane to display the information for the critical task.

2. Click the Units column of the bottom pane and type a new value, as shown in Figure 6.6.

Figure 6.6
You can add more
resource units to
shorten the task
duration.

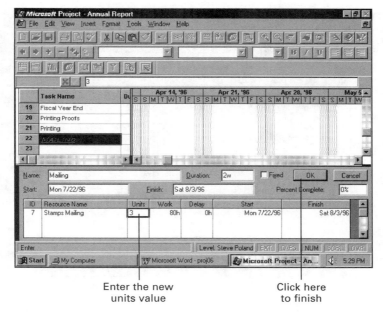

Enter the new
units value

Click here
to finish

3. Click the OK button in the bottom pane of the Task Entry
view to finish the entry. Project adjusts the Duration for the
task to reflect that the added resource units will finish the task
more quickly.

You also can change the Units setting via the Resource Assignment
dialog box. To do so, click the critical task in the Task Sheet of Gantt
Chart view or in the upper pane of Task Entry view. Click the
Resource Assignment button on the Standard toolbar or Resource
Management toolbar. Or, open the Insert menu and click Resource
Assignment. Click the Units column for the resource assigned to the
task, type a new value (see Fig. 6.7), and press Enter or click the Enter
button to finish changing the entry.

If you don't have the option of increasing the number of resource units
available to handle the task, you can add more resources to enable you
to reduce the number of hours of work the driving resource must allocate to the task, thereby shortening the task's duration. This isn't automatic, however—when you add the new resource to the task, you
must adjust the work hours for each resource to ensure that you don't
have too many resources assigned to the task, and to let you control
exactly what proportion of the work each resource handles.

Figure 6.7
This is another way
to adjust resource
units.

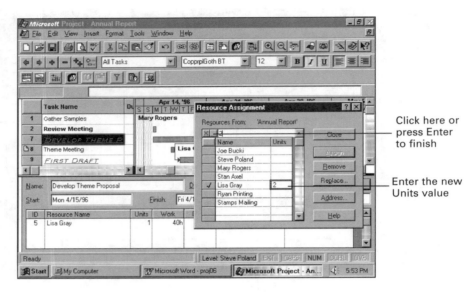

Click here or
press Enter
to finish

Enter the new
Units value

Follow these steps to add more resources to a critical task and decrease the task's duration:

1. Change to Task Entry view.

2. In the upper pane, click to select the critical task for which you want to add more resources.

3. In the lower pane, click in the first blank row of the Resource Name column. A drop-down list arrow appears at the far right end of the text entry box above the upper pane.

4. Click to display the drop-down list, then click a resource in the list to select it (see Fig. 6.8).

5. Click the OK button in the lower pane or the Enter button beside the text entry box to finish your entry. The new resource appears in the lower pane (see Fig. 6.9). If you refer to Figure 6.8, you'll notice that the Work column for the original resource held 80h, for the 80 hours of work required to complete the task in the assigned duration. In Figure 6.9 you can see that these working hours have not been adjusted in light of the new resource; in fact, the new resource also offers 80h in the Work column, for a total of 160h between the two resources. The Duration entry is 2w in both figures. This shows that simply adding the resource doesn't

shorten the task duration; instead, it creates a situation where you have too many hours assigned to the task.

Figure 6.8
Here's how to add another resource to a task

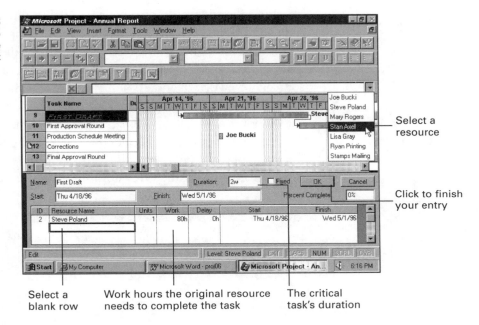

Select a resource

Click to finish your entry

Select a blank row

Work hours the original resource needs to complete the task

The critical task's duration

Figure 6.9
After you add the new resource, you have to adjust the working hours.

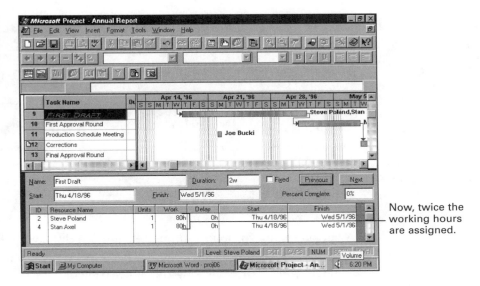

Now, twice the working hours are assigned.

6. The next step is to adjust the Work hours for each resource so that their total matches the number of work hours available for only the original resource. You also can control the proportion of work each resource has, splitting the work evenly between the two resources or letting the driving resource retain the bulk of the work. Using the examples in Figures 6.8 and 6.9, we can specify 60 hours of work for the original resource, Steve Poland, and 20 hours of work for the new resource, Stan Axel. The total work given for the two resources then equals the 80 hours originally scheduled for Steve Poland (see Fig. 6.10). To change each resource's Work entry, click in the Work column for the resource, type a new value (Project assumes you're specifying hours), and click the OK button in the lower pane.

Figure 6.10
Here are the same two resources with the working hours adjusted.

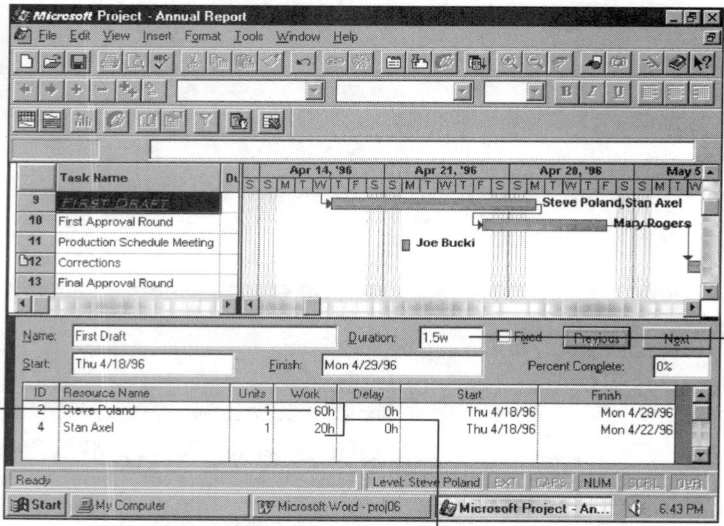

This resource works more, so it's the driving resource.

The duration is smaller, and reflects the work hours scheduled for the driving resource.

The work hours for both resources add up to the work originally scheduled for the first resource.

7. Repeat steps 3 through 6, if needed, to add more resources for the task.

As an alternative to steps 3 through 5, you can display the Resource Assignment dialog box (click the Resource Assignment button on the Standard toolbar after clicking the upper pane of Task Entry view), and drag new resources from the assignment box to the critical task. To do so, click the resource you want to drag, and then point to the gray box at the left of the resource name until you see the resource pointer (see Fig. 6.11). Press and hold down the mouse button, then drag the resource to the correct task name in the upper pane, and release the button.

Figure 6.11
You can drag a resource from the Resource Assignment box to the correct task name.

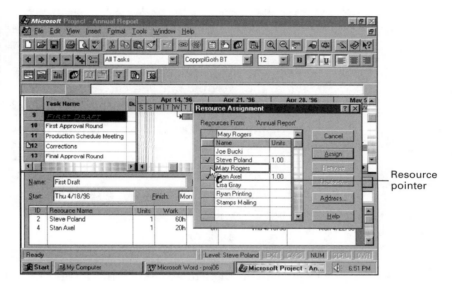

Resource pointer

CAUTION: You can add resources using the Resource Names columns of the Gantt Chart view, by typing in additional resource names and separating the entries with a comma. Or, you can use the Resources tab of the Task Information dialog box to add more resources. These methods, however, don't let you adjust the hours each resource will spend on the task to tighten up the task duration. Your best bet, therefore, is to add more resources using the technique just described.

Authorizing Overtime Work for a Task

Companies, particularly large ones, are obligated to compensate employees for overtime work. In some cases, you might also need to pay overtime charges for outside resources you bring in for your project. Overtime costs are required especially for any resources that are union workers. Thus, Project generally doesn't let you simply add extra shifts (overtime hours) for a resource by changing the Units entry to a value that's greater than one; as you learned earlier, changing the Units entry assumes that more than one worker from the resource will work on the task simultaneously.

You also can't specify overtime by simply changing the working calendar so that a resource has more hours in the day. (You can use that technique, however, to resolve overallocations for salaried resources.) Project forces you to enter overtime hours in another way for two reasons:

- To ensure that overtime costs are calculated correctly, according to the overtime rate you entered when you added the resource to the file (see Chapter 4, "Managing Resources")
- To ensure that you've approved the overtime work

The Task Entry view provides you the means to allocate overtime work for a task. After you add overtime, Project changes the task's duration to reflect the extra working hours, per day, provided by the overtime. Here's how to authorize overtime hours for a resource assigned to a critical task:

1. Change to Task Entry view.
2. In the upper pane of Task Entry view, click the critical task to which you want to assign overtime work. Information about the resource(s) assigned to the task appears in the lower pane.
3. Right-click the lower pane and click Resource Work. The pane changes to display more information about the resource's work schedule (see Fig. 6.12).

Figure 6.12
You can view
Resource Work
information in the
lower pane of Task
Entry view.

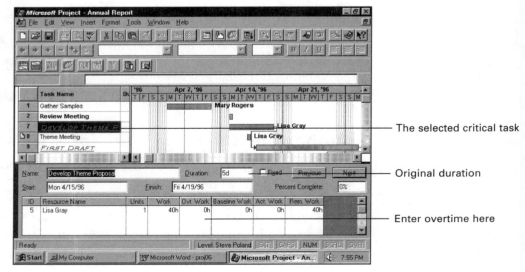

The selected critical task

Original duration

Enter overtime here

4. Click the Ovt. Work cell belonging to the resource for which you want to specify overtime hours. Type the number of overtime hours you want to authorize, then click the OK button in the lower pane. Project enters the overtime hours, and tightens the task's Duration entry accordingly (see Fig. 6.13).

Figure 6.13
Here's the revised resource work information.

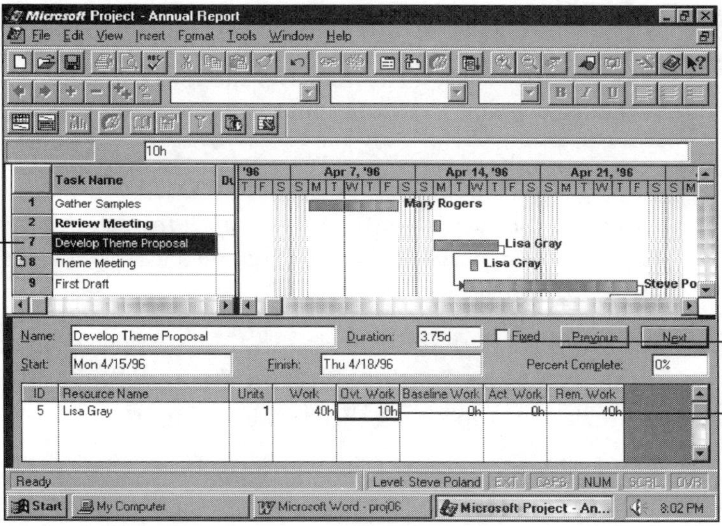

This task is no longer designated as critical.

New duration

Authorized overtime

NOTE: Adding overtime introduces slack in the schedule, which in turn might remove the critical designation for the task, depending on task relationships and other information you've specified about this task.

Working with Slack

Part of what defines a critical task is its impact on other tasks, depending on the relationships you've established between tasks. Sometimes, there's room between related tasks, so the task scheduled first can *slip* (be delayed or take longer to finish than scheduled) without delaying the start or completion of the successor task. That room between tasks is called *float time* or *slack*. Slack between tasks is called *free slack*. Slack between a particular task and the project finish date is called *total slack*, and basically tells you how long the task can slip without impacting the project finish date.

Total slack measurements also can be negative. That happens when you have two linked tasks, both of which are constrained to start on particular dates. If you change the duration of the predecessor task to make it longer, and don't add any lead time for the successor task (so it can start before the finish of the predecessor), you'll create negative slack.

TIP: In optimizing your schedule, make sure that you look for negative slack measurements and make changes to eliminate them, to ensure that the critical path is realistic.

If the total slack for a task is less than a minimum amount you've specified (which you'll learn to change shortly), Project identifies the task as a critical task.

You can display the free slack and total slack for the tasks in a schedule in the Task Sheet portion of Gantt Chart view or Task Entry view. Follow these steps to check the slack measurements for tasks:

1. Display Gantt Chart or Task Entry view.

2. Click anywhere in the Task Sheet portion of the view.

3. Open the <u>V</u>iew menu, point to Ta<u>b</u>le for a submenu of options (see Fig. 6.14), and click <u>S</u>chedule.

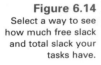

Figure 6.14
Select a way to see how much free slack and total slack your tasks have.

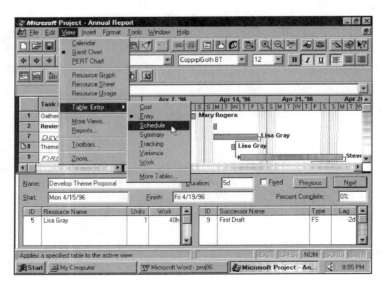

4. Use the scroll bar for that portion of the window to scroll right to display the Free Slack and Total Slack columns (see Fig. 6.15).

Figure 6.15
Here's what the slack columns look like when displayed in Task Entry view.

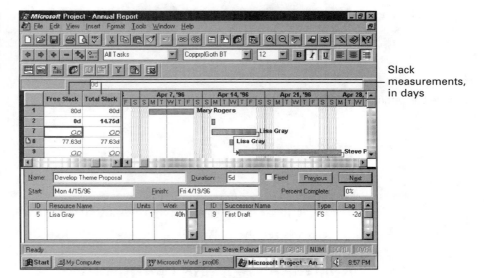

Slack measurements, in days

Changing How Much Slack Makes a Task Critical

Although Chapter 20, "Customizing Microsoft Project," covers how to adjust many important Project features, one feature relating directly to slack and critical tasks bears mentioning here. You can change the minimum amount of slack that tasks must have to avoid being designated as critical tasks. By default, any task with 0 or fewer days of total slack is designated as a critical task.

Increasing this setting designates more tasks as critical, giving you the opportunity to scrutinize them to look for ways to tighten the schedule. To change the option that controls which tasks are designated as critical, use these steps:

1. Open the Tools menu and click Options. The Options dialog box appears.
2. Click the Schedule tab to display its settings (see Fig. 6.16).
3. Double-click the entry in the Tasks Are Critical If Slack <= Days text box, and type a new entry. For example, type **3** to have Project designate any task with less than or equal to three days of slack as a critical task.

Figure 6.16
Use the Schedule
tab in the Options
dialog box to
control which tasks
are critical.

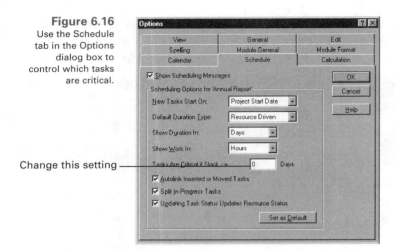

Change this setting ———

4. Click OK to close the dialog box. Project updates critical task designations in light of the new setting.

Adjusting Lead and Lag Times

Lead times and lag times can have a great impact on the slack available for a task as well as the critical path. (The "Working with Lead Times and Lag Times" section in Chapter 3 explains the basics of lead and lag times.)

You can, constraints allowing, add slack time by removing lead time or adding lag time. For example, you might change the Lag entry for a successor task from -2d to 0d to remove lead time. Adding slack time generally lengthens the schedule to some degree. Depending how much slack you add, Project might remove a task from the critical path. This can be beneficial in your planning if you're really unsure how well you've estimated the schedule for a task.

In contrast, to use lead and lag times to tighten the critical path, here are a few things you can do:

- Add lead time for a successor task where none exists, assuming that you can move up the start date of the successor task. For example, entering **-3d** creates three days' worth of lead time for a successor task.

- Add more lead time for a successor task with an FS link to its predecessor, as long as no constraint prohibits you from moving up the successor task.

- Cut back lag time, or eliminate it altogether, if constraints allow. For example, a 5d lag entry builds in five days of lag time; you might be able to change such an entry to **3d** or **2d**.

You can choose any of a number of techniques to adjust the lead and lag times for a task. For example, you can double-click a task name, click the Predecessors tab in the Task Information dialog box, then edit the Lag column in the Predecessors list. Or, you can use the lower pane of Task Entry view to work with lead and lag time, as follows:

1. In the upper pane, click the name of the critical task for which you want to work with lead and lag time.

2. Right-click the lower pane, then click Predecessors & Successors on the shortcut menu that appears. The lower pane changes to show other tasks linked to the selected task, either as predecessors or successors (see Fig. 6.17).

Figure 6.17
The bottom pane has been adjusted to let you work with linked tasks.

The selected critical task

Its successor, with lead time

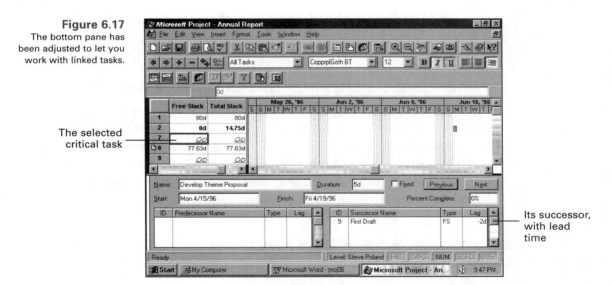

3. Click the cell in the Lag column for the link you want to edit. Type a new lag setting, then click OK in the lower pane. Project adjusts any task schedule as needed, according to your change. For example, Figure 6.18 shows the result of increasing the lead time assigned to row 7's successor task in row 9. The task in row 7 is no longer a critical task after the change.

Figure 6.18
Here's an example of working with linked tasks.

This task is no longer critical...

...due to the lead time added for its successor.

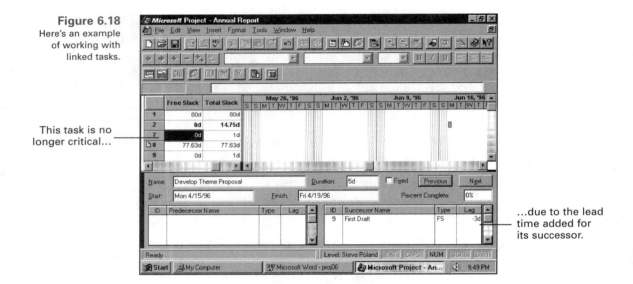

4. To adjust lead and lag times for another task, select the task in the upper pane, then make changes as needed in the lower pane.

Changing Constraints to Tighten the Schedule

Sometimes, constraints prohibit you from changing lead and lag time, or a schedule conflict arises if you try to do so. If you have Planning Wizard enabled, it warns you if a lead or lag time change will create such a conflict. For example, Figure 6.19 shows the message that appears if I try to reduce the lead time for a task that's constrained to Start No Later Than (SNLT) a particular date.

Figure 6.19
Constraints can keep you from making the schedule adjustments you want.

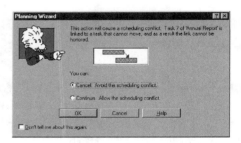

As such, you might want to review all the constraints you've assigned to tasks, looking for constraint changes that will allow you to tighten the schedule. In some cases, you might want to change constraints to ensure that a task stays on the critical path. Here are a few ideas of the types of constraint changes you can make:

- Change more tasks to As Soon As Possible (ASAP) constraints so that you can add lead times

- Remove Finish No Earlier Than (FNET) constraints for predecessor tasks, especially if they're linked to a successor with an FS link

- Use more Must Finish On (MFO) constraints to prevent predecessor tasks from slipping further out

To see a list of the constraints you've assigned to tasks so that you can quickly identify which constraints you want to change, do the following:

1. Change to Gantt Chart view or Table Entry view and click a task name in the list.

2. Open the View menu, point to Table, and click More Tables.

3. In the Tables list, double-click Constraint Date, or click it once and then click Apply. The Task Sheet changes to include Constraint Type and Constraint Date columns. You can drag the split bar from the upper pane, and use the scroll bar for the task list to display those columns (see Fig. 6.20).

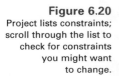

Figure 6.20
Project lists constraints; scroll through the list to check for constraints you might want to change.

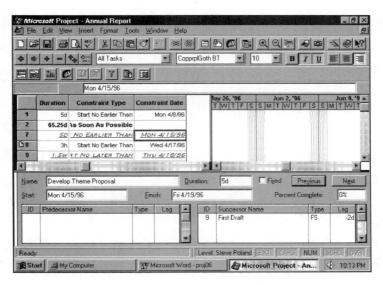

Chapter 3 covers the different types of task constraints in more detail. To quickly change constraints while the list of task constraints is on-screen, double-click the desired task name to display the Task Information dialog box. Click the Advanced tab. In the Constrain Task area, use the Type drop-down list and Date text box to specify a change to the constraint.

CHAPTER 7

COMPARING PROGRESS VERSUS YOUR BASELINE PLAN

Because a project often calls on a varied combination of resources, tasks, and other factors, you need to act as a "deejay" to ensure that the right tune plays at the right time (tasks stay on schedule), that the volume is right (everything's done correctly), and that all the dancers stay in step (your resources remain available and capable to work when you need them).

This chapter shows you how to compare actual progress on a project with the schedule you had planned, so that you can make adjustments, if needed, to meet your project goals. The chapter explains the following:

- How to capture the original project information and schedule

- Reporting work that has been completed

- Preserving the update information, and saving an interim plan

- Looking to see if your project's on time, ahead of schedule, or running behind

Creating the Baseline

When you're relatively young and the doctor puts you through your first thorough physical, the doc's not being paranoid and looking for imaginary illnesses. She's gathering your vital statistics while you're in good health, so that there will be a basis for comparison if you ever begin feeling ill. If your blood pressure is very low when you're healthy, a slight climb in the pressure can signal to your doctor that something serious is going on; however, if the doctor doesn't have your normal blood pressure reading, she might not catch the fact that your reading's higher than normal. Those original health measurements your doctor takes become the *baseline*—the starting point that your doctor uses for future comparison.

Project enables you to take a baseline reading of your schedule, too. Thus, you'll have a record of where you started that you can use to diagnose any problems that crop up in the schedule and budget. When you save a baseline for your schedule, Project records all the original details about your plan. Then you can compare information you've entered about the actual work performed and actual costs with the plans you started with (you'll learn how to do so later in this chapter).

The first time you save any project file after adding information to it, Project displays the dialog box shown in Figure 7.1, which asks whether you want to save the baseline for your new file. To save the baseline information, simply leave the top option button selected, and click OK. If you don't want to save the baseline at this particular time (because you haven't added all the information for the schedule), click the bottom option button, and then click OK.

Figure 7.1
When you've added information to your file and are trying to save it, Project asks if you want to add a baseline.

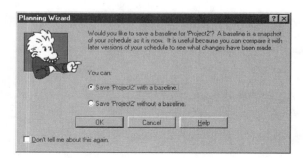

> **CAUTION:** Every time you save the baseline, the save process overwrites any baseline information you've previously saved. If you want to take a "snapshot" of your project at any given time and leave the baseline intact, save an *interim plan*. See the "Saving and Viewing an Interim Plan" section later in this chapter.

Don't worry if you opt not to create a baseline while saving. You have the option of saving baseline information at any point during the plan development process. You also can save a baseline for only part of the project, by selecting certain tasks to track in detail. Here are the steps for creating your schedule baseline:

1. Enter all the task and resource information you want to save as part of the baseline. It doesn't hurt to double-check to make sure that everything's in place, including links and fixed task costs you might have overlooked.

2. (Optional) If you want to save only certain tasks, select the rows you want in the Task Sheet in Gantt Chart view. (Make sure that you're at Gantt Chart view by opening the View menu and clicking Gantt Chart.) Select the tasks you want by pointing to the row number for the top row, and dragging down to highlight (select) the rows. To select noncontiguous rows, press and hold down Ctrl and then click each additional row.

3. Open the Tools menu and point to Tracking. A submenu of commands appears.

4. Click Save Baseline. The Save Baseline dialog box appears (see Fig. 7.2).

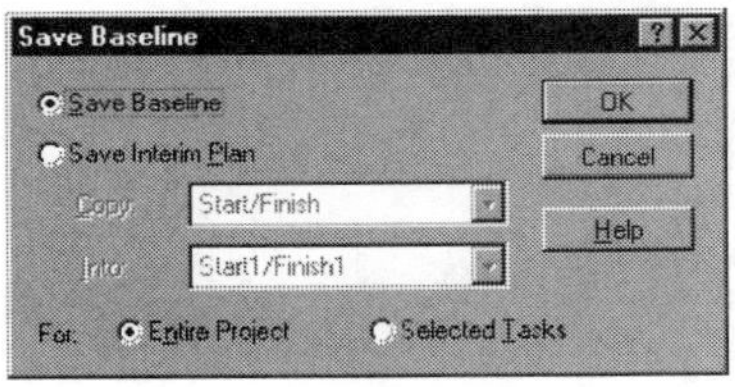

Figure 7.2
Using this dialog box, you can save baseline information easily at any time.

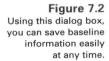

5. If you've saved baseline information for all the tasks, leave the Entire Project option button selected and click OK to continue. If you have selected specific tasks for the baseline, click the Selected Tasks option button, then click OK. In either case, Project stores the baseline information.

Viewing Baseline Information

After you've saved the baseline information, you might want to look at the baseline values for reference, or perhaps print them out for others on the team. To view the baseline information, use a variation of the Task Sheet called the *Baseline Table*. Although the "Choosing a Table" section in Chapter 9, "Working with the Different Project Views," provides more details, here are the steps for viewing this table of baseline information:

TIP: The baseline information also appears in one of Project's reports, the Project Summary report in the Overview category. For more on project reports, see Chapter 12, "Creating and Printing a Report."

1. Make sure that you're in Gantt Chart view by opening the View menu and clicking Gantt Chart. Gantt Chart view should appear with a cell selected in the Task Sheet.

2. Open the View menu, point to Table, and click More Tables. The More Tables dialog box appears (see Fig. 7.3).

Figure 7.3
Selecting a table here changes the columns that appear in the Task Sheet.

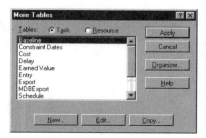

3. Make sure that you leave the T<u>a</u>sk option button selected at the top of the dialog box. From the <u>T</u>ables list, select `Baseline` by double-clicking it, or by clicking it once and then clicking App<u>l</u>y. Project displays the baseline columns in the Task Sheet.

4. Scroll the Task Sheet to the right a bit, and drag the vertical split bar to the right to display more of the Task Sheet, so that you can see the baseline columns (see Fig. 7.4).

Figure 7.4
You now can view the baseline information you've saved.

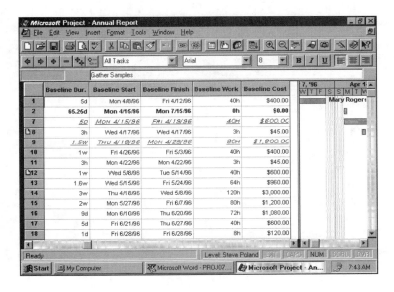

If you want to return to the regular Task Sheet view at any time, open the <u>V</u>iew menu, point to Ta<u>b</u>le, and click <u>E</u>ntry.

Entering Completed Work

Project would be an even better product if you could attach a "work meter" to each and every resource that would automatically capture what the resource does, and report that information to Project. Because the world isn't that high-tech yet—and such an approach has the scary feeling of a "Big Brother" society—you'll have to tell Project what actual work has been completed on scheduled tasks.

While Project offers you several means of entering information about actual work completed, one of the most convenient methods is the

Tracking toolbar. To display the Tracking toolbar, right-click any on-screen toolbar, and then select Tracking. The Tracking toolbar appears, as shown in Figure 7.5. You'll use several of these buttons as you update and view information about completed work, so I'll describe each button when you need it.

Figure 7.5
The Tracking toolbar offers buttons to speed the process of entering specific information about tasks.

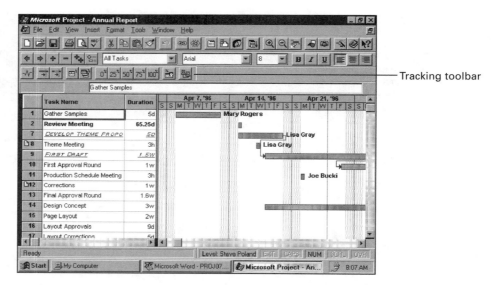

Tracking toolbar

Updating Task by Task

There are three key ways to tell Project about work that has been completed on a task or a selected set of tasks. The first method, updating completed work information with the mouse, is probably the most time-consuming, but enables you to have the greatest control over and familiarity with details about the completed work. With this method, you can update work using the calendar, indicating that, for example, someone has completed three out of five days of work scheduled for a task. Project calculates the percentage of work completed. To update task completion information using your mouse, work with the Gantt chart bars in Gantt Chart view. Point to the left end of the bar for the task you want to update, so that the mouse pointer changes to a percentage pointer. Press and hold the left mouse button and drag to the right (see Fig. 7.6). As you drag, a Task information box appears, telling you how many days will be marked as completed. When you release the mouse button, Project indicates the percentage of the task that has been completed by placing a dark completion bar within the Gantt chart bar for the task you've modified (see Fig. 7.7). If a task has not started on time and you need to enter information about the actual starting date, you should use the method described next to update the task.

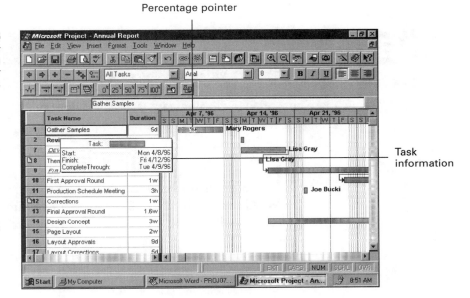

Figure 7.6
The percentage pointer indicates that you can update your task by dragging.

Figure 7.7
The dark bar within the Gantt chart bar for the first task shows the portion of work completed on that task so far.

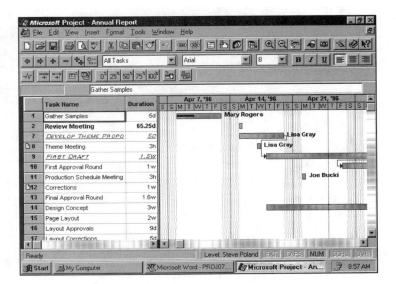

The second method also enables you to update tasks one at a time, but gives you some options about how you specify that the work is completed. This method enables you to specify the actual start and finish dates for the task when those dates differ from the dates you had scheduled. To use this method, follow these steps:

1. Select the task or tasks you want to update in the Task Sheet.

> **NOTE:** You can't select a summary task (the "master" task for a set of recurring tasks) to update it; you can only select the subtasks within a summary task. For more on working with summary tasks and subtasks, see Chapter 13, "Working with Outlining."

2. Open the Tools menu, point to Tracking, and click Update Tasks. Alternatively, click the Update Tasks button on the Tracking toolbar. The Update Tasks dialog box appears (see Fig. 7.8).

Update Tasks button

Figure 7.8
Here you enter actual data about a task's schedule and work completed.

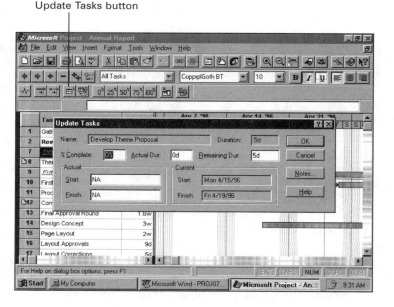

3. Enter information about the work that has been completed using one of the following three methods:

- Enter a percentage value, such as **10** for 10%, in the % Complete text box, which is highlighted by default when you display the Update Tasks dialog box. Project will change the duration settings for you when you finish updating the task.

- Enter the number of days of work completed in the Actual Dur text box. If you want to use a duration other than the default (days), enter the duration abbreviation with the value you enter, such as **w** for weeks. Project will calculate the percentage completed information and remaining duration information.

- Enter the number of days of work you estimate are remaining for the task in the Remaining Dur text box. Again, if you want to enter a duration that's not in days, include the appropriate duration abbreviation. When you specify work completed this way, Project will calculate the percentage completed and duration.

4. If it looks like the actual starting or finishing date for the task will differ from those dates entered in the Current area of the Update Tasks dialog box, change the Start and Finish text box entries accordingly. Enter the new dates in mm/dd/yy format. (By default, these text boxes contain NA if the actual date, according to your computer's date and time information, is later than the scheduled start date for the task.)

5. Click OK. Project updates the tasks, and will move and adjust any tasks as needed to reflect your changes in the Actual Start or Finish dates. It also uses a dark bar to mark the percentage of completed work you indicated for the selected task(s).

The final method for updating tasks is more "quick and dirty," and gives you less flexibility in specifying exact percentages or days of completed work. For this method, select the task or tasks you want to update in the Task Sheet, then click one of the five percentage buttons (0%, 25%, 50%, 75%, or 100%) on the Tracking toolbar. Project updates the Gantt bar(s) accordingly. Of course, you use the 0% button to remove any completed work that you previously specified. For example, if you thought an external resource had completed half a task, but you discover that no work has actually been completed (for instance, your contact person initially fibbed to you), you can select the task and click the 0% button to show the true percentage measurement.

CAUTION: If you select multiple tasks in the Task Sheet before displaying the Update Tasks dialog box, you can enter actual duration or actual start and finish information, but keep in mind that these changes apply to all the selected tasks. An instance where such a "global" change might be useful is if the project starting date becomes delayed, and you need to push out the actual starting dates for multiple tasks. Generally, you should select multiple tasks only when you want to enter the same % Complete value for all of them.

TIP: The Update As Scheduled button, second from the left on the Tracking toolbar, specifies work completed for the selected task(s) based on the scheduled start date(s) and the current date. Project assumes that all work scheduled between those dates has been completed, and enters the work update information accordingly, adding dark tracking bars to the Gantt chart.

Updating a Range of Tasks

If you want to update a range of tasks using the Update Tasks dialog box, but you don't want the same changes to apply to all tasks and don't want to have to open the dialog box time and time again, you can use the Update Task Range button on the Tracking toolbar to automate the process. Clicking this button runs a built-in Project macro that displays the Update Tasks dialog box for every task in the schedule, or for any group of tasks that fall within the date range you specify. (Because you don't enter update information for summary tasks, those are skipped by the macro.) Here are the steps for using this tool:

1. In Gantt Chart view, click the Update Task Range button on the Tracking toolbar. Project displays the Task Update Macro dialog box (see Fig. 7.9). Click Yes to continue.

Update Task Range button

Figure 7.9
Project asks whether you want to proceed with the Task Update Macro.

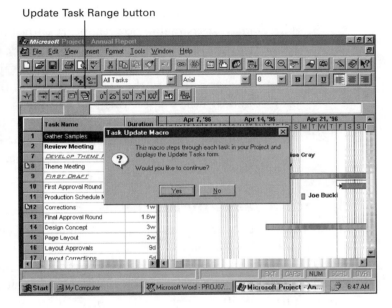

2. Project asks if you want to update all tasks in the schedule or a specific range of tasks (see Fig. 7.10). Click your choice to continue.

Figure 7.10
Tell Project which tasks to update in your schedule.

3. If you've chosen Specific Tasks, Project displays the Date Range dialog box, so you can enter the date that specifies the beginning of the range of tasks to update. Enter the date in mm/dd/yy format, and click OK. Enter the ending date for the range in the next dialog box that appears, and click OK. Project adjusts the Task Sheet so that it lists only the tasks in the specified range.

4. Next, whether you're updating all tasks or selected tasks, the Update Tasks dialog box appears, with the current information about the first task to be updated. Make any changes you want in this dialog box as described earlier in this chapter, then click OK.

5. The Update Tasks dialog box reappears with information about the next task to be updated. Again, enter or change information as needed, then click OK. Project makes the changes you specified to the task information, then moves on to the next task. Repeat this process each time the Update Tasks dialog box appears. After you update the last task, Project returns to the normal view of your schedule—and redisplays all the tasks, if you only updated specific tasks.

Updating Tasks by Resource

In some instances, you might not have information to enter about the work completed for all the tasks that were underway recently. Let's say that in the last week, you've only received a progress report from one resource, such as an outside contractor. When such a situation arises, you don't have to sift through the Task Sheet, hunting for each task handled by the resource so that you can update it. Click the Update Resources button on the Tracking toolbar. You'll see a message that Project is starting the Timesheet, which is an add-in program for updating resource information in Project. Soon, Project displays the Resource Update Options dialog box (see Fig. 7.11).

Figure 7.11
You can enter information about work completed for all the tasks handled by a certain resource.

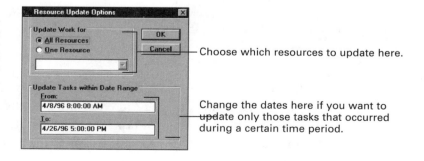

Choose which resources to update here.

Change the dates here if you want to update only those tasks that occurred during a certain time period.

In the Update Work For area at the top of the dialog box, you can leave the <u>A</u>ll Resources option button selected to list all resources for updating. To select a single resource, click the <u>O</u>ne Resource option button, then use the drop-down list that accompanies it to specify the resource for which you want to capture work completion information. If needed, edit the <u>F</u>rom and <u>T</u>o entries in the Update Tasks Within Date Range area of the dialog box to narrow the tasks to update to those occurring within the range you give. Click OK to continue. The Update Resource Work dialog box appears (see Fig. 7.12).

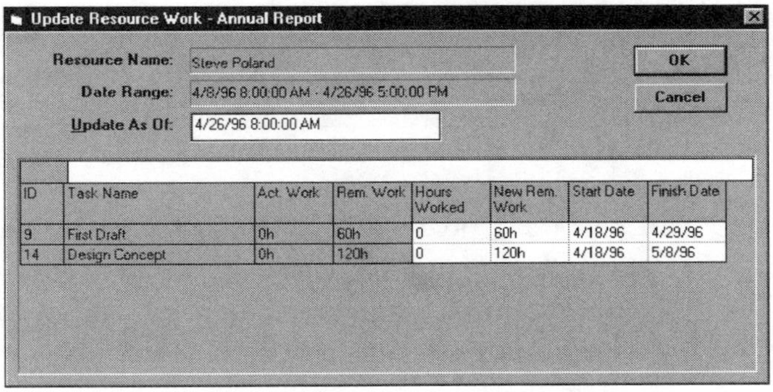

Figure 7.12
Double-check that the correct tasks to update are listed here before continuing.

By default, the <u>U</u>pdate As Of text box entry offers the current date and current time, rounded to the nearest hour. Leaving this entry as is tells Project to assume that all work scheduled for the selected tasks should be marked as completed through the present date and time. You can change the <u>U</u>pdate As Of entry, for example, if you know that work has been completed as of two days prior, but aren't certain whether more work has occurred during the last two days. Click OK to update the tasks. The Resource Update Options dialog box reappears, and you can select another resource to update, or click Close to finish.

Updating Project Information

As if the preceding methods weren't enough, Project offers one final path for indicating how much work has been completed for tasks you select, or for all the tasks in the project: the Update Project dialog box. To display and use this dialog box to update completed work information for the tasks in your schedule, follow these steps:

1. (Optional) If you want to update only selected tasks, select the tasks in the Task Sheet in Gantt Chart view by dragging over the task row numbers or dragging to select cells in the rows for the tasks you want.

2. Open the Tools menu, point to Tracking, and click Update Project. Project displays the Update Project dialog box (see Fig. 7.13).

Figure 7.13
This is yet another method for updating information about work completed.

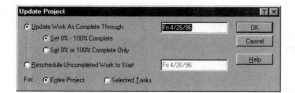

3. Leave the Update Work As Complete Through option button selected. If you don't have information that's absolutely current, you might want to change the date in the text box beside this option button to reflect the date through which you're certain work has been completed.

4. Choose among the following option buttons:

   • The Set 0%–100% Complete option button, which is selected by default and marks the work completed based on the percentage of work between the task's start date and the date specified in step 3.

   • The Set 0%–100% Complete Only option, which is an all-or-nothing choice that marks the task as 0% completed if its finish date is after the date specified in step 3, or 100% if it was scheduled to finish on or before the date specified in step 3.

5. If you selected a range of tasks in step 1, click to select the Selected Tasks option button at the bottom of the dialog box.

6. Click OK. Project closes the dialog box and marks the appropriate tasks with indicators of how much work has been completed.

Rescheduling Work

Things happen, and work doesn't always start as planned. For example, if you schedule painters to handle some outdoor painting, and it rains, there's no choice but to start the painting on a later, drier day. You might also encounter situations in which a resource begins work on a task, but can't finish it on the scheduled date due to problems such as scheduling conflicts or unforeseen absences from work. In such instances, you need to reschedule the task to a timeframe that's realistic—which means moving all or some of the work after the current date in the schedule. When a task needs to be rescheduled, it has *slipped.*

Of course, you have the option of dragging the Gantt chart bar for the task into a new position, or dragging to reschedule the finish date for a partially completed task, but Project also offers methods for quickly rescheduling all tasks for which work was to start (or finish) prior to the current date.

When you reschedule a task, if you've indicated that no work has been completed on it, Project moves the task so that its start date becomes the current date. If you've marked the task as partially completed, Project leaves the original start date in place but extends the task schedule so that the work yet to be done begins on the current date—this is called *splitting* an in-progress task.

NOTE: When you reschedule the remaining work for a partially completed task, Project is smart enough to know that you don't really add extra work hours for the task (or pay the resource for a dramatically increased number of hours). Even though the Gantt chart bar for the rescheduled task might look like the task has been dramatically expanded, if you check the Task Sheet or the Task Information dialog box, you'll find that the duration and the percentage of work completed on the task are consistent with what you originally scheduled.

Select the task(s) that you want to update in the Task Sheet, then choose one of the following methods to reschedule the task:

- Display the Update Project dialog box as just described. Click the Reschedule Uncompleted Work To Start option button (refer to Fig. 7.13), then enter the date when the rescheduled work should begin in the accompanying text box. Click the Selected Tasks option button, then click OK to let the work slip.

- Click the Reschedule Work button on the Tracking toolbar (the third button from the left) to move the selected task(s) so that uncompleted work begins on the current date.

Saving and Viewing an Interim Plan

While baseline plans let you look at where you started with your schedule and resource plans, an *interim plan* serves as a snapshot of changes you've made down the line, and how far you've come with a project. For example, you might set a milestone for the date when the project is 25% through its total schedule, and want a record of how things stand at that point. If you save an interim plan, it captures the current information (or information from a previous interim plan) in the fields for the start and finish dates for tasks.

For example, your resource might have completed Task 1, but it might have taken twice as long as you had anticipated. You might look at similar tasks later in your schedule, adjust them to reflect the new knowledge, and save an interim plan. Any changes you make subsequent to saving that interim plan are not added to the interim plan—they're added to the main scheduling fields for your project. You can save up to five interim plans to keep a record of where significant schedule changes occur.

TIP: If your company routinely uses follow-up meetings after the completion of a project to analyze what worked well and troubleshoot things that didn't work well, you should arm yourself for the discussion by creating interim plans and adding task notes about when and why key tasks slipped.

The initial steps for creating an interim plan resemble the initial steps for saving the baseline. Here are those initial steps, plus the rest of the steps needed to save your interim plan and view its information:

1. Enter all the task and resource information you want to save as part of the interim plan.

2. (Optional) If you want to save selected tasks, select the rows you want in the Task Sheet in Gantt Chart view.

3. Open the Tools menu and point to Tracking. A submenu of commands appears.

4. Click Save Baseline. The Save Baseline dialog box appears.

5. Click to select the Save Interim Plan option, which enables the Copy and Into drop-down lists.

6. From the Copy drop-down list (see Fig. 7.14), select the two fields of information from the Task Sheet you want to save in your interim plan. For the first interim plan, you should always select either the default Start/Finish or Baseline Start/Finish. For subsequent interim plans, you should choose the fields you specified in the Into drop-down list (see the next step) for the last interim plan you saved, so that the new interim plan gives you a record of which tasks have slipped more than once.

Figure 7.14
The interim plan captures information from two Task Sheet fields that you specify here.

7. Use the Into drop-down list to specify what Project will call the fields where it saves the interim plan dates. For your first interim plan, you should use Start1/Finish1, for your second interim plan, you should use Start2/Finish2, and so on.

8. If you want to save interim dates for only the tasks you selected in step 2, click to select the Selected Tasks option.

9. Click OK. Project saves the interim plan dates in new fields; you can add them to the Task Sheet to view their contents by completing the rest of these steps.

10. In the Task Sheet, click the column name of the column to the right of where you'd like to insert an interim plan field.

11. Open the Insert menu and click Insert Column (or right-click and then click Insert Column on the resulting shortcut menu). The Column Definition dialog box appears.

12. Click the drop-down list arrow to display the Field Name list, then scroll down and click the name of the interim plan field to be inserted at that location. For example, you would click Start1 to display the first field from your first interim plan (see Fig. 7.15).

Figure 7.15
You can choose to add an interim plan field to the Task Sheet.

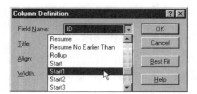

13. If needed, make changes to other fields in the Column Definition dialog box, then click OK to finish adding the field. It appears in the Task Sheet as shown in Figure 7.16.

14. Repeat steps 10–13 to add any other interim plan fields you want to view to the Task Sheet.

Viewing Baseline versus Actual Information

Because there are so many different kinds of information captured in your Project file, the baseline information you store and the actual information you enter about work completed doesn't display automatically. To close this chapter, I'll show you a few different ways to view this information, depending how much and what kind of detail you want to see.

The interim plan field

Figure 7.16
This interim plan field
has been added to the
Task Sheet.

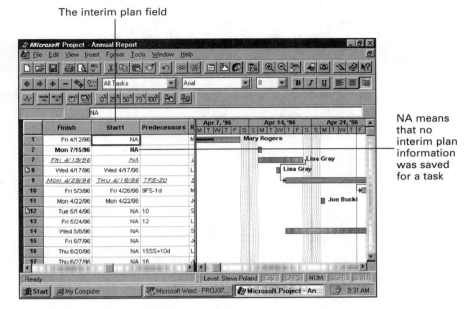

NA means
that no
interim plan
information
was saved
for a task

Using Tracking Gantt View

The Tracking Gantt view in Project lets you do virtually everything you can do in Gantt Chart view, such as dragging and moving tasks, updating links, or entering information about work that has been completed for a project. In addition, though, Tracking Gantt view uses Gantt bars that provide greater detail about work progress on tasks, so you can see at a glance which tasks are on schedule or falling behind. This is much more convenient than scrolling through various columns on the Task Sheet.

In this view, each Gantt bar is really two bars (see Fig. 7.17). The lower portion, usually gray even on a color monitor, shows you the baseline schedule for the task, assuming you've saved a baseline plan for the project. The top portion shows the current schedule for the project, in a lightly shaded bar. As you enter actual work information for the task, the portion of the bar representing the work completed becomes solid rather than shaded. By default, the top portion of the bar is blue if the task is on schedule or work has not yet begun on it. If the task is behind schedule (meaning that its finish date has passed but you haven't yet marked the task as 100% completed), the upper portion of the bar appears in red, a color commonly used to alert you that it's time to panic.

Figure 7.17
Tracking Gantt view
works like regular
Gantt Chart
view, but the
bars provide you
with more
information
about your tasks.

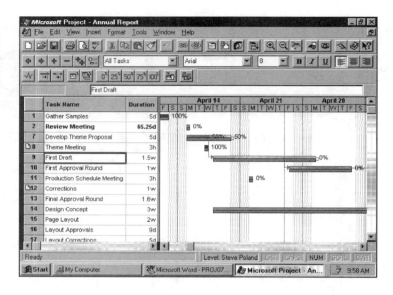

To display Tracking Gantt view, open the <u>V</u>iew menu and click <u>M</u>ore Views. In the More Views dialog box, scroll down the <u>V</u>iews list to display the Tracking Gantt choice. Double-click this choice (or click it once and click Apply).

> **CAUTION:** At times, Tracking Gantt view can be a bit unpredictable. If you switch to this view and don't see *anything* in the Gantt chart pane at the right, first make sure that Project hasn't scrolled the displayed dates beyond the schedule for the project. If that's not the solution, click the Goto Selected Task button on the Standard toolbar.

Other Tracking Views

If you want access to the baseline and tracking information in tabular form, you can change the Task Sheet display so that it displays the information you want. To do so in any view that contains the Task Sheet, click a cell in the Task Sheet, then open the <u>V</u>iew menu, point to Ta<u>b</u>le, and click <u>T</u>racking. The Task Sheet now displays tracking information (see Fig. 7.18).

NOTE: For this figure, I've expanded the size of the Task Sheet by dragging the vertical split bar to the right.

Figure 7.18
The Task Sheet now shows tracking information in tabular form.

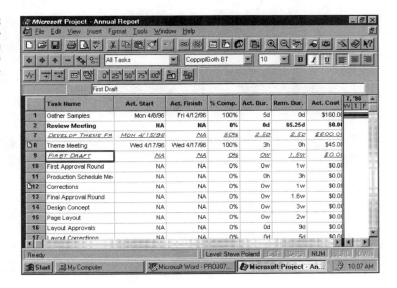

In Chapter 2, "Setting Up a Project," you learned how to display the Project Statistics box via the Project Info dialog box. The Project Statistics dialog box offers information about the baseline schedule for the project, including work and cost information, as well as the actual work completed and dollars spent. You also can display this dialog box by clicking the Project Statistics button (the first button) on the Tracking toolbar. The dialog box appears as shown in Figure 7.19.

Figure 7.19
As you enter actual
data about tasks
using the methods
covered in this
chapter, the
statistics for your
project change.

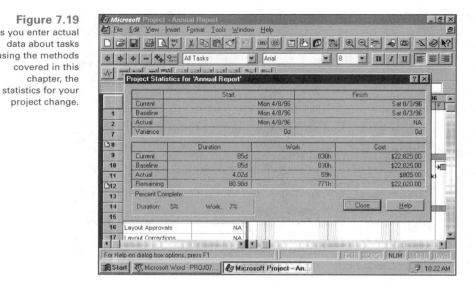

PART III

VIEWING, FORMATTING, AND PRINTING PROJECTS

CHAPTER 8

VIEWING AND MANAGING COSTS

When you're an independent contractor, you have to keep your eye on three key aspects of any project you manage for your client. First, you have to ensure that the work you deliver is of the highest quality. Second, you have get the job done on time—or even earlier. Finally, you have to track costs like a maniac to ensure that you not only charge the client a fair price but also make a fair profit.

As a project manager within a company, you also need to think like an independent contractor. The work your team delivers has to be top quality and on time, and must be delivered at a cost that helps your company stay profitable.

This chapter shows you how to get crucial mileage from all the resource and task information you've entered into Project. Specifically, this chapter shows you how to do the following:

- See how much a task has cost
- See how much a resource has cost
- See how much the whole project has cost
- Report to others about costs
- Manage costs and cash flow

Viewing and Finding Task Costs

Chapter 7, "Comparing Progress versus Your Baseline Plan," explains how to tell Project how much work has been completed on a task, and therefore how much of the task duration time has elapsed. In addition, though you might not be able to see it immediately, Project can use the task completion information you've entered to calculate the actual cost for that completed work, based on hourly rates for resources, and other cost information you've entered.

I say that you might not be able to see the costs immediately because Gantt Chart view doesn't display any cost information by default. You have to learn techniques for examining cost information in various ways, depending what type of information you want to view. Project enables you to view accumulated costs (costs based on actual work completed plus any fixed and per use costs) by task, by the whole project, or by the resource(s) completing the work. The remainder of this section describes how to access each of these types of cost information.

Making Sure That Costs Update Based on Work Completed

This technique took me a while to figure out, and it isn't easy to find guidance for it in Project's online Help system, so pay careful attention here. By default, Project *does not* automatically update the calculated costs for a task or resource when you update information about how much work has been completed on a task. You need to tell Project that you want calculated cost values (the number of hours of work completed for a task multiplied by the hourly rate for the resource completing the task). The primary reason not to have Project calculate these values as you go is to avoid calculation delays while you're updating information about the work completed on various tasks.

To ensure that Project correctly calculates information about actual costs based on the work you've marked as completed, follow these steps:

1. Open the Tools menu and click Options. The Options dialog box appears, with many tabs.
2. Click the Schedule tab to display its options (see Fig. 8.1).

Figure 8.1
The Schedule tab offers
options for controlling
how Project reacts
when you
enter scheduling
information.

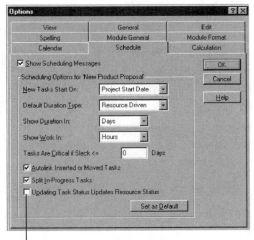

When this option is checked, Project automatically calculates actual expenses.

3. Select the Updating Task Status Updates Resource Status option (click to place a checkmark beside it). After you select this option, Project will update all calculated cost information whenever you update task completion information.

NOTE: Once you enable this option, it's enabled for all files you open in Project.

4. Click OK to close the Options dialog box. Your change takes effect immediately.

CAUTION: If you don't select the Updating Task Status Updates Resource Status option, the individual costs and total project costs aren't likely to calculate correctly, so you won't get the updated information you need. (Project instead will expect you to enter actual cost information, and who wants to do that?) It's essential to make sure that this option is selected!

Viewing Task Costs

One way to look at the expenses associated with your project is task by task. For example, your plan might include particular tasks for which you really need to watch expenses, such as work handled by an outside contractor with a particularly high hourly rate. Or, you might need to provide information about the costs you've estimated for a particular task to a team member negotiating to have that task completed, so the team member will know the highest price you're willing to pay to have the task completed.

Project offers a couple of methods by which you can take a look at how costs are adding up for a task based on the work completed for that task. Either method enables you to enter or edit cost information when you need to, such as when the actual fixed cost turns out to be less than the fixed cost you initially estimated.

The first method involves adjusting the columns shown in the Task Sheet; do this in any view that displays the Task Sheet, such as Gantt Chart view or Task Entry view. To display actual cost information in the Task Sheet, open the <u>V</u>iew menu, point to Ta<u>b</u>le, and click <u>C</u>ost. The Task Sheet changes to include several columns with cost information. Drag the vertical split bar (if there is one) to the right to display additional columns of cost information, as shown in Figure 8.2. To return the Task Sheet to its regular view, open the <u>V</u>iew menu, point to Ta<u>b</u>le, and click <u>E</u>ntry.

TIP: If Project doesn't automatically update actual cost information after you update task information, press Shift+F9 to manually recalculate the project information.

Displaying cost information in the Task Sheet as I've just described is useful when you want to view the costs for many tasks. There might be instances, however, when you don't want to change the Task Sheet's appearance, but do want to view the cost information for a particular task. You can do so by displaying the Cost Tracking form (you'll learn more detail about forms in Chapter 11, "Working with Forms"). Use one of the following methods to access the Cost Tracking form:

- Display the Custom Forms toolbar by right-clicking any toolbar on-screen and clicking Custom Forms. Click the Cost Tracking button (second from the left) on this toolbar.

- Open the Tools menu, point to Customize, and click Forms. The Custom Forms dialog box appears (see Fig. 8.3). Click to select the Task option button if it isn't already selected. In the Forms list, double-click Cost Tracking (or click it once and click Apply).

This task is partially completed, and cost information is adjusted accordingly.

This task is 100% completed.

Figure 8.2
You can adjust the Task
Sheet so that it displays
cost information.

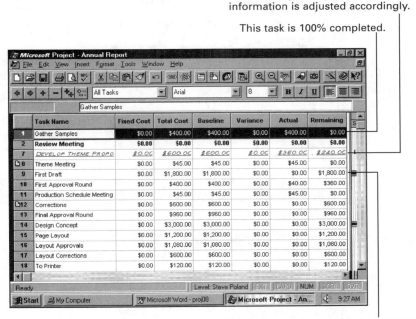

This task is underway, but costs accrue at the end, so no actual costs appear.

When you use either of the methods just described, the Cost Tracking Form appears (see Fig. 8.4). As you can see, this form offers several text entry boxes with various task cost information, including the baseline cost (how much you estimated the work on the task would cost), the actual cost of the work performed so far, and any remaining (Rem) budgeted cost. It also calculates the variance between the baseline cost and the actual cost. You can change several of the entries in this dialog box. Note, however, that if Project is calculating the task cost based on hourly cost rates you've entered for a resource, any edits you make in the Total text box will revert to the calculated value as soon as you close the dialog box. To close the dialog box after making the changes you want, click OK.

Cost Tracking button on the Custom Forms toolbar

Figure 8.3
Use this dialog box to display a form giving you cost information about a single task.

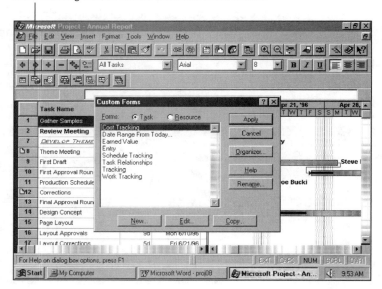

Figure 8.4
This form displays cost information for a single task.

TIP: A positive variance means that a task has gone over budget. A negative variance means that the task costs remain under the baseline budget.

Looking at Resource Costs

Chapter 5, "Resolving Overallocations and Overbooked Resources," covered how to identify when you've assigned too much work to a resource. Similarly, there might be situations where you want to review exactly how much each member or piece of equipment associated with your project is costing. This information can help you make intelligent decisions about cost cutting, or can help tease your memory about invoices that are coming due as the project schedule progresses. As usual, Project gives you several options for precisely how to view resource costs. Each of these is covered next.

> **NOTE:** If you haven't finished adding all the resources to your schedule, you can change the default standard hourly rate and overtime rate for new resources (so that it's no longer $0 for each). Do so using the General tab in the Options dialog box. Chapter 20, "Customizing Microsoft Project," covers setting this type of option.

Individual Resource Costs

The way you'll typically want to view resource costs is to view the total costs assigned to each resource. You can view this kind of information by adjusting the columns shown in the Resource Sheet, which Chapter 4, "Managing Resources," showed you how to use to add resources to your schedule. Here are the steps for displaying the Resource Sheet and displaying resource cost information in it:

1. If the Resource Sheet isn't currently on-screen, open the View menu and click Resource Sheet. The Resource Sheet appears as you've seen it in other chapters.

2. Open the View menu, point to Table, and click Cost. The Resource Sheet displays columns of cost information, as shown in Figure 8.5.

> **NOTE:** To return to regular Resource Sheet view, open the View menu, point to Table, and click Entry.

Figure 8.5
You can adjust the
Resource Sheet to
display cost
information, as
shown here.

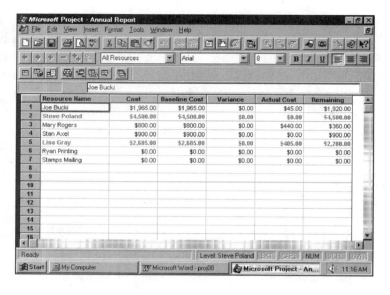

Each column in the Resource Sheet contains a particular type of cost information, and most are self-explanatory. One that isn't so obvious is the Cost column, which contains the current total cost of the work scheduled for the resource, as opposed to the baseline amount you initially planned. The cost information in all columns consists solely of calculated information; you can't edit any of these values. In fact, if you click a cell in one of the cost columns, you'll see that the entry in the text entry box above the Resource Sheet appears "grayed out"—if you try to edit it, you can't.

TIP: Once you change the Task Sheet or Resource Sheet to display cost information, you can print the information out. See Chapter 10, "Proofing and Printing a View," for more details.

Resource Group Costs

You might recall that one of the columns in the default version of the Resource Sheet is the Group column. In this column, you enter information to tell Project that a particular resource has something in common with other resources. For example, you might enter **Comm** in the Group column to identify each resource from the Communications department in your company. Or, you might enter **Contract** to identify each freelance or contract resource on the team. You might enter **Equipment** to distinguish non-human resources.

After you've displayed resource cost information as just described, you can reduce the list to display only resources that are part of a particular group and associated costs for only those resources. (This is a filtering operation—you'll learn more about filtering in Chapter 9, "Working with the Different Project Views.") To do so, follow these steps:

1. Display cost information in the Resource Sheet as previously described.

2. On the Formatting toolbar, click the arrow beside Filter to display a drop-down list (see Fig. 8.6).

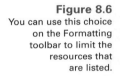

Figure 8.6
You can use this choice on the Formatting toolbar to limit the resources that are listed.

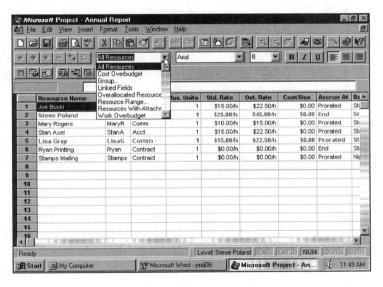

3. Click to select Group... from the Filter drop-down list. Project displays the Group... dialog box.

4. Enter the name of the group for which you want to view costs in the Group Name text box (see Fig. 8.7). You don't have to match the capitalization you used when you identified the resource group in the Group column (Project treats "comm," "Comm," and "COMM" as equivalent), but you do have to use the exact spelling.

Figure 8.7
Specify a resource
group for which
you'd like to see
cost information.

   5. Click OK to close the dialog box. The Resource Sheet displays
   cost information for only those resources you identified as
   part of the specified group (see Fig. 8.8).

Figure 8.8
Here's the cost
information for a
group of resources.

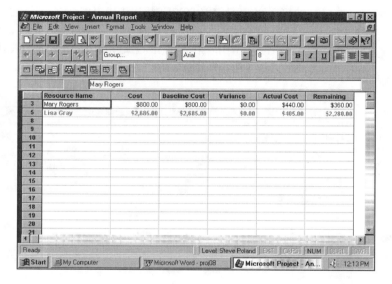

If you want to return to displaying all your resources in the Resource
Sheet, select All Resources from the Filter drop-down list on the Formatting toolbar.

Graphing Individual Resource Work and Costs

In addition to showing task information in graphical form with a
Gantt or PERT chart, you can show some resource information in a
chart. Although you'll learn more about adjusting various views in the
next chapter, here's a quick look at how to display graphical information about resource costs:

   1. Open the View menu and click Resource Graph. By default,
   Project shows a graphical representation of the work scheduled for the first resource listed in the Resource Sheet.

2. Right-click the right pane of the view (where the graphical information appears), or open the Format menu and click Details. On the shortcut menu (see Fig. 8.9) or submenu that appears, click Cost or Cumulative Cost. Project adjusts the graph in the right pane to show the exact cost amounts on the dates when they accrue (see Fig. 8.10), or a running total of the costs for the selected resource as they will accumulate (see Fig. 8.11).

Figure 8.9
You're en route to changing the resource information to graph.

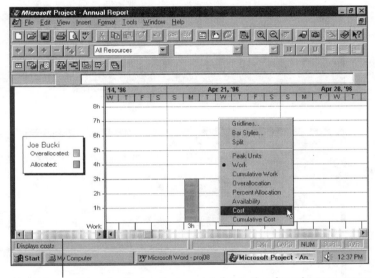

Use this scroll bar to display the graph information for other resources.

3. If you want to view a cost graph for another resource, use the scroll bar below the left pane where the resource name appears (refer to Fig. 8.9) to move between resources.

Viewing the Project Cost

In addition to viewing cost information about specific tasks or resources, you can view how costs are adding up for the entire project. Access information about project costs via the Project Info dialog box, which you've seen in a couple of earlier chapters in this book. To display total costs for your project, open the File menu and click Project Info. In the Project Info dialog box that appears for your project, click Statistics.

Figure 8.10
Here you're graphing the costs for a resource on particular dates.

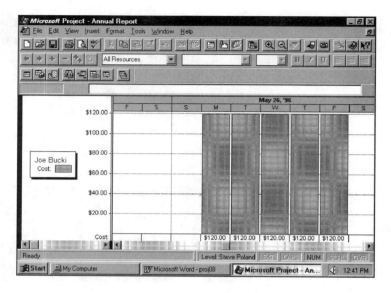

Figure 8.11
Here you're graphing how resource costs will accumulate over time.

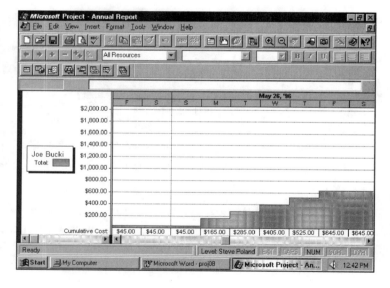

The Project Statistics dialog box appears (see Fig. 8.12). After you've reviewed the cost information, click Close to exit the Project Statistics dialog box.

Currently projected total cost (reflects any task or resource
cost changes you've made after saving the baseline)

Figure 8.12
This dialog box
contains information
about how much all
your project work is
costing.

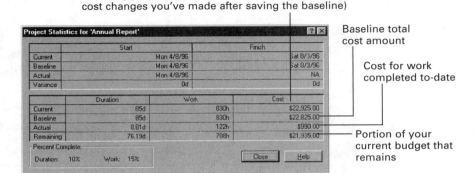

Baseline total
cost amount

Cost for work
completed to-date

Portion of your
current budget that
remains

A Word About Earned Values

The term *earned value* seems a bit misleading, because it's really a measure or whether or not particular tasks are on budget. In fact, when you view earned value information in either the Task Sheet or the Earned Value dialog box, you actually get to look at several statistics, which are listed in Table 8.1.

That's a lot of ways to slice up the information, and might be more than you ever want to know about the costs associated with your tasks. (For many project managers, the most relevant figure is the final variance.) There are two places to view all this cost information: the Task Sheet or the Earned Value dialog box. To display earned value information in the Task Sheet, follow these steps:

1. If you aren't already in Gantt Chart view, switch to it by opening the View menu and clicking Gantt Chart.
2. Open the View menu, point to Table, and click More Tables. The More Tables dialog box appears.
3. Make sure that the Task option is selected, then double-click Earned Value in the Tables list (or click it and click Apply). The Task Sheet now shows all the earned value amounts.
4. Drag the vertical split bar to the right so that you can review the earned value amounts (see Fig. 8.13).

If you want to view the earned value information for a single task in a convenient format, click its task row in any view that includes the Task Sheet. Next, click the Task Earned Value button on the Custom Forms toolbar, if you've displayed that toolbar as explained earlier in this chapter.

Alternatively, open the <u>T</u>ools menu, point to <u>C</u>ustomize, and click <u>F</u>orms; in the Custom Forms dialog box, make sure that the T<u>a</u>sk option is selected, and double-click `Earned Value` in the <u>F</u>orms list. Either way, the Earned Value dialog box appears (see Fig. 8.14). When you've finished viewing the earned value information, click OK to close the dialog box.

Table 8.1	Earned Value Statistics Tracked by Project
Abbreviation	**Description**
BCWS	*Budgeted Cost of Work Scheduled* is the cost you've budgeted for work scheduled up to the current date in your baseline plan.
BCWP	*Budgeted Cost of Work Performed* is calculated by multiplying the percentage of work actually completed on a task by the current date by the cost you've budgeted for the task in the same timeframe.
ACWP	*Actual Cost of Work Performed* calculates the cost for work performed to-date on a task, based on the hourly, per use, and fixed costs you've entered.
SV	*Schedule Variance* is the difference between BCWS and BCWP (BCWS–BCWP). This value compares the money you had planned to spend (in your baseline) by the current date to the money you had budgeted to spend for work performed by the current date; this figure simply shows how your budgeted costs have changed since you established the baseline. A positive SV value indicates that your current plan calls for spending more than your original plan did.
CV	*Cost Variance* shows how reality compares with the current budget; it subtracts BCWP from ACWP to tell you whether the work completed is over budget (indicated by a positive value) or under budget (indicated by a negative value).
BAC	*Budgeted At Completion* is the amount you've budgeted for the complete task, including fixed costs and per use costs. This amount is from your baseline plan.
FAC	*Forecast At Completion* is the amount presently budgeted for the complete task; it reflects any changes you've made to the amount of work scheduled, hourly costs, fixed costs, or per use costs since saving the baseline plan.
Variance	Compares the FAC with the BAC to see whether you'll be spending more (indicated by a positive value) or less (indicated by a negative value) than initially planned to complete the task.

Figure 8.13
You now can view a
listing of earned value
amounts.

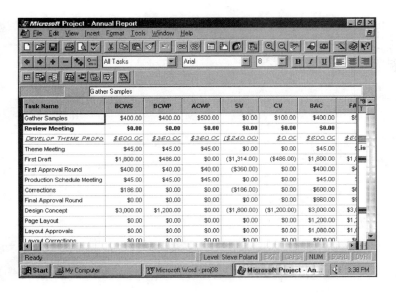

Figure 8.14
Project lets you see
earned value
information for a
single task.

A Preview of Cost Reports

Chapter 12, "Creating and Printing a Report," covers how to display,
format, and print various reports in Project. These reports gather and
calculate myriad types of data for you. Because budget information is
so important to any project planning process, Project provides many
types of cost and budgeting reports—five, to be exact. To display these
cost reports, open the View menu and click Reports. In the Reports
dialog box, double-click the Costs icon. The Cost Reports dialog box
appears, offering icons for five different reports; select and compile a
report by double-clicking its icon. Figures 8.15 through 8.19 show
examples of the available reports. Click Print in any report display to
print that report, or click Close to return to the Reports dialog box.

Figure 8.15
The Weekly Cash Flow report presents an update of how much you've spent per task each week.

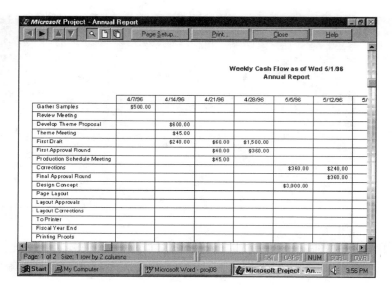

Figure 8.16
The Budget report presents the total costs you've scheduled for your project at the bottom, and the costs per task. This report sorts tasks from most expensive to least expensive.

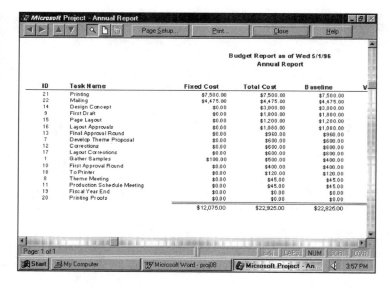

Figure 8.17
The Overbudget Tasks
report points out where
expenses are getting
out of hand.

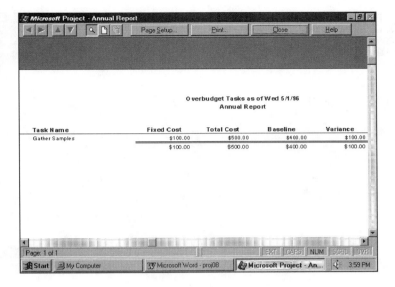

Figure 8.18
The Overbudget
Resources report
identifies when a
resource has had to
work more (and
therefore cost more)
than you had planned
in your baseline.

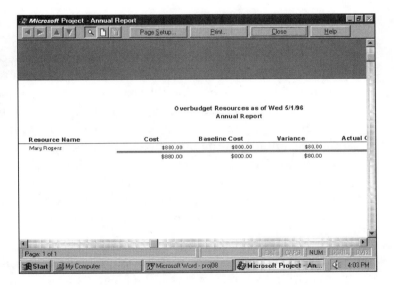

Figure 8.19
The Earned Value
report shows earned
value calculations for
each task, as well as
totals for the project.

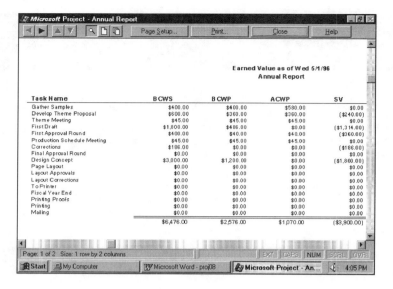

Changing How Costs Add Up

When you added resources to the project file using the default view of the Resource Sheet, you used the Accrue At column to note when costs for work performed should be charged to the project as an actual cost. Most costs will accrue in a *prorated* fashion, meaning that for each percentage point of the task that's marked as completed, a corresponding amount of the budgeted expense is charged as an actual cost. For tasks that have the Start setting in the Accrue At column, the total budgeted cost for the task becomes an actual cost as soon as any work is completed on the task. In contrast, for tasks where Accrue At is set to End, no actual costs accumulate until you mark the task as 100% completed.

In most cases, cash flow is as important to project management as the ultimate bottom line is. One of the biggest scams a consumer can fall prey to occurs when dealing with certain unscrupulous home repair contractors. The contractor gives the best estimate for a repair job, but asks for all or a large part of the money up-front. You hand over a check, and the contractor disappears into thin air without doing anything. Just as you'd certainly want to delay payments to a home repair contractor, it's in the interest of any business to delay project expenses until the work is completed to your satisfaction.

If you review task costs and it seems that too many have accrued too early in the schedule, look for tasks for which you can postpone accrued costs (negotiate with your resources, of course, to ensure that your changes reflect reality). You want to be able to change as many tasks as possible to accrue at the end of work on the task (although this isn't the realistic choice for most internal resources, which cost your company as soon as you use them). Where you can't have tasks accrue at the end, at least lobby for prorated cost approval and minimize the number of tasks that accrue at the start of work on the task. To review or change Accrue At information, display the Resource Sheet or right-click a task and then click Resource Information to display the Resource Information dialog box for that task. Change the entry in the Accrue At column or <u>A</u>ccrue At drop-down list box as needed.

NOTE: If you've changed the Resource Sheet to display earned value or other information instead of the default entry information, you need to change it back to adjust how costs accrue. With the Resource Sheet on-screen, open the <u>V</u>iew menu, point to Ta<u>b</u>le, and click <u>E</u>ntry.

Changing a Fixed Task Cost

After work has been completed on a task, most external resources present you with a bill. Alternatively, your company's accounting department might inform you how much of an allocated (shared) cost your group or department has to pay for the completion of a task. Whether the actual (fixed) cost for a task is higher or lower than you had budgeted in the Task Sheet, when you receive the actual bill or charge, you need to compare it with the Fixed Cost entry you made for the task, and adjust the entry upward or downward. Follow these steps to enter the actual, final fixed cost for a task after work on the task has been completed:

1. If you're not already in Gantt Chart view, change to it by opening the <u>V</u>iew menu and clicking <u>G</u>antt Chart.

2. Open the View menu, point to Table, and click Cost. The Task Sheet adjusts to show columns of cost information.

3. Click the Fixed Cost cell in the row for the task for which you want to enter actual data.

4. Click the task entry box above the Task Sheet, then edit the entry (see Fig. 8.20).

Click here to finish your edit.

Figure 8.20
You must edit the Fixed Cost amount when a task is completed, to reflect actual expenses or billing for a task.

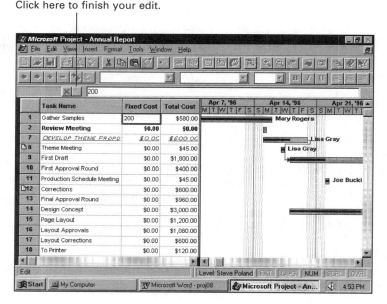

5. Click the Enter button or press Enter to finish your edit.

Overriding a Calculated Resource Cost

Just as a your original Fixed Cost entry might not reflect the final, actual cost, a calculated expense based on the amount of hourly work completed by a resource might not reflect the final charge to you for that work. This might happen when a resource (particularly a freelance resource) has to work more hours or days than you had estimated would be needed to complete the task, but because of a contractual obligation, the resource only bills you the original amount. Other times, a resource might have reason to bill you more for a task than had been initially agreed upon, even if the days or hours of work completed remained consistent with your estimate.

In either case, you need to adjust the actual costs for the task without changing the number of hours or days worked on the task. There's only one way to do so, and it involves the following steps:

1. Switch to Gantt Chart view and click the task for which you want to enter an actual cost that's different from the cost calculated by Project.

> **CAUTION:** You can override a calculated resource cost only after you've marked a task as 100% completed, and remaining costs (Rem. Cost) for the tasks are calculated as $0. Otherwise, Project will recalculate the actual cost (Act. Cost) based on the percentage of work completed, and your change will not take effect.

2. Open the <u>V</u>iew menu and click <u>M</u>ore Views. The More Views dialog box appears.

3. Scroll down the <u>V</u>iews list and double-click the Task Entry selection (or click it and click <u>A</u>pply). Project displays the Task Entry form in the lower pane.

4. Right-click the lower pane and click Resource Cost. The pane changes to display cost information about the resource.

5. Click the Act. Cost column and edit the entry as needed (see Fig. 8.21).

6. Click OK to finish your entry.

7. (Optional) Use the Pre<u>v</u>ious and N<u>e</u>xt buttons to display information about the resource work for other tasks, and repeat steps 5 and 6 to edit the Act. Cost entries.

To remove the lower pane and return to regular Gantt Chart view, open the <u>W</u>indow menu and click Remove Split.

Figure 8.21
You can edit the actual cost for a resource's work, when it's different from the calculated amount.

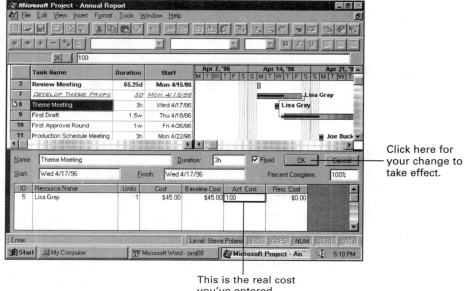

Click here for your change to take effect.

This is the real cost you've entered.

Cutting Back Costs

When you're developing your overall project schedule, or after work is underway and you're seeing that some of your actual cost amounts are exceeding amounts you've budgeted, you might need to look for ways to cut back costs. Here are just a few ways that you can reduce your overall budget:

- Look at the schedules for more expensive tasks—the Budget report (refer to Fig. 8.16) can help you identify these—and see if you can decrease the scheduled work for them, or negotiate a more favorable fee or hourly rate.

- Cut back the working time allotted for later tasks.

- Return to your cost estimates, and see if you have time to substitute less expensive resources for more expensive ones.

- Cut back the amount of work being handled by an expensive resource, perhaps by adding resources with less expensive hourly rates to share the expensive resource's workload.

CHAPTER 9

WORKING WITH THE DIFFERENT PROJECT VIEWS

Project enables you to capture a huge amount of information about the tasks and resources associated with your plan. In theory, you could use a spreadsheet program or word processor instead of Project to store all these details. To a limited degree, those kinds of programs let you chart or display information in alternative formats, but they do not provide the same flexibility in viewing and presenting your information that Project does.

Project offers this variety to enable you to be efficient at entering schedule and resource information, and to be proficient at reviewing the schedule and gleaning key facts. The different ways that Project presents information are called views, and this chapter reviews the views, including the following topics:

- The various view components
- How to display a view
- Working with tables, including how to control table information by sorting and filtering
- Using GanttChartWizard
- Adjusting whether charted information is displayed on a weekly, monthly, or other timescale
- Creating your own views and organizing views

Reviewing the Views

Earlier chapters in this book periodically explained how to change the view so that you could work with different kinds of information. The views used in earlier chapters included the Gantt Chart, Resource Graph, Resource Sheet, Resource Usage, and Task Entry views.

Project views can present information in a table or spreadsheet-like grid (as the Task Sheet and Resource Sheet do), in a graphical format (as Gantt chart bars do), or in a fill-in form format where you select fields or text boxes and then enter the information you want to view. Some views use a single method to present information, and some present information in various ways by having multiple panes on-screen. When a view uses only one method to organize information, such as a form, it's called a *single-pane view.*

TIP: Project prints information using the currently selected view. However, Project doesn't print information in forms, so a view comprised of only a form won't print at all. When printing is unavailable, the Print button on the Standard toolbar is disabled (grayed out).

In addition to thinking about how views appear on-screen, you need to select a view based on the type of information you want to work with. Some views primarily provide information about tasks, and other views primarily provide information about resources. Here are the predefined views you'll find in Project:

- **Calendar**—This single-pane view (see Fig. 9.1) displays tasks on a monthly calendar, using a bar and label to indicate each task duration.

- **Delay Gantt**—In this variation of Gantt Chart view, the Task Sheet includes a Delay column to indicate any tasks that Project delayed when you used automatic resource leveling (refer to Chapter 5, "Resolving Overallocations and Overbooked Resources," to learn more about resource leveling).

- **Detail Gantt**—In this variation of Gantt Chart view, the Task Sheet includes Delay information, and the Gantt bars indicate slack time and any task slips (changes in the task schedule since you saved the baseline). Figure 9.2 shows Detail Gantt view.

Figure 9.1
Use the Calendar view to show a monthly calendar for a project.

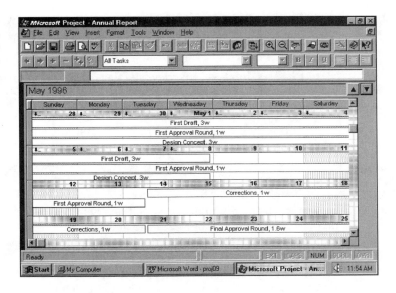

Slippage bar

Figure 9.2
Detail Gantt view presents more information than regular Gantt Chart view.

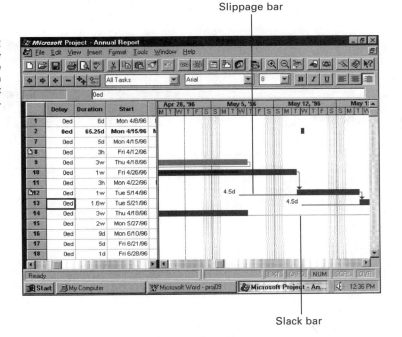

Slack bar

- **Gantt Chart**—This is the default view in Project; it includes the Task Sheet in the left pane and Gantt bars showing task durations and relationships in the right pane.

- **Module Editor**—This view enables you to view and edit macros and Visual Basic commands, and displays the Visual Basic toolbar.

- **PERT Chart**—This view displays tasks in a format resembling a flow chart (see Fig. 9.3). You can drag to link tasks, or right-click a task and click Task Information to make adjustments to the task schedule and resource assignments.

> **NOTE:** On the PERT chart, you also can drag to add new tasks to the schedule. Drag diagonally to create a box with the mouse. Right-click the new task box, then click Task Information. Provide the details about the task in the Task Information dialog box, then click OK. To delete a task in PERT Chart view, drag over an area that is larger than and surrounds the box to delete. When you release the mouse button, a gray selector appears around the box. Press the Delete key to remove the task box from the chart.

Figure 9.3
If you prefer a flow chart-like format, use PERT Chart view.

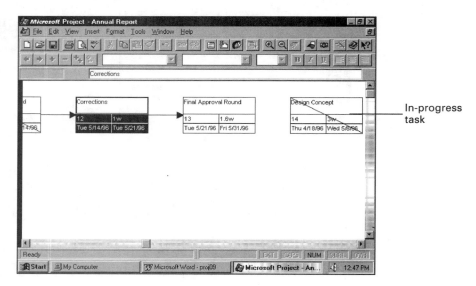

In-progress task

- **Resource Allocation**—This view presents the Resource Usage view in the upper pane, and presents the Task Sheet and Gantt chart in the lower pane.

- **Resource Form**—This is a form you use to enter and edit information about a specific resource. It lists all the tasks assigned to that resource, resource cost information, and more (see Fig. 9.4).

Figure 9.4
The Resource Form view captures all the information about the displayed resource.

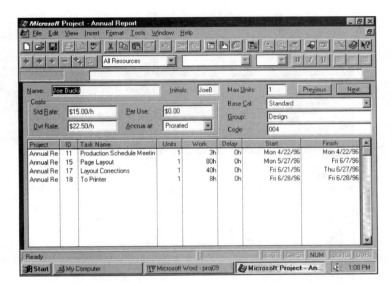

- **Resource Graph**—This view (examples of which are shown in Chapter 8, "Viewing and Managing Costs") can graph various information about a resource's daily and cumulative costs, scheduled work and cumulative work, overallocated times, percentage of work allocated, and availability. To change which information is graphed, right-click the chart area of the view and use the resulting shortcut menu to choose which information is charted.

- **Resource Name Form**—This abbreviated version of the Resource Form lists the resource name and its assigned tasks.

- **Resource Sheet**—Chapter 4, "Managing Resources," covers the Resource Sheet in detail. This view provides a grid of cells you can use to add resources to your project file.

- **Resource Usage**—This view (see Fig. 9.5) combines the Resource Sheet on the left with a grid on the right that you can adjust to show daily and cumulative costs, scheduled work and cumulative work, overallocated times, percentage of work allocated, and availability. To change which information is graphed, right-click the chart area of the view and use the resulting shortcut menu to choose which information is charted.

Work scheduled each day

Figure 9.5
In many views, you can right-click to select other types of information to chart or display.

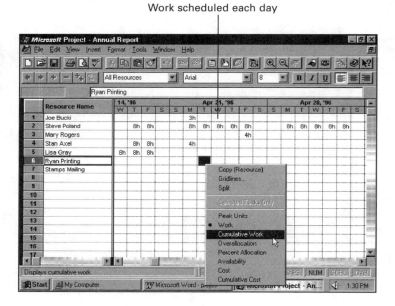

- **Task Details Form**—Similar to the Resource Form, this full-screen form displays task scheduling information, constraints, assigned resources, and more. You can view or edit information in this form, as you can in others.

TIP: You can right-click forms, also, to adjust what they display.

- **Task Entry**—This view displays the Gantt chart in the upper pane and the Task Form in the lower pane. It lets you perform detailed editing of task information in the lower pane, so you can see how your changes affect the Gantt chart. You can right-click the Task Form to select which information it displays.

- **Task Form**—This form enables you to change the task name, schedule, work completion information, and assigned resource(s).

- **Task Name Form**—This is the simplest variation of the Task Details Form. It enables you to change the task name and assigned resource(s).

- **Task PERT**—In a format resembling a flow chart (see Fig. 9.6), this view provides information about task links.

Figure 9.6
Task PERT view lets you focus on task links.

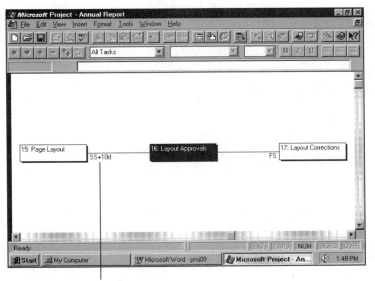

Link information

- **Task Sheet**—This view shows the Task Sheet at full-screen size rather than in combination with other view panes.

- **Tracking Gantt**—Chapter 7, "Comparing Progress versus Your Baseline Plan," discusses this variation of regular Gantt Chart view. In Tracking Gantt view, the Gantt chart bars are divided into upper and lower segments. The lower portion of each bar shows the task's original schedule, and the upper portion shows the task's current schedule.

Choosing a View

It's pretty obvious where to begin when you want to select a new view—the View menu. The top six commands on this menu take you directly to the specified view: Calendar, Gantt Chart, PERT Chart, Resource Graph, Resource Sheet, and Resource Usage.

If you want to display a view that's not listed on the menu, follow these steps:

1. Open the View menu and click More Views. The More Views dialog box appears (see Fig. 9.7).

Figure 9.7
The More Views dialog box enables you to choose a view that's not on the View menu.

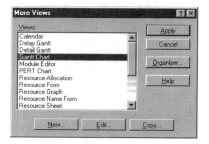

2. Scroll the Views list, if needed, to display the view you want to choose.

3. In the Views list, double-click the name of the view you want to display (or click the name and click Apply).

In views that include multiple panes, click within the pane you want to work in to make that pane the *active view*. The Active View bar along the edge of the screen darkens to indicate which pane you've selected to work in.

NOTE: If you're changing from a combination view that includes more than one pane to a view that includes only a single pane, the extra pane often won't close on its own. To close it, open the <u>W</u>indow menu and click Remove <u>S</u>plit (or double-click the dividing line between the panes).

NOTE: If you switch to any view that includes a Gantt chart and don't see *anything* in the Gantt chart pane, first make sure that Project hasn't scrolled the displayed dates beyond the schedule for the project. If that's not the solution, click the Goto Selected Task button on the Standard toolbar.

Adjusting a Sheet

The Task Sheet and Resource Sheet present information in various columns (fields) of information. Depending on the operation at hand, you may want to view columns that contain different information. For example, Chapter 8, "Viewing and Managing Costs," explains that you can display columns of actual and projected cost information in the Task Sheet. You also can control which rows appear in the current sheet, and the order in which those rows appear. This section covers how to make adjustments to the information presented in the Task Sheet or Resource Sheet.

Choosing a Table

In Project, each particular group of columns shown in a Task Sheet or Resource Sheet is called a *table*. To display one of the predefined sets of columns, therefore, you choose a different table for the currently displayed sheet. Of course, different tables are provided for the Task Sheet and Resource Sheet, as you track different information for tasks than you do for resources. When you select a particular table for a sheet, and then print the view that includes the sheet, Project prints only the columns that are part of the presently-selected table. Table 9.1 lists the many tables that are available.

Table 9.1   Tables Available for a Task Sheet or Resource Sheet

Table	Description
Task Sheet Tables	
Baseline	Displays the baseline schedule dates for tasks
Constraint Dates	Lists key constraint dates you've entered for tasks
Cost	Shows fixed cost information you've entered for a task, as well as calculated resource costs
Delay	Tells you when a task has been delayed as a result of resource leveling
Earned Value	Includes columns that identify planned costs versus actual costs, and more
Entry	The default; provides columns that enable you to set up new tasks
Export	When you export task data to an MPX file, Project uses this table, which includes all task fields
MDBExport	When you export task data for use in a database program, Project uses this table, which includes all task fields
Schedule	Presents task start and finish information, as well as information about slack time
Summary	Presents scheduled task start and finish dates, % of work completed, and budgeted cost and work hours
Tracking	Presents information you've entered about actual task start and finish dates, remaining duration, and actual costs
Variance	Lists baseline start and finish dates along with the current dates, and shows the variance between the two sets of dates
Work	Enables you to track work statistics, like the baseline number of hours scheduled for a task, the actual hours worked, variance between the two, and so on
Resource Sheet Tables	
Cost	Displays the baseline cost you've estimated for a resource, the current scheduled cost, the cost actually incurred, and more
Entry	The default; provides columns that enable you to set up new resources
Export	When you export resource data to an MPX file, Project uses this table, which includes all resource fields
MDBExport	When you export resource data for use in a database program, Project uses this table, which includes all resource fields
Summary	Includes information about hourly rates and work hours scheduled for a resource on a project, and more
Usage	Displays the resource name and number of hours of work by that resource scheduled for the project
Work	Lists scheduled and actual work hours by resource, overtime work authorized, percentage of work completed, and more

When you want to establish which table is used by a Task Sheet or Resource Sheet, first select the sheet. Next, open the <u>V</u>iew menu, point to Ta<u>b</u>le, and click the name of the table you want. If the desired table is not listed, click <u>M</u>ore Tables. The More Tables dialog box appears (see Fig. 9.8). If needed, select T<u>a</u>sk or <u>R</u>esource at the top of the dialog box to list the appropriate kinds of tables. Select a table from the <u>T</u>ables list by double-clicking it (or by clicking it and clicking Appl<u>y</u>).

Figure 9.8
Here's where you choose a table that's not on the Ta<u>b</u>le submenu.

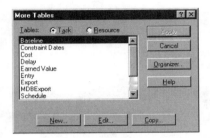

Filtering the Task Sheet or Resource Sheet

By default each Task Sheet or Resource Sheet displays all the tasks or resources you've entered for the project, no matter which table you've selected. There might be an occasion, though, when you'd like to see only some of the tasks or resources listed. For example, if you need to provide your boss with a list of tasks that have been completed, or a list of all resources from a particular resource group, you can *filter* the sheet to display only certain rows.

TIP: Filtering a sheet and then printing it is a "quick and dirty" method of creating a "report" about key facts from your schedule.

To filter the current sheet, use the Filter drop-down list on the Formatting toolbar (see Fig. 9.9). The available Filter choices differ depending on whether a Task Sheet or Resource Sheet is currently displayed. (This figure shows the Task Sheet choices.) Some filter choices are followed by an ellipsis (...), which indicates that if you choose that particular filter, Project will ask you to supply more information to help it select the rows to display. For example, if you select Date Range…, Project displays the dialog box shown in Figure 9.10 asking you to enter a date to begin specifying the timeframe within which the displayed tasks must fall. In this case, you would enter a starting date, click OK, enter an ending date, and click OK again so that Project could filter the list.

To return to the full listing of tasks or resources after you're done with the filtered version, select All Tasks or All Resources from the Filter drop-down list.

The ellipsis (…) beside a filter means that Project will prompt you for details about which rows to select.

Figure 9.9
Use the Filter drop-down list to control which rows appear in a sheet.

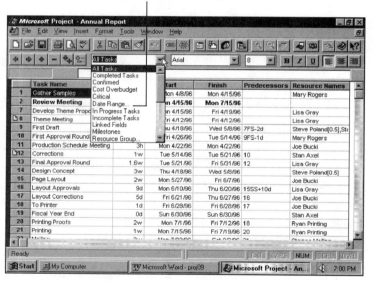

Figure 9.10
A filter might request that you provide more information—in this case, you need to enter the first date for a range.

If you prefer not to display the Formatting toolbar, but still want to filter tasks and resources, open the Tools menu, point to Filtered For to display a submenu, and click the name of the filter you want. If the name doesn't appear, click More Filters to display the More Filters dialog box (see Fig. 9.11). Use this dialog box to select the filter you want.

NOTE: Optionally, you can click the Highlight button in the More Filters dialog box to apply a highlight color to the filtered tasks or resources, rather than hiding the rows that don't contain the right type of information. If you do this, all rows are displayed on-screen, with the filtered tasks appearing in the highlight color.

Highlights the filtered tasks

Figure 9.11
Access more filters via this dialog box.

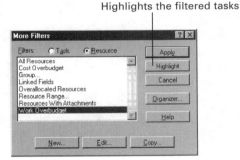

Sorting Information

By default, the information in your Task Sheet or Resource Sheet (and any accompanying charts in the view you've selected) appears in the order in which you added it to the project. Even if you select a different table or filter, the basic order in which the rows appear remains static—unless you adjust that order. For example, you might want to sort the Resource Sheet by the name of the resource.

CAUTION: If you're sorting by name, keep in mind that Project by default sorts by the first letter listed, which is generally the first name if the resource is a person.

To sort a sheet, open the Tools menu, point to the Sort submenu, and click the name of the field (column) to sort by. The fields listed vary depending on whether you're working in a Task Sheet or a Resource Sheet. For a Task Sheet, you can sort by Start Date, Finish Date, Priority, Cost, or ID. For a Resource Sheet, you can sort by Cost, Name, or ID. If the field you want to sort by does not appear on the Sort submenu, click Sort By. The Sort dialog box appears (see Fig. 9.12).

Click the Sort by Date button in the Task Sheet to quickly sort the tasks by start date.

Figure 9.12
Use this dialog box
to access more fields
to sort by.

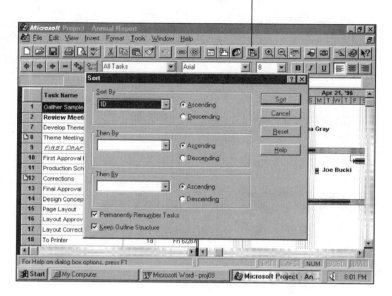

Click to display the Sort By drop-down list, then select the name of the field that contains the information you want to sort by. Select Ascending or Descending to specify whether the information should be sorted in lowest-to-highest order (A–Z) or highest-to-lowest order (Z–A). For example, when you sort tasks by the Cost field, Project by default reorders them from most expensive to least expensive—you might prefer to see the least expensive items first.

To sort by additional fields, as well, use the other drop-down lists provided in this dialog box. Click OK to complete the sort.

TIP: Click the Undo button on the Standard toolbar (or open the Edit menu and click Undo) immediately after a sort if its result is not what you needed or anticipated.

> **CAUTION:** When you select the Permanently Renumber Tasks/Resources check box, Project changes the ID numbers for the sorted tasks and resources to reflect their new order. If you've filtered tasks or resources already, or if you've deselected the Keep Outline Structure check box in the Task Sheet, the permanent renumbering option is unavailable.
>
> If Keep Outline Structure is deselected, subtasks will not remain with their summary tasks after the sort.

Quick and Dirty Gantt Chart Formatting

Chapter 14, "Other Formatting," details all the options for formatting bars in a Gantt chart, as well as for formatting information in the Task Sheet and elsewhere. Right now, however, you might want a quick way to adjust the Gantt chart bars appearing in any view that includes a Gantt chart. To avoid the need to master the commands on the Format menu, you can use GanttChartWizard to walk you through the key steps for adjusting how the Gantt chart bars look. To start GanttChartWizard, click the GanttChartWizard button on the Standard toolbar (third button from the right), or open the Format menu and click GanttChartWizard. The GanttChartWizard—Step 1 dialog box appears. Click the Next button to display the GanttChartWizard—Step 2 dialog box (see Fig. 9.13). In this dialog box, click to select the type of information you want to appear in your Gantt chart.

> **NOTE:** If you select any custom option (they're listed last in each GanttChartWizard dialog box), the dialog box that follows enables you to specify details about the option. Obviously, the details you can specify vary depending on the particular option. Also, the step number of the subsequent dialog box varies depending on the dialog box from which you've selected the custom option.

GanttChartWizard button

Figure 9.13
GanttChartWizard
idiot-proofs
the process
of changing the
appearance of your
Gantt chart bars.

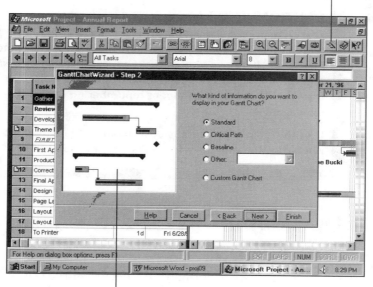

This sample changes to reflect the option button you select.

Make your selection, and click <u>N</u>ext to continue. The GanttChartWizard—Step 9 dialog box appears, enabling you to indicate what kinds of labels you want to appear with the Gantt chart bars. (The step numbers on the dialog boxes are not sequential—they vary depending on the choices you make.) The default is to label the task bars with both the resources and dates assigned to the task, but you can change this. Specify your choice, then click <u>N</u>ext. The GanttChartWizard—Step 13 dialog box appears. Select whether or not you want Project to include lines indicating links between tasks in the Gantt chart, then click <u>N</u>ext. The GanttChartWizard—Step 14 dialog box appears so that you can finish the process. Click Format It, and Project formats your Gantt chart exactly as you've specified.

Changing and Zooming the Timescale

The graphical portion of any view usually presents information in terms of a schedule. The schedule units used in that portion of the view, usually shown along the top of the view, are called the *timescale*. By default, Project uses a weekly timescale at the top of the graphical display; this is the *major timescale.* Below each week, the *minor timescale* slices the schedule into days.

Why would you want to change the timescale? Well, you might want to make the schedule more compact for easier printing (select a monthly timescale) or more extended to provide greater detail. To change the timescale, follow these steps:

1. Make sure that the pane that includes the graphical display is the active view.

2. Open the Format menu and click Timescale. The Timescale dialog box appears (see Fig. 9.14). You also can right-click the timescale on-screen, then click Timescale.

Zoom In the Timescale ————   ——— Zoom Out the Timescale

Figure 9.14
Adjust how your chart measures time by changing the timescale.

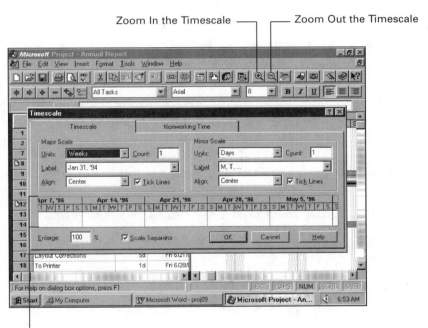

Previews the timescale selections

3. Set up the major timescale in the Major Scale area. Use the Units drop-down list to adjust the measurement (days or months, for example). In the Count text box, enter a value to control how many of the timescale units are labeled; for example, **3** means that Project will label every third unit on the major timescale (the top row of time units, which shows the

larger units of time you're displaying on the timescale). Select a date numbering style from the Label drop-down list, and use the Align drop-down list to specify how the labels will be aligned. Finally, select the Tick Lines check box if you want vertical dividing lines to appear between timescale units.

4. Set up the minor timescale in the Minor Scale area. (The minor timescale is the bottom row of time units, which shows smaller units of time to subdivide the major timescale. For example, if the major timescale is set to days, the minor timescale might show hours.) These settings work just like the ones described in step 3.

5. If needed, adjust the percentage shown in the Enlarge text box to show more or less of the charted information in the same space.

6. The Scale Separator check box, when selected, adds a horizontal line to separate the major and minor timescales. Select or deselect this option as you prefer.

7. If the Nonworking Time tab is available for the selected Gantt chart, click that tab to display its options (see Fig. 9.15). This tab enables you to control how nonworking time (such as holiday and weekend time) is charted. By default, nonworking time appears as gray vertical bars on the timescale.

Figure 9.15
You can use these options to specify whether or not nonworking time is charted.

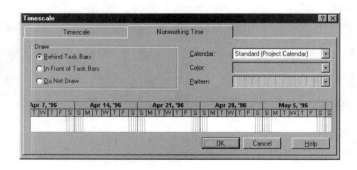

8. If you want to change how the working time is charted for a calendar other than the Standard calendar for the entire project—for example, if you want to specially highlight nonworking time for a particular resource—select the calendar to adjust from the Calendar drop-down list.

9. Use the Co<u>l</u>or and <u>P</u>attern drop-down lists to specify the charted appearance of the nonworking time.

10. In the Draw area, select an option button to control how the charted nonworking time interacts with the charted tasks. <u>B</u>ehind Task Bars means that Project always draws the task bars over the nonworking time. <u>I</u>n Front of Task Bars means that the nonworking time "bars" appear in front of the charted task bars. <u>D</u>o Not Draw tells Project not to indicate nonworking time at all.

> **CAUTION:** If you specify nonworking time in days, you must schedule the minor timescale in days or smaller units. Otherwise, Project is unable to chart the nonworking time.

11. Click OK to finish making your timescale settings. Your chart adopts a new appearance, as shown in Figure 9.16.

Major timescale, in months

Figure 9.16
This Gantt chart reflects the adjusted timescale.

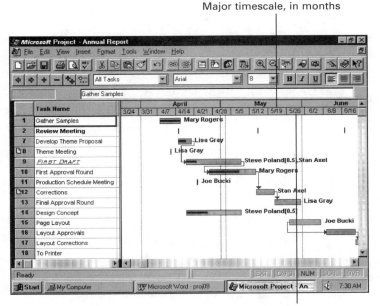

Minor timescale, in weeks

NOTE: You can change the timescale in the Calendar view by right-clicking one of the day's names, then clicking Timescale. For the Calendar view, the Timescale dialog box offers three tabs: Week Headings, Date Boxes, and Date Shading. Use the Week Headings tab to specify how the monthly, weekly, and daily headings appear on the calendar. You can specify whether each week displays 7 days or 5 days (the latter means that weekends are hidden). Also, select the Previous/Next Month Calendars check box if you want the calendar to include small thumbnail views of the months before and after the current month. Use the Date Boxes tab to control what appears in the gray shaded area along the top of each date box, or to display another shaded row (and control its contents) at the bottom of each date box. You specify what appears at the left or right side of each shaded area, and can control the pattern and color of the shading. Finally, use the Date Shading tab to control the shading for working days, nonworking days, and other types of dates in the base calendar for the schedule.

Creating a Table or Filter

The More Tables and More Filters dialog boxes each contain New and Copy buttons at the bottom. You can use these buttons to create tables and filters, either from scratch or based on an existing table or filter. For example, you might want to be able to quickly display a few added fields (columns) in a particular sheet. Or, you might want to create a set of fields that's completely different from the tables Project provides (for example, you might want only the task name, resource initials, and remaining work for tasks).

NOTE: You can use the Edit button in the More Tables, More Filters, or More Views dialog box to edit the selected table, filter, or view. Make changes using the dialog box that appears, then click OK to finish.

To create and save a custom table, follow these steps:

1. Display the More Tables dialog box. To do so, open the View menu, point to Table, and click More Tables.

2. (Optional) If there's an existing table similar to the table you want to create, click to select its name in the Tables list.

3. Click the New or Copy button. No matter which button you choose, the Table Definition dialog box appears (see Fig. 9.17).

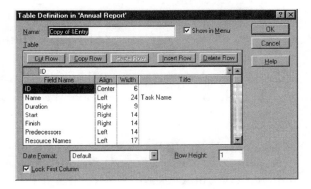

Figure 9.17
You can add and
remove fields here to
create a custom table.

4. Edit the Name for the table, if needed.

5. If you want the custom table to appear as a choice on the Table submenu, leave the Show in Menu check box selected. Otherwise, clear this check box so that the table is only listed in the More Tables dialog box.

6. To remove a row that appears (if you're working on a copy of an existing table), click the Field Name cell in that row, then click the Cut Row button.

7. To add a new field, click the Field Name cell in the first blank row. Next, click the drop-down list arrow at the right end of the text entry box to display a scrolling list of all available fields. Click the field you want. If needed, edit the Align, Width, and Title columns for the new field.

8. Continue adding and adjusting field rows. You can use the Copy Row, Paste Row, and Insert Row buttons to move selected rows, or to insert a new, blank row between existing rows.

9. If your table includes date fields and you want to change how they appear (for example, you want to spell out the month name), use the Date Format drop-down list to select a format.

10. If you want each table row to have more height (to make it more attractive or legible), increase the value in the Row Height text box by clicking and editing the existing entry.

11. The Lock First Column check box "freezes" the far left column so that you can't edit it, and it won't scroll out of view. Clear this check box if you don't want either condition to apply.

12. Click OK. Project saves your table and adds it to the Tables list in the More Tables dialog box.

13. Click Close to exit the More Tables dialog box without applying the table, or click Apply to apply the new table to the current sheet.

Just as you can save a custom table, you can save a custom filter using a process very similar to the one just described. Open the Tools menu, point to Filtered For, and click More Filters. In the More Filters dialog box, select the filter you want to use to create the custom filter, if any. Click the New or Copy button. The Filter Definition dialog box appears (see Fig. 9.18).

TIP: I strongly recommend creating a custom filter by copying an existing filter, because it's much easier and faster to edit filtering criteria than to create new ones from scratch.

Figure 9.18
In this case, a custom filter is being created by copying an existing filter.

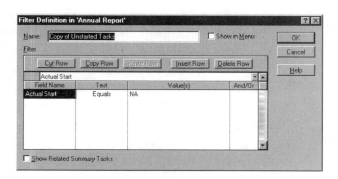

Edit the filter name and specify whether you want it to appear as a choice on the Filtered For submenu. Each row you edit or create in the Filter list area contains a single filter criterion. The Field Name cell for each row contains the name of the field you want to filter by. To specify a field, click the Field Name cell, then click the arrow at the right end of the text entry box to display the list of field names. Click the one you want. Next, click the Test cell for this criterion. This holds the operator that Project uses to evaluate the selected field. To change the test, click the arrow to display the text entry box drop-down list (see Fig. 9.19), and click the operator you want.

Figure 9.19
Project offers
numerous ways to
evaluate data.

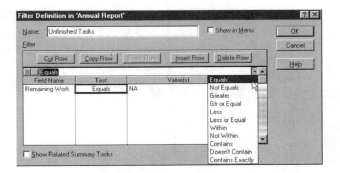

Next, use the Value(s) column to specify what data the test will compare to the field contents. You can type a value or date in this column, or use the text entry box drop-down list to select another field to compare the data with. If you enter a value that involves a work amount or schedule amount, be sure to include a time abbreviation with your entry. For example, you might build a criterion with Remaining Work under Field Name, Not Equals under Test, and 0h under Value(s). Finally, if you want to filter by more criteria, use the And/Or column to specify whether the filtered rows must match all entered criteria (And) or just one of the entered criteria (Or).

Click to select the Show Related Summary Tasks check box if you want the filtered list to display summary tasks that match the filter specifications. Click OK to finish creating the filter, then close the More Filters dialog box by clicking Apply. Project applies your new filter to the current sheet.

Creating a View

Unlike when you create a table or filter, it's often easiest to create a new view from scratch rather than edit an existing view. Project enables you to create and save a single-pane view that combines a specified table and filter. Thus, if you want to create a view that uses a custom table or filter, you need to create the custom table or filter first. To create a new single-pane view, follow these steps:

1. Open the View menu and click More Views. The More Views dialog box appears.

2. Click the New button. Project uses the Define New View dialog box to ask if you want to create a Single View or Combination View. Leave Single View selected, and click OK. The View Definition dialog box appears (see Fig. 9.20).

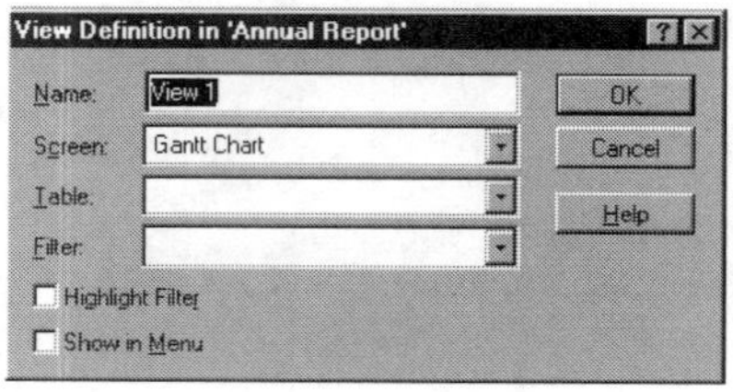

Figure 9.20
Project helps you view your schedule exactly as you want to.

3. Enter a Name for your new view.

4. Use the Screen drop-down list to specify whether you want your view to offer a sheet, form, or chart. For example, select Task PERT to display task information in your view using the abbreviated form of the PERT chart.

5. If you've selected a sheet style for your screen, use the Table drop-down list to specify a table that controls which columns of information appear in your view.

6. Use the Filter drop-down list to control which rows of information appear in your view.

7. If it's available, click Highlight Filter to highlight data that matches the filter, rather than hiding the data that doesn't match the filter.

8. Click to select the Show in Menu check box if you want the new view to appear as a choice on the View menu.

9. Click OK to finish creating your view, then apply the view by clicking Apply, or simply close the More Views dialog box by clicking Close.

A *combination view* displays two single-pane views in upper and lower panes on-screen. If you want a combination view to include a custom single-pane view, you need to create the single-pane view first, then create the combination view.

To create a combination view rather than a single-pane view, select Combination View in the Define New View dialog box (step 2 in the previous set of steps). The View Definition dialog box appears again, but this time it resembles Figure 9.21.

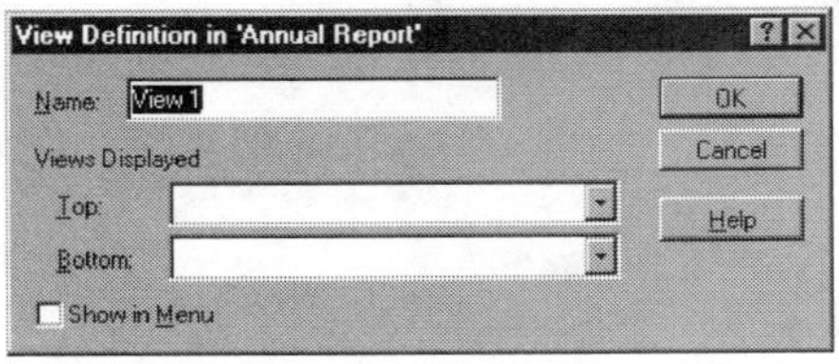

Figure 9.21
This dialog box is where you specify details of the combination view you're creating.

Type the Name you want for the view. Use the Top drop-down list to select the view that will appear in the upper pane, and use the Bottom drop-down list to select the single-pane view that will appear in the lower pane. Select the Show in Menu check box if you want the new view to appear as a choice on the View menu, then click OK to finish making the view and return to the More Views dialog box. Exit this dialog box as described in the previous set of steps.

Dealing with the Organizer

By default, the custom tables, filters, views, reports, and other items that you create are saved with the open, active project file only. This means that you can select one of these custom items only when that particular project file is open and active. If you want a custom view, filter, or other item to be available to other project files, you need to copy the custom item to the Global.mpt master file. To do this, you use the Organizer, which enables you to specify where custom items are stored.

You might have noticed earlier in this chapter that the More Tables, More Filters, and More Views dialog boxes each contain an <u>O</u>rganizer button. Clicking that button in any dialog box displays the Organizer dialog box (see Fig. 9.22). The tab that appears on top in this dialog box varies depending on which dialog box you clicked the <u>O</u>rganizer button from; for example, if you were in the More Views dialog box, the Views tab is selected when the Organizer dialog box opens. To deal with a different type of item, click the appropriate tab.

Figure 9.22
The Organizer enables you to move custom items between files.

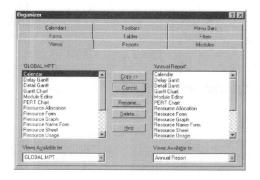

Each tab in the Organizer dialog box contains two lists. The list on the left shows the views (or tables, filters, or whatever) that are saved in Global.mpt. The list on the right shows the elements that are saved in the current project file. To copy an item from the list on the left to the list on the right (that is, from Global.mpt to the current project file), click the item name and then click <u>C</u>opy>>. To copy an item from the project file to Global.mpt, click the item name and then click <<**C**opy.

TIP: Use the Views A<u>v</u>ailable In drop-down list (in the lower-left corner of any tab in the Organizer dialog box) to control the file for which you're listing items on the left side of the tab. Similarly, use the Views Availa<u>b</u>le In drop-down list (in the lower-right corner of the tab) to control the file for which you're listing items on the right side of the tab. If you want to copy a view or other item between two project files, rather than between a project file and Global.mpt, make sure that you change the Views A<u>v</u>ailable In selection on the left to display the name of the second project file.

If you select an item from either list and then click Rename, Project displays the Rename dialog box. Type a new name, and click OK. If you select an item from either list and then click Delete, Project permanently deletes the item from the list for that file only, not from any other files that use the same item. Deleting an item from the Global.mpt file makes it inaccessible to all files, unless you've previously copied the item to an individual schedule file. If you have copied a custom item to multiple individual schedule files, remember that you need to remove it from each and every file to permanently delete it.

When you're finished working in the Organizer, click the Close button, and click Close again to exit the More... dialog box that's open.

To save an item like a view or table that you've added to any project file, be sure to save the file. When you exit Project, the application automatically saves changes that have been made to Global.mpt.

CHAPTER 10

PROOFING AND PRINTING A VIEW

Unless you've developed telepathic capabilities or are connected to everyone involved with your project via a network or via e-mail, you're going to need some kind of method of sharing information. The most traditional method of sharing information is via printed *hard copies*. While "virtual" information sharing has its benefits, certain situations—such as meetings or bound proposals made for clients—call for printouts.

Like other Microsoft applications, Project provides you with a great deal of control over what you print and how it appears in the hard copy. This chapter focuses on the steps you need to take to prepare and print information from your schedule, covering these key issues:

- Making sure that you've spelled everything correctly

- Telling Project and Windows which printer you want to use, and what settings it should use

- Setting up the appearance of the printed pages

- Adjusting which page information appears on

- Getting a sneak preview of your printed document

- Printing your document

Spelling Checking the Project

I'm probably revealing too much about my age by saying this, but I remember when hand-held calculators began dropping in price so that non-engineers began to use them. When kids started bringing them into school (at least I'm young enough to have been in school then), some teachers acted as if doomsday had arrived, predicting that we youngsters would lose all ability to cipher without a calculator, or at least our fingers and toes. Obviously, this didn't happen. There are even a handful of diehards like me who attempt to balance a checkbook without the benefit of an automated math device.

While a program's spelling checking capabilities also can't take the place of one's basic ability to come up with what appear to be words in English, spelling checkers provide an essential backup for your brain.

To put your best, most professional foot forward, you should always—I repeat, *always*—spelling check your Project files and any other business documents you create.

Project's Spelling feature checks all the information in your schedule for correct spelling, starting from the first task in the Task Sheet and progressing through all your task and resource information. It even checks any information you've entered as a Task Note or Resource Note. To spelling check a project file, follow these steps:

1. Make sure that the file you want to check is the open, active file.

2. Open the Tools menu and click Spelling. Alternatively, press F7 or click the Spelling button on the Standard toolbar. The spelling check starts, and when the spelling checker encounters a word it doesn't recognize, it displays the Spelling dialog box (see Fig. 10.1).

3. Look at the Not In Dictionary entry to see which word Project doesn't recognize, then use one of the following methods to adjust its spelling, if needed:

   • If the word isn't misspelled, click Ignore to leave it intact, or Ignore All if you know that the word is used several times in the file. For example, if "Blalock" is in your company name and appears several times in the file, you want the Spelling feature to ignore all uses of "Blalock," meaning that for the rest of the spelling check, it assumes "Blalock" is spelled correctly.

The best suggestion

The unrecognized word

Figure 10.1
The Spelling feature asks you to tell it how to deal with each word it doesn't recognize.

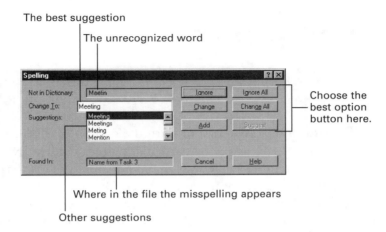

Choose the best option button here.

Where in the file the misspelling appears

Other suggestions

- If the word is wrong and the spelling in the Change To text box is correct, click Change or Change All. Change corrects only the presently highlighted instance of the word, and Change All corrects it everywhere it appears in the Project file.
- If the word is wrong and the Change To spelling isn't correct either, you can edit the Change To text box entry, or click another spelling in the Suggestions list to place that spelling in the Change To text box. Then, click either Change or Change All.

NOTE: If you edit the Change To entry and want Project to remember that spelling as a correct word for future files, click the Add button to include the spelling in Project's dictionary.

4. After you tell Project how to adjust the unrecognized word, it displays the next unrecognized word so that you can adjust that one. Deal with each unrecognized word as explained in step 3.

5. When the Spelling checker has reviewed the entire file, it displays a message alerting you that the spelling check is finished (see Fig. 10.2). Click OK to close the dialog box.

Figure 10.2
Project alerts you
when it has
checked the
entire file.

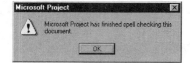

To learn to type, you had to learn the pattern of the letters on the keyboard. If you learned a particular pattern incorrectly, chances are that you'll tend to make the same typographical error (typo) over and over for the rest of your typing career. Or, you might be a fine typist, but would like a way to quickly enter certain words that you use often and are tricky to type. For example, you might not want to have to type "Blalock" each time it's needed in a file.

Project's AutoCorrect feature can help in either of these situations. In essence, you train Project to automatically replace your frequent typos (or abbreviations) with the correct (or full) terms you're trying to type. This ensures that certain terms are entered correctly in the first place, so you don't have to rely on the spelling checker to catch those errors. Use the following steps to create an AutoCorrect entry:

1. Click to open the Tools menu, then click AutoCorrect. The AutoCorrect dialog box appears (see Fig. 10.3).

Figure 10.3
This is your
chance to train
Project to help
you type more
effectively.

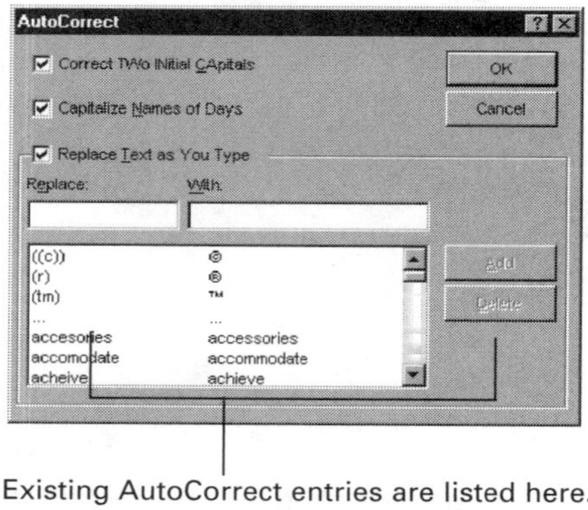

Existing AutoCorrect entries are listed here.

2. If you want Project to change the second letter in any word from uppercase to lowercase if you mistakenly type two capital letters, leave the Correct TWo INitial CApitals check box selected. Otherwise, clear this check box. You might want to clear it, for example, if you'll be typing a lot of state abbreviations.

3. Leave the Capitalize Names of Days check box selected if you want Project to automatically capitalize day names when you type them.

4. For AutoCorrect to work, make sure that a checkmark appears beside the Replace Text As You Type check box. If this option is not checked, Project will not make automatic replacements.

5. To create a new AutoCorrect entry, type the typo or abbreviation you want Project to catch and replace in the Replace text box. For example, you might type **bl** as the abbreviation you want to use for "Blalock." You can't include any spaces or punctuation in the Replace entry, but it can be up to 254 characters long.

NOTE: AutoCorrect doesn't make the correction until you type a full word and press the spacebar. So, you don't have to worry if the typo or abbreviation you enter as the Replace choice is the beginning of other words. For example, even though "bl" is the beginning of words like "black" and "blue," you can still use "bl" as an AutoCorrect abbreviation.

6. In the With text box, enter the correction you want AutoCorrect to make (for example, **Blalock**).

7. Click Add to finish creating the AutoCorrect entry. Project adds this entry to the list of AutoCorrect entries, as shown in Figure 10.4.

8. Click OK to close the AutoCorrect dialog box. New AutoCorrect entries take effect immediately.

Figure 10.4
Project adds your
AutoCorrect entry
to its list.

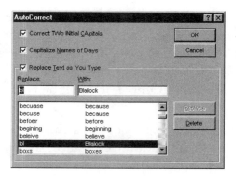

Changing Printer Settings

If you're using Project in a small business or home office, you'll probably
have only one printer attached to your computer system. If you work in
a larger company, however, you might have access to multiple printers—
say, one in your office and one attached to your company network. In
any environment, your computer also might have a built-in
FAX/modem that you can "print" to, thereby faxing documents without
making a hard copy—this is the same as having multiple printers.

If you have multiple printers attached to your system, you need a way
to select the one you want to send your Project file to. In addition,
each printer offers slightly different capabilities. For example, your
laser printer might be capable of printing at 600 dots per inch (dpi),
but for everyday printing you might want to print at 300 dpi to
ensure faster printing. Similarly, many dot matrix and inkjet
printers offer a choice between letter quality and draft modes.

CAUTION: If you're using an older dot-matrix printer, any
Project printouts that include graphical information might
not appear as crisp and clean as you desire. In addition,
depending on the printer, Project might present fewer
options for altering the Page Setup, based on the printer's
limitations. If you need to print many Gantt or PERT charts,
you should buy a laser printer. Quality laser printers are
now available for as little as $500.

Before you set up your printout pages in Project, you should first select the printer you want to use and set the options you prefer for that printer. Select and set up the printer first, if needed, because different printer capabilities might affect the page setup options available in Project. Note that you don't have to set up a document or open any project file to print before setting up the printer. Once you adjust printer settings, they remain in effect until you change them or exit Project.

To select and set up a printer, use the steps that follow. As there's quite a bit of variation between printers, and it's impossible to cover every option for every printer, I've highlighted the most important options for you to be concerned with.

1. Click to open the File menu, then click Print. Alternatively, press Ctrl+P. The Print dialog box opens (see Fig. 10.5).

Use this drop-down list to select a printer that's set up on your system.

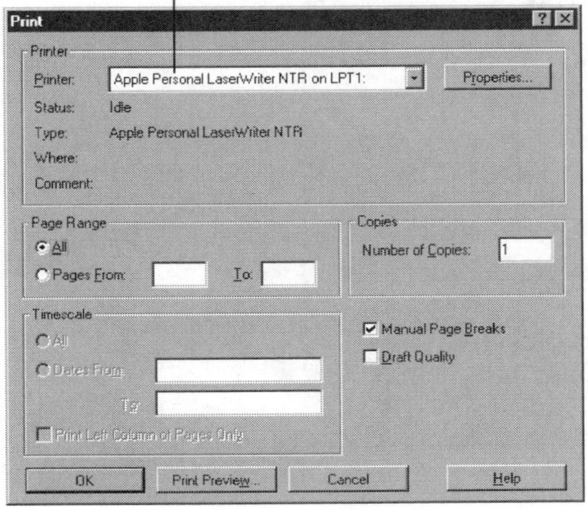

Figure 10.5
Part of the purpose of the Print dialog box is to enable you to choose and set up a printer.

2. Click the drop-down list arrow to display the Printer selections. The printers listed here are ones that have already been installed to work with Windows on your system or with a Windows NT network you're connected with. (To learn to set up a printer using the Windows Control Panel, see the Windows documentation or online help.) In this list, click the name of the printer you want to print your Project files to.

3. After you've selected the correct printer, click the P<u>r</u>operties button beside it. If this is the first time you've worked with printer properties during the current Project work session, Project displays a dialog box alerting you that your printer settings will apply to all documents you subsequently print—not just the currently displayed view.

4. Click OK to continue. The Properties dialog box for the selected printer appears on-screen, as shown in Figure 10.6.

TIP: In Windows 95, *properties* include information about a file, program, or piece of hardware, as well as the settings or options available for that file, program, or hardware.

Figure 10.6
The Properties dialog box offers different options, depending on the capabilities of the selected printer.

5. On the first tab, you adjust settings for paper. Most printers enable you to control the following options:

- Paper si<u>z</u>e—Use the scrolling list to display the size you'll be using, and click the appropriate thumbnail example to select it.

- <u>O</u>rientation—Select whether you want to print in a format where the paper's taller than it is wide (<u>P</u>ortrait) or wider than it is tall (<u>L</u>andscape). The thumbnail picture in the

Orientation area shows you what effect your selection there will have on your document's printed layout.

- Copies—Change the entry here if you want Project to print more than one copy of each document, by default.

- Restore Defaults—This command button appears on each tab of the Properties dialog box. Clicking it restores the tab's settings to the defaults for that printer.

TIP: If you need information about one of the Properties settings for your printer, click the question mark icon near the right side of the Properties dialog box title bar, then click with the question mark mouse pointer on the item you want information about.

6. After you've completed changing the settings you want on the Paper tab, click the Graphics tab to display its options (see Fig. 10.7). The two options on this tab that are available for most printers are Resolution and Scaling. Adjust the Resolution setting, if needed, to adjust how "fine" the appearance of printed graphics is. Adjust the Scaling setting to specify the size of the printed image as a percentage (from 25% to 400%) of the original size.

Figure 10.7
The Graphics tab offers options that are especially useful when you print a Gantt or PERT chart.

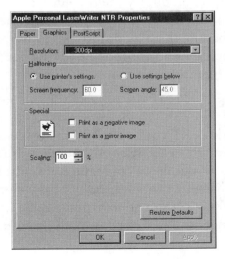

7. After setting the Graphics tab options, click the final tab, which for PostScript printers is the PostScript tab, and for non-PostScript printers is the Device Options tab. This tab usually offers a single drop-down list. On the PostScript tab, it's the PostScript output format list, which offers options that let you print faster—or with higher quality—in PostScript format. On the Device Options tab, the single drop-down list is for Print quality, enabling you to specify whether to print a document in draft or letter quality.

8. After you've specified all the property settings for your selected printer, click OK to close the Properties dialog box and return to the Print dialog box.

9. At this point, you can click the Close button to return to Project and alter the Page Setup for your project file, as described in the next section. Or, you can use the Print dialog box to print your document, as described in the last section of this chapter, "Finishing the Print Job."

Controlling the Page Setup

In Project, the first step to determining what appears on your printout is to select a view. Project creates a printout of that view, so if you've displayed Gantt Chart view, the printout contains the Task Sheet Task Name and Duration columns at the left, and the Gantt chart bars on a schedule at the right. If you display the Resource Sheet only, Project prints the contents of the Resource Sheet. In a Task Sheet or Resource Sheet, you need to be sure that you display the correct table and filter the information if needed before printing (see Chapter 9 to learn more about selecting and filtering a table).

There are only a couple of limitations on what you can print. Project doesn't print any information or view pane that's a form. It also doesn't let you print the Task PERT chart, which is an abbreviated version of the standard PERT chart. In the selected view, you also need to specify formatting—such as adjusting the appearance of Gantt bars, changing the timescale, and changing column breaks (see the next section in this chapter)—to control how information appears in the final printout. The formatting changes you make appear both on-screen and in the printed document.

Send Us
YOUR COMMENTS

Dear Reader:

Thank you for buying this book. In order to offer you more quality books on the topics *you* would like to see, we need your input. At Prima Publishing, we pride ourselves on timely responsiveness to our readers' needs. If you complete and return this brief questionnaire, *we will listen!*

Name (First) _____ (M.I.) _____ (Last) _____

Company _____ Type of business _____

Address _____ City _____ State ____ ZIP _____

Phone _____ Fax _____ E-mail address: _____

May we contact you for research purposes? ❑ Yes   ❑ No

(If you participate in a research project, we will supply you with the Prima computer book of your choice.)

---

❶ How would you rate this book, overall?

❑ Excellent   ❑ Fair
❑ Very good   ❑ Below average
❑ Good   ❑ Poor

❷ Why did you buy this book?

❑ Price of book   ❑ Content
❑ Author's reputation ❑ Prima's reputation
❑ CD-ROM/disk included with book
❑ Information highlighted on cover
❑ Other (please specify):_____

❸ How did you discover this book?

❑ Found it on bookstore shelf
❑ Saw it in Prima Publishing catalog
❑ Recommended by store personnel
❑ Recommended by friend or colleague
❑ Saw an advertisement in:_____
❑ Read book review in:_____
❑ Saw it on Web site:_____
❑ Other (please specify):_____

❹ Where did you buy this book?

❑ Bookstore (name):_____
❑ Computer store (name):_____
❑ Electronics store (name):_____
❑ Wholesale club (name):_____
❑ Mail order (name):_____
❑ Direct from Prima Publishing
❑ Other (please specify):_____

❺ Which computer periodicals do you read regularly?_____

_____

_____

_____

❻ Would you like to see your name in print?

May we use your name and quote you in future Prima Publishing books or promotional materials?

❑ Yes   ❑ No

---

❼ Comments & suggestions: _____

_____

_____

8 I am interested in seeing more computer books on these topics

❑ Word processing ❑ Databases/spreadsheets ❑ Networking ❑ Programming
❑ Desktop publishing ❑ Web site development ❑ Internetworking ❑ Intranetworking

9 How do you rate your level of computer skills?

❑ Beginner
❑ Intermediate
❑ Advanced

10 What is your age?

❑ Under 18 ❑ 40–49
❑ 18–29 ❑ 50–59
❑ 30–39 ❑ 60–over

SAVE A STAMP

Visit our Web site at **http://www.primapublishing.com**

and simply fill out one of our online response forms.

PRIMA PUBLISHING
Computer Products Division
701 Congressional Blvd., Suite 350
Carmel, IN 46032

PLEASE
PLACE
STAMP
HERE

NOTE: Page Setup options are different from formatting changes, such as choosing a new font for text or adjusting how Gantt chart bars look. To learn more about formatting your project, see Chapter 14, "Other Formatting."

In contrast, the Page Setup options control only how the printed information appears. For example, you can adjust the header or footer that appears on each page of a printout, or can specify how many pages you want the printout to occupy. To adjust the Page Setup options before printing, click to open the File menu, then click Page Setup to display the Page Setup dialog box for the selected view (see Fig. 10.8).

Figure 10.8
The Page Setup dialog box offers options specific to the selected view, which in this case is Gantt Chart view.

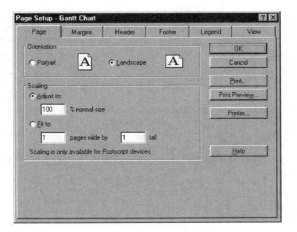

The available options vary slightly, depending on the selected view. The choices for each option that Project suggests also differ, depending on the selected view (in Figure 10.8, for example, Project suggests printing the Gantt chart in the Landscape orientation). Finally, some of the settings you see in the Page Setup dialog box resemble the ones provided in the printer Properties dialog box. Remember that the printer Properties settings become the default for all Project files printed. Any Page Setup options you select for the current view take precedence over the Properties settings.

The remainder of this section describes the settings on each tab of the Page Setup dialog box. (Keep in mind that some of them might not be available in your selected view, in which case they'll be grayed out.) After you've chosen the settings you want from all tabs, click the OK button to close the dialog box and have your changes take effect. (Or, using one of the other option buttons, you can preview your print job or jump directly to the Print dialog box to finish printing. Each of these operations is described later in this chapter.)

Page Tab Settings

Figure 10.8 shows the first tab in the Page Setup dialog box, the Page tab. In the Orientation area of the dialog box, specify whether you want the printout to appear in Portrait (tall) or Landscape (wide) format. If the printer you've selected is a PostScript printer (meaning that it uses the PostScript page description language rather than another printing technology that builds your printout dot by dot), the Scaling options are available. When the Adjust to option button is selected, you can enter a percentage that makes the printed image smaller (down to 25%) or larger (up to 400%) than its original size. I prefer, however, to use the Fit to option, which enables you to enter values telling Project how many pages wide and tall to make the printout. This is my preference because in most professional situations, I prefer to have a printout that's one page tall but as many pages as needed wide, making it easier for an audience to understand if it's included in, for instance, a bound report. For a Task Sheet or Resource Sheet printout, on the other hand, you might prefer a result that's one page wide and multiple pages tall.

Margins Tab Settings

The second tab in the Page Setup dialog box is the Margins tab. Click the tab to display its options (see Fig. 10.9). When you change the margin settings, you're changing the amount of white space that Project leaves around the information printed on a page. The Margins tab offers four text boxes—Top, Bottom, Left, and Right—where you can type the margin setting you want to use for your printout, in inches by default. To change one of the settings, double-click its text box and type the new value.

This sample shows how wide the specified margins will look.

Figure 10.9
Use this tab to control the margins (white space) that appear around the information in your printout.

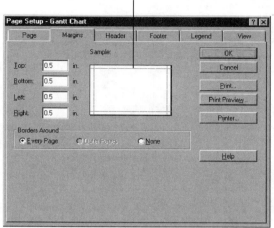

By default, Project also prints a thin border around the information on Every Page of the printout. If you wish, you can change that setting in the Borders Around area of the Margins tab. If the selected view is the PERT chart, you can click to select the Outer Pages option button, which prints a border around only the first and last pages of the printout. For other views, you can click the None option button to completely eliminate borders from the printout.

TIP: Headers, footers, and legends print within any border included on the printout, not within the margin area.

Header Tab Settings

Moving on, you can click the Header tab in the Page Setup dialog box to display the options shown in Figure 10.10. A *header* appears at the top of a printout and provides information about the printout. A header can consist of any text you want to type in; for example, you might want to designate the printout as "First Draft" or something similar. Alternatively, you can build the header components using the tabs and buttons in the Alignment area of the Margins tab.

Click a tab to specify a header at the left, center, or right at the top of the printout.

Figure 10.10
Project hasn't specified any header information for my Gantt Chart view.

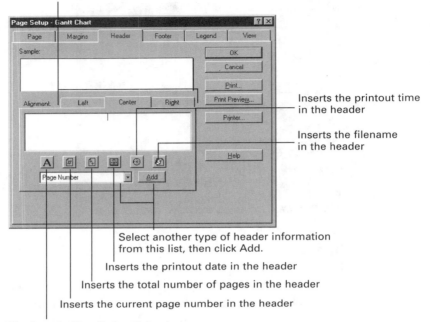

Inserts the printout time in the header

Inserts the filename in the header

Select another type of header information from this list, then click Add.

Inserts the printout date in the header

Inserts the total number of pages in the header

Inserts the current page number in the header

Displays the Text Styles dialog box so you can format selected header text

Start by clicking a tab in the Alignment area to select whether the entered header information will align to the left, center, or right. (Note than you can designate header information to appear simultaneously in two—or even all three—of these tabs.) To enter information simply by typing, click in the blank area below the tab and type the information you want—it appears in the Sample area as you type.

As indicated in Figure 10.10, you can use several of the buttons in the Alignment area to enter calculated fields of header information. For example, suppose that I want my header to include the printout date. I would click within any information already entered for the header to specify where the date should be inserted, then click the button that inserts the printout date. A code identifying where the printout date will be positioned appears in the header I'm building, as shown in Figure 10.11.

Project enables you to automatically insert other kinds of information, such as the schedule Start Date, in the header by using the drop-down list at the bottom of the Alignment area. First, click to indicate where you want the information inserted in the header. Click the drop-down list to see the kinds of information you can insert, click the name for the type of information you want to insert, then click the A̲dd button beside the drop-down list. Project inserts a code for that kind of information in the header.

Figure 10.11
Build a header using a variety of techniques.

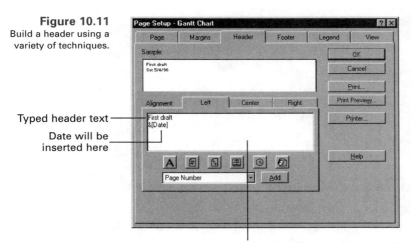

Typed header text ⎯

Date will be
inserted here

You can click in this area to position the
insertion point, or drag over text to select it.

You can format the appearance of the text in any header area by dragging to highlight it, then clicking the formatting button in the Alignment area (this button is on the far left and has the letter "A" on it). Project then displays the Text Styles dialog box, in which you can choose a new F̲ont, S̲ize, and so on for the selected text. Chapter 14, "Other Formatting," covers how to use the Text Styles dialog box, which also appears when you format text in a Task Sheet or Resource Sheet. Suffice it to say here that you can make the changes you want, then click OK to return to the Page Setup dialog box.

Footer Tab Settings

Click the next tab to move to the Footer options (see Fig. 10.12). A *footer* resembles a header, but appears at the bottom of each printed page. You create a footer just as you would a header, so refer to the preceding information about creating a header to learn how to work with the Footer tab options.

Figure 10.12
The Footer options work just like the Header options.

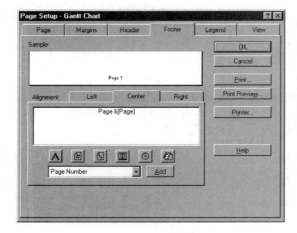

Legend Tab Settings

A *legend* appears on printouts that include graphical information, to explain what the graphical chart symbols mean. To specify whether or not a legend appears on such a printout, click the Legend tab in the Page Setup dialog box. The Legend tab options appear as shown in Figure 10.13.

Figure 10.13
For graphical printouts, you can include a legend—and set it up—on this tab.

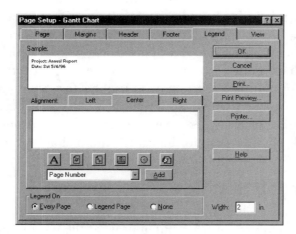

Because a legend can include text, Project offers the kind of text formatting options available for creating headers and footers. Those settings work just like the ones on the Header and Footer tabs, so I won't explain them again here.

The Legend On area at the bottom of the tab enables you to control whether or not the legend appears. By default, Every Page is selected, meaning that the legend appears on every page of the printed hard copy. If you select the Legend Page option button, Project prints the legend only on its own, separate page, so that there is more room for the schedule's graphical information on the other printed pages. The None option causes the printout to have no legend at all. You can control how wide the legend area is with the entry in the Width text box. If you need more room in the legend area—to include more detailed text in the legend, for example—double-click the Width text box and type the new setting you want to use.

View Tab Settings

Clicking the final tab in the Page Setup dialog box, the View tab, enables you to set a few final options specific to the selected view. Figure 10.14 shows how this tab looks for Gantt Chart view. Here's how to work with each of the listed options, when they're available:

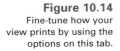

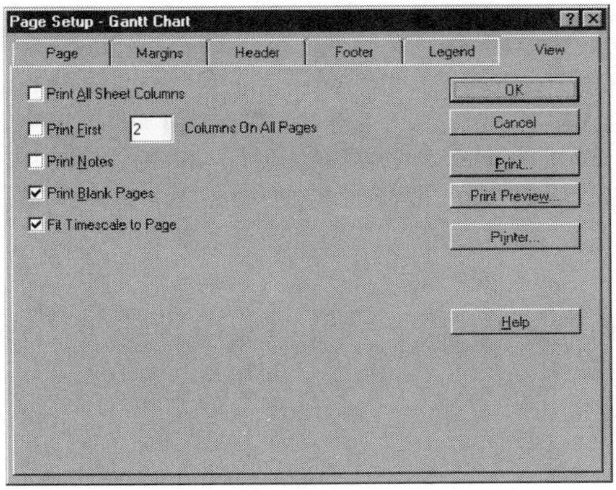

Figure 10.14
Fine-tune how your view prints by using the options on this tab.

- Print <u>A</u>ll Sheet Columns—When a view contains a chart with a timescale, Project by default prints only the columns in the accompanying Task Sheet or Resource Sheet that appear on-screen. If you drag the split bar so that only one sheet column is visible, then only that column prints. Click to select the Print <u>A</u>ll Sheet Columns check box if you want to print all the sheet columns, not just the presently displayed columns.

- Print <u>F</u>irst... Columns On All Pages—If you want to choose exactly how many columns in a Task Sheet or Resource Sheet print, click to select this check box and then, in the accompanying text box, type the number of columns to print. You can only use this option if you're printing a view that includes information charted on a timescale. This option doesn't always behave as you'd expect, however. If your printout is more than a page deep and more than a page wide, then all the far left pages include the visible columns, not the number of columns you specify here. Thus, you ideally want to use this option only when you're sure that the printout will be one page deep but many pages wide. If you can't ensure that, then you'll have to drag the vertical split bar in the view to adjust the number of visible columns.

> **NOTE:** Keep in mind that Project will print the columns from the table that's presently applied to the Task Sheet or Resource Sheet portion of your view, as well. If you want Project to print cost information in the Task Sheet portion of Gantt Chart view, rather than the basic task information, you have to click the <u>V</u>iew menu, point to Ta<u>b</u>le, and click <u>C</u>ost before printing.

- Print <u>N</u>otes—When you click to select this option for the views where it's available, Project prints the notes you've attached to a task or resource on a separate page at the end of the printout.

- Print <u>B</u>lank Pages—For some of the views that contain charted information, you might end up with pages that don't actually contain any data. An example is the lower left page of any Gantt chart printout that's more than one page deep and one page wide. If you want to save paper by not printing these blank pages, clear the checkmark beside this option. However, if you plan to assemble the multiple pages of your printout into a large, single chart—perhaps by taping them together and hanging them on the wall of your office—leave this option selected.

- Fit Timescale To Page—You've seen earlier in this chapter that if your printer allows it, you can scale your printout by a certain percentage to control how small or large it prints. That's somewhat of an eyeball approach, and it doesn't ensure that your schedule fits neatly on the printed pages. You might end up, for example, with half a blank page at the end of your printout. If you want to ensure that the graphical portion of your printout (the timescale) takes advantage of all the available space on your pages, make sure that this check box is selected. Project then stretches the timescale (for example, by making each day take up slightly more space) to ensure that the graphical information fills the last printout page.

Controlling Page Breaks

You just learned that in any view that combines a Task Sheet or Resource Sheet with graphical or timescale information at the right side of the page, you must drag the vertical split bar to control how many columns of the sheet appear in the printout.

In addition, you might want to control which rows of task or resource information appear on each page of a printout. For example, you might know that you've entered a milestone task in row 15 of your Task Sheet. You can control where the pages break in printouts of Gantt Chart view, Resource Usage view, and Task Sheets or Resource Sheets by inserting a *manual page break*. A manual page break tells Project to stop printing on the current page with a particular row, and to begin the next page down with the information in the next row.

TIP: Manual page breaks don't affect how many pages wide your printout is. They only affect how many pages tall it is.

To add a manual page break, follow these steps:

1. Switch to the view you want to print.

2. In the Task Sheet or Resource Sheet, click to select a cell in the row that should be at the top of a new page. (You also can select the whole row by clicking its row number.) Project will insert the manual break above the selected row.

3. Open the Insert menu and click Page Break. Project inserts a dotted line in the sheet to show you where the page break will occur (see Fig. 10.15).

Figure 10.15
A manual page break appears as a dotted line above the row you've selected.

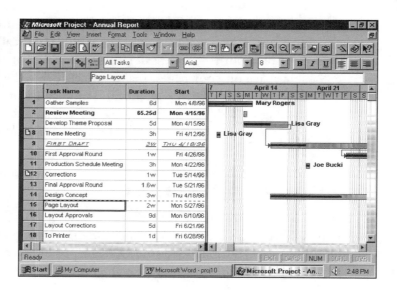

CAUTION: Inserted page breaks can cause unexpected printouts in reports that you generate (see Chapter 12, "Creating and Printing a Report," for an in-depth look at reports). I recommend removing manual page breaks after you use them, unless you're sure that you won't be working with any reports.

To remove manual page breaks, either select the row above the break by clicking its row number, or click the Select All button in the upper-left corner of the sheet. Open the Insert menu and click Remove Page Break.

Previewing the Printing

You've been diligent and have selected the proper view to print, then have designated which table columns should print and where you want page breaks to appear. You've chosen the correct printer and adjusted its properties, and have double-checked all the options in the Page Setup dialog box. Despite all this, you still might not have a good idea how your printout will look.

You can waste a lot of paper by repeatedly printing your schedule and then making adjustments to ensure that the final version is exactly what you want. Or, you can preview the print job on-screen, make any necessary adjustments, and only create a hard copy when you've got it right. To switch to the print preview for the current view of your schedule, click the Print Preview button on the Standard toolbar (it's the fifth button from the left and looks like a page with a magnifying glass over it), or open the File menu and click Print Preview. A preview version of your printout appears on-screen, as shown in Figure 10.16.

Figure 10.16
Preview a printout to see what setup changes you need to make without wasting paper.

Arrows

Zoom in

Show one full page

Show multiple pages

Command buttons

Zoom pointer

Tells you that the printout has more than one page

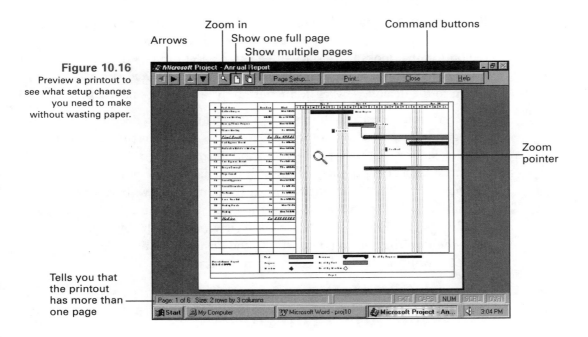

At first, Print Preview shows you the first page of your printout in a reduced view that provides a look at the overall page layout. You'll see whether the printout includes a legend (the one in Fig. 10.16 does), how the margin spacing looks around the data, where the headers and footers appear, and more.

If the printout includes more than one page, you can use the left and right arrow keys to move forward and backward through the pages. The up and down arrows only activate if there are too many rows to fit on a single page. You can use the up and down arrows to view the extra rows, which will be on separate pages when you print the hard copy.

You might, however, want to zoom in to read particular details in the printout before printing; for example, you might want to check to see if a heading you've added looks the way you want it to. You can either click the Zoom button at the top of the preview to zoom in on the upper left corner of the page, or use the zoom pointer to zoom in on a specific area. After you've zoomed in, you can click the button for displaying one full page (this button has a page on it) to return to the default view.

If the printout has more than one page and you want to view multiple pages, perhaps to see how the information is divided between pages, click the button that looks like a stack of papers. Project displays multiple pages of the printout on-screen, as shown in Figure 10.17. Again, to return to the default view, click the button for displaying one full page.

If the printout doesn't look the way you want it to, you need to make changes. For example, I want to move up the graphic in the lower left page of Figure 10.17 to try to squeeze my printout onto three pages. To make such changes that require you to return to the normal schedule view, click the Close button to exit the print preview. If you need to change a page setup option, click the Page Setup button to display the Page Setup dialog box. Or, if the preview meets with your approval, click the Print button to go directly to the Print dialog box and complete the printout, as explained in the next section.

Finishing the Print Job

Figure 10.18 shows the Print dialog box, which you saw earlier in this chapter when you learned to select and set up a printer. To display the Print dialog box, open the File menu and click Print (or press Ctrl+P).

Figure 10.17
If the printout has multiple pages, you can preview more than one page at a time.

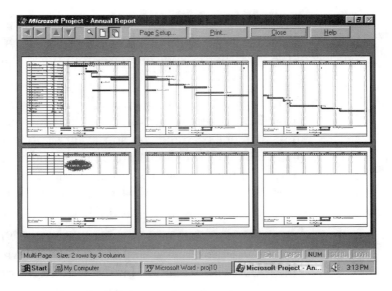

Figure 10.18
Make your final settings before sending a job to the selected printer.

Print button

Print Preview button

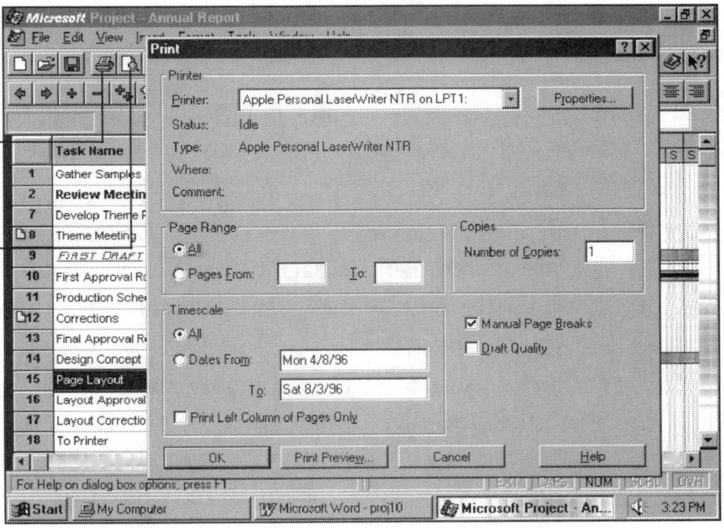

TIP: If you want to print your schedule without going through the Print dialog box to specify final options, click the Print button on the Standard toolbar. When you print using this method, Project automatically prints with the current printer settings and current Page Setup options.

The settings in the Print dialog box override any settings you've made elsewhere, such as when you initially set up your printer. Here's a review of the final choices you can make from this dialog box before sending your schedule to the printer:

- In the Page Range area, leave the <u>A</u>ll option button selected to print all the pages in your schedule. Or, if your printout includes more than one page and you don't want to print the entire document, click the Page <u>F</u>rom option button and then enter the page number of the first page you want to print. In the <u>T</u>o text box, enter the page number of the last page you want to print.

- To print more than one copy, double-click the Number of <u>C</u>opies text box and then type the number of copies to print.

- You can use the Timescale options to control which tasks print. Leave the A<u>l</u>l option button selected to print all the tasks. Or, to print only tasks starting within a particular range of dates, click the Dates Fro<u>m</u> option button and enter the starting date for the range in that text box. In the T<u>o</u> text box, enter the ending date for the range. If you want only one page's worth of Timescale tasks to print, click to select the Print Left Column of Pages Onl<u>y</u> check box.

- When the Manual Page <u>B</u>reaks check box is selected, the printout uses any manual page breaks you've inserted. If you don't want to remove the page breaks you've set up, but don't want Project to use them for this particular printout, clear the check box for this option.

- Click to select the <u>D</u>raft Quality check box if you want to print a quick-and-dirty version of your printout that might be less attractive, but will print faster and give you an adequate opportunity to review the information before printing a final version.

Once you've finished changing the Print dialog box settings as needed, click OK to send your schedule to the printer.

CHAPTER 11

WORKING WITH FORMS

In Chapter 9, you learned how to change the view that Project uses to display and organize your schedule information on-screen. You learned that some views include (either alone or with other types of information) *forms* that are intended to make it easier to enter and edit information.

This chapter shows you how to work with forms on their own, rather than working with them as part of a view. You'll learn about these specific topics:

- How working with forms differs from working with views, tables, and filters

- How to select a form to display

- How to create a unique form

Understanding Forms

Years ago, people had to communicate with programs run on large mainframe computers using punch cards. They would punch a pattern of numbers on a card, and the computer would read (and presumably understand) the data from the card. For obvious reasons, this was one of many factors that discouraged lots of people from working with computers—so that computing became a geeks-only affair.

Over time, many easier ways of communicating with programs have evolved. You've seen so far in Project that you can enter information via spreadsheet-like tables or sheets, by dragging on a Gantt chart or PERT chart, via dialog boxes, and more. Forms are yet another method for entering data.

Forms resemble dialog boxes in that they include text boxes to let you enter and edit information, and also display other information, such as calculated costs, that you cannot edit. Although some views consist solely of a large form—or include a form in a lower pane—you also can display a form in its own floating dialog box (see Fig. 11.1).

Figure 11.1
When you display a form independent of a view, it appears in its own dialog box.

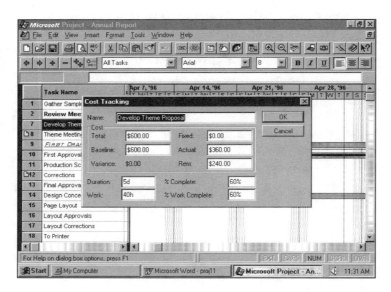

Project offers some forms for resource information (see Fig. 11.2) and others for task information. Table 11.1 lists the predefined forms available in Project.

Figure 11.2
Here's an example of a form displaying resource information.

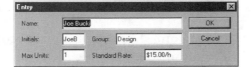

Table 11.1   Task Forms and Resource Forms in Project

Form Name	Description
Task Forms	
Cost Tracking	Displays cost information for the selected task, including baseline budget, current budget, and actual costs to the current date based on work performed
Date Range From Today	Lets you specify a range of tasks to display
Earned Value	Displays earned value information, such as the variance between the originally budgeted cost and currently budgeted cost (see Chapter 8 to learn more about costs); only lets you edit the task name and completion percentage
Entry	Enables you to enter or edit basic information about the selected task, including its name, duration, start date, and finish date
Schedule Tracking	Shows the selected task's baseline and currently scheduled start and finish dates, and calculates the variance between the original and current dates
Task Relationships	Displays and lets you edit the predecessors and successors linked to the selected task
Tracking	Enables you to enter actual start and finish dates, as well as completion information, for the selected task
Work Tracking	Enables you to specify how much work has been completed on a task, in terms of a percentage or number of hours worked
Resource Forms	
Cost Tracking	Displays cost information for the resource selected in the Resource Sheet, including baseline cost, total cost (currently budgeted), and actual cost for work performed to-date; none of these values can be edited
Entry	Enables you to edit the basic information defining the resource, such as the resource's name, initials, and standard rate
Summary	Summarizes the amount of work and budget for costs scheduled for the resource, among other things
Work Tracking	Displays the amount of work scheduled for a resource, the percentage completed, and variance in work completed to-date; these calculations can't be edited

Selecting a Form

The process for selecting a form differs a bit from selecting some of the other types of view information, because there's no way to directly display a form via a menu or submenu choice. You have to use the Custom Forms dialog box, as described in the following steps:

1. Display the Task Sheet or Resource Sheet, and select the task or resource for which you want to display form information by clicking the Task Name or Resource Name cell in the appropriate row.

CAUTION: If you're working in a task view, you can't display resource forms, and vice versa. Thus, it's critical to select a task or resource to ensure that the correct form choices are available.

2. Open the <u>T</u>ools menu, point to <u>C</u>ustomize to display its submenu, and click <u>F</u>orms. The Custom Forms dialog box appears (see Fig. 11.3).

Figure 11.3
Use this dialog box to select and manage forms.

3. In the <u>F</u>orms list, select the form to display by double-clicking its name (or by clicking the name once and then clicking Apply). Project closes the Custom Form dialog box, and displays the form you selected on-screen. Figure 11.4 shows an example.

Figure 11.4
An example
resource form is
displayed on-
screen here.

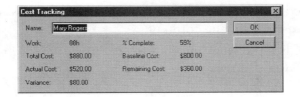

4. If you need to edit any information in the form (and the form offers editable text boxes), double-click each text box and then edit its contents.

5. Click OK when you're finished displaying the form.

Creating a Custom Form

You might find that none of the custom forms in Project capture the information you'd like to show. For example, you might need a quick way to check actual task costs, along with the resource name and group, to keep an eye on how much work by another department in your company you'll need to pay for—that is, track the costs for work performed by resources from another group that are coming from your project budget.

Project enables you to create your own custom forms, and to do so you don't need any programming experience. You simply need to be able to click and drag. You can add text to your form, or you can add information from any field in the Task Sheet or Resource Sheet. If a field contains a calculated value that you shouldn't edit, Project automatically formats the field so that it can't be edited on your form.

While there's a nearly infinite number of custom forms that you can create, the following steps and the example shown with them should give you a good start. Afterward, you can experiment on your own to discover the combinations of form information you'll find most useful.

1. Open the Tools menu, point to Customize to display its sub-menu, and click Forms. The Custom Forms dialog box appears.

2. Click either the Task or Resource option button at the top of the dialog box to indicate whether your form will display information from the Task Sheet or Resource Sheet. This is a

critical step, because your choice here affects which fields you can add to your form.

3. Click the <u>N</u>ew button. Project displays the Define Custom Form dialog box (see Fig. 11.5).

Figure 11.5
This dialog box
enables you
to begin defining
your custom form.

4. Enter the form name in the <u>N</u>ame text box. For example, if you're creating a form showing actual task cost, resource name, and resource group information, you might enter **Cost and Group**.

5. If you want to be able to use a shortcut key combination to display the custom form, enter the second key for the combination in the <u>K</u>ey text box. Project allows only letters here; you can't enter numbers, function keys, or special characters such as punctuation marks.

6. Click OK to continue defining the form. Project displays the form editor, with a new blank form background, as shown in Figure 11.6. Notice that most of the toolbar tools have been disabled, and that the available menus have changed to reflect that you're working with the form editor functions.

7. By default, a dotted outline appears around the border of the blank form dialog box to indicate that this box is selected. (If this boundary outline doesn't appear, you can display it by opening the <u>E</u>dit menu and clicking Select <u>D</u>ialog.) If needed, you can change the size of the form by clicking and dragging the dotted line on any side of the dialog box, as shown in Figure 11.7.

8. Now, it's time to begin adding elements to the form. Usually, you'll want to add a text label for each field you display. To add a text label, open the <u>I</u>tem menu and click <u>T</u>ext. Project adds placeholder text to the form, surrounded by dotted boundary lines. If you point to this text and a four-headed

arrow appears (see Fig. 11.8), you can drag it to a different location. You can adjust the size of the text by dragging one of its boundary lines.

Figure 11.6
Create custom forms
with the Form Editor
shown here.

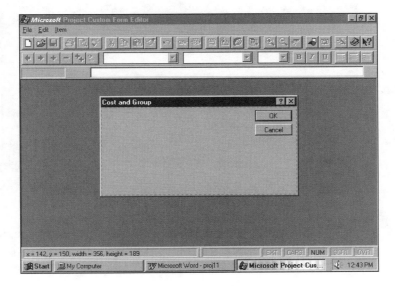

Figure 11.6
Create custom forms
with the Form Editor
shown here.

Figure 11.7
It's easy to resize the
form by clicking
and dragging its
boundary lines.

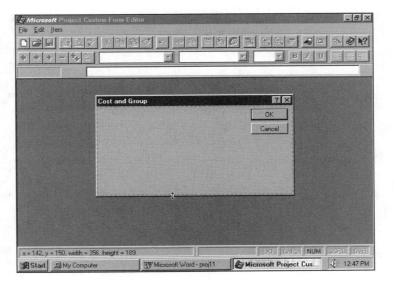

Figure 11.8
You can drag the text box placeholder into the position you prefer on the form.

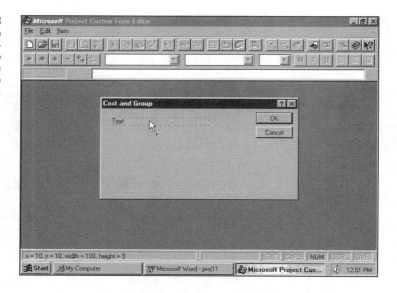

9. After you've positioned and sized the text placeholder, double-click it on the form (or open the Edit menu and click Info). The Item Information dialog box appears, as shown in Figure 11.9.

Figure 11.9
Once you've placed an item on the form, you need to edit the information it displays.

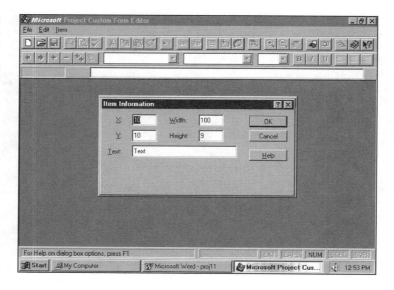

10. You shouldn't need to edit any of the top four text boxes, because you already defined the placeholder's size and position

in step 8. Simply double-click the <u>T</u>ext text box, and then type the text you want to appear in that area of the form; for example, I'll type **Task Name**. Click OK to close the Item Information dialog box.

11. To add a field to the form, open the <u>I</u>tem menu and click <u>F</u>ields. Project displays the Item Information dialog box immediately, because you have to specify which field to display.

12. (Optional) If you didn't add a text label for the field earlier (which we did add in steps 8 through 10), you can now type a label for the field in the <u>T</u>ext box.

13. Display the <u>F</u>ield drop-down list, and click the name of the field you want to appear on the form. For example, I'll select <u>N</u>ame to display the task name, as shown in Figure 11.10.

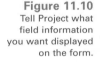

Figure 11.10
Tell Project what field information you want displayed on the form.

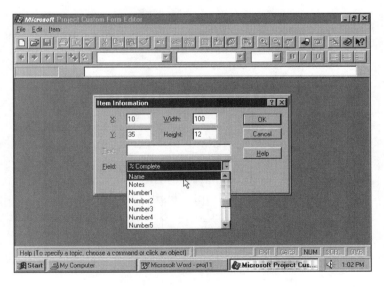

14. If you know that a field typically appears in an editable format on forms—as the Name field usually does—then click to select the <u>S</u>how As Static Text check box if you want Project not to enable editing of the field information.

15. Click OK. The field appears on the form, ready for you to resize and drag into place (see Fig. 11.11).

Figure 11.11
A field has just been
added to the form.

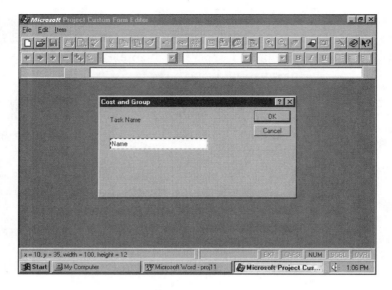

TIP: To delete any item you've added to a form, click the item once so that dotted boundary lines appears around it, then press the Delete key.

16. Continue adding items to the form, using the same general process of making a choice from the Item menu, displaying (if needed) the Item Information dialog box to define what the item displays, resizing the item, and dragging it into position. For example, Figure 11.12 shows my completed form. I've used the Group Box selection on the Item menu to create the Stats box.

17. Open the File menu and click Save to save your form with the name you provided in step 4.

18. Open the File menu and click Exit. Project closes the form editor, and returns to the Custom Forms dialog box. Your new form appears there, as shown in Figure 11.13.

19. At this point, if you displayed the appropriate sheet before creating the form, you can double-click the form name to display it. (If you're at the wrong sheet view, you have to close the Custom Forms dialog box, switch to the appropriate sheet,

redisplay the Custom Forms dialog box, and then select your form.) Figure 11.14 shows how my custom form appears when displayed.

Figure 11.12
Here's how my final form looks.

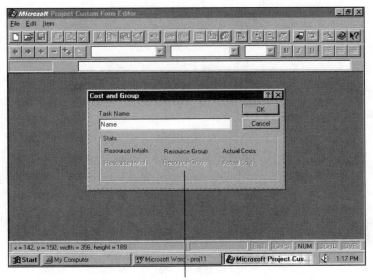

This indicates that a field will be displayed as static text that you can't edit.

My custom form

Figure 11.13
You select the forms you've created via the Custom Forms dialog box.

It takes a little practice, but soon you can create a variety of useful forms. Pay attention to every detail if you want to achieve professional results. For example, make sure that your text boxes and field boxes align at both the left and right sides of the form whenever possible, and make sure that information looks centered when you intend it to.

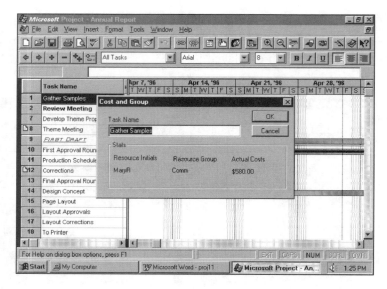

Figure 11.14
A custom form
that you create
can look just as
good as the forms
that come with
Project.

NOTE: Custom forms that you create are saved with only the current project file, until you either copy them to Project's Global.mpt master file or delete them. To make a form available to all files or to delete a form, click the <u>O</u>rganizer button in the Custom Forms dialog box, and use the Forms tab of the Organizer to make your changes. Chapter 9, "Working with the Different Project Views," discusses working with the Organizer.

Creating a Toolbar Button to Display a Form

Note that each form only lets you display information about one task or resource at a time. Unlike forms used as part of a view, forms that you display on their own don't offer Pre<u>v</u>ious and N<u>e</u>xt buttons to enable you to display information about other resources or tasks without closing the form. Because it can become tedious to use the <u>T</u>ools menu to display a form over and over, and a shortcut key can be difficult to remember, you might want to add a button that displays this form to a toolbar.

CAUTION: While you can change an existing toolbar tool so that it displays a form rather than executing its currently assigned command, I don't recommend doing so, because it might prove very difficult (or impossible) to recall what the button's original command was if you ever want to reinstate it.

Here are the steps for adding such a button to a toolbar:

1. Drag a new toolbar button onto a toolbar by right-clicking any toolbar, clicking Customize, then dragging the button you want from the Customize dialog box onto the appropriate toolbar. (A copy of the button you select remains in the Customize dialog box, with its original command assignment intact.) Ideally, the graphic on the button you select should reflect the contents of the form the button will display. Click Close to close the Customize dialog box.

2. Right-click the button you just dragged onto the toolbar, then click Customize Tool. The Customize Tool dialog box appears (see Fig. 11.15).

I dragged this button onto the Standard toolbar, then right-clicked it and selected Customize Tool.

Figure 11.15
You can change the command for any toolbar button using this dialog box.

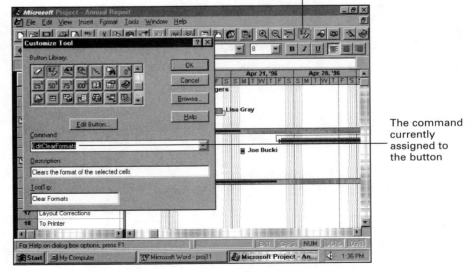

The command currently assigned to the button

3. Click the down arrow to display the <u>C</u>ommand drop-down list. Scroll down the list to select the form you want the button to display. Figure 11.16 shows the selection of my custom Cost and Group form.

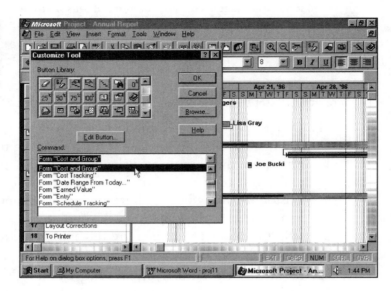

4. In the Customize Tool dialog box, enter a <u>D</u>escription for the button (to explain the button in the status bar) and a <u>T</u>oolTip (to describe the button whenever the user places the mouse pointer on it).

5. Click OK to finish creating the button. Figure 11.17 shows an example.

Figure 11.17
Here's a custom
form toolbar
button with its
ToolTip displayed.

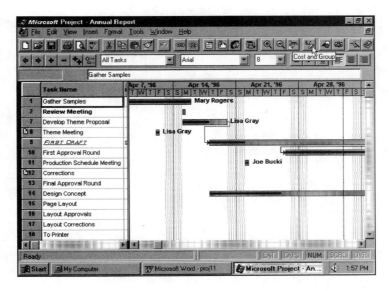

CHAPTER 12

CREATING AND PRINTING A REPORT

Software developers have placed a good deal of
emphasis on offering more ways to work with the
information you gather in a particular program. That's
because the typical business person needs to share
information with a variety of audiences, and each
audience needs only a particular subset of the
information.

For a Project file, for example, you might need to
prepare a weekly report of the current expenses for a
project to give to your boss, a listing of upcoming tasks
to give to the participants in a planning meeting, or a
weekly to-do list for yourself, to tickle your memory
about issues you need to follow up on.

Project can generate these kinds of reports (and more)
automatically. This chapter introduces you to reporting
in Project, including the following:

- Learning what predesigned reports Project offers

- Selecting the correct report

- Fine-tuning and printing a report

- Designing a unique report

Understanding the Report Types

The predefined reports offered in Project provide the most common types of summary information that you might need to provide to others within and outside of your organization. In Chapter 10, "Proofing and Printing a View," you learn how to select and filter different views for printing, to control the information appearing in your printout. While that method of selecting and printing information works fine in many cases, it has a few drawbacks:

- It frequently requires several steps to display just the facts you want to see.

- It's tough to filter data for just the current week, and you often can't capture totals for data in the format you prefer.

- There are some kinds of lists you just can't print from a view, such as a list of working days for the schedule.

Project's reports address these issues for you, providing a streamlined approach for selecting and printing information. In addition, using a report rather than printing a view yields a printout with an attractive layout that's suitable for distribution to readers whom you need to impress. Finally, the reports capture information in key columns; there's no need for the reader to wade through extraneous data in a report printout.

To create reports in Project, you work with the Reports dialog box. To display the Reports dialog box, start from any view. Open the View menu and click Reports; the Reports dialog box appears (see Fig. 12.1). This dialog box offers five icons (pictures) of different categories of reports: Overview, Current Activities, Costs, Assignments, and Workload. The sixth icon, Custom, enables you to create more unique reports, as described later in this chapter, in the "Creating a Custom Report" section.

To select a report category, click the icon for the category and then click Select (or simply double-click the icon). Project displays a dialog box showing the different kinds of reports available in that category, including an icon for each report that shows a thumbnail view of what the report looks like. While there's not room in this book to show you a printout of every report type, the rest of this section introduces you to the reports in each category, via the dialog box for that category. The reports that work best for you will depend on what information you're required to report to others, as well as how concerned you are about having frequent updates on specific information, such as upcoming tasks or tasks that are underway. After you review the dialog boxes shown here for the various report categories, spend some time on your own experimenting to discover which reports you prefer to work with.

Figure 12.1
Use this dialog box to select from the report categories offered in Project.

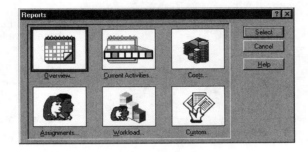

 TIP: Clicking Cancel from any dialog box listing specific reports closes that dialog box and redisplays the Reports dialog box.

Overview Reports

When you select the Overview Reports icon in the Reports dialog box, Project displays the Overview Reports dialog box (see Fig. 12.2).

Figure 12.2
Reports that provide project summaries at a glance.

Reviews numbers of tasks and resources, schedule by project and task, costs, and start and finish dates

Lists milestones, summary tasks, and notes

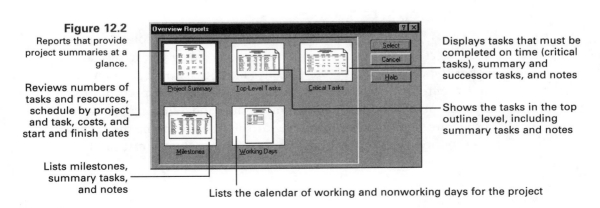

Displays tasks that must be completed on time (critical tasks), summary and successor tasks, and notes

Shows the tasks in the top outline level, including summary tasks and notes

Lists the calendar of working and nonworking days for the project

Current Activities Reports

The next category of reports, Current Activities, appears in the Current Activity Reports dialog box (see Fig. 12.3) that appears after you select <u>C</u>urrent Activities in the Reports dialog box.

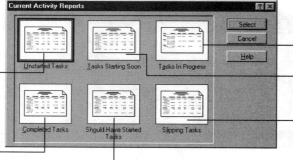

Figure 12.3
Reports that provide project summaries at a glance.

Provides a month-by-month overview of tasks for which work has begun but has not been completed, along with resources

Lists tasks for which work hasn't started, including notes, predecessor tasks, and resources

Creates a list of upcoming tasks, along with needed resources and notes

Compiles a month-by-month list of completed tasks

Indicates tasks that might not be completed when scheduled, with summary and succession tasks, and notes

Lists tasks scheduled to start by a particular date, showing successor tasks, summary tasks, and notes

NOTE: Two of the report types in the Current Activities category, <u>T</u>asks Starting Soon and Sh<u>o</u>uld Have Started Tasks, require you to enter dates. Whenever Project prompts you to enter a date, type it using mm/dd/yy format, then click OK to continue.

Costs Reports

To take a look at the dollars and cents you're spending on your project, select the Cos<u>t</u>s category in the Reports dialog box to display the report types shown in Figure 12.4. It's likely that you'll get a lot of mileage from these report formats, as one of the key aspects of project management is monitoring the bottom line and adjusting planned expenditures as required. These reports not only compile the expenses you specify, but also total various expenses by column (category).

Figure 12.4
These reports track and sum up costs.

Compiles a week-by-week summary of costs of each task

Lets you know which resources might cost more than you've planned

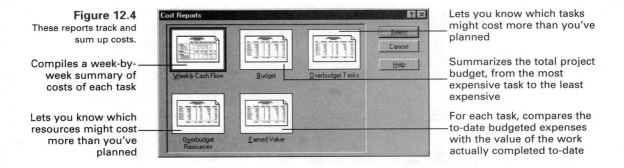

Lets you know which tasks might cost more than you've planned

Summarizes the total project budget, from the most expensive task to the least expensive

For each task, compares the to-date budgeted expenses with the value of the work actually completed to-date

Assignments Reports

The Assignments selection in the Reports dialog box displays four report types in the Assignment Reports dialog box (see Fig. 12.5). Although you can print much of the same information by printing a Gantt chart, the report formats summarize the information in a more accessible format that's suitable for presentation—for example, you can bind them as part of a project plan to be distributed at a meeting.

Figure 12.5
Some reports enable you to provide information about task assignments.

Lists all task schedules

Creates a week-by-week to-do list for a resource

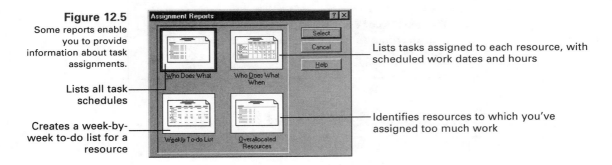

Lists tasks assigned to each resource, with scheduled work dates and hours

Identifies resources to which you've assigned too much work

Two of these reports provide particularly valuable management tools. The Weekly To-do List lets you prepare a list of all the scheduled tasks for a resource you select, when prompted, from the Using Resource dialog box. The Overallocated Resources report provides you with ammunition you might need to help you request more resources for a project—or for particular tasks—during a given timeframe, by showing when currently available resources have too many assignments.

Workload Reports

While the Assignments reports focus on enabling you to view work schedules by resource, the two reports available when you select Workload in the Reports dialog box enable you to examine the total workload scheduled during each day of the project. The schedule can be grouped by either Task Usage or Resource Usage (see Fig. 12.6).

Figure 12.6
These report options generate crosstab reports that summarize the working hours scheduled for each day in your project.

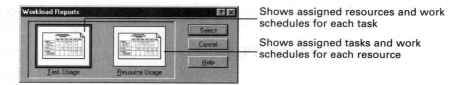

Shows assigned resources and work schedules for each task

Shows assigned tasks and work schedules for each resource

NOTE: The Workload reports and some of the other reports you've seen are referred to as *crosstab reports* because they present information in rows and columns separated into specific cells of information by a grid. At the intersection of each row and column is a cell with specific information about the resource or task listed in that row, on the date indicated by the selected column.

Selecting, Setting Up, and Printing a Report

As noted at the beginning of this chapter, the report creation process begins with the Reports dialog box. After you've selected the report you want, Project compiles the report information and displays the report on-screen in Print Preview mode. Once the report is on-screen, you can make some modifications to its layout before printing it out. This section describes how you can tackle all these tasks.

To select the report you want to work with and print out, open the project file that you want to create the report about, and then follow these steps:

1. Open the <u>V</u>iew menu and click <u>R</u>eports. The Reports dialog box appears on-screen.

2. In the Reports dialog box, select the category of report you want by double-clicking a category icon (or by clicking the icon once and then clicking <u>S</u>elect). Project displays the dialog box for the report category you've selected.

3. Select the thumbnail icon for the type of report you want to use. Do so by double-clicking the icon (or by clicking the icon once and then clicking <u>S</u>elect).

4. Some report types require you to specify a date or resource name, and prompt you to do so with a dialog box. If a date is requested, enter it in mm/dd/yy format as shown in Figure 12.7. If the dialog box prompts you to select a resource, do so using the drop-down list that's presented. After you specify either a date or a resource, click OK to finish. (Some report formats prompt you for another date; if this happens, enter the date and click OK again to finish.)

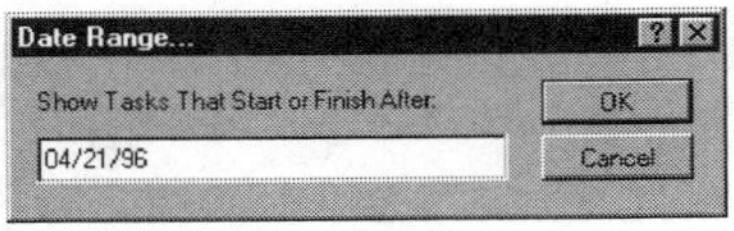

Figure 12.7
Project may prompt you to specify a date or select a resource to report about.

After you complete the preceding steps, Project compiles the report and presents it on-screen for viewing, fine-tuning, or printing.

You might encounter instances, however, when you have selected a report type that Project cannot compile, or have entered a date for which there's no data to report. For example, if you try to print a report about T<u>a</u>sks In Progress from the Current Activities category, and there are no tasks underway on the date on which you try to print the report, Project displays the dialog box shown in Figure 12.8. Click OK to close the message dialog box, and Project redisplays the Reports dialog box so that you can try again. Select a different report type, or try specifying a different date for the report you want.

At any time, to close the preview area where the report appears, click the <u>C</u>lose button near the top of the screen. Project returns to the Reports dialog box. Click the Cancel button to put away that dialog box and return to the active view for the project file.

Navigating in the Report

The report you've selected appears on-screen in a Print Preview view like the one you learned about in Chapter 10. This view offers a few special tools and icons that enable you to view different parts of the report, or to take a closer look at particular items in the report (see Fig. 12.9).

Figure 12.9
Project offers
special tools that
enable you to
work with a
report preview.

Arrows

Zoom in

Show one full
page

Zoom pointer

Tells you that
the report has
more than one
page

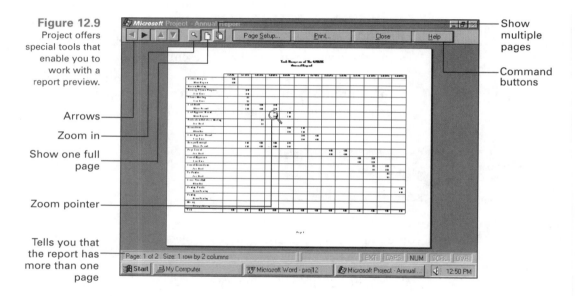

Show
multiple
pages

Command
buttons

Use the left and right arrow keys to move forward and backward through the pages in the report. The up and down arrows are enabled only if there are too many rows to appear in a single report page. You can use the up and down arrows to view the extra rows, which appear on separate pages if the report is printed.

By default, you'll see one page of the report, shown in a size that keeps the whole page visible in the preview. You might, however, want to zoom in to read particular details in the report before printing. You can click the Zoom button at the top of the preview to zoom in on the upper-left corner of the report, or use the zoom pointer to zoom in on a specific cell. After you've zoomed in, click the button for displaying one full page (the button has a page on it) to return to the default view.

> **TIP:** Obviously, you won't always want to print the reports you generate. Reports often are a fast way to check information such as the current budget total. You can generate the report, zoom in to check a detail or two, then click the <u>C</u>lose button to exit the preview and the Cancel button to close the Reports dialog box.

If the report has more than one page and you want to view multiple pages, perhaps to see how the information is divided between pages, click the button that looks like a stack of papers. Project displays multiple pages of the report on-screen, as shown in Figure 12.10. Again, to return to the default view, click the button for displaying one full page.

Figure 12.10
Sometimes you'll want to look at multiple report pages.

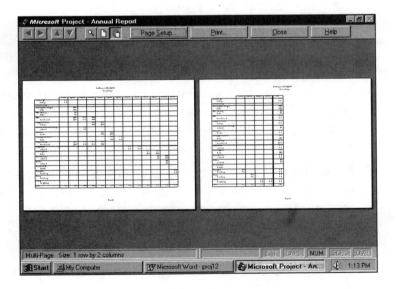

Viewing Setup Options

As you learned in Chapter 10, "Proofing and Printing a View," you have control over numerous aspects of how a printout appears. For example, you can adjust margins to allow for more or less space around printed data, or you can specify whether a page number appears on every page. You adjust these options using the Page Setup dialog box, which you display from the Print Preview view by clicking the Page Setup button at the top of the screen. The Page Setup dialog box for the report appears (see Fig. 12.11).

Figure 12.11
This dialog box enables you to adjust how the final printout will look.

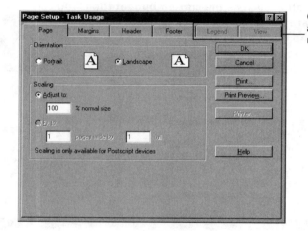

Grayed out tabs aren't available for the current report.

Although the dialog box offers six tabs, two of them aren't available for many reports. These are the Legend and View tabs, which offer options that apply when you're printing certain charts and views. Additionally, other tabs may become disabled (grayed out) when you select a report type for which they don't apply. For example, you cannot adjust the header or footer for a Project Summary report.

As you learned in Chapter 10, to change a page setup option in the Page Setup dialog box, first click to select the tab that offers the option, make your changes, then click OK to close the Page Setup dialog box or click Print to send the report to the printer. The four tabs of available Page Setup options for reports are:

- **Page**—Enables you to specify whether the printout is wide (landscape) or tall (portrait); also lets you scale the printed information by entering a size percentage or the desired number of pages for the printout.

- **Margins**—Enables you to enter a separate measurement for the margin for each of the four page edges, or to specify a printed border for report pages.

- **Header**—Enables you to edit the header that appears at the top of the report pages (see Fig. 12.12), including what it contains (page number, company names, and so on) and whether it's centered or aligned left or right (see Chapter 10 for more information about creating printout headers and footers).

- **Footer**—Offers options similar to those found on the Header tab, but places the specified text at the bottom of each printed report page.

Figure 12.12
You can specify the header for the report pages on the Header tab; the Footer tab is nearly identical.

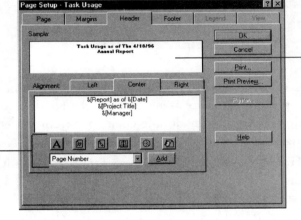

The header or footer is previewed here.

Use these buttons and this drop-down list to add new header or footer contents.

Printing

Once you've checked to ensure that you've chosen the report you need, and have made any changes you want in the Page Setup dialog box, you're ready to print your report. To initiate the print process, click the Print button found in either the Page Setup dialog box or the Print Preview screen. The Print dialog box appears (see Fig. 12.13).

This dialog box is covered as part of Chapter 10's in-depth look at printing; however, a few options in the dialog box might be particularly attractive to you when you're printing reports. They are as follows:

- **Page Range**—By default, Project prints All pages in a report if the report has more than one page. You might, however, only want to print part of a report. To do so, click the Pages From option button in the Page Range area, then enter the starting page in the From text box and the final page in the To text box. For example, enter **4** and **5** to print only pages 4 and 5 of the report.

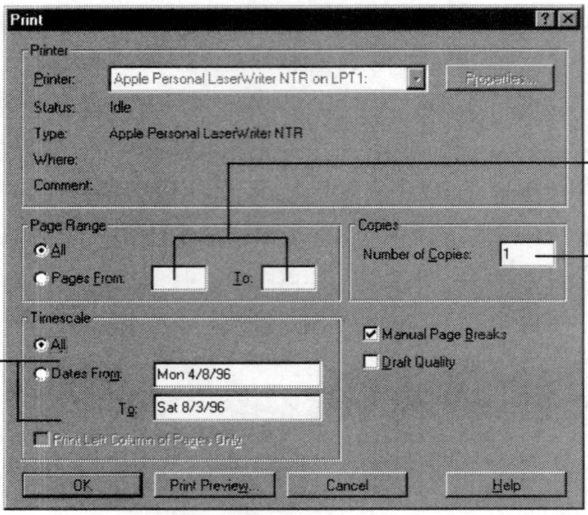

Figure 12.13
When you click the Print button, Project displays this dialog box so that you can set a few more options.

Use these text boxes to print only selected pages.

Change this entry to print more than one copy of the report.

Use this option button and its accompanying text boxes, when enabled, to limit the timeframe the printout covers.

- **Copies**—To print more than one copy at a time (such as 10 copies to distribute at a meeting), change the Number of Copies text box by double-clicking the current entry, and typing a new entry (such as **10**).

- **Timescale**—Normally, unless a report by default asks you for a particular timeframe, the report covers the full duration of the project schedule. If you want to print only the report pages that pertain to particular dates in the schedule, click to select the Dates From option button in the Timescale area, then enter the starting date in the From text box and the last date of the range you want to print in the To text box.

After you've specified the options you prefer in the Print dialog box, click OK. Project sends the report to the printer, and closes the print preview for the report. To close the Reports dialog box, which reappears on-screen after printing, click Cancel.

Creating a Custom Report

The sixth category icon in the Reports dialog box, the Custom button, enables you to control various features of any available report, create a new report based on an already existing report, or start from scratch to build an entirely unique report to suit your needs. The report features you can change vary depending on the report you start working with. For some reports, such as the Base Calendar report, you can only change the font and text formatting to adjust the report's appearance. For other reports, Project displays a dialog box enabling you to edit such elements of the report as its name, the time period it covers, the table it's based upon, filtering, and more.

To change, copy, or create a custom report, you work in the Custom Reports dialog box (see Fig. 12.14). To display this dialog box, double-click the Custom option in the Reports dialog box (or click Custom once and then click Select). The scrolling Reports list in this dialog box enables you to select a report to customize, if needed.

Figure 12.14
The Custom Reports dialog box enables you to show and format specific report information.

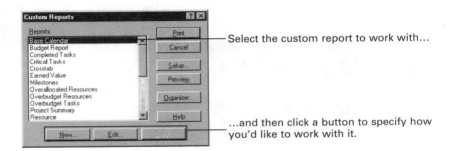

Select the custom report to work with...

...and then click a button to specify how you'd like to work with it.

From the Custom Reports dialog box, after you select a report in the Reports list, you can use the Preview button to display the selected report in Print Preview mode, the Setup button to go to the Page Setup dialog box for the report, or the Print button to go to the Print dialog box for the report. After selecting one of these buttons, you can work with the preview, setup, or printing options for the report just as described previously in this chapter. Click Close to close the Custom Reports dialog box, then click Cancel to close the Reports dialog box.

Making Changes to an Existing Report

The fastest way to customize a report and arrive at both the report contents and formatting you need is to choose the report that most closely resembles what you want, then make changes to it. To start this process, click the name of the report to edit in the Reports list of the Custom Reports dialog box. Then click the Edit button.

What happens next depends on the report you've selected for editing. If you've selected the Base Calendar or Project Summary report for editing, Project only enables you to change the fonts specified for the report, and thus displays the Report Text dialog box shown in Figure 12.15. Use the Item to Change drop-down list if you want the change to apply only to the Calendar Name or Detail information in the report, then use the Font, Font Style, and Size lists to select the text attributes you want. The sample area shows a preview of what your selections will look like when applied to text in the report. To underline the text, for example, select the Underline check box, and to specify a color for text, use the Color drop-down list. After you've made the desired font selections, click OK to implement your changes and return to the Custom Reports dialog box. From there, you can preview or print the edited report.

Figure 12.15
For some reports, you can only change the appearance of printed text.

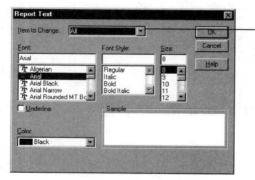

Use this drop-down list to specify what elements the font changes apply to.

CAUTION: Once you make changes to a report offered in your project file, the changes remain in effect until you specifically return the report to its original format. There's always a chance, however, that you might forget what the original format was. If you're planning to make major changes to a report, you're always safer working from a copy of the report as described next, rather than working from the original.

For other reports you select from the Reports list, a different dialog box appears when you click the Edit button. Depending on the selected report type, the dialog box that appears is named Task Report, Resource Report, or Crosstab Report. Each of these dialog boxes has three tabs, but the tab contents vary slightly, depending on the report category (as described next). After you specify the options you want in one of these dialog boxes, click OK to implement your changes. From the Custom Reports dialog box, you then can preview, set up, or print the report.

Task Reports

A *task report* generally has the word "task" or "what" in its name in the Reports list of the Custom Reports dialog box. When you select one of these reports and then click the Edit button, the Task Report dialog box appears (see Fig. 12.16). The first tab of this dialog box, the Definition tab, enables you to work with the most basic information about the report, such as the report name. You might want to change the report name to reflect your changes, perhaps calling it "Weekly Budget Report" instead of simply "Budget Report." This tab also enables you to control the timeframe for which information is reported, and to specify whether or not to apply a filter to display only some tasks in the project (Chapter 9, "Working with the Different Project Views," covers filtering in detail).

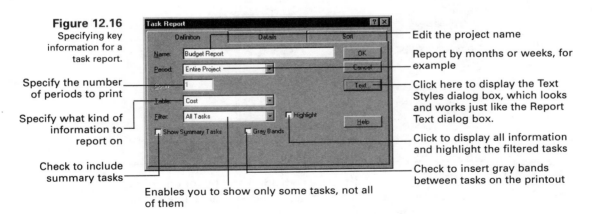

Figure 12.16
Specifying key information for a task report.

Specify the number of periods to print

Specify what kind of information to report on

Check to include summary tasks

Enables you to show only some tasks, not all of them

Edit the project name

Report by months or weeks, for example

Click here to display the Text Styles dialog box, which looks and works just like the Report Text dialog box.

Click to display all information and highlight the filtered tasks

Check to insert gray bands between tasks on the printout

After you've set the project definition options, click the Details tab. The options on this tab (see Fig. 12.17) control which details appear for the tasks you've chosen to display using the Definition tab.

Figure 12.17
Here's where you specify which details appear in the report.

Check to choose each task detail you want in the report

Check to place a border around the details

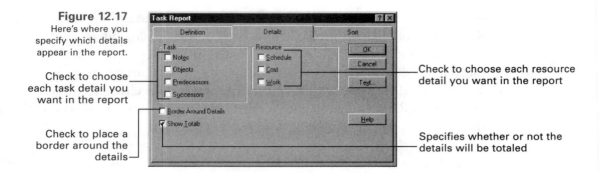

Check to choose each resource detail you want in the report

Specifies whether or not the details will be totaled

Finally, click the Sort tab to determine how to sort the tasks that appear in your report. Click to display the Sort By drop-down list (see Fig. 12.18), then choose the name of the field that contains the information you want to sort by. Select Ascending or Descending to specify whether the information is sorted in A-Z (lowest-to-highest) order or Z-A (highest-to-lowest) order. For example, by default the Budget Report lists the most costly tasks first, but you might want to see the least expensive items first. To sort by other fields, as well, use the additional drop-down lists provided on this tab.

Figure 12.18
The final touch in organizing your report information is to sort it.

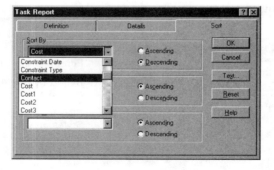

TIP: To specify that there's no field to sort by for one of the drop-down lists in the Sort tab, select the blank line at the top of the drop-down list.

Resource Reports

A *resource report* provides information about resources, and generally includes the word "resource" or "who" in the report name. For example, the "Overallocated Resources" and "Who Does What" reports are examples of resource reports. When you select a resource report from the Reports list in the Custom Reports dialog box, then click the Edit button, the Resource Report dialog box appears. This dialog box offers three tabs that look and work exactly like the tabs for the Task Report dialog box (refer to Figs. 12.16 through 12.18).

Crosstab Reports

A *crosstab report* is the last type of custom report you might want to customize. These reports summarize information in a grid of rows and columns, and include reports like "Weekly Cash Flow." When you select a crosstab report from the Reports list in the Custom Reports dialog box and then click the Edit button, the Crosstab Report dialog box appears (see Fig. 12.19). You'll notice that the first tab here differs from that for the two previous report types. Use the Row drop-down list to specify whether the rows contain task or resource information. In the Column area, type an entry for how many units of time to display, and then (if needed) change the time unit type to something like months using the drop-down list beside your entry—these choices determine how many columns appear in the crosstab (for example, **4 weeks** or **2 months**). Then, in the drop-down list below your time selections, select what kind of information about the task or resource to display in each column below the date.

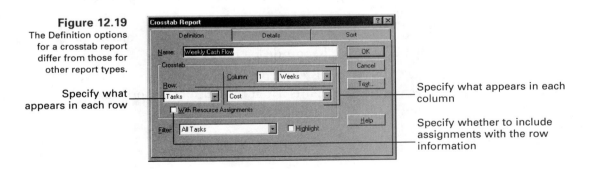

Figure 12.19
The Definition options for a crosstab report differ from those for other report types.

Specify what appears in each row

Specify what appears in each column

Specify whether to include assignments with the row information

The Details tab also offers a couple of unique choices for crosstab reports. On this tab, click to select the Show Zero Values check box if you want to have zeros displayed rather than blank cells. Make sure that the Repeat First Column on Every Page option is selected if you want to repeat the names of the listed tasks or resources on every report page for easier reference. Finally, use the Date Format drop-down list to control the appearance of any dates listed for your crosstab report.

The Sort tab for crosstab reports works just like the Sort tab for the Task Report dialog box (refer to Fig. 12.18).

Creating a Report Based on an Existing Report

If you want to leave an existing report intact, but create a new report based on it, follow these steps:

1. Display the Custom Reports dialog box.

2. In the Reports list, click to select the name of the report that you want to use as the basis for your custom report.

3. Click the Copy button. Depending on the type of report you selected, the appropriate Report dialog box (such as the Task Report dialog box) appears.

4. In the Name text box of the Report dialog box, Project shows Copy of plus the name of the report you selected in step 2. Be sure to edit this name to ensure that your custom report has a name you'll recognize. For example, you might edit it to read **Monthly Budget Report** if that's the kind of report you're creating.

5. Make any changes you desire to the various options in the three tabs of the Report dialog box.

6. Click OK. Your custom report appears, with the name you've given it, in the Reports list of the Custom Reports dialog box (see Fig. 12.20).

Figure 12.20
The highlighted report name is the custom report I've created based on the Budget Report.

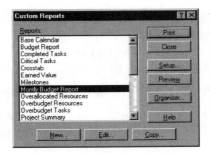

NOTE: Custom reports that you create are saved with the current project file, until you either copy them to Project's Global.mpt master file or delete them. To make a report available to all files or to delete a report, click the Organizer button in the Custom Reports dialog box, and then use the Reports tab to make your changes. Chapter 9, "Working with the Different Project Views," discusses working with the Organizer.

Saving a Unique Report

If you ever want to define a new report completely from scratch, to avoid the possibility of making an unwanted change to one of your existing reports, you can do so by clicking the New button in the Custom Reports dialog box. The Define New Report dialog box appears (see Fig. 12.21).

Figure 12.21
This dialog box enables you to build a report from scratch.

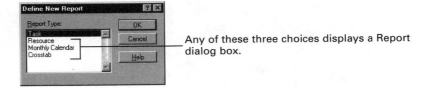

Any of these three choices displays a Report dialog box.

In the Report Type list, select the type of report you want to create, then click OK. If you select Task, Resource, or Crosstab, Project displays the Task Report, Resource Report, or Crosstab Report dialog box, respectively. You work in any of these dialog boxes (refer to Figures 12.16 through 12.18) just as described earlier in this chapter when you learned how to edit different types of reports. Make sure to edit the report Name on the Definition tab (it starts out as "Report 1," "Report 2," or another sequentially numbered name) to make it more descriptive. Select any other options you want on the applicable tabs, then click OK. Your report appears in the Reports list of the Custom Reports dialog box.

If you click the Monthly Calendar choice on the Define New Report dialog box, Project displays the Monthly Calendar Report Definition dialog box, as shown in Figure 12.22. Most of the options in this dialog box work just like options you've seen on various tabs of the Report dialog boxes. Some options, however, are unique to calendar formats.

For example, use the Calendar drop-down list to specify whether the calendar is based on one of the default schedule base calendars (Standard, Night Shift, or 24 Hours), or the calendar for a particular resource. Use the Solid Bar Breaks and Show Tasks As options to specify whether or not to gray out nonworking days, and to control how the bars representing tasks appear on the report. Finally, use the Label Tasks With check boxes to specify whether each task is identified with its ID number, resource Name, or task Duration (or any combination of these pieces of information). When you've finished setting all these options, click OK to close the Monthly Calendar Report Definition dialog box and add your new calendar report to the Reports list of the Custom Reports dialog box.

Figure 12.22
This dialog box offers some options particular to calendar reports.

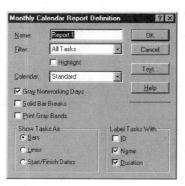

CHAPTER 13

WORKING WITH OUTLINING

At one time many artists and writers used a particular style or method called *stream of consciousness*, which basically meant that the creator would sit down and just let the brushstrokes or words come out, leading where they would. The artist or writer would make no effort to impose any type of structure on his or her output.

We humans, by nature, tend to prefer a more orderly approach to work of any kind—especially in the business world, where the most effective professionals excel at spelling out expectations and providing clear direction for what others need to do.

To help you become more orderly as you build your list of tasks, Project provides outlining capabilities. This chapter helps you learn how to outline, covering these topics:

- A brief look at how outlining works and what benefits it offers

- Knowing how to promote and demote tasks, and what the difference is between a summary task and a subtask

- How summary tasks can help you optimize the critical path

What Outlining Does for You

Different project leaders definitely have different styles. Some fancy themselves "big picture thinkers" and like to sketch out overall plans first; such a leader might even hand a project off to someone else charged with "figuring out the details." Other leaders treat project tasks as a puzzle, first laying out all the pieces, then grouping together pieces for the edge, the sky, the grass, and so on before proceeding to put the puzzle together. No matter which approach best describes you, you'll find that Project's outlining features can accommodate you.

If you prefer to build a schedule using a top-down approach where you identify and arrange major, general tasks before filling in the details, you can enter those major categories, then break them down into more specific action items. Conversely, if you like to simply do a brain dump and list every possible task (the bottom-up approach), you can later group your list into logical areas.

When you use outlining in Project, the major tasks within your Task Sheet are called *summary tasks*, because they summarize a series of actions in a given timeframe. Each of the tasks that's part of the work required to complete a summary task is called a *subtask*. Because Project allows for 10 outline levels, keep in mind that you can have summary tasks within summary tasks.

Project uses special formatting to help you identify summary tasks and subtasks on-screen, as shown in Figure 13.1. Summary tasks usually appear in bold text in the Task Sheet, and use a special summary Gantt bar. Subtasks are indented in the Task Name column of the Task Sheet; if a task is a summary task of a summary task, it's indented twice.

Summarizing work in this way not only gives you an idea of where major milestones in your project will occur, but also can help you make resource assignment decisions. For example, you may examine a particular summary task and its subtasks, and decide to farm the whole mess out to a contractor who can provide multiple people to complete and add continuity to the summary task. Or, you may see that the start and finish dates for two summary tasks are about the same, and realize that those tasks are creating a "crunch period" in your schedule, during which you'll need as many resources as possible, or might need to authorize overtime hours.

Outdent button
Indent button
Show Subtasks button
Hide Subtasks button
Show All Tasks button
Outline Symbols button

Figure 13.1
The Formatting toolbar
offers several buttons
that make outlining
more convenient.

Subtasks are indented—

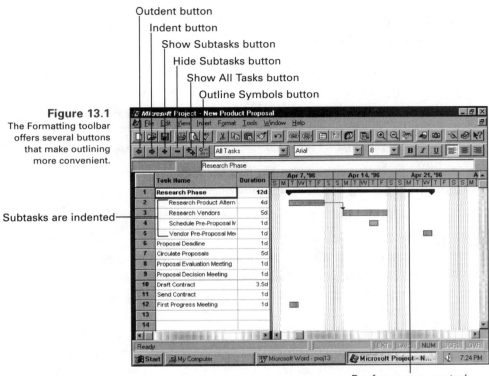

Bar for a summary task

CAUTION: Microsoft Word and Excel for Windows 95
also provide outlining features. Unfortunately, however,
if you copy outlined information from Word or Excel and
paste it into Project, Project does not recognize the outline
levels you assigned in Word or Excel. You still, however,
save the time and effort of retyping the information.

You apply outlining in the Task Sheet for your schedule, from any
view that includes the Task Sheet. The fastest way to work with outlining is to use the outlining tools on Project's Formatting toolbar. The
Formatting toolbar appears on-screen by default, but if you need to
display it, right-click any toolbar and then click Formatting. Refer to
Figure 13.1 to identify the outlining tools.

Promoting and Demoting Tasks at the Outline

Whether you're using outlining for a list of existing tasks, or are using the outlining tools to organize a list of tasks that you're building, the process is generally the same. You select the Task Name cell (or entire row) of the task for which you want to define an outline level, then you *outdent* (or *promote*) it to a higher level, or *indent* (or *demote*) it to a lower level.

To promote the selected task, use one of the following methods:

- Click the Outdent button on the Formatting toolbar.

- Open the Tools menu, point to Outlining, and click Outdent.

- If the task is a subtask and is not on the top level of the outline, select the entire task by clicking its row number, then right-click the row and click Outdent on the shortcut menu that appears.

- If the task is not on the top outline level, point to the first letter of the task name, press and hold the mouse button, and drag to the left to move the task up a level. A vertical gray line appears to indicate the outline level to which the task is being promoted.

If a task is already at the top level of the outline, meaning that it does not appear indented in the Task Name column, Project will not let you promote it. If PlanningWizard is active when you attempt to promote such a task, PlanningWizard appears on-screen to inform you that the task can't be promoted (see Fig. 13.2). Simply click OK to close the PlanningWizard dialog box. Project returns you to your Task Sheet without making any changes. When you promote a task, the tasks listed below it that were previously on the same level become subtasks of the promoted task, and the promoted task is reformatted accordingly.

Figure 13.2
If you try to promote a task that's already at the top level, PlanningWizard tells you that it can't make the change.

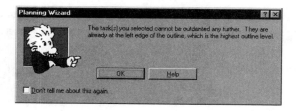

To demote a selected task to the next lowest level, you have similar choices:

- Click the Indent button on the Formatting toolbar.
- Open the Tools menu, point to Outlining, and click Indent.
- Select the entire task by clicking its row number, then right-click the row and click Indent on the shortcut menu that appears.
- Point to the first letter of the task name, press and hold the mouse button, and drag to the right to move the task down a level. A vertical gray line appears to indicate the outline level to which the task is being demoted.

The demoted task is automatically formatted as a subtask, and the task above it is formatted as a summary task. Just as Project prevents you from promoting a task that's already at the top level of your outline, it prevents you from demoting a task if doing so would skip a level in the outline and result in some task ending up two outline levels below the task above it.

TIP: You can select multiple tasks that are on the same outline level and demote them simultaneously. To do so, drag across the row numbers to select the group of tasks, then click the Indent button on the Formatting toolbar.

NOTE: If you promote or demote a summary task, Project promotes or demotes its subtasks, as well.

Inserting a Summary Task

If you're using a bottom-up approach to building your schedule, you may have a list of tasks, into which you want to insert summary tasks. It would be nice if Project simply allowed you to simultaneously demote all the tasks you've typed in and then insert higher-level tasks, but it doesn't work that way. Instead, follow this multi-step process:

1. Insert a blank row above the tasks you want to summarize. To do so, right-click the top task in the group you want to summarize, then click Insert Row in the shortcut menu.

2. Enter the Task Name for the new task. You don't have to specify any other task details, such as Duration. Project will make those entries for you when you define the subtasks for the summary task.

> **CAUTION:** If the task above the inserted row is a subtask, you need to promote the inserted task before going on to step 3.

3. Drag over the row numbers for the tasks you want to convert to summary tasks (to select those rows), then click the Indent button on the formatting toolbar. Alternatively, you can open the Tools menu, point to Outlining, and click Indent; or right-click the selected tasks and then click Indent on the shortcut menu (see Fig. 13.3). Figure 13.4 shows how the tasks in Figure 13.3 look when the indent operation is completed. A summary bar has been added in the Gantt chart for the newly designated summary task in row 6.

Inserting Subtasks

To insert a subtask, you need to insert a new row for it in the Task Sheet. As you learned in the preceding section, when you insert a new row into a Task Sheet, the task in that row adopts the outline level of the task above it. Therefore, one of two situations might develop:

- If the task above the inserted row is at the summary level, you need to enter the Task Name, then demote the task in the newly-inserted row.

- If the task above the inserted row is at the correct subtask level, just enter the Task Name. Notice that if you insert a new task row within a group of several subtasks, Project does not demote the tasks in rows below the newly inserted row to a lower outline level. Instead, Project assumes that all tasks in the group should remain at the same level until you tell it otherwise.

Figure 13.3
You can use the shortcut menu to demote selected task rows.

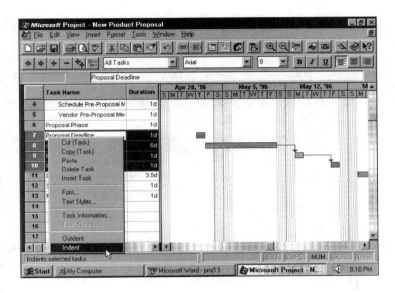

New summary bar

Figure 13.4
The newly inserted row is designated as a summary task.

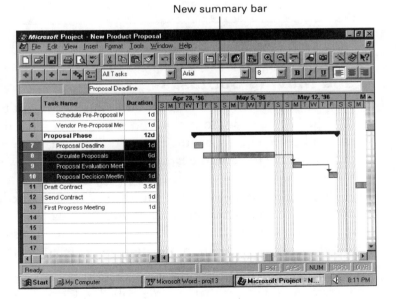

Similarly, when you're entering brand new tasks into blank rows at the bottom of the Task Sheet, Project assumes that each newly entered task should adopt the outline level of the task above it. For example, if I type a new Task Name into row 16 of the Task Sheet shown in Figure 13.5, Project assumes it to be a subtask of the row 13 summary task, just like the subtask in row 15.

Figure 13.5
If I create another task in row 16, it becomes a subtask like the two tasks above it.

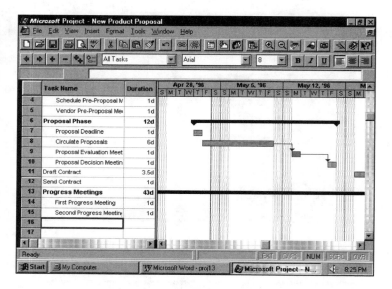

Adjusting Subtask Scheduling and Moving Subtasks

If you've experimented at all with outlining, you might have noticed that the summary task duration and summary task bar on the Gantt chart adjust to encompass the earliest task start date for any subtask of the summary task, and the latest task finish date for any subtask. For that reason, I think it's a little easier to create your entire list of tasks, apply the outlining you prefer, and then adjust the scheduling information as needed for all subtasks. If you enter dates for a task, convert it to a summary task, and then later demote it to be a subtask, you lose the original duration information you entered for the task.

You can change the schedule for a subtask using any of the methods for rescheduling tasks that were described in Chapter 3, "Fine-Tuning Tasks." The duration, start date, finish date, and Gantt chart summary bar for the summary task all adjust automatically to reflect the change. Figures 13.6 and 13.7 show an example of how dragging to lengthen a subtask changes the summary task.

Original summary task duration   Original summary task bar

Figure 13.6
I'm dragging to increase the subtask schedule.

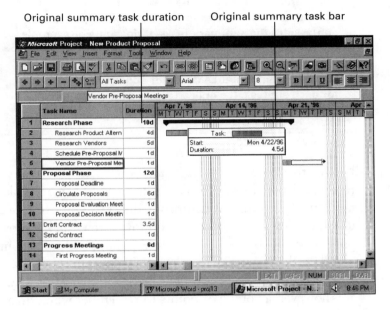

Figure 13.7
After I've rescheduled the subtask, notice that the summary task duration has changed.

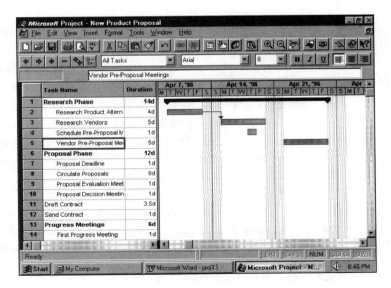

> **NOTE:** You can display the Task Info dialog box for a summary task. When this dialog box appears, it won't let you edit certain information, such as the summary task duration. Don't assume that all the information you can enter for the summary task also applies to all subtasks of the summary task—it doesn't. For example, if you assign a resource to the summary task, such as a supervisor who'll manage all the resources handling the subtasks, that resource does not appear as a resource for each subtask. It's only a resource for the summary task.

No creative process is perfect, and you might find that you've incorrectly positioned several tasks, including a summary task and its subtasks, in the outline. When this is the case, you can move the tasks as usual, by dragging task rows. To move a row, click its row number, point to a row border, then press and hold the mouse button while you drag the row to its new location, dropping the row into place whenever the gray insertion bar reaches the location you want. There are, however, a couple of points to remember when dragging outlined tasks:

- **Subtasks travel with their summary task.**—Therefore, if you drag a summary task to a new location in the task list, when you drop it into place, its subtasks will appear below it.

- **Dragging tasks around can disturb links.**—If you insert a group of subtasks linked by a series of Finish-to-Start links within tasks already linked by Finish-to-Start links, the results are unpredictable. This is yet another argument for nailing down your outline as much as possible before progressing too far with information about scheduling, resources, or links.

> **TIP:** You can link a summary task to other tasks in many instances, as simply as dragging between bars in the Gantt chart. The only restriction is that you cannot link a summary task to one of its subtasks.

- **A moved task adopts the outline level of the task above it.**—When you move a task, Project assumes that you want the task to be on the same outline level as the task above it in its new location. Project even demotes or promotes a moved task more than one level, if needed. For example, if you move a task to a Task Sheet row directly below a task that's two outline levels lower, Project demotes the moved task (and any subtasks that travel with it) two levels.

Work Breakdown Structure Information

The *work breakdown structure (WBS)* for a list of tasks is simply a method of hierarchically numbering tasks in a traditional outline numbering format. WBS numbers are also called *outline numbers*. Tasks at the top outline level are numbered sequentially. For example, the WBSs for the first ten top-level outline tasks are numbered 1 through 10. Subtasks on the first level use the top level number for their summary task plus a decimal value; for example, the first three subtasks of summary task 2 are numbered 2.1, 2.2, and 2.3. For the next outline level down, Project adds another decimal; for example, the first two subtasks under task 2.1 are numbered 2.1.1 and 2.1.2.

When you use outlining, Project assigns the WBS numbers automatically. As you move, promote, and demote tasks, Project updates the WBS numbers accordingly. Your company might follow a specific set of WBS numbers that you need to follow. If you need to assign a WBS to a task that's different from the WBS that Project assigns, click the task, then click the Information button on the Standard toolbar (or right-click the task, then click Task Information on the shortcut menu). In the Task Information dialog box, click the Advanced tab. Double-click the entry in the WBS Code text box, and type the new entry you want, as shown in Figure 13.8. Click OK when you've finished editing the entry.

You can add a field (column) to the Task Sheet to display WBS numbers, or can even sort by WBS numbers, if you want. You also can display WBS numbers along with the task name in the Task Sheet. To do so, open the Tools menu and click Options. On the View tab of the

Options dialog box, click to place a check beside the Show Outline Number option. The assigned outline number appears to the left of each task name, as shown in Figure 13.9.

Figure 13.8
If your company requires specific WBS codes, you can change the ones that Project creates in the WBS Code text box.

Figure 13.9
If your company prefers, you can display each task's WBS number with the task name.

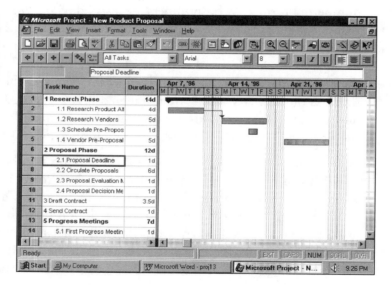

NOTE: Other aspects of how the outlined information appears are controlled on the View tab of the Options dialog box. For more information about setting Project options, see Chapter 20, "Customizing Microsoft Project."

NOTE: If you copy the Task Name column into Word as unformatted text (see Chapter 15, "Using Information from Another Project or Application"), the WBS numbers are not copied with the Task Name entries, even if the WBS numbers were displayed in Project. If you need to include accurate WBS numbers in documents in other applications, insert a WBS column into the Task Sheet by right-clicking a column head, then clicking Insert Column on the shortcut menu. In the Column Definition dialog box, select WBS as the Field Name, then click OK.

Controlling the Outline Display

As when you're outlining in a word processing application or spreadsheet program, one of the advantages of outlining in Project is that outlining enables Project to give you visual cues about how you've structured your outline. This can help you to make intelligent decisions about scheduling changes and resource assignments. This section explains how you can work with the outlining display features.

Displaying and Hiding Outlining Symbols

Outlining symbols help you differentiate summary tasks from subtasks. Any task that has subtasks below it is considered a summary task, and is indicated with a plus (+) outlining symbol. Any task that has no subtasks below it, even top-level outline tasks with no subtasks below them, are indicated with a minus (–) outlining symbol. When you display outlining symbols, they appear for all tasks in the Task Sheet, at the left of the task names.

To display outlining symbols, click the Outline Symbols button on the Formatting toolbar. Outlining symbols appear in the Task Sheet, as shown in Figure 13.10. To hide the outlining symbols, click the Outline Symbols button again.

Outline Symbols button

Figure 13.10
Outlining symbols
appear beside each
task name.

Summary task
outlining
symbols

Outlining
symbol for a
task with no
subtasks

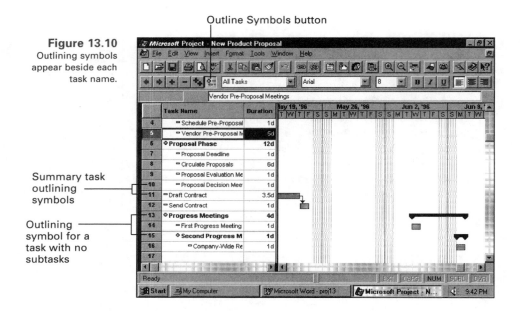

NOTE: In Chapter 3, "Fine-Tuning Tasks," you learned
how to create a recurring task, which behaves
somewhat like a summary task. When you display
outline symbols, they appear on a recurring task (and
each of its subtasks) just as they do on real summary
and subtasks. However, the Gantt chart bar for a
"summary" recurring task never looks like the Gantt
chart bar for a summary task created via outlining.

Specifying Which Outline Levels Appear

Summary tasks wouldn't provide much of a summary if you could
never view them without their subtasks. Consequently, Project enables
you to hide subtasks from view for your convenience. There are a couple of reasons why you might want to hide some or all subtasks in
your schedule. First, you might want to print the schedule and have
the printout only include summary tasks, not the details shown in
subtasks. Second, if you have a lengthy list of tasks in your project,
you might find it easier to move up and down through the Task Sheet
if you hide subtasks until you need to view or work with the information for a particular subtask.

When you hide and redisplay subtasks, you do so for a single summary task by selecting that summary task first. To hide or redisplay subtasks for all the summary tasks in the Task Sheet, first select the whole Task Sheet by clicking the Select All button in the upper-left corner, or select the whole Task Name column by clicking that column heading.

Then, to hide subtasks, click the Hide Subtasks button on the Formatting toolbar. Alternatively, open the Tools menu, point to Outlining, and click Hide Subtasks. Figure 13.11 shows a Task Sheet with the subtasks for one summary task hidden. Notice that not only the subtask rows but also the corresponding Gantt bars are hidden, leaving only the summary task bar on the Gantt chart.

Figure 13.11
The task in row 1 is a summary task; its bold formatting and the plus sign beside it tell you that it contains subtasks.

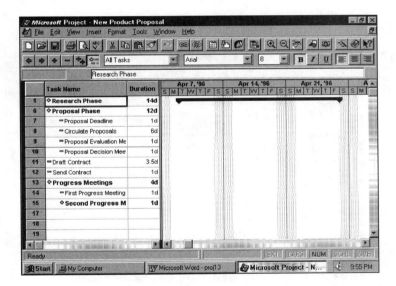

To redisplay subtasks for selected summary task(s), click the Show Subtasks button on the Formatting toolbar. Alternatively, open the Tools menu, point to Outlining, and click Show Subtasks. If you want to redisplay all subtasks without taking the time to select particular summary tasks, click the Show All Tasks button on the Formatting Toolbar.

Rolling Up Subtasks

If you have a long list of subtasks within a summary task, you might lose track of how a particular task compares to the summary schedule.

Or, you might have a particular task near the middle of the summary task range that you want to highlight by having it appear on the summary bar as well as its usual location. To achieve this effect, you *roll up* the subtask to its summary task.

Click to select the summary task to roll up, then press and hold Ctrl while you click to select the subtask to roll up. Click the Information button to display the Task Information dialog box. On the General tab of this dialog box, click to select the Rollup Gantt Bar to Summary option, then click OK. The subtask bar is then displayed on the summary bar, as shown in Figure 13.12. To remove the effects of a roll up, select the summary task and subtask, redisplay the Task Information dialog box, and clear the Rollup Gantt Bar to Summary check box.

Figure 13.12
A subtask has been rolled up on the summary task in row 1.

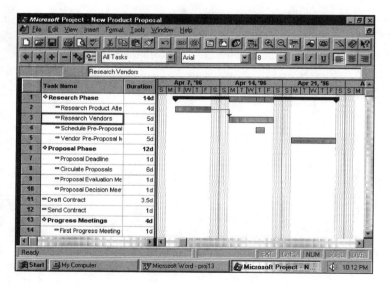

CAUTION: Do not select the Hide Task Bar check box in the General tab of the Task Information dialog box when you're rolling up tasks. If you do so, you won't be able to see the rolled up task or any text that accompanies it.

If you want to roll up a summary task and several of its subtasks simultaneously, drag over the row numbers to select the rows. Display the Task Information dialog box, select the Rollup Gantt Bar to Summary option, and click OK.

> **TIP:** You can reformat the bars for summary tasks so that they display dates or have a different appearance that makes them stand out more when rolled up. For example, you can make the Gantt bar for a particular subtask red so that it stands out when rolled up. To learn how to reformat a Gantt bar, see Chapter 14, "Other Formatting."

Using Summary Tasks to Reduce the Critical Path

As you learned in Chapter 6, "Optimizing the Schedule," the critical path for your schedule identifies tasks that can't slip without causing the overall project finish date to move. When you finish setting up all your schedule information, you might find that the schedule is longer than you'd like it to be. If that's the case, working with your summary tasks (perhaps hiding subtasks in the process), can help you to identify critical tasks. Here are a few ideas about how you can use summary task information to identify ways to condense the critical path:

- Look for ways to remove slack time between summary tasks.

- If none of your summary tasks overlap in timing, check to see if you can move up the schedules for some later summary tasks, so that some summary groups run concurrently.

- Create a Gantt bar style for bars that indicate both summary and critical path information. See Chapter 14, "Other Formatting," for more details about bar styles.

CHAPTER 14

OTHER FORMATTING

When you're learning to use Project, the way that text and other elements look may be the farthest thing from your mind. At first, you worry about setting the schedules for your tasks, figuring out how different kinds of links work, determining how to allocate resources most effectively, and working out any kinks that unnecessarily extend your overall schedule.

After you set everything, however, you may begin to look at your schedule in a new light. You may become more interested in ensuring that your schedule not only is attractive, but also highlights key facts clearly. This chapter examines the tools that enable you to control the appearance of information in Project. You learn the following things:

- How to change the appearance of selected text in a Task Sheet or Resource Sheet

- How to work with a single chart bar or box

- How to control gridlines that appear on a chart

- How to adjust the appearance of a particular style of sheet text or a particular style of chart bar or box

- How to control the display of details and choose a layout for links

- How to work with Project's drawing tools

Formatting Selected Sheet Text

Fonts are different types of lettering used for text. Within Project, you can select a different font—along with a particular font size, color, and so on—for any cell, row, or column that you've selected in a Task Sheet or Resource Sheet. The fonts you can choose depend on the fonts that you installed to work with Windows on your system. When you reformat selected text, the formatting changes appear both on-screen and in printouts, including the formatted text.

TIP: Font sizes are measured in *points*. Each point is 1/72 inch; 12 points equal 1/6 inch.

An easy way to apply formatting to selected text is to use the tools in the Formatting toolbar (see Fig. 14.1). To display the Formatting toolbar, right-click any toolbar and then click to select Formatting.

Figure 14.1
Select text in a Task Sheet or Resource Sheet, then use a tool in the Formatting toolbar to change its appearance.

Text with a different, larger font; the row automatically becomes taller to accommodate the new size

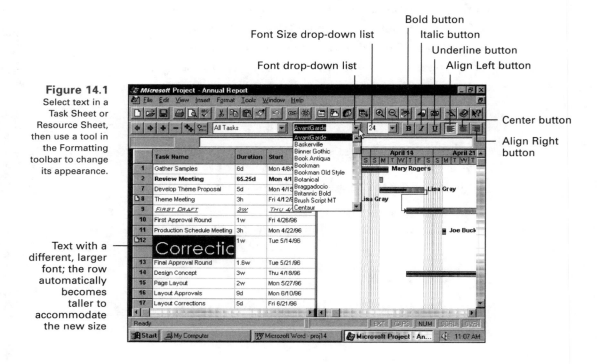

Note that the three alignment buttons—Align Left, Center, and Align Right—realign all cells in the sheet column, even if you have selected a single cell in the column. If you select a single row and then click an alignment button, all columns in the sheet are realigned.

In addition to using the Formatting toolbar, you can format text by using the Font dialog box. Follow these steps:

1. Select the cell that contains the text that you want to format. Alternatively, click a column header to select the entire column, or click a row number to select an entire row.

2. Open the Format menu and click Font, or right-click and then click Font on the shortcut menu. The Font dialog box appears (see Fig. 14.2).

Figure 14.2
The Font dialog box enables you to specify formatting for selected text.

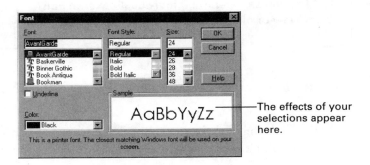

The effects of your selections appear here.

3. Scroll the Font list and select the font you want to use.

4. If you want to format the text with an effect such as bold or italic, select the effect from the Font Style list.

5. Scroll the Size list and select the font size you want to use, or double-click the Size text box and type the appropriate size.

6. If you want to apply an underline to the selected text, click the Underline check box.

7. If you want to format the selected text with a particular color (perhaps to call more attention to it on-screen or in printouts on a color printer), select the color from the Color drop-down list.

8. Click OK to close the Font dialog box and apply your selections.

Formatting the Bar for a Selected Task

Just as you can use formatting selections to call attention to specific text in a Task Sheet or Resource Sheet, you can reformat the Gantt bars for selected tasks in your schedule. Suppose that you want to call attention to the Gantt bars for all the tasks that begin next week. You could make each of those bars yellow, so that they're brighter on-screen or in a printout. Alternatively, you could include the text of a particular field of task information (such as the Actual Start date) in the Gantt chart bar.

NOTE: You can't reformat individual boxes in PERT Chart view or individual bars in Resource Graph view.

To adjust formatting options for one or more Gantt chart bars, follow these steps:

1. Click the Task Name cell to select the task you want to reformat, or select row numbers to select multiple rows. (You must select the entire row when you reformat multiple Gantt bars.)

TIP: If you want to skip step 1 and display the Format Bar dialog box to reformat a single Gantt bar, double-click the Gantt bar.

2. Open the Format menu and click Bar. The Format Bar dialog box appears (see Fig. 14.3).

3. Click the Bar Shape tab to display the Bar Shape options. This tab enables you to specify the appearance of the selected Gantt bar(s), including overall thickness, color, and ending shapes or symbols.

Figure 14.3
The Format Bar dialog box contains numerous options for formatting the selected Gantt bar(s).

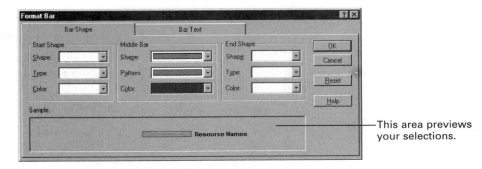

This area previews your selections.

4. To add a symbol to the left end of the selected bar(s), select it from the Shape drop-down list in the Start Shape area. Then use the Type drop-down list to specify the ending shape, such as Solid. (If you leave this option blank, the Start Shape will be invisible.) Finally, to apply a color to the selected Start Shape, select that color from the Color drop-down list. Figure 14.4 shows some possible Start Shape selections.

Figure 14.4
I've added a start shape for the selected Gantt bar.

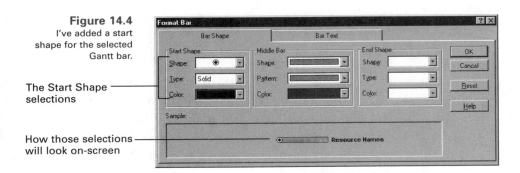

The Start Shape selections

How those selections will look on-screen

5. In the End Shape area of the dialog box, use the Shape, Type, and Color drop-down lists to specify and format a shape for the right end of the selected Gantt bar(s). These options are the same as the corresponding options in the Start Shape area.

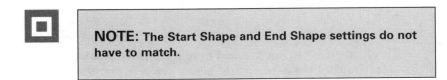

NOTE: The Start Shape and End Shape settings do not have to match.

6. In the Middle Bar area, specify how the center of the selected bar(s) will look. The Shape drop-down list enables you to specify how thick you want the bar to be and how you want to position it in relation to the start and end shapes—slightly up or down, or centered.

7. If the bar Shape that you specified is more than a thin line, use the Pattern drop-down list to adjust the relative density and hatching of the color used for the bar.

8. Select a Color for the bar.

   Figure 14.5 shows some selected bar shapes.

Figure 14.5
The final result of my bar-color and shape adjustments.

9. Click the Bar Text tab to display the Bar Text options. You use this tab to specify how you want to display text in relation to the selected Gantt bar(s): Left, Right, Top, Bottom, or Inside. The tab offers a separate line for each of these options; you can enter text in any of them or a combination of them. (By default, resource names are displayed to the right of each bar.)

10. To add text to appear with a particular part of the bar, click the cell beside the area name; then type the field name for the text that you want to display and click Enter. Alternatively, you can select the field from the drop-down list of fields (see Fig. 14.6).

11. Use the technique described in step 10 to edit any of the other text areas.

TIP: If you want to remove text from a particular display area, highlight the existing field name, delete it, and then click the Enter button.

Figure 14.6
You can specify a field of text to appear at the left end of the Gantt bar.

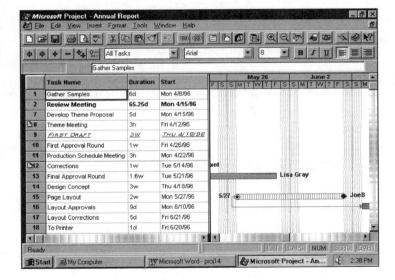

12. When you finish setting options in the Bar Shape and Bar Text tabs, click OK to close the Format Bar dialog box. (Figure 14.7 shows a sample formatted bar.)

Figure 14.7
The Gantt bar has new starting and ending markers, a patterned bar in the middle, and new labels.

TIP: To return a Gantt bar to its default formatting, select the bar, display the Format Bar dialog box, and click the **Reset** button.

Working with Gridlines

Gridlines in Project, like gridlines in other applications that display graphical information, help your eye determine whether objects line up or where particular measurements occur. If you add gridlines to separate Gantt bars, you can easily tell which Gantt bars align with which Task Sheet rows. By default, the timescale in Gantt Chart view shows vertical gridlines that identify the major columns, which generally represent work weeks.

> **NOTE:** The lines that separate the rows and columns in Task Sheets and Resource Sheets are also considered to be gridlines, and can be removed or reformatted. These gridlines are identified as the Sheet Rows and Sheet Columns options in the Lines to Change list of the Gridlines dialog box.

Some gridlines are horizontal, such as those that identify Gantt bar rows. Other gridlines are vertical. Generally, if the items for which you want to add gridlines appear in rows, the gridlines will be horizontal; if the items for which you want to add gridlines are organized in columns, the gridlines will be vertical.

When you change gridline settings, your changes apply to the entire schedule file; you can't change only the gridlines that correspond to selected tasks.

To add gridlines to a graphical view in Project, follow these steps:

1. Open the Format menu and click Gridlines, or right-click the graphical area of the view (such as the Gantt chart) and then click Gridlines on the shortcut menu. The Gridlines dialog box appears (see Fig. 14.8).

2. In the Line to Change list, select the item for which you want to add or edit a gridline. If the selected item already has some type of gridline applied, the specified formatting options for that gridline appear on the right side of the dialog box.

Figure 14.8
The Gridlines dialog
box enables you to add
gridlines to the Gantt
chart area of your
view.

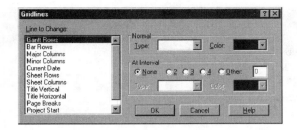

3. In the Normal area (the upper-right portion of the dialog box), specify the gridlines that you want for your Line to Change choices. Use the Type drop-down list to select the overall gridline appearance, such as dotted or dashed. Use the Color drop-down list to apply a color to the gridlines.

NOTE: If you want to remove displayed gridlines for the selected Line to Change item, select the blank option at the top of the Type list. If you want gridlines to appear at intervals and not for every column or row, make sure that no line Type is selected.

4. In the At Interval area, you can specify the appearance of gridlines at a specified interval. If the normal gridlines are black, for example, you may want every fourth gridline to be red. Click the 2, 3, 4, or Other option button (and edit the default Other value, if necessary) to specify which gridlines should use the alternative formatting. Then select the alternative gridline Type and Color.

5. Click OK to close the dialog box and display your gridlines.

Figure 14.9 shows dotted gridlines used to separate Gantt rows. Every fifth gridline is a solid red line.

Figure 14.9
This Gantt chart
shows gridlines
separating the
Gantt bar lines.

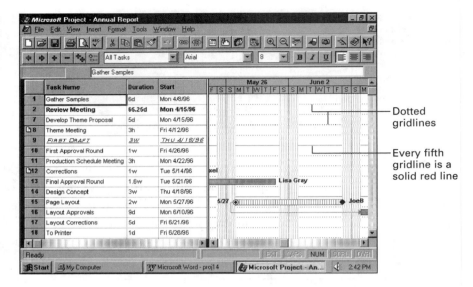

Dotted
gridlines

Every fifth
gridline is a
solid red line

Formatting Text Styles

Based on the information you add to your schedule, Project classifies certain tasks based on their impact. The program marks all tasks on the critical path as being critical tasks, for example, or treats summary tasks differently from subtasks. Even though Project can track task categories easily, tracking might be a bit more difficult for you. To make the job easier, Project enables you to apply special text formatting to any category of task or resource information in the Task Sheet or Resource Sheet. In Project, when you apply formatting to a particular category of information, you're defining a special *text style*.

To work with a text style, follow these steps:

1. Display the view that includes the Task Sheet or Resource Sheet to which you want to apply the style.

2. Open the Format menu and click Text Styles. Alternatively, select a column, right-click it, and then click Text Styles on the shortcut menu. The Text Styles dialog box appears.

3. Select the category of information for which you want to adjust formatting from the Item to Change drop-down list (see Fig. 14.10). If you want to change the font size of summary tasks, for example, select Summary Tasks here.

NOTE: The Item to Change list contains even such items as column and row heads. The list is rather long, so check out everything that you can change.

Figure 14.10
You select a style to change and then set its options.

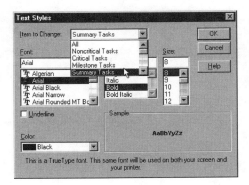

4. Specify the text-formatting options for this category of information, just as you did for selected sheet text in the "Formatting Selected Sheet Text" section earlier in this chapter. The text-formatting options here work just like those you saw in Figure 14.2.

5. (Optional) If you want to set the formatting for other categories of information, repeat steps 3 and 4.

6. Click OK to close the Text Styles dialog box and apply the styles. All text in that category displays your formatting changes. (Figure 14.11 shows an increased font size for summary tasks.)

Adjusting the Bar or Box Styles for Charts

Just as Project applies a particular style of text to different categories of tasks or resources, it applies a particular style of formatting to the corresponding charted information. The adjustments that you can make in charted information depend on the selected view in Project. The formatting options are different for Calendar view bars, Gantt Chart view bars, PERT Chart view boxes, and Resource Graph bars. The following sections provide an overview of the most important options for each type of display.

Figure 14.11
The summary
tasks in rows 1,
6, and 13
now appear in a
larger font size.

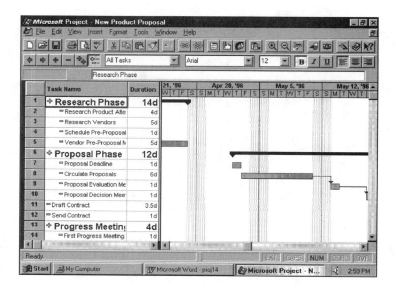

NOTE: The formatting options that are available for bars and boxes vary, depending on whether the graphical information appears in a combination view or in a single pane. The options also might change based on the type of information displayed.

For all views but Calendar view, you can display a dialog box that contains the appropriate bar- or box-formatting options by double-clicking the chart area. For all charts, you can right-click the chart area and then click Bar Styles or Box Styles on the shortcut menu. If you prefer to use menu commands, open the F̲ormat menu and click Bar S̲tyles (for Calendar, Gantt Chart, or Resource Graph view) or Box Styles (for PERT Chart view). After you make changes in one of these dialog boxes, click OK to close the dialog box and apply your selections to the appropriate bars and boxes.

Style Options in Gantt Chart View.

Figure 14.12 shows the Bar Styles dialog box that appears in Gantt Chart view. To adjust a bar style, edit the column entries and Text and Bars tab settings. To add a new bar style, scroll down the list, enter the information for the style in each column, and then specify the Text and Bars tab options. To delete a style, select it in the Name list and then click the Cut Row button near the top of the dialog box.

Figure 14.12
These options enable you to adjust Gantt-chart bar styles.

Each row represents a bar

These tabs and their options work exactly like those in the Format Bars dialog box.

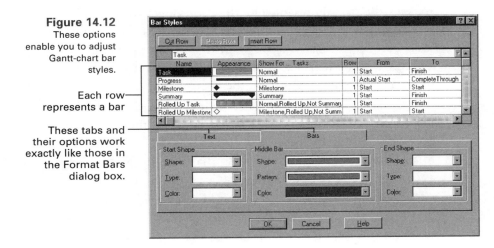

Figure 14.13 shows an example of the formatting possibilities for the summary task bars.

Figure 14.13
This example shows reformatted Gantt bars for summary tasks.

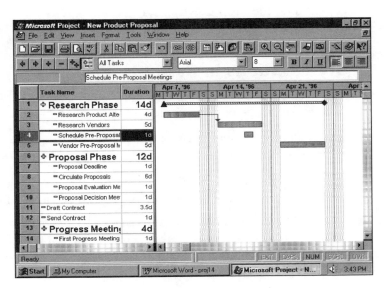

Not all the style columns are self-explanatory, so the following list reviews them:

- The Name column displays the name you enter for the style.

- The Appearance column displays the style's settings, which you specify by using the Text and Bars tabs at the bottom of the dialog box.

- The Show For... Tasks column specifies which fields or types of tasks the bars represent. Use the drop-down list to select a field. (You could, for example, create a bar style that applies to tasks Not Started Yet.) If you want to add multiple fields, type a comma in the text box after the last listed field and then select an additional field from the drop-down list.

- If you want to display multiple bars for each task (as in Tracking Gantt view), enter a value other than 1 in the Row column for a style. If you create a new style for tasks Not Started Yet, for example, you might enter **2**, so that the Not Started Yet bar appears below the task's default bar.

- The From and To columns also can display fields. The fields that you select determine the length of the Gantt bars for the style. For the Not Started Yet bars, for example, you might want to specify `Baseline Start` in the From column and `Start` (for the currently scheduled start) in the To column. Those options draw a bar that leads up to the default bar for the task. Use the drop-down list at the far right of the text box to make your entries for these columns.

Style Options in Calendar View

Select a Task Type from the list in the upper-left corner; then choose the various Bar Shape options (which work just like those for Gantt charts).

This dialog box offers a few options that are unique to Calendar view (see Fig. 14.14):

- If you choose the Shadow option, Project displays a drop shadow below bars of that style to provide a 3-D appearance.

- The Bar Rounding option makes bars of that style appear in full-day increments, even when an actual task's duration is less than a full day.

Figure 14.14
Change the bar styles for Calendar view by using these options.

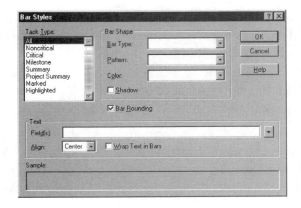

- The Field(s) box enables you to specify what field information is used to label bars of the selected style. You can select fields from the drop-down list at the far right of the box. Again, you can separate multiple fields in the text box with commas.

- The Align options enable you to specify where in the bars the specified text should appear.

- The Wrap Text in Bars option allows the specified text to occupy more than one line, if necessary.

Style Options in Resource Graph View

Figure 14.15 shows the Bar Styles dialog box for Resource Graph view.

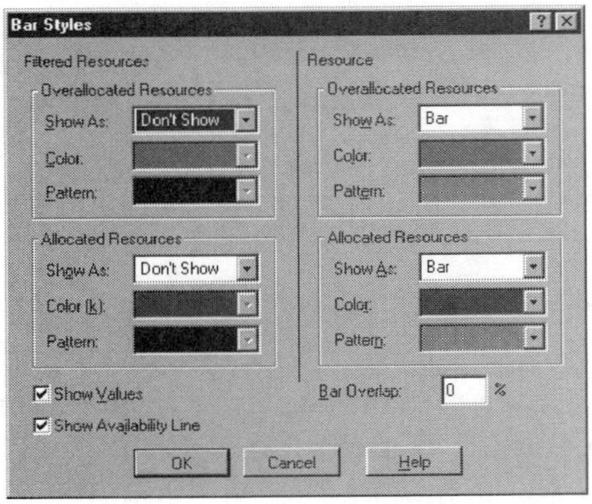

Figure 14.15
Resource Graph view offers these bar-style options.

The options available in this dialog box vary radically, depending on whether this graph appears by itself or in the lower pane of a combination view. The Filtered Resources options apply only to filtered resources when the Resource Graph appears by itself on-screen; otherwise, the settings apply to all resources. The Resource options apply to the displayed resource.

Another factor that affects the options in this dialog box are the details that you have chosen to display (see the "Working with Details" section later in this chapter). If you have chosen to display cost information in the graph, for example, the Bar Styles dialog box looks like Figure 14.16.

Figure 14.16
The Resource Graph bar-style options have changed because cost information now appears in the graph.

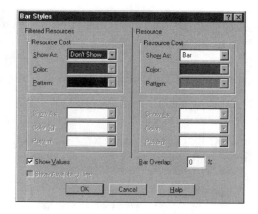

No matter which kinds of information you can format, the options are similar:

- Use any Show As drop-down list to specify whether the information appears as a bar, line, area, or other type of chart indicator.

- Select a color for the graphed information from the corresponding Color drop-down list.

- Select a pattern from the corresponding Pattern drop-down list.

- The Show <u>V</u>alues option displays the values for the charted information at the bottom of the graph.

- The Show Availability Line option displays an indicator that shows whether the resource has any available working time.

(This option is available when you're charting work information, as opposed to cost information.)

- If you want to display more than one type of bar for each time period in the graph, you can specify a <u>B</u>ar Overlap % option to allow the charted bars to overlap slightly, so that more information fits into less horizontal space. Figure 14.17 shows bars with a 25 percent overlap. The legend at the left side of the display shows what each style of charted information means.

Figure 14.17
Creating overlapping bars is only one of your options in Resource Graph view.

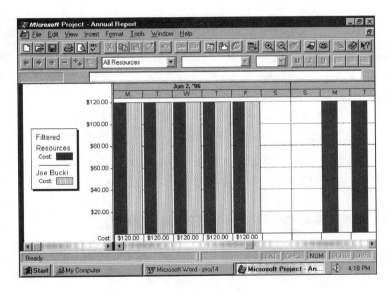

Style Options in PERT Chart View

In PERT Chart view, you adjust box styles (instead of bar styles) by using the Box Styles dialog box shown in Figure 14.18.

Figure 14.18
Full PERT Chart view enables you to control the appearance of the boxes.

This area resembles the grid within each box; from each drop-down list, select the information you want to appear in the corresponding box "cell."

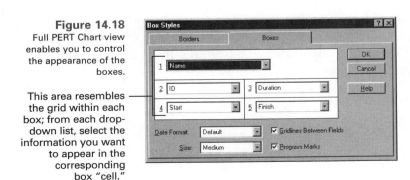

When you display this dialog box, the Boxes tab appears. This tab contains the following options:

- By default, each PERT chart box is divided into five cells. Drop-down lists <u>1</u> through <u>5</u> let you specify what field information appears in each cell.

- The <u>D</u>ate Format drop-down list enables you to specify the way dates are displayed in the boxes.

- The <u>S</u>ize list specifies the size of the boxes.

- When you select the <u>G</u>ridlines Between Fields option, lines separate the cells in the boxes.

- The <u>P</u>rogress Marks option (selected by default) displays one diagonal slash through each in-progress task in the PERT chart box, and crosses out completed tasks with an X.

- Clear the <u>P</u>rogress Marks check box to prevent Project from indicating whether tasks are underway or completed.

Click the Borders tab in the Box Styles dialog box to display the options shown in Figure 14.19.

Figure 14.19
You can adjust the appearance of the boxes in each task category by making choices in this dialog box.

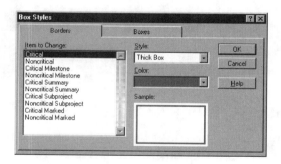

Select the style of box (for a particular type of task) from the <u>I</u>tem to Change list; then select a <u>S</u>tyle and <u>C</u>olor for that type of box. You subsequently can select other task types from the <u>I</u>tem to Change list and adjust each box's <u>S</u>tyle and <u>C</u>olor.

Working with Details

In the "Graphing Individual Resource Work and Costs" section in Chapter 8, you learned that you can right-click the graph area on the right side of Resource Graph view to display a shortcut menu, from which you select the information you want to view. You can select Percent Allocation, for example, to display a daily percentage of how much of the workday a resource will spend on a given task.

Similarly, you learned in Chapter 9 that you can right-click any form that's part of a combination view to display a shortcut menu that enables you to specify which information the form displays. In the lower pane of Task Entry view, for example, you can right-click the form and then click Predecessors & Successors on the shortcut menu. The form then displays information about all predecessor and successor tasks that are linked to the selected task in the Task Sheet.

The equivalent of these shortcut menus is the Details submenu of the Format menu (see Fig. 14.20). This submenu becomes available only when you select a pane that can "morph" to display different information. The submenu options vary, depending on the nature of the selected pane. Simply select the type of information you want to display in the selected pane—the submenu closes, and the display changes accordingly.

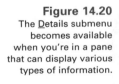

Figure 14.20
The Details submenu becomes available when you're in a pane that can display various types of information.

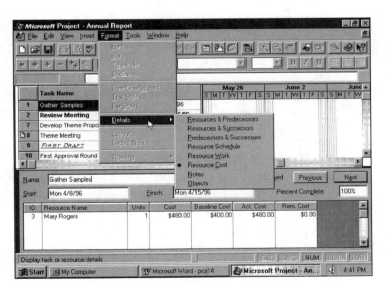

Choosing a Layout

The layout features control how graphed bars appear in relation to one another in Calendar, Gantt Chart, and PERT Chart views. The layout options for bar and box styles vary, depending on the selected view. To display the layout options for one of these views, open the Format menu and click Layout, or right-click a blank space of the chart area and then click Layout on the shortcut menu.

Layout Options in Calendar View

The layout options for Calendar view are simple, as Figure 14.21 shows. If you want each week to show more task information, select the Attempt to Fit As Many Tasks As Possible option. Select the Automatic Layout option to tell Project to adjust the calendar to accommodate inserted and moved tasks.

Figure 14.21
The layout options are limited in Calendar view

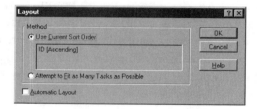

NOTE: As you might surmise from the presence of the Automatic Layout option in the Layout dialog box, Calendar view doesn't update automatically when you move or reschedule tasks in Gantt Chart view; neither does PERT Chart view. If you need to update Calendar view or PERT Chart view to reflect the current schedule and task relationships, open the Format menu and click Layout Now.

Layout Options in Gantt Chart View

Figure 14.22 shows the Layout dialog box for Gantt Chart view.

Figure 14.22
The Gantt Chart view
layout options enable
you to control the
appearance of links and
more.

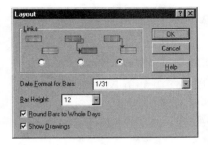

This dialog box contains the following options:

- Select the Links option to specify how (and whether) you want task-link lines to appear.
- The options in the Date Format for Bars drop-down list enable you to control the display of any date information that accompanies Gantt bars.
- The Bar Height option enables you to make all bars (and their rows) larger or smaller.
- The Round Bars to Whole Days option enables you to format each bar as a full day—even for, say, a three-hour task.
- If you added a drawing to the Gantt chart area, make sure that the Show Drawings check box is selected, so that the drawing appears. To hide the drawing temporarily (for printing, for example), clear this check box.

Layout Options in PERT Chart View

Figure 14.23 shows the Layout dialog box for PERT Chart view.

Figure 14.23
These layout options
are available for PERT
Chart view.

This dialog box contains the following options:

- As you can for a Gantt chart, you can use the Links option to specify how links appear on a PERT chart.

- Use the Show Arrows option to specify arrows on the link lines that indicate the flow of work.

- Select Show Page Breaks to display dotted lines in the view, so that you'll know which PERT boxes will print together on a page.

- Make sure that the Adjust for Page Breaks option is selected. Later, when you open the Format menu and click Layout Now, Project moves task boxes that appear on a page break to one page or the next, so that the box doesn't split in the printout.

Creating a Drawing in Project

In Chapter 15, "Using Information from Another Project or Application," you learn how to insert a drawing from another application into your Gantt chart as an object. Although Project is by no means a drawing application, it includes some basic drawing tools that you can use to add simple graphics to your Gantt chart. You might want to display a box with some text to call attention to a particular task, for example. If you have a great deal of time, you can be creative, layering numerous drawn objects for a nice effect. By default, the drawn objects that you add appear both on-screen and in any printout of a view that contains your Gantt chart.

The drawing tools in Project work like those in Word, Excel, and many other Microsoft applications. Although an exhaustive discussion of drawing is beyond the scope of this book, this section shows you how to draw objects, select and format them, and position them in relation to the correct date or task in the Gantt chart. Follow these steps:

1. In Gantt Chart view, scroll the chart to display the blank area where you want to create the drawing.

2. Display the Drawing toolbar (see Fig. 14.24). To do so, open the Insert menu and click Drawing; click the Drawing tool on the Standard toolbar; or right-click any toolbar on-screen and then click Drawing.

The Drawing button

Figure 14.24
The tools in the
Drawing toolbar allow
you to add basic
objects to the Gantt
chart.

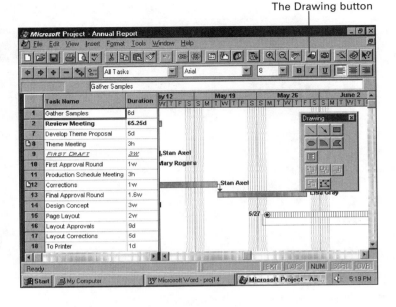

3. The top seven tools in the Drawing toolbar—Line, Arrow, Rectangle, Ellipse, Arc, Polygon, and Text Box—allow you to create those objects. To use each of these tools, you basically click and drag. (There are two exceptions: to use the Polygon tool, you have to click for each point and double-click to finish; to use the Text Box tool, you have to type text.) When you finish drawing the object, release the mouse button—the object appears with black selection handles around it.

Figure 14.25 shows an example of using the Ellipse tool.

4. Double-click the object you just drew; the Format Drawing dialog box appears (see Fig. 14.26). Alternatively, click the object to select it (if it's not already selected), then open the Format menu, point to Drawing, and click Properties.

5. Choose the Line and Fill options that you want to use. The Preview area shows the result of your choices.

6. Click the Size & Position tab, which contains the following options:

   • You probably don't need to worry about the Size options near the bottom of the dialog box, because you defined the size when you created the object.

Figure 14.25
Click a drawing
tool and then drag
to create a shape.

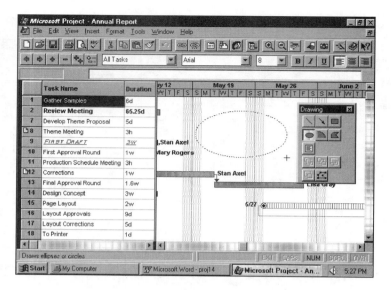

Figure 14.26
Format an object
with this
dialog box.

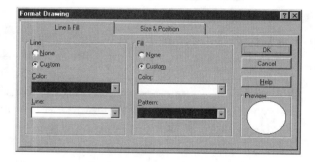

- The Position options enable you to attach the drawing to a particular date (the Attach to Time<u>s</u>cale option button) or task (the Attach to Tas<u>k</u> option button) in the Gantt chart.

- By default, Attach to Timescale is selected, with the <u>D</u>ate and <u>V</u>ertical entries reflecting the way that you positioned the object when you created it.

- The Attach to Tas<u>k</u> option attaches the drawn object to the Gantt bar for the specified task in the list; however, you might not be satisfied with the results of selecting this option.

7. When you finish selecting options, click OK to close the Format Drawing dialog box.

8. Create another object, if you want. Figure 14.27 shows a newly created text box.

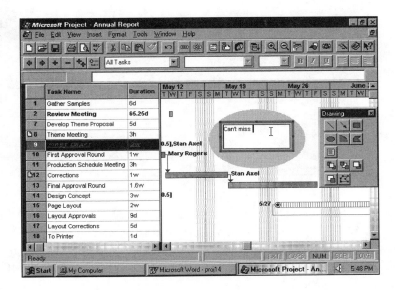

Figure 14.27
This is a second new object.

9. Double-click the new object to set its formatting options. If you're adding a text box over an oval, for example, and you want the text to look like part of the oval, choose <u>N</u>one as the <u>L</u>ine option (on the Line & Fill tab) in the Format Drawing dialog box, and give the text box the same Fill Colo<u>r</u> as the oval. Figure 14.28 shows the result.

10. Save the file to save your drawing on the Gantt chart. If you close the Project file without saving it, you lose your drawing.

TIP: You have to use a special method to format the text in a drawn text box. Click the box to select it; then drag over the text within the box to select (highlight) it. Next, open the Fo<u>r</u>mat menu and click <u>F</u>ont; finally, use the Font dialog box to specify the formatting you want.

Figure 14.28
A text box layered
over another
object can be an
attention-getting
reminder.

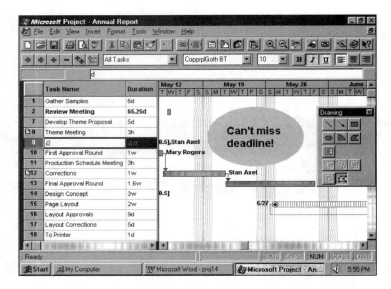

The objects you draw appear in invisible layers, with the object drawn most recently appearing on the top layer. You can use the Bring to Front or Send to Back button on the Drawing toolbar to send the selected object to the top or bottom layer, respectively. If you want to move the selected drawing object up or back by a single layer, use the Move Forward or Move Backward button.

PART IV

HANDLING MULTIPLE PROJECTS

CHAPTER 15

USING INFORMATION FROM ANOTHER PROJECT OR APPLICATION

There's no shame in using shortcuts—in fact, smart businesspeople seek them out and use them as tools for repeating successes. If you wrote a new-sales-call follow-up letter that enabled you to close a sale, you'd be silly to write a new follow-up letter after the next call. Instead, you'd reuse as much as you could of the letter that had already worked for you.

When you have invested a good deal of time entering information about resources and certain kinds of tasks in Project, and when you find that information to be valuable, you may want to reuse that information. If different projects that you manage have similar tasks or use some of the same resources, you can save time by copying or moving information between those projects. You can even share information between Project and other Windows applications. This chapter covers the following topics:

- Copying and moving data between projects

- Enhancing a project's Gantt Chart views with graphics from other applications

- Copying Gantt charts and other Project images into other applications

- Using OLE objects to create dynamic links between applications

Copying Information Between Projects

When you copy or move information in Windows applications, Windows leaves the original information intact and places the copied information in the Clipboard—a holding area in your computer's memory. When data is in the Clipboard, you can paste it into a new location, or into several locations. The file or location from which you copy or move information is called the *source*, and the place where you paste the information is called the *destination*.

The following sections show you how to copy information between two Project files. The steps that you take vary a bit, depending on whether you're copying all the information about a particular task or resource, or only part of the information.

> **NOTE:** You can copy and move information within a Project file as well. Simply select the information, cut or copy it, select another location for it in the Task Sheet or Resource Sheet, and then paste it in place.

Copying Task and Resource Information Between Projects

When you select and copy an entire task row (or multiple rows), the entire set of information related to that task—the task name, resources assigned to that task, the duration, the start time, task notes, and so on—is copied. If you select two or more linked tasks and paste them into another project, the link information that connects the tasks is copied, too.

You also can copy resource information to other projects. Copying resource rows picks up all the fields defined in your Resource Sheet.

> **TIP:** If you frequently copy the same resource information to new projects, choose <u>T</u>ools, Multiple <u>P</u>rojects, Share <u>R</u>esource to create a common set of resources that are available to multiple projects. To learn more about shared resources, see Chapter 17, "Creating and Printing a Report."

To copy tasks or resources between projects, follow these steps:

1. Open the files for the two projects in question, select the same view in each project window (Gantt Chart view, for example), and arrange the project windows so a portion of each window is visible. You can open the <u>W</u>indow menu and click <u>A</u>rrange All to tile the project windows automatically.

2. Select the entire task or resource row to copy by clicking the row number. To select multiple consecutive rows, hold down the Shift key and clicking each row. To select multiple non-consecutive rows, hold down the Ctrl key and click each row.

3. Open the <u>E</u>dit menu and click <u>C</u>opy (Task) or <u>C</u>opy (Resource). Alternatively, do any of the following: right-click the selection and then click <u>C</u>opy (Task) or <u>C</u>opy (Resource) from the shortcut menu; press Ctrl+C; or click the Copy button on the Standard toolbar. (The command name reflects the type of information that you've selected—task or resource.)

4. If you're copying the information to another Project file, click a portion of the destination window (such as the title bar) to tell Project that you want to copy information to that file; then select the first cell of the row in which you want to place the copied information.

5. Open the <u>E</u>dit menu and click <u>P</u>aste. Alternatively, do any of the following: right-click the row to paste to, then click Paste on the shortcut menu; press Ctrl+V; or click the Paste button on the Standard toolbar. The task or resource information is pasted into the selected row.

You also can use Project's drag-and-drop feature to copy task or resource rows between project windows. Follow these steps:

1. Open the project files, and arrange the windows so that the source and destination rows are visible.

2. Select the rows to copy by clicking the appropriate task or resource row numbers.

3. Position the mouse pointer on the border of the selected area. The pointer changes to an arrow.

4. Drag the selected information to the first cell of the destination row. As you drag, the pointer changes to an arrow and a plus sign, indicating that the copy operation is process.

5. Release the mouse button to drop the copied information in the new location.

Figure 15.1 shows the drag-and-drop operation in process.

Figure 15.1
You can use the drag-and-drop feature to copy Task Sheet or Resource Sheet rows to other Project files.

Cut button

This pointer appears when you drag to copy information

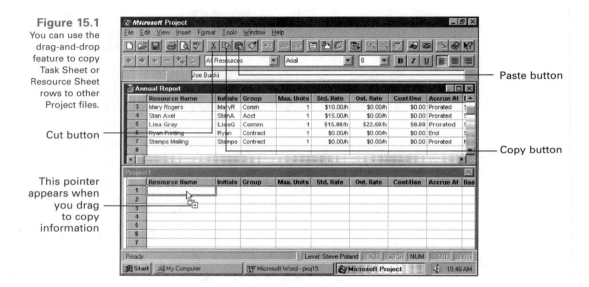

Paste button

Copy button

> **CAUTION:** If you try to paste a copied or cut row of information between existing rows, Project inserts a new row for the pasted information. Otherwise, when you're pasting cells or column selections, Project pastes the information over any information that currently appears in the destination location. When you paste information, make sure that you're not pasting over other information that you need.

Copying Cell and Column Information Between Projects

In some cases, you want to copy selected information about tasks or resources from one Task Sheet or Resource Sheet to another. You can copy a list of task names only, for example, or you can copy the hourly and overtime rates for one resource to the corresponding cells for another resource.

When you copy information from cells, all the original information for the task or resource is left behind; only a copy of the cell contents is placed in the destination project. When you copy partial task or resource information to another project, the default values for Duration and Start Date (tasks), Accrue At and Baseline (resource), and so on are assigned to the task. You can edit those settings as necessary.

> **CAUTION:** Keep the field (column) format types in mind when you copy information between Task Sheets or Resource Sheets. Typically, you should copy only between fields of the same type—from a Task Name field to a Task Name field, for example. Otherwise, you may get unexpected results. In some cases, if you try to paste an entry into a cell that needs a different kind of data (if you're trying to paste a name into a cell that contains an hourly rate, for example), Project displays a warning, as shown in Figure 15.2. Also, Project does not allow you to paste information into any calculated field.

Figure 15.2
You see a message if a copy operation could create unwanted results.

I tried to copy this name...

...to this rate cell.

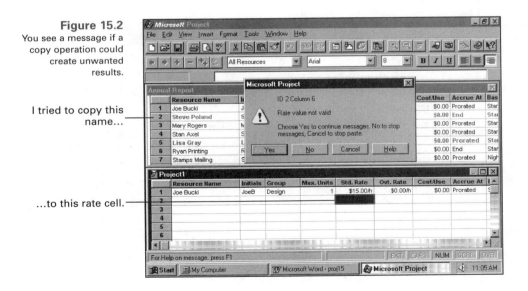

To copy cell information between projects, follow these steps:

1. Open the two projects between which you want to copy information, select the same view in each project window, and arrange the project windows so that a portion of each is visible.

2. Select one or more cells to be copied. To select multiple consecutive cells (a range or block of cells), select the upper-left cell of the range, and then hold down the Shift key and click the lower-right corner of the range (see Fig. 15.3). To select multiple nonconsecutive cells, hold down the Ctrl key and click each cell that you want to copy.

Figure 15.3
You can select a range of

Click this cell...

...then hold down the Shift key and click this cell.

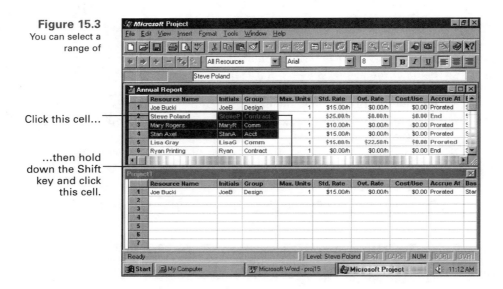

3. Open the <u>E</u>dit menu and click <u>C</u>opy (Cell). Alternatively, right-click your selection and click Copy (Cell) on the shortcut menu; press Ctrl+C; or click the Copy button on the Standard toolbar. (The command name reflects the type of information that you've selected—in this case, a cell.)

4. If you're copying the information to another Project file, click a portion of the destination window (such as the title bar) to tell Project that you want to copy information to that file; then select the first cell of the row in which you want to place the copied information.

5. Open the Edit menu and click Paste. Alternatively, do any of the following: right-click the selection you're pasting to, then click Paste on the shortcut menu; press Ctrl+V; or click the Paste button on the Standard toolbar. The cell information is pasted in the selected area.

As you would expect, you can use the drag-and-drop feature to copy cell information between projects. Select the cells that you want to copy, point to the selection border so that you see the arrow pointer, drag the information to the destination, and release the mouse button to drop the information in place.

You also can copy and paste entire columns of information from one project to another. Suppose that you are creating a new project that has all the same tasks as an existing project, but the associated Duration, Start, and Finish entries—and the resources—are different.

To copy the Task Name entries from the existing project to the new one, click the column heading (Task Name, in this case) to select the entire column. Then do any of the following: open the Edit menu and click Copy (Cell), press Ctrl+C, or click the Copy button on the Standard toolbar. In the window for the new project file, click the Task Name column heading. Then do any of the following: open the Edit menu and click Paste, press Ctrl+V, or click the Paste button on the Standard toolbar. The entire list of task names is pasted into the new project.

TIP: If you often work with multiple projects at the same time, you can save the open projects and window positions as one unit. Save each of the open projects individually, then open the File menu and click Save Workspace. Give the workspace a meaningful name, and click OK to save the workspace. The next time you open the workspace file, the project windows open in the place where you last left them. Chapter 1, "Getting Started with Project," covers saving a workspace in more detail.

Finally, you can make entering information in a single column easier by *filling*—an operation that's similar to copying. Start by selecting the cell that contains the information you want to copy to other cells that are lower in the list. Next, hold down the Shift key and click the bottom cell of the group of cells that you want to fill, or hold down the Ctrl key and click other noncontiguous cells lower in the column. Then open the Edit menu and click Fill Down (or press Ctrl+D). Project fills all the selected cells with the information that appears in the first cell that you selected.

Moving Information Between Projects

In addition to copying, you can move information between Task Sheets or Resource Sheets in open Project files. Moving information is almost identical to copying, except that you cut the information from the source file, leaving the selected row, column, or cells empty, rather than leaving the information in place, as you do when you copy. Then you paste the information where you want it.

As in copying, the moved information replaces existing information unless you're moving an entire row, in which case the moved information is inserted between existing rows. Finally, moving an entire row of information carries all the task or resource information for that row, except for linking information.

> **TIP:** To ensure that the information you're moving doesn't overwrite existing entries in your destination Task Sheet or Resource Sheet, open the Insert menu and click Insert Task or Insert Resource before you perform the move. Project inserts a new row in the location of the currently selected cell, and moves existing rows down in the sheet.

The possibilities for moving information are almost endless. You may want to move information if you have more than one project under way and decide to move a resource from one project to another. In such a case, you need to move the contents of the row that contains that resource from the Resource Sheet of the first project file to the Resource Sheet of the second project file.

To move information between two Task Sheets or Resource Sheets, follow these steps:

1. Open the files for the two projects in question, select the same view in each project window (Gantt Chart view, for example), and arrange the project windows so that a portion of each is visible. You can open the <u>W</u>indow menu and click <u>A</u>rrange All to tile the project windows automatically.

2. Select the task or resource row, column, or cells that you want to move.

3. Open the <u>E</u>dit menu and click Cu<u>t</u> (Task) or Cu<u>t</u> (Resource). Alternatively, do one of the following: right-click the selection and then click Cut (Task) or Cut (Resource) on the shortcut menu, or click the Cut button on the Standard toolbar. (The command name reflects the type of information that you've selected—task or resource.)

   Cutting removes the information from its original location and places the information in the Windows Clipboard.

CAUTION: Information stays in the Clipboard only while your computer is on. If you shut off the computer, or if it loses power for some reason, the Clipboard empties. Also, if you cut or copy anything else to the Clipboard, the new information wipes out the existing Clipboard contents. Therefore, make sure that you paste information as quickly as possible after cutting it.

4. If you're moving the information to another Project file, click a portion of the destination window (such as its title bar) to tell Project that you want to move information to that file. Then select the first cell of the row in which you want to place the moved information.

5. Open the <u>E</u>dit menu and click <u>P</u>aste. Alternatively, do any of the following: right-click the selection you're pasting to, then click Paste on the shortcut menu; press Ctrl+V; or click the

Paste button on the Standard toolbar. The task or resource information is pasted into the area.

To use the drag-and-drop feature to move information between projects, you use a process that's similar to copying. First, select the information that you want to copy. Next, point to the selection border so that you see the arrow pointer, hold down the Ctrl key, and drag the information to the destination. Then release the mouse button to drop the information in place.

Affecting Links When You Copy and Move Information

Many of the tasks in the Project files that you create are part of a series of tasks linked via Finish-to-Start (FS) links. The tasks are strung together like beads on a string. If one of the beads cracks and falls off, the remaining beads slide together to fill the gap.

When you copy or move a group of linked tasks from one project file to another, the links stay intact within the group. If you move or copy a single task, linked information doesn't travel with the task.

By default, when you move a task that's linked, via FS links, to a series of other tasks within a Project file, Project adjusts the linking information so that the linked tasks still flow continuously. If you move the linked task to a location that's higher or lower in the Task Sheet list, the links update to reflect all new task predecessors and successors.

In Figure 15.4, for example, the tasks in rows 1 and 4 are linked via an FS link, as are the tasks in rows 2 and 3. If you drag the task from row 1 to a location between tasks 2 and 3, the links rearrange, as shown in Figure 15.5. If the linking change would create a scheduling problem, PlanningWizard warns you (by default), as shown in Figure 15.6.

Pasting a copied task within a series of linked tasks also can disturb the linking relationships. If you want to be able to move tasks that are linked by FS relationships without changing the links, click to open the Tools menu and then click Options to display the Options dialog box. Click the Schedule tab, clear the Autolink Inserted or Moved

Tasks check box, and click OK. Otherwise, you can avoid screwing up links simply by not moving or pasting tasks within a series of linked tasks, or by moving only tasks that aren't connected to a predecessor or successor via an FS relationship.

Figure 15.4
These two pairs of tasks are linked via Finish-to-Start (FS) links.

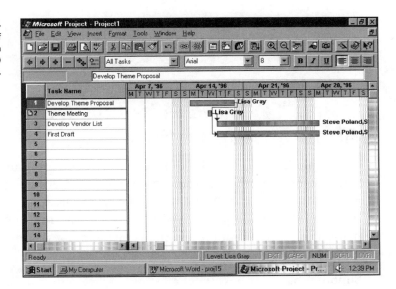

Figure 15.5
Moving the task that was originally in row 1 changed the links.

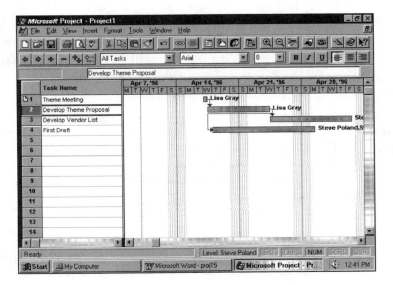

Figure 15.6
If moving or copying tasks would cause a linking problem, PlanningWizard warns you.

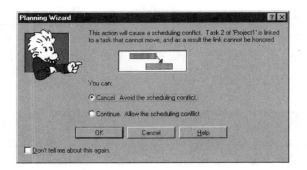

Using Text and Graphics from Another Application

As a companion to the Microsoft Office suite of applications, Project was designed with information-sharing in mind. All Office applications (and many other Windows applications) are built to enable you to share information between applications easily. You can create information in one application and then copy and use that information in another application.

Suppose that your boss types a list of key operations for a project in a word processing program—say, Microsoft Word. The list is about three pages long. If you're not a skilled typist, typing such a list could take you an hour or more. If you have Word installed on your computer, however, and if your boss will give you a copy of the file that contains the list, you can get the job done in minutes by copying the list from the Word file to a file in Project.

> **TIP:** Every time you retype information, you have the potential to make errors. When information has already been spell-checked or proofed for errors, always copy it rather than retype it.

Following are just a few other examples of text and graphics from other applications that you can copy and paste into Project:

- You can convert a to-do list created in Word to a list of tasks in Project.
- You can use a list of committee members who are assigned to a project as the foundation of a Resource Sheet list.
- You can paste the names of people in your department from a spreadsheet to a Resource Sheet.
- You can include graphic images, such as company logos, in a Gantt chart to make the printouts more attractive and informative.
- You can paste electronic images of product designs or chart images of product information in the Objects box of the Task Form for particular tasks.
- If you have scanned-in photos of colleagues or of equipment to be used to complete a task, you can add those images to the Objects box for the resources in the Resource form.

The procedures for copying text and graphics are different, so the following sections cover the procedures separately.

> **NOTE:** When you paste information into blank rows in a Task Sheet or Resource Sheet, Project automatically creates new tasks or resource entries in those rows, and adds the default settings for fields (columns) into which you do not paste information. If you paste a to-do list in the Task Name column of a Task Sheet, for example, Project adds a default duration of 1d (one day) for each task and sets the defaults for the remaining columns.

Using Lists from Other Applications

You can copy information from any application that supports OLE (see "Working with OLE Objects," later in this chapter) and allows you to create lists—this includes most Windows-based word processing and spreadsheet programs—and then paste that information into a Project file. When you paste, you're restricted to pasting the information into a

Task Sheet or Resource Sheet. Therefore, you can paste information into any view that shows the Task Sheet or Resource Sheet, or into any table that's a variation on those sheets.

Keep in mind that if you're copying cells from a spreadsheet program (such as Excel), Project tries to paste to an area that's similar in shape—say, three columns wide by two rows deep. Also, no matter what kind of application you're pasting from, Project won't allow you to paste a type of information that's inappropriate for the destination. You can't paste text information into a cell that calls for an hourly rate, for example.

In most cases, you probably will simply paste a one-column list into the Task Name or Resource Name column of the Task Sheet or Resource Sheet.

> **CAUTION:** Text information that you paste replaces any information that's in the selected destination cells. Be sure to select only a blank area of the Task Sheet or Resource Sheet if you don't want to wipe out any existing information.

To copy text information from an application and paste it into a Project sheet, follow these steps:

1. Open the document that contains the text that you want to copy to Project.

2. Select the text; then open the Edit menu and click Copy (or click the Copy button, if available). Figure 15.7 shows an example.

3. Open or switch to the Project application. (You can press Alt+Tab or click the Project button on the Taskbar to switch to Project.) Then use the Windows Start menu to start Project.

4. Select or open the Project file into which you want to paste the copied information.

5. Select the view that you want to use, such as Gantt Chart or Resource Sheet.

Figure 15.7
You can copy
information from a
word processing
program.

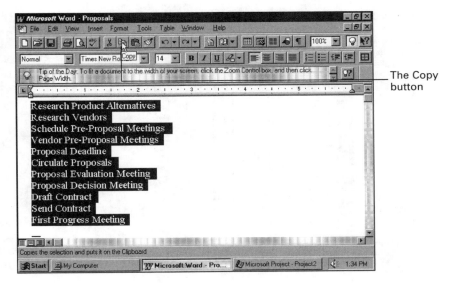

6. Select the upper-left corner of the range of cells into which you want to paste the information. To paste a list of tasks, for example, you could click the top cell of the Task Name column.

7. Open the Edit menu and click Paste. Alternatively, do any of the following: right-click the selection to paste to, then click Paste on the shortcut menu; press Ctrl+V; or click the Paste button on the Standard toolbar. The text is pasted into the selected cells.

CAUTION: When you copy-and-paste specially formatted text from another application into Project, be prepared to lose the special formatting. For example, if you copy an outline from Word and paste it into Project, you end up with simple text that lacks the outline formatting.

Figure 15.8 shows the text copied from Figure 15.7 pasted into the Task Sheet.

Figure 15.8
The word processing list is now a list of tasks.

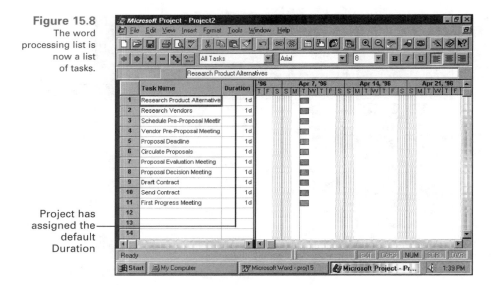

Project has assigned the default Duration

NOTE: Be sure that you have enough room in your Project file for the copied information. If you copied five rows of names from a Word document, for example, you need five blank rows in the Resource Sheet. You can insert more rows in your Task Sheet or Resource Sheet by opening the Insert menu and clicking Insert Task (Gantt Chart view) or Insert Resource (Resource Sheet view).

Using Graphics to Enhance Your Project

You can copy graphics—such as electronic images of company logos, products, and charts—created in other applications into Microsoft Project graphic areas. These graphics can range from purely decorative (an image that you use to jazz up a Gantt chart) to purely informational (a graphic of a resource that enables widely separated team members to recognize one another). Although Project offers drawing capabilities, you may want to use a graphic that was created in another application or that may need to be created with tools that Project doesn't offer (as with scanned images). For these reasons, Project allows you to use graphics copied from other graphics applications.

You can copy a graphic to any view that shows a Gantt chart, such as Gantt Chart view (see Fig. 15.9). When you paste a graphic into a Gantt chart, Project allows you to format the graphic just as you would format a drawing that you created in Project. (For more information on formatting, refer to Chapter 14, "Other Formatting.")

Figure 15.9
Here's an example of a graphic pasted into a Gantt chart.

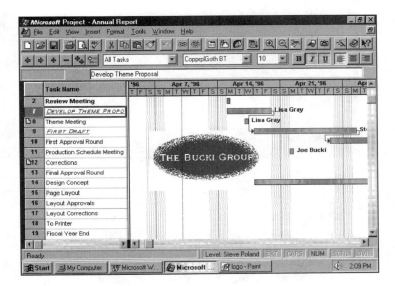

You also can paste a copied graphic into the Objects box of the Task Form or Resource Form, or into any view that offers one of these forms. The Task Form, for example, appears as the bottom pane of Task Entry view.

To display the Task Form or Resource Form, open the <u>V</u>iew menu and click More <u>V</u>iews to display the More Views dialog box; then double-click Task Form or Resource Form in the <u>V</u>iews list. To display the Objects box for the form, right-click the form and then click Objects on the shortcut menu. The Objects box is the big blank area at the bottom of the form. Figure 15.10 shows a graphic pasted into the Task Form.

To copy a graphic image from another application, follow these steps:

1. Start the application that contains the graphic object that you want to copy to Project. (All Windows users have at least one graphic program, called Paint, for working with graphic images.)

2. Open the file for the graphic image, or create the new image.

Figure 15.10
Here's an
example of a
graphic pasted
into
the Task Form.

Objects box

> **NOTE:** Graphics files can be rather large. If you'll be sharing your Project files with other people via e-mail or floppy disks, adding numerous graphics to your project files can make transfer more time-consuming and difficult. Under such circumstances, you should use graphics files sparingly.

3. Select the image (or any portion of the image) that you want to use in Project, using the program's selection method.

Figure 15.11 shows a graphic selected in Paint.

4. Open the <u>E</u>dit menu and click <u>C</u>opy to copy the graphic to the Clipboard.

5. If this object is the only one that you need to copy, exit the application.

6. Open or switch to the Project application. (You can press Alt+Tab or click the Project button on the Taskbar to switch to Project.) Then use the Start menu to start Project.

7. Select or open the Project file into which you want to paste the copied information.

Figure 15.11
The dotted line borders
the selected area that
will be copied.

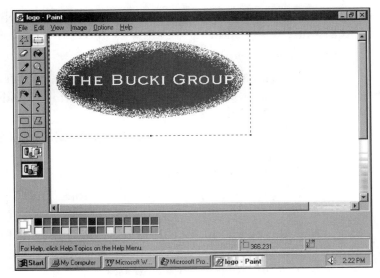

8. Select the view that you want to use, such as Gantt Chart view; or display either the Task Form or Resource Form to paste the information into the Objects box on the form.

9. In a Gantt chart, scroll to the section of the view where you want the graphic to appear. In a Task Form or Resource Form, click the Objects box.

10. Open the Edit menu and click Paste. Alternatively, right-click the selection to paste to, then click Paste on the shortcut menu (or press Ctrl+V). The graphic object is placed in the upper-left corner of the Gantt chart area or Objects box.

If you don't like the location of the graphic in the Gantt bar chart area, you can drag the object to the exact position you want. Place the mouse pointer on the object. The pointer changes to a four-headed arrow, indicating that you can drag the object to a new location. In an Objects box, however, you can't move an object after it's been placed.

Using Project Information in Other Applications

You can copy almost all the information and views in Project to other applications. Copying information into Project saves time and reduces errors; copying information from Project and using it elsewhere does the same thing. Following are a few examples of how you can use Project information in other applications:

- You can copy Gantt chart timelines as pictures (graphics that can't be edited) and paste them into a weekly status report in Word.

- You can copy resource cost tables, showing how much time various people have spent on the project, and paste that information into a spreadsheet.

- You can paste a list of tasks from Project into a project-update memo for company executives.

- If you added the e-mail addresses field to your Resource Sheet, you can copy resource names and addresses into a note for distribution to all team members.

Project allows you to copy information as straight text, as an object (for more information on objects, see "Working with OLE Objects" later in this chapter), or as a picture. Information that appears in the timescale area on the right side of a view—such as the Gantt-chart portion of Gantt Chart view or the schedule portion of Resource Usage view—can be copied only as a picture or an object, not as text. In addition, the table information that appears to the left of the charted information is always copied as well. You can't copy a picture of a few Gantt-chart bars without copying a picture of the accompanying task information.

Copying Project Information as Text

The procedure for copying text from Task Sheets or Resource Sheets in Project depends on what kind of application you're pasting to. When you paste to a spreadsheet program, such as Excel, Project assumes (by default) that you're pasting the information as text. When you paste to a word processing program, such as Word, Project assumes that you want to paste an object; you have to tell Project to paste the information as unformatted text, meaning that the pasted cell entries are to be separated by simple tab characters.

If you select the task or resource row before copying, the entire set of task or resource fields is copied and pasted at the destination. If you want to copy only some fields (columns) from the Task Sheet or Resource Sheet, select the individual cells that you want to copy and paste.

> **NOTE:** The text in Calendar and PERT Chart views cannot be copied to other applications. These views can be copied only as picture or Microsoft Project objects.

To copy information from Project as text, follow these steps:

1. Select the Project view that contains the text that you want to copy to another application.

2. In the Task Sheet or Resource Sheet, select the task or resource row or the individual cells that you want to copy.

3. Open the Edit menu and click Copy (Task), Copy (Resource), or Copy (Cell). Alternatively, right-click the selection and then click the appropriate command on the shortcut menu (or simply press Ctrl+C). The command name on the Edit or shortcut menu reflects the type of information you've selected—task, resource, or cell. The text is copied to the Windows Clipboard.

4. If you copied from Resource Usage view, Project displays a dialog box, asking whether you want to copy Table Only (the selected cells in the Resource Sheet) or Table and Timescale (both the selected cells from the Resource Sheet and the corresponding rows in the Timescale area on the right side of the view). Make your selection; edit the dates below the Table and Timescale options, if necessary; then click OK to continue.

5. Exit Project, if this is the only copy operation you need to perform.

6. Open or switch to the destination document.

7. Select the area in which you want the Project text to appear.

   In a spreadsheet application, select the upper-left cell of the range of cells in which you want to paste the text. In a word processing application, position the insertion point where you want to paste the text.

NOTE: As in any copy-and-paste operation, make sure that you have room for the information that you want to paste. Pasting into some applications, such as word processing programs, inserts the pasted information. In other applications, such as spreadsheet programs, pasting overwrites (or replaces) existing text.

8. Open the Edit menu and click Paste Special. The Paste Special dialog box appears, listing the paste options that are available for the information on the Clipboard. These options vary, depending on the application to which you're pasting. Figure 15.12 shows the options for pasting into Microsoft Excel.

Figure 15.12
The Paste Special options in Excel appear in a list.

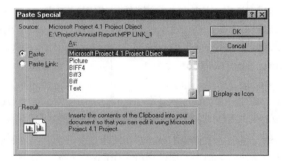

NOTE: Working with the paste options for a particular application may take some experimentation. Excel's options, for example, include weird-looking items called BIFF, BIFF3, and BIFF4. These options represent different kinds of Excel text and will paste the copied information into a group of cells, for example.

9. Select the Unformatted Text or Text option in the As list box.
10. Click OK to paste the text into the document. The text appears in the document as unformatted text.

Figure 15.13 shows some resource information pasted into Excel.

CAUTION: If you use the Paste button on the Standard Toolbar, you can paste Project tasks or resources as Microsoft Project graphic objects, not as text objects. For that reason, you must use the Paste Special command on the Edit menu. The single exception is Excel, which allows you to use the Paste button to paste as text. Using the Paste Special command is crucial, however, for pasting into Word.

Figure 15.13
Resource information pasted into Excel appears where you specify.

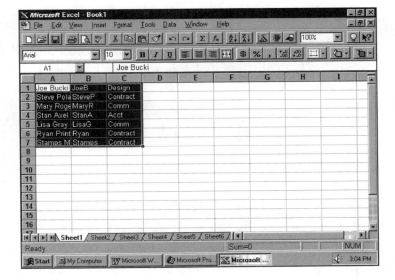

Pasting a Picture of Project Information

Pasting a picture of Project information allows you to insert that image into the destination application as a graphic. This method can be a good way to go if you won't need to edit the information in the destination application; if you don't want to reformat any text after pasting; and if you want to include Gantt bars, PERT charts, or timescale information in the destination application.

To copy Project information as a picture of the information, rather than text that can be edited, follow these steps:

1. Select the Project view that contains the information that you want to copy.

NOTE: When you copy and paste Project information as a picture-formatted object (a non-editable graphic), only the portion of the current view that corresponds with the selected Task Sheet or Resource Sheet information is copied. Whether you are in Calendar view, Gantt Chart view, or any of the Resource views, be sure to scroll to the appropriate section of the view and select the right rows in the table before using Copy or Cut.

2. Select the task row, resource row, or PERT chart area that you want to copy.

3. Click the Copy Picture button on the Standard toolbar. The Copy Picture dialog box appears (see Fig. 15.14).

Figure 15.14
The Copy Picture dialog box enables you to select the picture format— For Screen or For Printer.

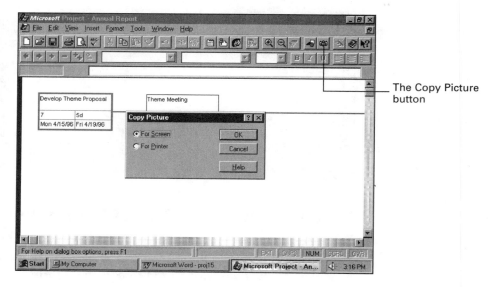

The Copy Picture button

4. If you want to copy only the information in the same size as the current screen view, leave For Screen selected. If you want to copy a larger view, select For Printer.

5. Click OK to copy the Project view to the Windows Clipboard.

6. Switch to (or open) the document into which you want to paste the picture.

7. Place the insertion point where you want the picture to appear.

8. Open the <u>E</u>dit menu and click <u>P</u>aste. Alternatively, press Ctrl+V or click the Paste button on the Standard toolbar. The Project picture appears in the document.

Figure 15.15 shows a PERT chart selection copied to a Word page.

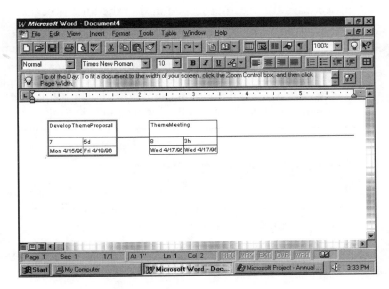

Figure 15.15
PERT-chart information can be copied to a Word document.

Working with OLE Objects

Object linking and embedding (OLE) allows applications to share information dynamically. Basically, the information is created with the *source* application or its tools; then that information is displayed in the *container* application.

If the information in the container application is linked to the original information in the source application, you can make changes in the source document, and those changes show up in the linked information in the destination document.

Embedding enables you to edit an object that was created in another application within the current application. You can edit a chart created in Excel and embedded in a Word document by using the menus, commands, and other features of Excel from within Word. You don't have to exit Word, start Excel, edit the object, cut or copy the object, and paste it back into your Word document.

Numerous books cover OLE and the various ways that you can put it to work for you, so detailed descriptions of all the possibilities are beyond the scope of this book. The following sections cover the basic procedures for creating linked and embedded objects.

> **TIP:** The steps described in the following sections explain how to create linked and embedded objects based on Project data. Keep in mind that you can do the reverse—link and embed information from other applications in Project files.

Creating a Linked Object

When you link information from a view, the linked object looks like a picture in the container document. Thus, the linked object can include Gantt bars and timescale information.

To link information from Project to a document in a container application, follow these steps:

1. Select the information that you want to place in another document. The information can be from a Task Sheet, a Resource Sheet, or even a PERT chart.

2. Open the Edit menu and click Copy. Alternatively, do any of the following: right-click the selection and then click Copy on the shortcut menu; press Ctrl+C; or click the Copy button on the Standard toolbar. Project copies the information to the Windows Clipboard.

3. Open or switch to the document into which you want to paste the linked Project object.

4. Position the insertion point where you want the linked object to appear.

5. Open the Edit menu and click Paste Special. The Paste Special dialog box appears (see Fig. 15.16).

6. Click the Paste Link option.

Figure 15.16
The Paste Special
Dialog box lists the
object types that can be
applied to the object in
the Windows Clipboard.

This option creates a —
linked object

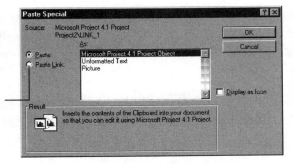

7. Notice that the Microsoft Project 4.1 Project Object type is selected in the As list box by default. You also can select the Picture object type in the As list box if you want to paste the object as a bitmap graphic. The bitmap object will still be linked to the Project document.

8. Click OK. The Project information appears in the destination document, as shown in Figure 15.17.

Figure 15.17
Linked Project
information looks like
this in a Word
document.

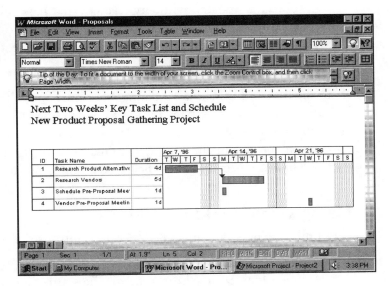

Managing a Link's Update Setting

By design, a linked object is updated each time the object's source document is changed or updated. By using the Links command, you can specify when the changes in the source document are reflected in the linked object. You have two choices of link-update timing. You can update the linked object automatically each time the source document changes, or you can update the object manually by making menu and dialog-box choices.

To select a link's update setting, follow these steps:

1. Open the document that contains the linked OLE object.
2. Click the linked object to select it.
3. Open the Edit menu and click Links. The Links dialog box appears, displaying a list of linked objects in the document.

    The dialog box lists the link name and the path name of the source document, and indicates whether the link is set to update automatically or manually. Also, the name of the object that you selected in step 2 is highlighted.
4. Click to select the Manual option button at the bottom of the dialog box.
5. Update the link by clicking the Update Now button. The object is updated with any changes that have taken place in the object's source document.
6. Click OK. The Links dialog box closes, and the link is set for manual updating.

With the link set for manual updating, you must open the Links dialog box and click the Update Now button to update the object with the latest changes in the source document. In some cases, depending on the application and document holding the linked information, you can right-click the linked object and then click Update Link on the shortcut menu.

Using Other Linking Options

The Links dialog box contains a few other buttons that enable you to manage the links to objects in your documents:

- The Open Source button opens the source document of the currently selected link. With the source document open, you can make changes in the source object, investigate surrounding information, or just refresh your memory as to the name and location of the source file.

TIP: You can open any OLE object's source application
quickly by double-clicking the object.

- The Change Source button displays the Change Source dialog box, which enables you to select a new file as the source document for the linked object.
- The Break Link button removes the link information to the selected object. If you click this button, a dialog box appears, asking whether you are sure that you want to break the link to the selected object. If you are sure, click OK; otherwise, click Cancel. After you break a link, you must perform a cut-and-paste operation to reestablish the linked object.

Creating Embedded Objects

The process of creating an embedded Project object is similar the process of creating a linked object, but the connection between the source document and the destination document is different. The information in the embedded object does not depend on the source document—that is, you can make changes in the embedded object that don't show up in the source document.

NOTE: Unlike the situation with a linked object, when you embed an object, Project copies all the tasks or resources in the selected Task Sheet or Resource Sheet. This means that after you open the Edit menu and click Paste Special to place the embedded information in the container document, click the object and then drag the black resizing handles to control how much of the information appears.

To create an embedded Project object, follow these steps:

1. Select the Task Sheet or Resource Sheet that you want to use to create the embedded object.

2. Open the Edit menu and click Copy. Alternatively, do any of the following: right-click the selection and then click Copy on the shortcut menu; press Ctrl+C; or click the Copy button on the Standard toolbar.

3. Open or switch to the destination document.

4. Position the insertion point where you want the embedded object to appear.

5. Open the Edit menu and click Paste Special. The Paste Special dialog box appears (refer to Figure 15.16), listing the available paste options.

   The default Paste Special options are set up to create an embedded object. The Paste option should be selected, and the object type Microsoft Project 4.1 Object should be highlighted. Notice that the Results area of the dialog box indicates that the selected settings allow you to use Microsoft Project 4.1 to edit the object.

6. Click OK to paste the object. The object appears at the insertion-point location.

CAUTION: You cannot create an embedded object from an image that you copied by using the Copy Picture button on the Project toolbar. The Copy Picture button creates a bitmap image of the selected area; it does not maintain the information that is necessary for embedding.

Editing an embedded object is a simple, straightforward process—and one in which the primary advantage of embedding comes into play, because you do not have to recall the name and location of the source document that created the object. You simply double-click the object, and the source application (Project) starts, enabling you to edit the object.

When you finish making changes in the object, open the File menu and click Update. The source application closes, and you return to the container document. (In some applications, you may have to open the File menu and click Exit to close the source application.)

Importing Other Project-Management Files

Project enables you to work with information stored in a variety of file formats. If you need to bring in information from an application that saves information in tabular format (such as a spreadsheet or database program), you can import that information rather than copy it. Table 15.1 lists some of the file formats that you may be able to import.

Table 15.1	The Most Common File Types That Project Can Read
Application	**File Format**
Microsoft Project	MPP, MPX, MPT
Microsoft Excel	XLS
Microsoft FoxPro	DBF
Plain text (ASCII)	TXT
Comma-separated values	CSV
dBASE III and IV	DBF
Lotus 1-2-3	WKS, WK1, WK3

TIP: If your database program isn't listed in Table 15.1 (Microsoft Access is notably absent), see whether the program allows you to use its Save As command to save files in one of the listed formats.

The procedure for importing a file is similar to the procedure for opening a file that you learned in Chapter 1, "Getting Started with Project." Follow these steps:

1. Open the File menu and click Open; press Ctrl+O; or click the Open button on the Standard toolbar. The File Open dialog box appears.

> **NOTE:** Microsoft offers the Microsoft Project Converter program, which converts files from several other project-management programs to the MPX format, which Project can use. Project Converter converts files from Symantec Timeline 5.0 for MS-DOS, Symantec Timeline 1.0 for Windows, ABT Project Workbench 1.x for Windows, ABT Project Workbench 3.0 for MS-DOS, and CA-SuperProject 3.0 for Windows formats. If you're working with a vendor or other resource that can report project information to you in one of these formats, you should obtain the Project Converter. You can buy the program directly from Microsoft by calling (206) 635-7155, or you can download it from the Microsoft Project forum on the Microsoft Network, if you belong to that online service.

2. In the Look In drop-down list, select the drive where the file that you want to import is stored.

> **TIP:** Select `Network Neighborhood` in the Look In drop-down list if the file is on a drive that is connected to another network.

3. Double-click a folder to display the contents of that folder. (You may need to double-click subfolder icons to display the file that you want to open.)

4. In the Files of Type drop-down list (see Fig. 15.18), select the format for the file that you want to import.

5. When the file that you want to open appears in the list, double-click its name, or click it and then click Open to load the file into Project. The Import dialog box appears, as shown in Figure 15.19.

6. In the Read area of the dialog box, select Tasks (if you want Project to treat the imported information as Task Sheet information) or Resources (if you want Project to treat the imported information as Resource Sheet information).

Figure 15.18
Select the type of file to import.

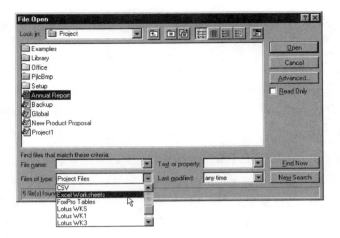

Figure 15.19
Tell Project how to treat the information that you're importing.

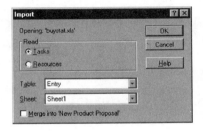

7. In the Table drop-down list, specify what kind of sheet table (and what column headings) will be used for the imported information.

8. If you're importing a multi-part document, such as a worksheet file that contains numerous sheets, use the Sheet drop-down list to select the information to import.

9. Select the Merge into Filename check box if you want the imported information to be added to a currently open file rather than a new file.

10. Click OK to finish the import operation.

If necessary, Project adds default information for columns that are not filled in by the imported information, such as the Duration column.

Exporting Project Files

The flip side of importing is exporting. When you export information from a Project file, you save it in a format that another application can use. The formats to which you can export generally are the same as the import formats listed in Table 15.1 earlier in this chapter.

An export operation resembles a Save As operation. Follow these steps:

1. Open the File menu and click Save As. The Save dialog box appears.

2. Navigate to the drive and folder where you want to save the file, using the Save In drop-down list and the folders that appear below it. (Double-click a folder icon to open that folder so you can store the file there.)

3. In the File Name text box, type the name you want to give the file.

4. Use the Save as Type drop-down list to specify the file format to export to.

5. Click the Save button. The Export dialog box appears (see Fig. 15.20).

Figure 15.20
You can save Project information in a different format.

6. In the Write area, specify whether you want to export All Tasks, Filtered Tasks only, or All Resources (not tasks).

7. Use the Table drop-down list to specify what table format to use for this export. This setting specifies which columns of information appear in the exported file.

8. Click OK. Project exports the file, saving it with the name and format you've specified.

Sharing Project Data with Microsoft Access and Other Databases

Project comes with a Database Utility that enables it to share information with database programs that are *ODBC-compliant*, meaning that those databases can communicate in a particular way. Not every *ODBC driver* (the software that lets a database or other program communicate via ODBC) works with the Database Utility, but the Microsoft Access 7.0 and Microsoft SQL drivers definitely do. This means that you can save Project data in an Access 7.0 database (or a database from any other ODBC-compliant database application which you discover works), or use information from an Access database in Project.

The Database Utility doesn't install with the typical Project installation. You can tell whether or not it's installed by clicking Tools, clicking Multiple Projects, then clicking Open From Database or Save To Database. If either of these commands doesn't work, then you need to install the Database Utility. To do so, follow these general steps:

1. Rerun the Project Setup program by double-clicking the MS Project Setup icon in the Project folder on your hard disk.

2. When Setup prompts you, insert Setup Disk 1 or the Setup CD-ROM for Project, and click OK or press Enter to continue.

3. When Setup prompts you, verify the folder where Project is stored, and click OK to continue.

4. In the Setup dialog box that asks you to specify what kind of installation to perform, click Custom.

5. The next Setup dialog box lists different features to install. Make sure that a checkmark appears beside Tools (click it if no checkmark appears), then click Change Option.

6. Click to place a checkmark beside Database Utility in the Setup dialog box that appears, then click OK.

7. Click Continue, then follow the on-screen prompts to swap disks and finish updating your setup.

After you install the Database Utility, Project information can be saved as a database. Also, database information can be used with Project. You might want to display the Workgroup toolbar by right-clicking any toolbar and then selecting Workgroup. This toolbar offers the Save To Database and Open From Database buttons, which are equivalent to the corresponding commands in the Multiple Projects submenu of the Tools menu.

> **NOTE:** Only text or numerical information from the project is stored in the database, such as task names, start and finish dates, resource names, and resource assignments. No formatting or graphical information is stored.

Saving Project data as an Access database requires two general operations. First, you have to create the database file if it doesn't already exist. Next, you save the Project data in the database. Use the following steps to accomplish both operations:

1. Create and save your schedule information in Project.

2. Click to open the Tools menu, point to Multiple Projects to display its submenu, and click Save To Database. Alternatively, you can click the Save To Database button on the Workgroup toolbar.

3. Project might ask you to enter a title for the project (see Fig. 15.21), if you haven't already specified one as part of the properties for the Project file. Enter the title you want in this text box, then click OK to continue.

4. In the SQL Data Sources dialog box, click the New button.

5. In the Add Data Source dialog box that appears, click Microsoft Access Driver (*.mdb) and click OK. The Database Utility displays the ODBC Microsoft Access 7.0 Setup dialog box shown in Figure 15.22.

6. Type a Data Source Name entry (this assigns a name to the data source you're creating to hold the database file), then click the Create button. The New Database dialog box appears (see Fig. 15.23).

Figure 15.21
Project prompts you to
provide a title for the
database.

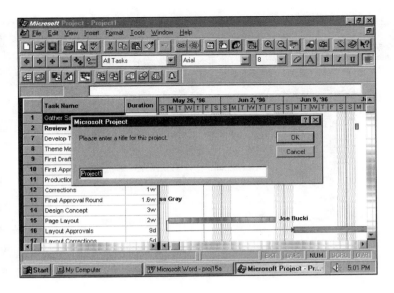

Figure 15.22
This dialog box enables
you to create an Access
database to save to.

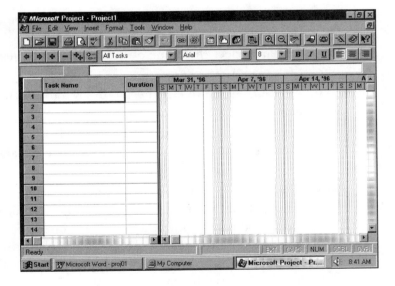

7. Type a name for the database file in the Database Name text box. If necessary, use the Directories and Drives lists to specify a different location for saving the database file. Click OK.

8. When a message box informs you that the database file has been created, click OK again.

Figure 15.23
Assign a name for
your Access
database file.

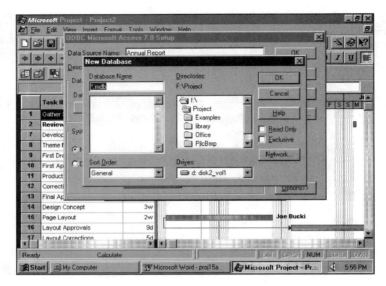

9. In the ODBC Microsoft Access 7.0 Setup dialog box, click the Select button. In the Select Database dialog box that appears, select the name of the database you just created, then click OK.

10. Click OK again to exit the ODBC Microsoft Access 7.0 Setup dialog box.

11. In the SQL Data Sources dialog box, click the name of the data source you just created from the Select Data Source list, then click OK.

12. The Database Utility displays a message asking whether you want to build the needed tables for your data in the database file. Click Yes to continue. A message box appears on-screen to keep you informed as information is saved to the database file. When this message box disappears, the Database Utility has finished saving your new database file.

After information from a schedule has been saved as an Access database, you need to open it from the database file to use it again in Project. Follow these steps to retrieve the information from the Access file:

1. Open the Tools menu, point to Multiple Projects to display its submenu, and click Open From Database. Alternatively, click the Open From Database button on the Workgroup toolbar.

2. In the Select Data Source list in the SQL Data Sources dialog box, click the name of the data source you created when you saved the file. Click OK.

3. In the Open from Database dialog box, click the title you assigned to the project data (in step 3 of the previous set of steps) in the Existing Projects list.

4. Click OK. The Database Utility opens the information from the Access database file.

CHAPTER 16

WORKING WITH TEMPLATES

Clothing makers a century or two ago had to have strong powers of visualization. Unless one had an old garment to take apart and copy the pieces from, he or she had to envision how each piece of fabric should be shaped to come together into a garment that looked like a fashionable piece of apparel rather than a misshapen clown suit.

Then, some genius determined that you could make a prototype for a garment out of cheap muslin and the muslin pieces could be copied as a paper pattern to use when cutting fabric for duplicates of the garment.

The pattern does the grunt work, freeing the user to focus on improvements and fine-tuning—and that's exactly what a *template* file does for you in Microsoft Project. You'll learn in this chapter how to put a template to use, including the following specific topics:

- ■ **Formatting Documents Automatically**
- ■ **Organizing Your Thoughts**
- ■ **Writing Efficiently with the Help of Shortcut Keys**
- ■ **Making Spell Checking Painless**
- ■ **Finding Just the Right Word**
- ■ **Checking Your Grammar**

Why Templates Can Save Time

When you save a file in Project, it's saved by default as a regular Project or schedule file, and includes all the task and resource information you've entered. When you open the file, it opens the one and only copy of that file, and when you save the file, it save changes to that file.

Under this scenario, it's not necessarily convenient to reuse all the information stored in your Project file. If you have a similar project and want to save the trouble of reentering all the information, you'll have to do some careful saving (and saving as) to reuse the information you want without overwriting the original file.

A better way to make your basic task and resource information available for reuse is to save that information as a *template file*. The template file is like a pattern of project tasks and resources that you can use as many times as you want. Using a template saves you the trouble of entering similar task and resource information over and over.

The template file sets up your basic task and resource information for you, then you can edit it to fine-tune it for the unique requirements of your current project. Before I launch into describing the templates Project provides and how to work with them, here are just a few situations where you might want to create a template:

- You have a project, such as a newsletter or publication, that recurs on a regular basis.

- You have a schedule file into which you've entered a tremendous amount of task or resource information, and you think you might have other projects that are similar.

- You want to create an example file of how numerous links work, so you don't have to create the links again.

- Members of your company's sales force need a basic tool for plotting out schedules for customers, and you want to provide a schedule blueprint with typical task durations.

- You're training others to manage a particular type of project in your company, and you want to provide a framework to help them with planning and to ensure that they don't miss any steps.

Using a Template

When you install the typical Project features, the Setup process copies a number of predesigned templates to your system. While you can create your own templates (as you'll learn later in this chapter), and the process for using one of your own templates is the same as the process for using a template provided with Project, it's worth reviewing the templates that come with Project in the hopes that some will be useful to you. Table 16.1 lists the templates that ship with Project.

Table 16-1. Custom Templates Installed with Project	
Template files	**Description**
Audit	Provides a basic plan for performing a financial audit of a business
Eventpln	Maps out a plan for setting up a special event
Iso9000	Provides a plan for implementing ISO9000 quality standards and management in a company
Isoaudit	Sketches out the steps for performing an internal audit of compliance with ISO9000 quality standards
Laninst	Identifies the basic steps for installing a company local area network (LAN); initially appears in PERT Chart view, and offers Cue Cards to help you get started
Lansub	Can be a subproject of installing a LAN; covers the phase of analyzing needs, planning implementation, seeking approval, and announcing the project
Mktplan	Provides a plan for a full-scale marketing/advertising campaign, including research
Pert	Provides a variety of custom tables for you to compare an optimistic schedule with a pessimistic schedule, and so on
Rollout	Suggests a schedule for testing, selecting, and rolling out a new piece of software in your company
Rollup	Offers a special table, the Rollup table, and the Milestone Date Rollup and Milestone Rollup custom views
Softdev	Maps out the process of developing new software, and provides custom reports

Project and Windows identify template files with an MPT filename extension (which normally is hidden) instead of the MPP extension used for normal Project schedule files. Because the template files are identified differently "behind the scenes," opening a template file is slightly different from opening a regular Project file.

To open a template file—one that you've created or one that comes with Project—use these steps:

1. Open the File menu and click Open (or press Ctrl+O). Alternatively, click the Open button on the Standard toolbar (it's second from the left and has an open file folder). The File Open dialog box appears.

2. Click to open the Files of type drop-down list, then click Template, as shown in Figure 16.1. After you make this selection, the Look in list in the dialog box adjusts to list only folders and template files.

Figure 16.1
In the File Open dialog box, specify that you want to look for template files.

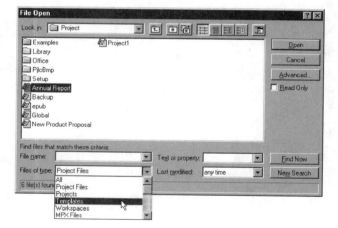

3. Use the Look in drop-down list and the folder icons to navigate to the folder that holds the template you want to use. To access the templates that come with Project, double-click the Library subfolder within the Project folder (refer to Fig. 16.1) to display the templates shown in Figure 16.2.

4. In the Look in list, double-click the name of the template file you want to open, or click the filename once and then click

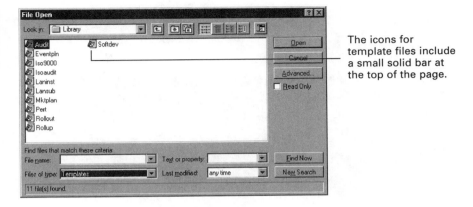

Figure 16.2
The File Open dialog box lists the templates stored in the selected folder.

The icons for template files include a small solid bar at the top of the page.

the Open button. The template opens on-screen. Figure 16.3 shows an example of how one of Project's templates, the Mktplan template, appears when it's opened.

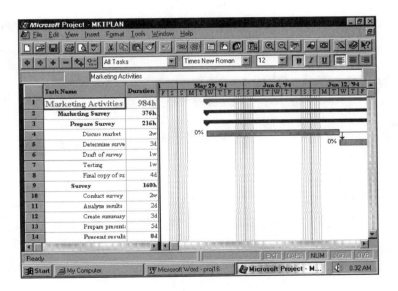

Figure 16.3
Project's Mktplan template is open on-screen.

5. Before you make any changes, I recommend immediately saving the template as a Project file. By default, when you try to save a template file, Project assumes you want to save a *copy* of the template file as a regular Project file. To start the save, open the File menu and click Save (or press Ctrl+S). Alternatively, click the Save button on the Standard toolbar.

PlanningWizard, if enabled, asks whether or not you want to save the file with a baseline (see Fig. 16.4).

Figure 16.4
You can save a baseline if you want, but it won't be valid because you haven't entered any real schedule information.

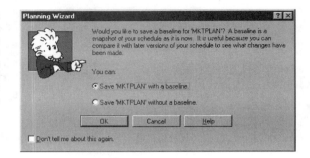

6. I recommend saving the plan without a baseline, because you haven't yet entered your real schedule information. Click to select the Save "MKTPLAN" without a baseline option button, then click OK. The File Save dialog box appears, as shown in Figure 16.5.

Figure 16.5
When you save a template, you're really saving a copy of it as a new schedule file, so the original template remains intact. This enables you to use the basic template again and again.

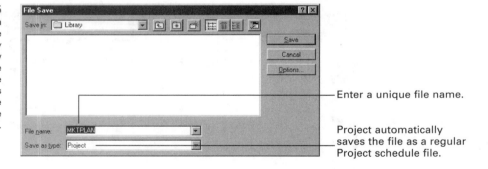

Enter a unique file name.

Project automatically saves the file as a regular Project schedule file.

7. (Optional) Navigate to a different folder in which you want to save the file.

8. If you want, edit the suggested File name to save the file with a name that's different from the template name—usually one that's more descriptive of your project. For example, you might include the name of the product you're marketing in the file name for your copy of the MKTPLAN template, as in **Super Software Mkt Plan**.

9. Click Save to finish saving your file.

After you've opened the template you want, and have saved a copy of it as a regular file, you can begin editing it to include your actual schedule information. The types of edits you need to make—and the available bells and whistles—vary, depending on the contents of the template. For example, the Mktplan template (refer to Fig. 16.3) provides a suggested list of tasks and a suggested duration for each task, so all you need to do is to enter correct start dates for tasks in the Task Sheet. In the Mktplan template, the text and Gantt bars are already attractively formatted and color-coded (for example, milestones are in green) to make them easy to tell apart. Other templates might include special tables and views you can apply, or other kinds of formatting. Simply make the edits and formatting changes you want, saving and printing when needed. After you've saved your copy of the template, it behaves completely like other Project files do.

Creating a Template

Because a template works like a pattern, it can consist of just a few pieces, or as many pieces as are needed to create the final product. Thus, a Project planning template can include numerous pattern pieces (types of information) that anyone opening the template can make use of. Any template you create can include these kinds of information and tools, among others:

- Lists of tasks in the Task Sheet, including suggested durations and links
- Lists of resources in the Resource Sheet; for example, if a particular project always requires a resource like a shipping company that charges a per use and hourly rate, include information about that resource (especially its costs) with the template
- Text formatting applied in the Task Sheet or Resource Sheet, including formatting applied to individual cells as well as Text Style changes for categories of information
- Formatting applied to chart elements like Gantt bars
- Custom views, tables, reports, and filters that you've created
- Macros and custom toolbars or toolbar buttons (see Chapter 21 for more information about macros)

To build your own template, start by opening a new file and creating all the elements you want the template to include, such as the types of elements just listed. Or, if you want to use a project file you've previously created as a template, open that file. For example, if you've created a New Product Proposal schedule that has worked well for you, such as the one shown in Figure 16.6, you can save it as a template.

Figure 16.6
This project schedule file worked well, so I'll save it as a template to reuse it.

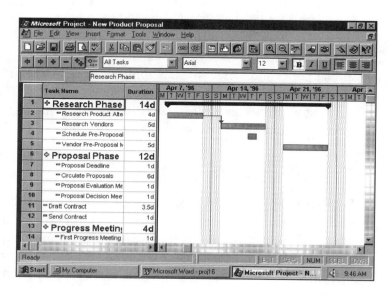

> **TIP:** Make sure that you include as much file Properties information and as many Task Notes and Resource Notes with your template as possible. This information will remind you and other users how to correctly use the template and will help you recall what particular entries mean.

Next, follow these steps to save your creation as a template:

1. Open the File menu and click Save As. The File Save dialog box appears.

2. Navigate to the folder where you want to store the template file. If you want to store your custom template along with Project's template, select the \Project\Library folder.

3. Click to open the Files of type drop-down list, then click Template.

4. Edit the File <u>n</u>ame entry to make it easy to see that the file is a template, as shown in Figure 16.7.

Figure 16.7
Edit the File <u>n</u>ame entry
to clarify that the file's a
template.

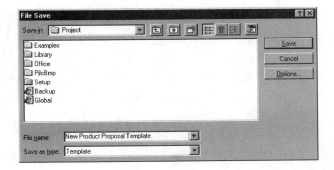

5. Click the <u>S</u>ave button. Project warns you, as shown in Figure 16.8, that any linked or embedded OLE objects in the file (see Chapter 15 to learn more about OLE) will not be saved with the file. Click <u>Y</u>es to finish saving the template. The title bar for the file changes to indicate that the currently opened file is a template file.

Figure 16.8
Project warns you that
OLE objects won't be
saved with the file.

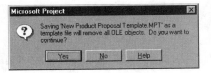

6. Open the <u>F</u>ile menu and click <u>C</u>lose. This removes the template file from the screen. At any time, you can reopen the template file and save a copy of it as described in the previous section to begin working with the copy.

Sometimes you might want to make changes to one of your custom template files, or one that came with Project. Say, for example, that you've got a template file in which you've included resource information, and you discover that the standard hourly rates and overtime rates for several of the resources have increased. You can open the template file, edit the template, and resave it as a template file. Here are the steps:

1. Open the template file, as described in steps 1 through 4 of the earlier section, "Using a Template."

2. Make any changes you want to make in the template.

3. Open the File menu and click Save As.

4. In the File Save dialog box, select Template from the Save as type drop-down list. Leave all other settings intact to ensure that your changes are saved within the same template file.

5. Click Save. Project asks you to confirm that you want to overwrite the existing template file, as shown in Figure 16.9.

Figure 16.9
Project asks you to confirm that you want to change the template file.

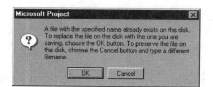

6. Click OK to finish saving the template. You then should open the File menu and click Close to close the template file. If you want to use it immediately to create a schedule, reopen it and save a copy.

Finding and Using TemplateWizard

The Typical Setup (installation) process for Project installs a separate program named TemplateWizard. TemplateWizard is a tool that you can use, when needed, to walk through the various entries needed to create a schedule file based on a template. What TemplateWizard does is to ask you whether you want to include each of the various task and resource entries from the template in the schedule you're creating based on the template. Eventually, TemplateWizard builds a Project schedule file (not a template file) for you, so you can save it and work in it as needed.

Project doesn't provide an easy way to access TemplateWizard. You have to do a bit of work to make it available in general, but there is a trick you can use to make it available with particular templates.

> **NOTE:** TemplateWizard is a rather large, complex program that can take some time to load, especially on older systems with limited RAM. You might want to use TemplateWizard only the first time or two you use a template, or might only want to start it automatically in those templates that will be used by inexperienced Project users.

Creating a Button to Run TemplateWizard

The TemplateWizard application icon (Tmpltwiz) is included in the same folder where Project is installed on your system (see Fig. 16.10). In theory, you can start Project, then launch TemplateWizard from the Project folder by double-clicking its icon. While this works, it's less than convenient.

Figure 16.10
TemplateWizard has a program icon in the Project folder.

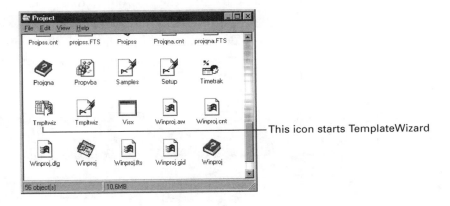

This icon starts TemplateWizard

A better solution is to create a toolbar and button for the TemplateWizard application. While you can create a TemplateWizard button on an existing toolbar, it makes more sense to put it on its own toolbar, so that you can easily include that toolbar with only certain template files. Here are the steps for adding a TemplateWizard toolbar and button in Project:

1. Open the <u>V</u>iew menu or right-click a toolbar to display its shortcut menu, then click <u>T</u>oolbars. The Toolbars dialog box appears, as shown in Figure 16.11.

2. Click the <u>N</u>ew button. In the New Toolbar dialog box that appears, type a <u>N</u>ame for the toolbar, such as **TemplateWizard**, then click OK. The Customize dialog box appears, along with a new, blank toolbar.

3. The Customize dialog box offers categories of buttons that you can add to a toolbar. There's a better way, however, so click Close to close the Customize dialog box.

4. Move the mouse pointer to the blank area on your new toolbar. Hold down the Ctrl key and click the blank area. A blank button appears on your toolbar, and the Customize Tool dialog box appears (see Fig. 16.12).

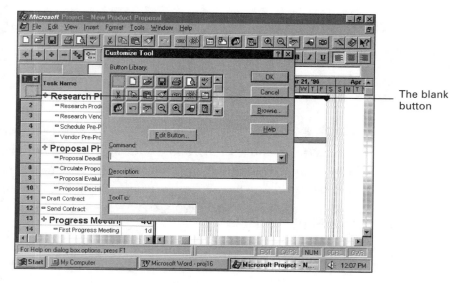

The blank
button

5. Select the actual button to use by clicking it in the scrolling Button Library at the top of the dialog box.

6. In the Command text box, type

AppExecute Command:="c:\project\tmpltwiz.exe"

where c:\project\ represents the actual drive and folder on your computer's hard disk where Project is installed. You must correctly capitalize and punctuate the full command line.

> **NOTE:** If you installed Project with other Microsoft Office applications, your Project folder might be something like c:\office95\project.

7. Drag to highlight the Description text box entry, then type a unique entry, such as **Launches the TemplateWizard**. The Description will appear in the status bar whenever you point to the new button.

8. Click the ToolTip text box and make an entry, such as **TemplateWiz**. The ToolTip will appear whenever you place the mouse pointer over the new button. At this point, the Customize Tool dialog box should resemble Figure 16.13.

Figure 16.13
Just hold down Ctrl and click to add a button to the toolbar.

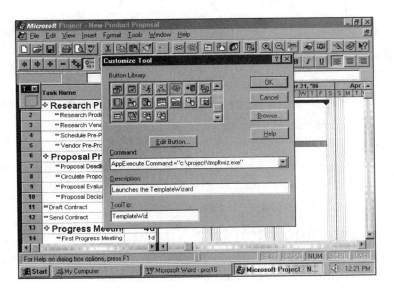

9. Click OK to finish the button. It appears in your custom toolbar.

The custom toolbar that you've created is stored in the Global.mpt template that stores your Project settings. You can display and use it with any template file; however, if you'll be using the template file on a different computer system or e-mailing it to another user, you'll need to save the toolbar with the template file. Use the following steps:

1. Open the template file to which you want to add the custom toolbar.

2. Open the View menu (or right-click your toolbar to display its shortcut menu), then click Toolbars. The Toolbars dialog box appears.

3. Click the Organizer button. The Organizer dialog box appears, with the Toolbars tab selected.

4. In the list at the left, which shows the toolbars stored in the Global.mpt file, click the name of your custom TemplateWizard toolbar, as shown in Figure 16.14.

Figure 16.14
In the Organizer, copy your custom toolbar to the template file.

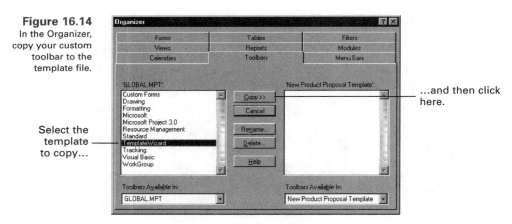

5. Click the Close button to close the Organizer, then click Close again to exit the Toolbars dialog box.

Running TemplateWizard

To use Template Wizard, first open the template you want to use with TemplateWizard. Then click the TemplateWiz button on your custom toolbar. TemplateWizard begins loading, which might take a few minutes. When it's finished loading, it appears as shown in Figure 16.15.

NOTE: TemplateWizard won't work unless there's at least one task in the current project.

Figure 16.15
TemplateWizard takes a
little while to load.

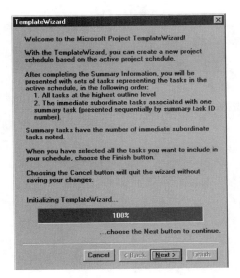

Click the <u>N</u>ext button to ask TemplateWizard to begin walking you through the template entries. TemplateWizard first gives you the opportunity to enter summary (Properties) information about the schedule file it's creating for you (see Fig. 16.16). Enter the information you want to use to identify the file, then click <u>N</u>ext.

The next step of TemplateWizard, which resembles Figure 16.17, enables you to begin selecting which information will appear in the schedule file that TemplateWizard builds. By default, all entries are selected. To remove one, click OK to clear the check box beside it. When you've finished reviewing and selecting certain entries for the current TemplateWizard step, click <u>N</u>ext. Another group of entries appears with the next step. Continue making your entries and clicking <u>N</u>ext. After you've worked through all the available entries, click the Create Schedule button, and TemplateWizard builds a new project file that includes all the template information you specified.

Figure 16.16
You can enter summary informatio nfor the schedule file.

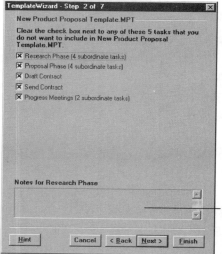

Here's how many steps TemplateWizard will lead you through.

Figure 16.17
TemplateWizard enables you to select which template information is included in your new schedule file.

If the template offers a note about the particular task or resource selection, it appears here.

CAUTION: Project must be running for TemplateWizard to work. Even though TemplateWizard is a separate program and provides a great deal of automation, it's not capable of launching the main Project application and opening a template.

CHAPTER 17

CONSOLIDATING PROJECTS

Once you become a Microsoft Project guru (I know you will with this book in hand), you'll use it to manage more forms of work than you could have imagined. You can have two, three, or more schedules running simultaneously. In such a situation, the challenge for you as the project leader becomes to understand and prioritize work *between projects,* as well as to understand and prioritize work between tasks in a project.

This chapter shows you how to better manage all the work on your plate by consolidating information from multiple project files. In particular, you'll discover the following:

- What it means to consolidate projects, and situations where consolidation might be helpful

- How to consolidate projects

- Using the consolidated information

- Sharing resources between projects that aren't consolidated

When to Combine Projects

If you need a single printout of the tasks from two projects, you can print them out separately, trim the excess, tape the two together, and make a photocopy so that you have a single, solid document. This solution, however, is clearly inelegant and forces you to do the dirty work rather than having your computer do it.

Project offers a workaround for situations like this; it's called *consolidating projects*. When you consolidate two or more schedule files, Project places all the information from each of the selected files into a single, consolidated file. Then you can change the view, print, and otherwise work with the combined information.

Here are just a few situations in which you might want to consolidate projects into a single file:

- You're managing multiple projects, and you want a list of in-progress tasks to jog your memory about tasks that you need to follow up on. You consolidate the tasks, then filter the Task Sheet so that it lists only the in-progress tasks.

- You'd like to display a list of all the tasks in your projects that will start in the near future. You can print them before a meeting with your boss, so the two of you can discuss shifting priorities and identify some tasks to reschedule.

- You want to print a list of all the resources you're using for all projects.

- You have two projects using the same resources, and you want to see if there are any resource overallocations. You can consolidate the files and switch to Resource Usage view to find overallocations.

Combining Projects

Consolidating schedule files places all the information from the specified individual files into a new file that is the *consolidated file*. By default, the consolidated file has a name beginning with "Multi" and a number. The first consolidation file you create during a Project work session is named Multi1, the second is named Multi2, and so on. You can save a consolidated file in order to reuse the information it contains. When you save it, you can assign it a unique name of your choosing. The rest of this section explains the details of creating and working with a consolidated file.

Consolidation Methods

Consolidated files can work in two different ways. The consolidated file can exist completely independent of the files from which its information came. This situation is fine if you want to work with the consolidated file on a one-time basis only. If, however, you want to reuse the consolidated file over a period of days, weeks, or longer, the schedules for the individual, original project files might change, making the consolidated file obsolete—unless you link it to the original files when you create it.

No matter how you prefer your consolidated file to work, the steps for creating a consolidated file are similar. To create a consolidated file, do the following:

1. If needed, update schedule information and save any of the files that will make up the consolidated file. It's not necessary, however, to have the files open to consolidate them.

2. Open the Tools menu, point to Multiple Projects to display the submenu, and click Consolidate Projects. The Consolidate Projects dialog box appears (see Fig. 17.1).

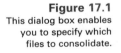

Figure 17.1
This dialog box enables you to specify which files to consolidate.

3. With the first cell in the <u>F</u>ile Name column selected, click the <u>B</u>rowse button. The Browse dialog box appears, enabling you to select a file that you want included in the consolidated file. Navigate to the folder containing the files you want to consolidate. If you'd like to consolidate multiple files in that folder, select all of them by clicking the first one, then pressing and holding the Ctrl key as you click additional ones (see Fig. 17.2). Click the Add Files button to add the selected files to the list in the Consolidate Files dialog box.

NOTE: If you know the full drive, folder, and filename for a file you want to consolidate, you can type this full path in a <u>F</u>ile Name cell. Using the <u>B</u>rowse button, however, saves you the trouble of remembering the path information, and also prevents the possibility of typos.

Figure 17.2
You can browse to specify the files you want to consolidate.

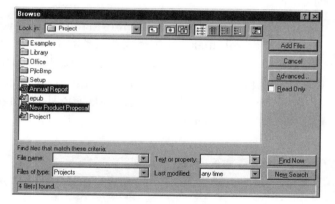

4. By default, Project enters Read-Write in the Open File column for each <u>F</u>ile Name in your list. This means that you'll be able to make changes to the information in your consolidated file. If you want to prevent editing of the consolidated information (especially if the consolidated file will be linked to the source file, and you don't want to inadvertently change the source file), click the Open File cell beside the name, click the drop-down list arrow beside the text entry box, and click to select Read-Only.

5. Repeat steps 3 and 4 to add the names of any additional files to consolidate.

NOTE: The order in which you enter source projects in the Consolidate Projects dialog box controls the order in which the project information appears in the consolidated file. If you want the files to appear in a particular order, you must add them to the list in the Consolidate Projects dialog box in that order.

6. In the Options area, make sure that a checkmark appears beside the <u>A</u>ttach to Source Projects option if you want to link the consolidated file with the original (source) files you're con- solidating. Then, any information you change in the consoli- dated file also changes in the source file, and vice versa. This means that you can use the consolidated file over and over, and the information it contains will remain up-to-date. Conversely, if you're using the consolidated file to relieve resource overallo- cations between projects, then working in a linked consolidated file saves you the trouble of making changes to multiple files.

7. If some of the consolidated projects use some of the same resources, you can select the Combine <u>R</u>esource Pools check box to have Project "merge" the resource lists into a single list. This way, if a resource is used by two projects, it's listed only once in the consolidated project, and the scheduled work from the two projects gets added together. You must select this option to see if a given resource is overallocated across projects.

8. If you want the consolidated file to appear with the names of the consolidated files as summary tasks, and with the individ- ual project tasks (subtasks) hidden, click to select the Hide <u>S</u>ubtasks option.

9. Click OK. Project consolidates the files, informing you briefly as it adds each individual file to the consolidated file. When Project finishes, the consolidated file appears on-screen, as shown in Figure 17.3.

10. Click the Save button on the Standard toolbar (or open the <u>F</u>ile menu and click <u>S</u>ave) to save the consolidated file. Depending on the options you selected when consolidating (linking, shared resources, and so on), Project might prompt

you to save changes to one or more of the consolidated files, as shown in Figure 17.4.

11. Unless you want to decide whether or not to save changes to individual source files (in which case you should click the Yes or No button for each file), click the Yes to All button to continue.

Figure 17.3
This is how a consolidated file appears on on-screen.

The name of a consolidated project; notice that it has no row number

The default name for the consolidated file

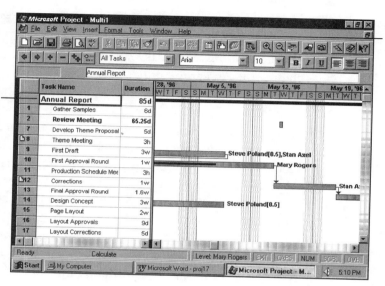

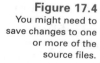

Figure 17.4
You might need to save changes to one or more of the source files.

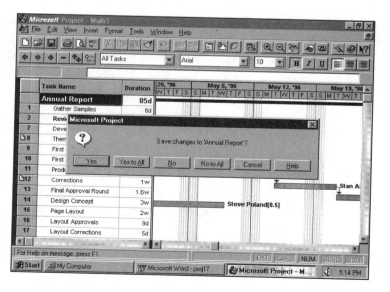

12. In the File Save dialog box that appears, specify the folder to which you want to save the consolidated file, then enter a unique File name such as **All Projects**, and click Save. Project saves the consolidated file. You can work in it, print it, or close it as needed.

There is a somewhat faster way to create a consolidated file, but as usual with such matters, you have to give up a little flexibility to save time. To use this method, begin by opening each of the files you want to consolidate. Make any changes you want to the files, and save them. Open the Window menu and click New Window. The New Window dialog box appears. In the Projects list, click the name of the first file to consolidate. Press and hold down the Ctrl key, then click to select the additional files (see Fig. 17.5). Click OK, and Project compiles the consolidated file on-screen. (By default, the consolidated file is linked to the original source files. In addition, the resource pools for the individual files are not consolidated.) You then can save and work with the consolidated file.

Figure 17.5
This is a quicker, but less flexible method to select files for consolidation.

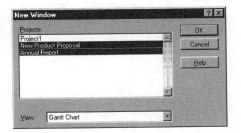

Working with Your Consolidated Information

When you're working with the consolidated file, you can do everything that you can do in an individual Project file. You can change any entries you want, or change the view. For example, open the View menu and click Resource Sheet to view the Resource Sheet for a consolidated project file. If you've combined the resource pools for the consolidated files, any resource overallocations are highlighted (see Fig. 17.6) in bold, red text. Also, if you have combined resource pools, you can open the View menu and click Resource Graph. When you display a resource that's assigned to more than one project, the overallocated hours for that resource are graphed (see Fig. 17.7).

Figure 17.6
Here's the Resource Sheet for a consolidated file with pooled resources.

Resources that are overallocated across projects

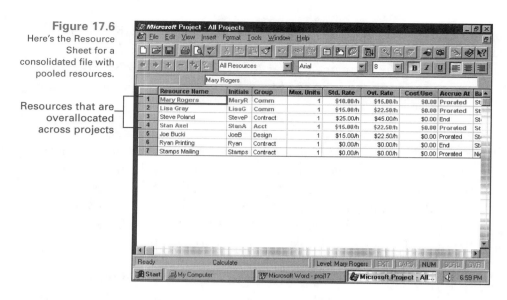

Figure 17.7
Here's the Resource Graph for a consolidated file with pooled resources.

Overallocations

Dividing line between work scheduled for different projects

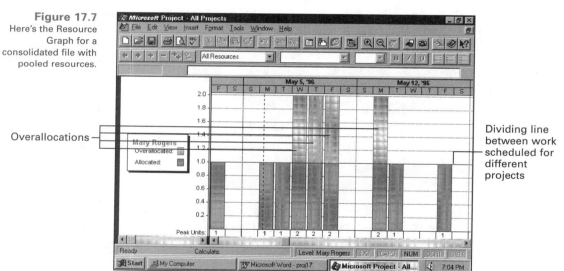

Another thing to note when you're working with the information in a consolidated file is that the name for each of the source project files you've consolidated appears as an unnumbered row in the Task Sheet of any view that includes the Task Sheet (such as Gantt Chart view). These rows are treated by Project as summary tasks at the highest level of the outline (see Chapter 13 to learn more about outlining). The top-level tasks from the source files appear as subtasks of the source files. All tasks that were subtasks within the original project files are hidden, and all individual project tasks holding subtasks appear in bold (see Fig. 17.8).

Figure 17.8
Project provides cues to help you identify which tasks came from which source files, and which tasks include subtasks.

Information from the next source file starts here.

These bold tasks were top-level tasks in the source file, and include subtasks.

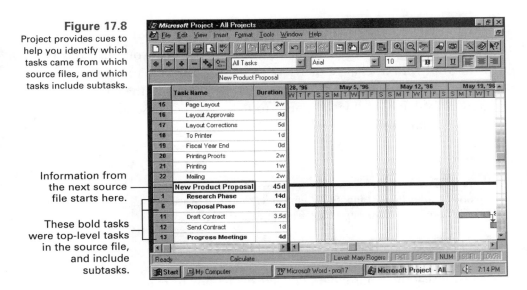

If you click the Task Name column and then click the Hide Subtasks button on the Formatting toolbar, the Task Sheet displays only the names of the consolidated files (see Fig. 17.9).

Figure 17.9
This file is a consolidation of two other files.

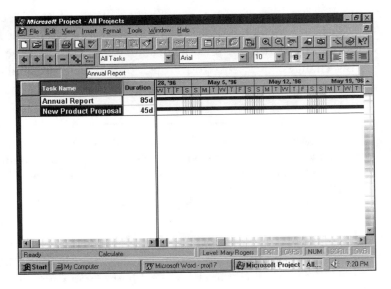

By now, you get the idea. The consolidated file behaves much like other project files in terms of how you can change its contents.

Adjusting the Consolidated File

At any time after you save and close a consolidate file, you can reopen it to work with it, change the view, and edit the information it contains. You eventually might want to remove a file from the consolidation, or add another file. You need to redisplay the consolidated file so that you can edit its contents.

NOTE: You open a consolidated file just as you open any regular Project file. See Chapter 1, "Getting Started with Project," if you need a refresher about opening files.

To redisplay the Consolidate Projects dialog box to make changes to the options specified for the consolidated file, first open the consolidated file. Open the Tools menu, point to Multiple Projects, and click Consolidate Projects. Project asks you to verify that you want to edit the open consolidated project rather than creating a new one; click Yes to proceed. The Consolidate Projects dialog box appears. In this dialog box, you can enter the name of a new file to add to the consolidation in a blank row. Or, you can click a row and use the Cut Row button to remove that file from the consolidation. When you've finished making changes, click OK, and Project updates the consolidated file. Make sure that you save the consolidated file following the changes.

TIP: When you save or close a consolidated file in which the individual files share resource pools, you might be prompted to save the resource pool as a separate file. Follow the prompts to do so.

If you close a consolidated file after making changes to it and saving it, Project might prompt you to save changes to the linked files (refer to Fig. 17.4), but also is likely to ask whether you want to update baseline information. You have the option of updating only tasks that presently lack baseline information, all tasks, or no tasks (see Fig. 17.10). Click the option you want, then click OK.

Figure 17.10
You might need to save
baseline information
when you close a
consolidated file.

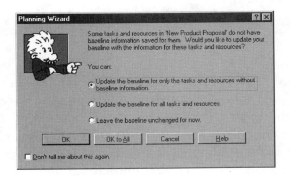

Working with Resource Pools

Another name for the list of resources you create in the Resource Sheet for a particular project is the *resource pool*. You can assign any of the resources in that pool to any task in the project file. Each list of resources is saved along with the project file where you created it. It's important to realize, though, that any Project file can access the resource pool that's saved with another file.

When you start a new project file and want to use the entries in the Resource Sheet saved with another file, rather than typing in a whole new list of resources, you can do so by *sharing resources*. Here are the steps, which assume that you've already created and saved the Project file containing the resources you want to reuse:

1. Open the file in which you've already created and saved the resource information that you want to reuse.

2. Open or create the file that will share the existing resource information.

3. Open the Tools menu, point to Multiple Projects to display the submenu, and click Share Resources. The Share Resources dialog box appears.

4. Click the Use Resources option button, then use the From drop-down list to select the file containing the resources you want to share (see Fig. 17.11).

Figure 17.11
Select the file
containing the
resource pool you
want to reuse.

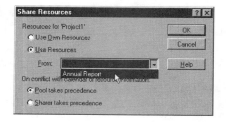

Figure 17.11
Select the file
containing the
resource pool you
want to reuse.

5. In the On conflict with calendar or resource information area, select Pool takes precedence (meaning that Project will adjust resource assignments in a way that makes sense for all the projects using the pool) or Sharer takes precedence (meaning that Project will adjust to accommodate any assignment change you make in a particular consolidated file).

6. Click OK to finish sharing the resources. The resource pool from the file you specified is now used for the current file. Save the current file to save the resource sharing information.

When you save and close a file that uses the resource information from another file, Project saves that "link." When you reopen the file containing the "link" to resource information, Project must open the other file, and informs you that it's doing so. If you've made changes to the Resource Sheet in the file you're sharing information from, those changes appear in the file that shares the information.

If you open a file that uses resource information from another file, you can edit the resource "link" information. To do so, redisplay the Share Resources dialog box by opening the Tools menu, pointing to Multiple Projects, and clicking Share Resources. In this dialog box, make the changes you prefer (such as selecting another file to use resources from, or opting not to use resources from another file at all), then click OK. Project closes the dialog box, and your resource sharing changes take effect. Make sure that you save the current file to save these changes.

NOTE: In practical terms, this means that you can create a project file that's strictly for listing resources. For example, if you use the same resources over and over, you can create a single file named Resources where you store every resource you use for every project. You then can specify that every other schedule file you create uses the resources stored in the Resources file.

CHAPTER 18

WORKING WITH MASTER PROJECTS AND SUBPROJECTS

Henry Ford is credited with having a revolutionary idea that became a classic business case study. Prior to Ford, product manufacturing was slow because most craftspeople put together an entire product (or most of it) without help from anyone else. Because each person spent so much time switching gears between different types of tasks, and perhaps was more skilled at some tasks than others, this approach greatly extended the overall timeframe for making the product. Ford realized that by breaking up the process into smaller, easier-to-master tasks, each worker could become more focused. He then put the goods on an orderly assembly line, so that workers wouldn't have to spend time moving around from place to place.

This divide-and-conquer approach can be applied to many processes—even to schedules you create in Project. *Master projects* and *subprojects* are Project's equivalent of a divide-and-conquer technique. This chapter helps you learn to use master projects and subprojects for efficiency, covering the following issues:

- Situations where subprojects might be helpful

- How subproject and master project information can interact

- Adding a subproject file to a master project

- Opening subprojects

When to Use Subprojects

Chapter 15 discusses Object Linking and Embedding (OLE), where you link or embed information from one application or file (called the *source*) in another document or application (called the *container*). You can think of a master project as a kind of container. The master project file contains the names of the subprojects plus any other information you want to appear in the master project. Each subproject is a separate, independent schedule file that's linked to the master project file.

Basically, Project's master project capabilities provide a simplified, specialized way to link files. The advantage to the master project method is that it displays only the name of each subproject file and the overall duration of the subproject schedule, rather than displaying all the tasks in the subproject, which would occur if you linked the files by using OLE (refer to Chapter 15) or creating a consolidated file (refer to Chapter 17). Thus, the master project file provides you with an abbreviated view of the full project schedule, and the major areas of activity that will occur.

Before we look at how to set up a master project and subprojects, you should identify some project planning situations in your company where it might make sense to break down a project into parts. These might include the following situations:

- You need to distribute summary printouts of your schedule, but want an alternative to creating them by outlining.

- Your project is massive, requiring hundreds of steps, and you want an easier way to work with that bulky information. You computer loads smaller files faster than larger ones, so you prefer to work with smaller subsets of tasks.

- You want other team members to schedule and manage certain parts of the project, but you want to bring their files together easily in an overview file.

- You need to create reports and printouts for particular sets of tasks. If sets of tasks are included in a project file along with other sets of tasks running in the same timeframe, it's difficult to filter just the tasks you want. Thus, you want to keep each subset of tasks in separate files for reporting reasons.

- A particular subset of tasks might fit into two master projects. For example, you might be developing an advertising campaign to promote two new products, with the same ad campaign as part of the overall schedule for introducing each product.

Adding Subprojects

Each subproject is linked to a single Task Sheet line in the master project. In a row of the master project Task Sheet, you create the link to the subproject file; usually, you'll want to specify the name of that file as the task name, too. You don't see all the tasks for the subproject—instead, you see a single Gantt bar summarizing the subproject. By default, the start date entered for the subproject in the master project file controls the scheduled start date for the subproject file; the subproject file uses the start date specified in the master project file. The duration of the full schedule for the subproject file becomes the duration for the subproject task entry in the master project Task Sheet. So, if all the tasks listed in the subproject will take 95 days to complete, the master project shows 95d as the Duration entry for the subproject task, and you can't edit that entry.

NOTE: There will be times when you need to readjust the start date for a subproject. See the "Controlling Dates in Master Projects and Subprojects" section later in the chapter for more details.

You have to create the subproject files before adding them to the master project file. If you try to add a subproject that doesn't exist, Project warns you that it doesn't exist, and displays a dialog box prompting you to select another file. You don't, however, have to initially create the tasks within the subproject file. You can simply open and save the file with the name you want, then close it and add it to the master project. You can reopen the subproject file at any time to enter its tasks.

TIP: The approach just mentioned works best in many cases, because it ensures that you don't have to go back and manually update a subproject start date.

To set up a master project and its subprojects, follow these steps:

1. Create, save, and close the subproject files.

2. Create or open the file that you want as the master project file.

3. Click the Task Name cell for a blank Task Sheet row in which you'd like to display subproject information.

4. Open the Insert menu (or right-click the Task Name cell to display a shortcut menu) and click Task Information. The Task Information dialog box appears.

5. Click the Advanced Tab to display its options, as shown in Figure 18.1.

Specify the subproject file here.

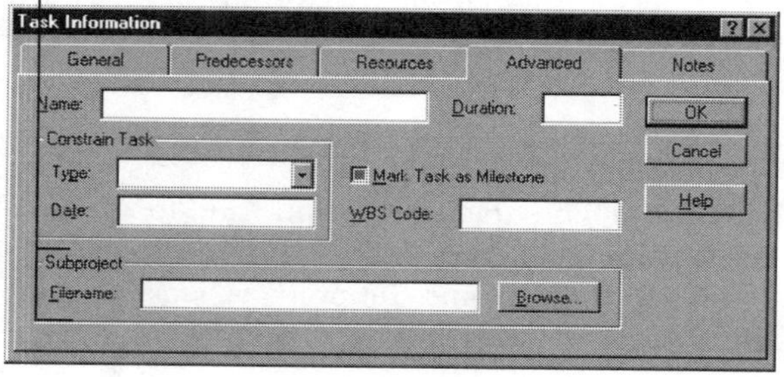

Figure 18.1
Use the Advanced tab in the Task Information dialog box to link a subproject to the currently selected Task Sheet row in the master project.

6. Click the Filename text box in the subproject area of the dialog box. If you know the full disk, folder, and filename path for the subproject file, simply type it in. Otherwise, click the Browse button to open the Subproject dialog box (see Fig. 18.2).

7. Select the subproject file you want by navigating to it with the Look in folder icons, then double-clicking it in the Look in list. You return to the Task Information dialog box, where the Filename you've specified appears in the Subproject area.

8. Type a Name for the subproject task. Usually, you'll want to use the same name as the subproject file name (see Fig. 18.3).

9. Click OK. The Task Information dialog box closes, and the subproject task appears in the file, as shown in Figure 18.4.

10. With the subproject task selected, press F9. Project recalculates and adjusts the task's Gantt bar to match its Duration value.

11. After this recalculation, Project tells you if a subproject has any tasks with work scheduled to begin before the start date for the master project file (see Fig. 18.5).

12. Click OK to continue. Project displays the subproject task with the dates scheduled in the subproject.

13. You can reschedule the master project start date to match the start of the actual work performed on the subproject. To do so, open the File menu and click Project Info. Edit the Start Date entry to make it as early as needed, then click OK.

The Gantt bar doesn't match the duration.

Figure 18.4
The subproject appears, but its Gantt bar doesn't reflect the proper duration.

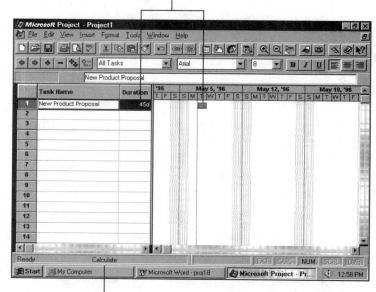

Project is telling you to recalculate to update the task.

Figure 18.5
If the start of actual work in the subproject precedes the master project start date, Project warns you.

14. Save the master project file to save the links to subprojects.

You can use the preceding steps to link other subprojects to the master project file.

TIP: If you want to delete the subproject, right-click its row number, then click Delete Task.

Opening Subprojects

Even though the subproject files and master project file remain as separate entities on disk, by design they share information so that they always reflect the same dates. For example, if you reschedule several tasks in a subproject to make the total subproject duration longer, you'll want the new duration to be reflected in the master project file. It helps to understand how this automatic updating occurs—it takes place through opening files. Basically, you have two options for triggering the updates:

- You can open each subproject file as normal, update its contents, and save it. Then you can open the master project file, which is automatically updated to display the latest information you've added into each subproject file. Make sure that you then save the master project file to save its changes.

- Open the master project, then double-click the Task Name for the subproject task (or the box for that subproject if you're in PERT Chart view). When you make changes in the subproject file, they immediately appear in the master project file. Be sure to save all the files before closing them.

Controlling Dates in Master Projects and Subprojects

Sometimes you'll need to make manual adjustments to ensure that the schedules in your subproject files and master project file are in synch.

For example, a subproject file might include old schedule information, so you might need to adjust its start date to match the subproject start date in the master project. This would happen, for example, if you created the subproject file on April 7, so that its original project Start Date was April 7, but didn't create the master project file until April 8, and accepted that date as the master project's Start Date. Even though the Start Date in the Project Information dialog box would change to April 8 when you added the subproject to the master project, the individual task schedules in the subproject would not adjust. You'd need to move out the task schedules manually. Similarly, if you changed the start date for an individual subproject in the master project, you'd want to make sure that the change was reflected in the subproject file. To update a subproject file so that its task schedule reflects the start date you've entered in the master project, use these steps:

1. Open the master project file.

2. In the Task Sheet, double-click the Task Name for the subproject file that needs updating. The subproject file opens on-screen (see Fig. 18.6).

The "before" dates

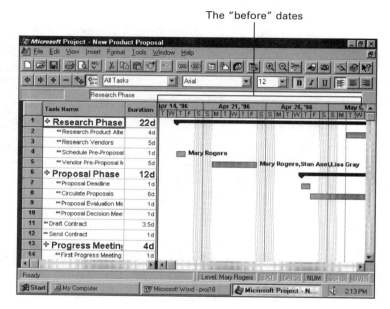

Figure 18.6
Here's the subproject before you adjust it to the master project start date entry.

3. Open the Tools menu, point to Tracking to display the submenu, and click Update Project. The Update Project dialog box appears (see Fig. 18.7).

4. Click to select the Reschedule Uncompleted Work to Start option button. Beside it, the start date specified in the master project file for the subproject appears automatically as the date to reschedule task start dates to. Leave the Entire Tasks option button selected.

TIP: If you've selected a single task to move out, click the Selected Tasks option button instead of the Entire Tasks option button.

Figure 18.7
The Update Project dialog box provides an easy method for rescheduling all the work in your subproject.

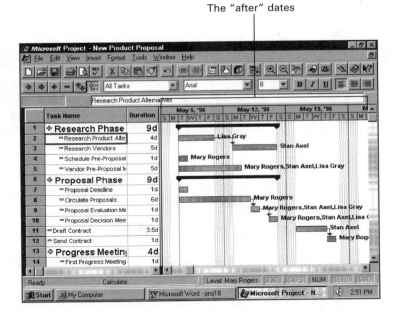

5. Click OK. Project displays the Calculate message in the status bar.

6. Press F9 to recalculate the schedule. Project moves out the tasks so that none start before the specified start date (see Fig. 18.8).

The "after" dates

Figure 18.8
Project has rescheduled the tasks.

TIP: All dialog boxes that warn you of schedule conflicts offer a Help button. You can click this button to identify exactly what the source of the conflict is.

Notice in Figure 18.8 that links have stayed intact. Because the process isn't perfect, from here I would need to reschedule some of the tasks to ensure that they started with the same timing in relation to each other as they did before I moved them out. For example, I would move out task 4 so that it begins when task 3 is about half completed. This is still easier, though, than moving tasks one by one.

In some cases, task constraints will interfere with your ability to move out one or more tasks. For example, if a task has a Must Start On, Must Finish On, Finish No Later Than, or Start No Later Than constraint entered in the Constrain Task area of the Advanced tab in the Task Information dialog box, and the associated constraint date is earlier than the date you want to reschedule the task to, Project warns you that there's a scheduling conflict when you try to move the task. Click OK to continue, then remove the task's constraint, or select another constraint type such as As Soon As Possible, As Late As Possible, Start No Earlier Than, or Finish No Earlier Than. (Remember that you can display the Task Information dialog box simply by double-clicking the task.)

Another problem occurs if you try to move out a single linked task rather than all the tasks. If you move a task and the link creates a scheduling conflict, you can remove the conflict by clicking the Task Name for the successor task, then clicking the Unlink Tasks button on the Standard toolbar.

NOTE: If the subproject contains work already marked as completed, and the start date for that work precedes the start date you've specified in the master project file, you can remove the conflict by removing the work specified as completed. To do so, open the <u>T</u>ools menu, point to Trac<u>k</u>ing, and click Update <u>T</u>asks. Edit the % <u>C</u>omplete entry to be 0, then click OK. Or, if the work really has started for the task, move the start date for the subproject entry in the master project to an earlier date, as described earlier in this chapter.

There's one last manual adjustment you can make. You might actually want the subproject schedule to control the start and finish dates that appear for the subproject task in the master project. You make this happen by creating a link between certain Task Sheet cells in the two files; this link overrides the automatic links created when you added the subproject to the master project. Here are the steps to follow:

1. Open both the master project and the subproject files. Make sure that the subproject file appears on-screen by selecting its filename from the <u>W</u>indow menu.

2. Right-click the row 1 row number for the Task Sheet, then click Insert Task. A new, blank row is inserted in the Task Sheet. This row serves as a summary task for all the other tasks in the subproject file.

3. Type a Task Name for the new summary task row.

4. Drag across the row numbers to highlight all rows except the top, summary row you've just added. Right-click the selected rows, then click Indent Task (see Fig. 18.9).

Figure 18.9
Tell Project that you want the top task to summarize the whole project.

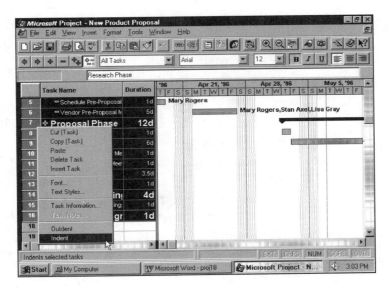

5. Click row 1 and press F9, if needed, to recalculate the duration and ensure that it's correct.

6. Scroll over and drag to highlight the start and finish dates in row 1 of the Task Sheet, as shown in Figure 18.10.

7. Right-click the selected date information, then click Copy (Cell) on the shortcut menu; alternatively, click the Copy button on the Standard toolbar. Project places a copy of the date information on the Windows Clipboard.

Figure 18.10
Select the subproject start and finish information.

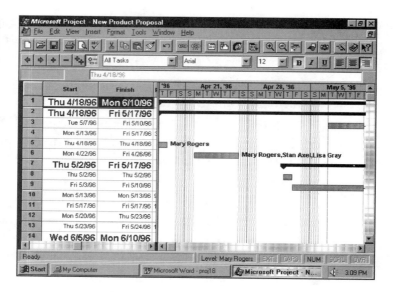

8. Open the Window menu and click the name of the master project file to display it.

9. In the row that contains the subproject, scroll over and drag to select the start and finish cells.

10. Open the Edit menu and click Paste Special. The Paste Special dialog box appears.

11. Click the Paste Link button (see Fig. 18.11), then click OK to finish the link. Project updates the master project information for the subproject, to reflect the start and finish dates pasted from the subproject—these dates will update dynamically if both files are open, and you edit the subproject cells you pasted from. Make sure that you save the files to preserve this link.

Figure 18.11
Once you paste the link, you can count on the appropriate master project information being updated automatically when you change the dates in the subproject.

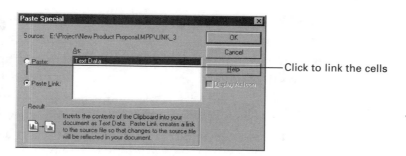

PART V

WORKING WITH ADVANCED FEATURES

CHAPTER 19

USING MICROSOFT EXCHANGE TO SHARE PROJECT INFORMATION

MIS Project offers paperless, automated alternatives through its workgroup message-handling capabilities. Workgroup messaging works in conjunction with Microsoft Exchange in Windows 95 to enable you to automatically send assignment and update information—and receive status reports—to and from resources that you communicate with via e-mail.

In particular, this chapter walks you through using workgroup messaging with Project and Exchange to do the following:

- Add an e-mail address for a resource
- Send a TeamAssign message to assign work
- Sent a TeamUpdate message to tell resources about changes in a task schedule or work completion status, or send a note about a task
- Request a status update for one or more tasks with TeamStatus
- Use Exchange to send these messages
- Respond to and use workgroup message information

Specifying E-Mail Addresses

Just as you have to address paper mail or regular e-mail, you need to tell Project what each resource's e-mail address is to ensure that Project properly addresses the messages you send.

> **CAUTION:** If the recipients of your messages don't have the full Project program installed, at the very least each recipient must install WGSETUP.EXE (available on Project Setup Disk 1 or on the Setup CD) to be able to work with workgroup messages, like TeamAssign messages. In addition, some e-mail systems (such as, surprisingly, Microsoft Mail) can't deal with workgroup messages unless WGSETUP.EXE is installed on both the sender's and recipient's systems.

To tell Project what a resource's e-mail address is, use these steps:

1. Switch to the Resource Sheet view (open the View menu and click Resource Sheet).

2. Double-click the Resource Name for the resource for which you want to specify the e-mail address.

3. In the Resource Information dialog box, click the Details button. Because you haven't previously specified an e-mail address, Project displays the Check Names dialog box. Click to select the Create a new address for… option button, then click OK. Project displays the New Entry dialog box.

> **NOTE:** If you know that the e-mail address is already in your Exchange Personal Address Book, click Change to and then click Show More Names. Click to select a name from the list that appears, then click OK.

4. From the <u>C</u>reate what kind of entry list, click the type of e-mail address you're creating (this identifies the kind of e-mail you use to communicate with that particular resource, which might vary from resource to resource), such as CompuServe or the Internet. Then click OK.

5. The New... Properties dialog box appears. The text boxes for the tab where you specify the e-mail address vary, depending on the type of address you're creating. Enter the address information.

6. Click <u>A</u>pply to save the address settings, then click the <u>Per</u>sonal Address Book button to add the address to your Exchange address book.

7. Click OK to finish creating the address, then click OK again to close the Resource Information dialog box.

8. Repeat steps 2–7 if you want to specify an e-mail address for another resource.

Sending Project Files to Exchange

There are instances, such as when the project schedule is finalized or when you receive a request from a superior to review the schedule, when you might want to send your entire project file as an attachment to an e-mail message. Of course, doing so assumes that the recipient of the message also has Microsoft Project installed, so that he or she can open and review the file.

TIP: The WorkGroup toolbar offers buttons for sending files and other workgroup messages. To display this toolbar, point to any toolbar on-screen, right-click, and then click WorkGroup.

When you send a file, it's sent to your Microsoft Exchange Outbox. You then have to launch Exchange and send the message from there, as described in the later section titled, "Sending the Messages from Exchange."

To send a project file as an attachment to an Exchange message, use these steps:

1. Open the file you want to send, make any last-minute changes you want, then save the file.

2. Open the File menu and click Send (or click the Send Mail button on the WorkGroup toolbar—it's the second button from the left). If Exchange prompts you to specify an Exchange profile, select a different one from the drop-down list, if needed, and click OK to continue. The Microsoft Exchange message window appears, with the project file already inserted as a file attachment, as shown in Figure 19.1.

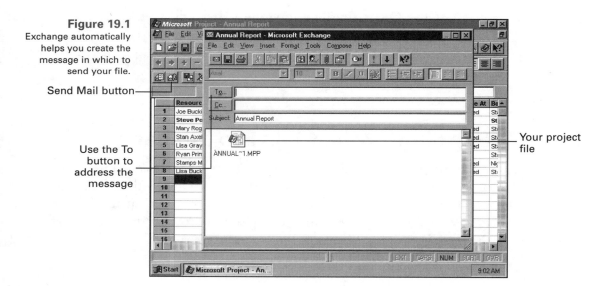

Figure 19.1
Exchange automatically helps you create the message in which to send your file.

Send Mail button—

Use the To button to address the message

Your project file

3. Click the To button to display the Address Book dialog box. Click a name in the list at the left, then click To to add the name to the list of Message recipients. Add other names as needed, then click OK.

4. If you want to include text—perhaps to describe what the file contains or to ask the recipient a specific question—click in the message area below the file icon, then type your message (see Fig. 19.2).

Figure 19.2
The message is
ready to go.

Send button

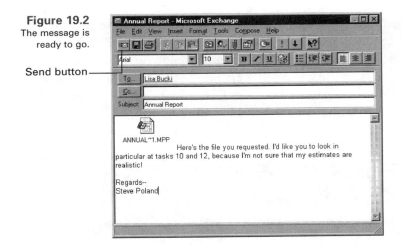

5. Open the File menu and click Send. Alternatively, click the Send button at the left end of the top Exchange toolbar. The message with the file attachment is sent to your Exchange Outbox.

You can route a message including a file to a number of users, and have a copy automatically come back to you when the last recipient closes the file after working with it. You can send the message to all recipients at once, or set it up so that it goes to the first recipient, who then must forward it to the next recipient, and so on.

To route a file, open the File menu and click Add Routing Slip (or click the Routing Slip button at the left end of the WorkGroup toolbar). The Routing Slip dialog box appears. Click the Address button to display the Address Book dialog box. Click a name from the list at the left, then click To to add this name to the list of recipients at the right. Add all the names you want, then click OK to close the dialog box and return to the Routing Slip dialog box.

The Routing Slip dialog box shows the routing order (see Fig. 19.3). If needed, click a name in the To list and click one of the Move arrows to change the selected name's position in the list. Click and enter any Message Text you want to appear. In the Route to Recipients area, tell Exchange whether you want the message to be routed to the listed recipients One After Another or All at Once. Make sure that there's a checkmark beside the Return When Done option if you want

Exchange to automatically send a copy of the routed file back to you after the last recipient in the list works with the file and closes it. The Track Status feature, when checked (and when you're routing the file from one recipient to the next), generates a notification message to you when each recipient on the list forwards the file to the next recipient. Click Route after you've specified all the settings you want; this sends the routed file to your Exchange Outbox.

Figure 19.3
You can route a file to several recipients.

Routing Slip button

Routing order

Include text here, if needed

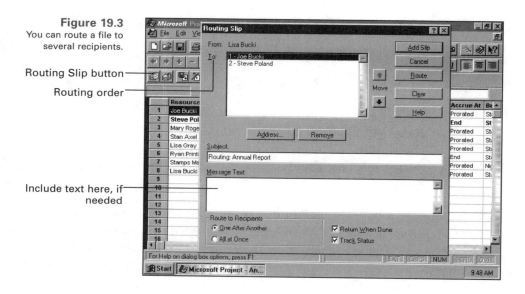

NOTE: When you use routing, even though the routing feature automatically creates return messages and posts them to the recipients' Outboxes, the recipients must send the messages from there.

Sending Assignments, Updates, and Status Requests to Exchange

The TeamAssign, TeamUpdate, and TeamStatus commands on the Workgroup submenu of the Tools menu all work in concert with Microsoft Exchange to enable you to share task information with the resources assigned to particular tasks. These Workgroup commands take advantage of the workgroup messaging feature that comes with

Project. Selecting any of these commands generates a special message in the workgroup messaging format, which is then sent to your Exchange Outbox as an attachment to a regular Exchange message.

CAUTION: Project's workgroup messaging is designed for communication over a network or dial-up network connection, in concert with Exchange or mail products like Lotus cc:Mail, if your workgroup uses one of them. Workgroup messaging doesn't work reliably when you're sending information via an online service or the Internet. If you try to send a TeamAssign message to a CompuServe address, for example, the recipient receives two separate messages. One includes a "system administration" warning saying that the recipient system can't handle the workgroup message. The other message includes the actual workgroup message as an "attachment." The recipient can view this "attachment" and see your message, but if the recipient tries to reply, the original message sometimes deletes itself and the reply message is rarely delivered. If you're have trouble sending workgroup messages to a particular recipient, check with your system administrator or get technical support help from Microsoft.

The workgroup message lists the resource(s) you're sending the message to, and key data about each of the tasks you've selected to send or request information about. It includes suggested message text, so you don't even have to type instructions if you don't want to. It lists the task name, start date, number of work hours completed, and number of work hours remaining. It also offers a comments column for each task. The recipient of each workgroup message can make changes to the task information, then automatically return the message to you via their Exchange Outbox.

Each of these commands has a particular purpose, so I'll review each of them in turn:

- TeamAssign—This type of message asks a resource to verify that he/she has accepted an assignment, as well as the schedule you've sent for it, as shown in Figure 19.4.

Figure 19.4
This workgroup
message asks a
resource to verify an
assignment.

Task information
appears here

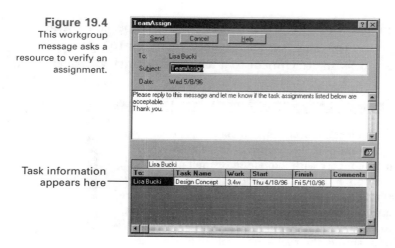

• Team<u>U</u>pdate—A message of this type (see Fig. 19.5) enables you
to report changing task information, such as a revised start or finish date. In order for this to work, you have to have previously
sent information about tasks and incorporated resource replies
into these tasks (as you'll learn to do later in this chapter). Otherwise, Project tells you that there are no tasks in the schedule to
update.

Figure 19.5
Workgroup messaging
makes it easy to
communicate an
update to a team
member.

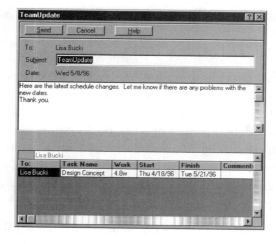

• Team<u>S</u>tatus—This type of message queries the recipient to tell
you how work is progressing on a task (see Fig. 19.6).

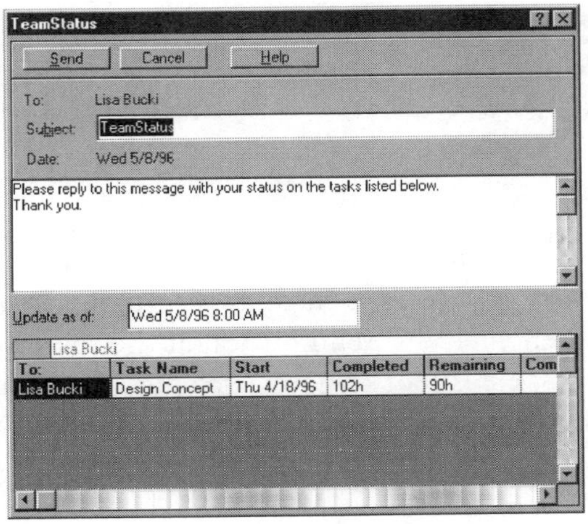

Figure 19.6
You can ask resources to report to you about progress on tasks.

The steps for sending each type of workgroup message are similar, and are as follows:

1. Update information in the schedule in Gantt Chart view, and save your file.

2. If you want to send a workgroup message about a particular task or group of tasks, click to select a single task, then hold down Ctrl while clicking any additional tasks you want to select.

3. Open the Tools menu, point to Workgroup to display a sub-menu, and click TeamAssign, TeamUpdate, or TeamStatus. Alternatively, click the TeamAssign, TeamUpdate, or TeamStatus button on the WorkGroup toolbar.

NOTE: Depending on how it's set up, Exchange might or might not prompt you to specify a profile when you send messages. Make the appropriate selection, if prompted, then click OK to continue.

4. The Workgroup Mail dialog box appears (see Fig. 19.7). Click to specify whether to send the message regarding All Tasks or Selected Tasks, then click OK.

5. The workgroup message appears on-screen. Edit any of the information you want, such as the Su**bj**ect or text of the message, then click the **S**end button at the top of the message. The message is sent to your Exchange Outbox. You'll learn shortly what to do with it from there.

Sending Notes to Exchange

Project can automatically set up an Exchange e-mail message for you, building the recipient list based on options you specify and enabling you to select whether the attached file should hold your entire schedule file or just a graphic picture (BMP file) of any tasks you've selected in the Task Sheet. This kind of note can be sent to e-mail addresses that you specify.

To send an automatically formatted message like this, follow these steps:

1. Update information in the schedule in Gantt Chart view, and save your file.

2. If you want to send a note message about a particular task or group of tasks, you need to select the task or tasks. Click to select a single task, then hold down Ctrl while clicking any additional tasks you want to select.

3. Open the **T**ools menu, point to **W**orkgroup, and click Send Sc**h**edule Note. The Send Schedule Note dialog box appears, as shown in Figure 19.8.

4. In the Address Message To area, specify the recipients for the message, and whether the list should include the **R**esources and **C**ontacts from the **E**ntire Project or **S**elected Tasks.

5. In the Attach area of the dialog box, specify whether the attachment message should be the entire **F**ile or just a **P**icture of Selected Tasks.

Figure 19.8
Specify who will
receive a note message
and what file
attachment it will
contain.

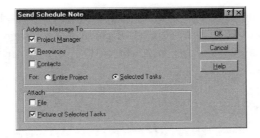

6. Click OK. If you haven't included an e-mail address for any of the selected recipients, you're prompted to do so. Specify the needed address(es) as described earlier in this chapter. The Exchange message appears on-screen, as shown in Figure 19.9.

Figure 19.9
The Exchange message
appears so that you
can type the note; the
correct recipients have
already been entered.

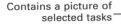

Contains a picture of
selected tasks

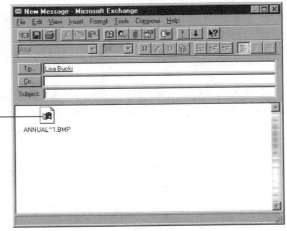

7. Type a subject for the message, then click in the message area below the attached file, and type the note you want to send.

TIP: You can delete the attached file from the message if you want. All your addressing information remains intact. To delete the attachment, click its icon, then press the Delete key.

8. Open the File menu and click Send. Alternatively, click the Send button at the left end of the top Exchange toolbar. The message with the file attachment is sent to your Exchange Outbox.

Sending the Workgroup Messages from Exchange

All the Exchange and workgroup messages you've learned to create so far in this chapter were sent from Project to your Outbox folder within Exchange. This makes sense, because Project and the workgroup messaging features aren't e-mail programs—they simply prepare your information to be sent via e-mail.

Now, you need to send your messages from the Outbox to the intended recipients. To send the messages from Exchange, follow these steps:

1. Go to your Windows 95 desktop and double-click the Inbox icon to start Microsoft Exchange. Alternatively, click the Start button on the Taskbar, point to Programs, and click Microsoft Exchange.

2. If the Choose Profile dialog box appears, select another profile, if needed, using the Profile Name drop-down list. Then click OK. Microsoft Exchange loads and appears on-screen, with your Inbox folder open.

3. Click the Outbox folder icon to open it and show outgoing messages (see Fig. 19.10).

4. Open the Tools menu and click Deliver Now. (If you have numerous e-mail services installed with Exchange, and your Outbox includes some regular Exchange messages with attachments being mailed to an online service or the Internet, the Tools command might be Deliver Now Using, in which case you need to click All Services).

5. Project connects to your mail system and delivers the messages, keeping you informed on-screen as the messages are delivered.

Figure 19.10
The messages you've prepared are lined up in the Outbox, waiting to be mailed.

The Outbox folder

Your workgroup messages

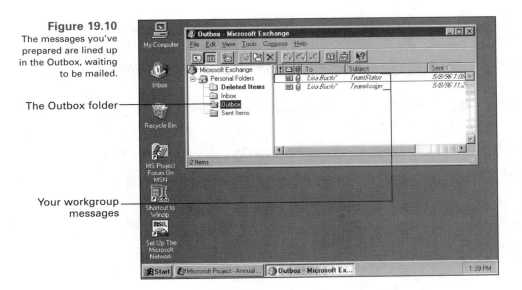

Responding to Assignments and Updates

When you're on the receiving end of workgroup messages, they appear in your e-mail or Microsoft Exchange Inbox folder along with other, normal e-mail messages. To read a workgroup message, double-click it. It opens and appears in a message dialog box on-screen (see Fig. 19.11).

NOTE: If you need to take any steps to retrieve regular messages from your e-mail system into Exchange to get those messages to appear in your Inbox, then you'll need to do the same for your workgroup messages.

Click the Reply button to prepare your response to the message. The window automatically adjusts to enable you to reply, and RE: appears beside the window title and in the beginning of the Subject text. An insertion point appears in the Message area; type your overall reply there. In your reply, you also can change any column of task information—the question marks in the cells prompt you to do so. To change an entry, click it, then drag over it in the text entry area, as shown in

Figure 19.12. Click the Send button to send the reply to your Exchange Outbox. From the Outbox, send the reply to the project manager using the steps outlined in the preceding section.

Figure 19.11
This is an example of how a workgroup message—a TeamStatus request—looks to its recipient.

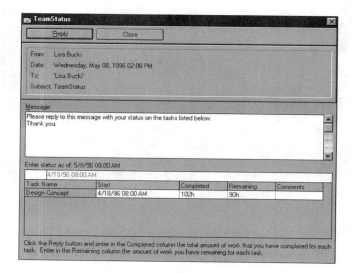

Figure 19.12
Here's a response to the status request from Figure 19.11.

Type your overall reply.

Click an entry here...

...then drag over it here, type a new entry, and click the Enter button.

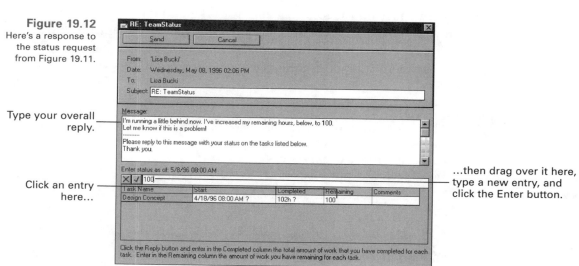

If you're a project manager, your resources will send replies to your assignment and status requests. Such responses appear in your e-mail or Exchange Inbox, and you can double-click each one to open it. For example, the response shown in Figure 19.12, after being sent to the project manager, resembles Figure 19.13 when the project manager opens it.

Figure 19.13
This status update has been received from a resource.

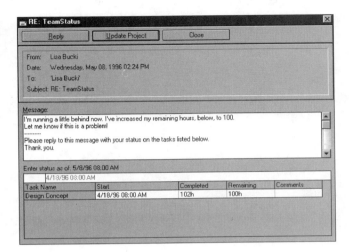

If the resource's response isn't satisfactory, click the Reply button to send a reply message. If the resource simply confirmed the existing schedule, you can click the Close button to close the message, and click No if you're asked whether to update the Project file. If the response suggests some schedule changes and you want to enter these changes into your project file, click the Update Project button. If Project isn't open, it starts and the file opens for updating. The schedule changes are made to the appropriate task in the schedule, and the status update message closes. Save your project file to keep these changes.

CHAPTER 20

CUSTOMIZING MICROSOFT PROJECT

Throughout the book, I've noted numerous situations where you need to tweak how Project reacts to your commands, or even how you communicate with Project to give it commands. This chapter provides an overview of all the customization options available to you in Project. It explains how to make Project look and work the way you want it to, including the following:

- Making adjustments to menus
- Hiding and displaying toolbars, and working with toolbar tools
- Working with the options on the nine tabs of the Options dialog box

Creating a Custom Menu

Early on, many computer programs deserved the reputation of being difficult to learn. Each program used its own terms for particular operations, such as opening a file (which was also called "getting," "retrieving," and so on). Moreover, each program had different menus that grouped commands differently. From one program to the next, you never knew exactly how to navigate. While software publishers have come a long way toward standardizing terms and menus so that what you learn in one program applies in another, they've been kind enough to leave in plenty of flexibility for controlling how menus appear.

In fact, in Project and many other applications, you can create custom menu bars, custom drop-down menus, and custom menu commands solely to suit your needs and working style. The commands you create can execute standard program commands, macros that come with the programs, or macros you create. To work with menus in Project, open the Tools menu, point to Customize, and click Menu Bars. Or, right-click the menu bar, then click Customize Menu Bar. The Menu Bars dialog box (see Fig. 20.1) displays the list of menu bars available in Project. Each menu bar offers a list of menus, which in turn list commands. To display a different menu on-screen, simply double-click its name in the Menu Bars list of the dialog box.

TIP: To display a different menu bar at any time, right-click the current menu bar, then select another one from the list.

Figure 20.1
Work with menus using this dialog box.

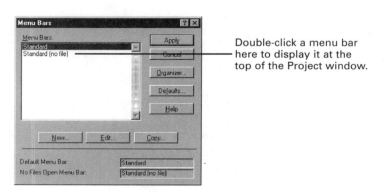

Double-click a menu bar here to display it at the top of the Project window.

You also can use the Menu Bars dialog box to add a new command to a menu, to add a new menu to a menu bar, or to create an entirely new menu bar. For example, to create a new menu bar, click the <u>N</u>ew button in the Menu Bars dialog box. The Menu Bar Definition dialog box appears, as shown in Figure 20.2. Type a name for the menu in the <u>N</u>ame text box.

Enter the menu name

Promotes or demotes the selected row entry, so you can specify whether it's a menu name or menu item

Cuts a row to remove it from the menu bar

Inserts a row to add it to the menu bar

Figure 20.2
You can create a completely new menu bar.

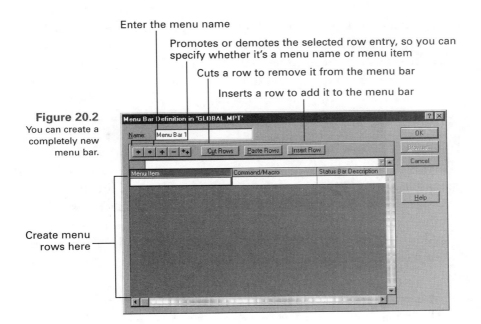

Create menu rows here

Next, you want to enter the name of the first menu on the menu bar. Click the first Menu Item cell, then type the name of the menu, such as **&Favorites**. Press Enter. Project knows that you intend the entry to be a menu name, and automatically formats it in bold. The ampersand (&) before the F is how you tell Project to format the letter "F" as a *selection letter;* for your custom menu, then, pressing Alt+F will open the Favorites menu.

TIP: The selection letter doesn't need to be the first letter of the item you're adding. For example, entering Favo&rites results in the same menu name, Favorites, but it makes "r" the selection letter, so that pressing Alt+R will open the Favorites menu.

NOTE: For obvious reasons, you can't use the same selection letter for two menu names on the same menu bar, or for two commands on the same menu.

In the next Menu Item cell, type the name for the first command you want to appear on the menu, using the ampersand before the letter that you want to be the underlined selection letter; press Enter. Reselect the cell, then click the right arrow to demote the entry to a menu command. Click the Command/Macro cell for the menu command, then click Browse. By default, GLOBAL appears as the Libraries/Projects choice. If you want the command to execute a macro, select the correct macro module choice from the Classes/Modules list at the left, then click the macro you want from the list at the right, and click Paste. If you want the custom command to execute an existing Project command, select MSProject from the Libraries/Projects list, then select a class at the left, select a command at the right, and click Paste. Back in the Menu Bar Definition dialog box, press Tab, then click the Status Bar Description cell for the entry. Type whatever description you want to appear for this command in the status bar.

TIP: If you want a command to display a submenu, enter that command as explained above, then enter the first command for the submenu in the following row. Select the row holding the submenu command and click the Indent button, moving the submenu command to two levels below the menu name, and one level below the command that displays the submenu.

Press Enter to finish adding the command, and press the left arrow key twice to move back to the Menu Item column. A new menu command looks like the one shown in Figure 20.3.

You might want to be able to group commands on your menu for easier access. You can do so by inserting a blank row or a separator line. To insert a blank row, just click the position where you want it to appear, and click Insert Row. The row is inserted with [Blank Item] grayed out in the Menu Item column. Unless you edit that entry, the row remains blank.

Figure 20.3
Here's a brand-new
menu command.

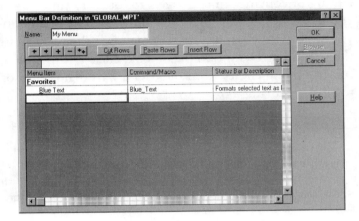

CAUTION: If you try to create a blank row by pressing Enter with the last row in the list selected, you just end up closing the Menu Bar Definition dialog box.

To insert a separator line, type a single hyphen (–) in the Menu Item column for a new or blank row, and press Enter. Project creates a separator line at that location in the menu.

Continue using the techniques just described to add additional commands to your menu. Anytime you want to start a new menu on the menu bar, enter its name in the Menu Item column, the click the promote button to promote it to a menu name. When you finish making all your menu bar entries, click OK to return to the Menu Bars dialog box, where the new menu is now listed.

While starting from scratch when creating a menu is fine, you're probably better off selecting an existing menu and clicking the Edit button to edit it. Or, try selecting an existing menu and clicking the Copy button in the Menus Bar dialog box, then selecting the name of the copied menu and clicking Edit. When you click Edit to edit a menu, it appears in the Menu Bar Definition dialog box. You can click Insert Row to insert a new command or menu name, or Cut Rows to remove commands or menu names that you no longer want. Not only does editing or copying a menu save a lot of entry time, but it also enables you to easily leave key menus, such as the File menu, on-screen while you work with your custom commands. When you finish working in the Menu Bar Definition dialog box, click OK to close it. Click to Apply a menu choice from the Menu Bars dialog box, or click Close to close the dialog box.

TIP: If you make changes to the Standard menu bar and later want to undo the changes, display the Menu Bars dialog box, click Standard in the menu list, and click Edit. In the Menu Bar Definition dialog box, click the Reset button.

NOTE: Your custom menu bars and toolbars are stored by default with the Global.mpt file where Project settings are stored. If you want to e-mail a schedule file and have it offer the custom menu bar or toolbar, you need to copy the custom menu bar or toolbar to that particular file. Click the Organizer button in either the Menu Bars or Toolbars dialog box to display the Organizer, which enables you to copy the custom feature. See Chapter 9, "Working with the Different Project Views," to learn more about the Organizer.

Working with Toolbars

Toolbars are much easier to customize than menu bars, and most users find them easier to use, as well. You've seen numerous instances elsewhere in this book where displaying different toolbars or working with particular toolbar tools can help you get the most out of certain Project features. This section shares more information about how you can work with Project's toolbars.

Displaying and Hiding Toolbars

Every toolbar is accessible via the other toolbars. You can right-click any toolbar to display a shortcut menu, then click the name of another toolbar you want to display or click the name of a toolbar that's already on-screen that you want to hide.

An alternative method of choosing which toolbars appear on screen and which don't, as well as accessing other commands for working with toolbars, is to open the View menu and click Toolbars. The Toolbars dialog box appears, as shown in Figure 20.4. To display the Toolbars dialog box using the mouse, right-click any toolbar, then click Toolbars.

Figure 20.4
Use the Toolbars dialog box to select which toolbars are on-screen and to work with toolbar options.

Click the name of any toolbar you want to display in the Toolbars list, then click Show. If you want to hide a toolbar that's on-screen, simply click its name in the Toolbars list. The Show button changes to a Hide button; click this to remove the toolbar from the screen. Click the Close button to close the Toolbars dialog box.

Customizing the Buttons on a Toolbar

You can make any changes that you want to the contents of a toolbar. You can remove buttons, add buttons, or edit the function of any button. To add and remove buttons on a toolbar, use the following steps:

1. Display the toolbar that you want to edit on-screen.
2. Open the View menu and click Toolbars. Click the Customize button in the Toolbars dialog box. Alternatively, you can right-click any toolbar and then click Customize. The Customize dialog box appears.

3. To add a button to one of the displayed toolbars, click one of the <u>C</u>ategories list choices to display the available buttons in that category, then drag a button onto the toolbar in the position you want, as shown in Figure 20.5. Release the mouse button to drop the new toolbar button into position.

Figure 20.5
You add a button to
a toolbar by
dragging the button
from the Customize
dialog box.

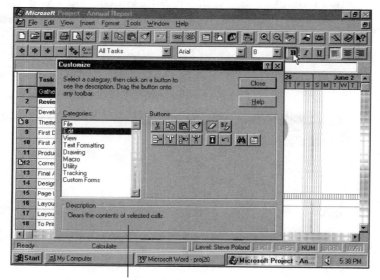

This description explains the selected button's function.

TIP: If you drag a button from the Customize dialog box onto the working area in Project rather than onto a toolbar, Project automatically creates a new toolbar and places the selected button on the new toolbar.

4. To move an existing toolbar button to a new position on the same toolbar, which you must do while the Customize dialog box is open, just drag the button and release it in the new location.

5. To remove a button from a toolbar, which you must do while the Customize dialog box is open, drag it off of the toolbar and release the mouse button. (Make sure that you don't accidentally drop it on another toolbar.)

6. When you've finished dragging buttons onto, off of, and around on toolbars, click Close to close the Customize dialog box.

The buttons available in the Customize dialog box are, for the most part, buttons that already exist on a Project toolbar. If you want to place a blank button on a toolbar, press and hold down the Ctrl key, then click the toolbar wherever you want the blank button to appear. Project inserts a blank button and displays the Customize Tool dialog box.

At the top of the Customize Tool dialog box, scroll through the Button Library and select the button design you want to use. If you can't find a button that's exactly what you need, click one that's close in appearance, then click Edit Button. The Button Editor appears on screen, as shown in Figure 20.6. Click a color or Erase in the Colors area, then click a square (called a *pixel*) on the Picture to change that pixel to the selected color. Click OK when you're done making changes. The edited button appears as a new choice at the end of the Button Library choices, and is selected in the Customize Tool dialog box.

Click a color or the Erase choice here...

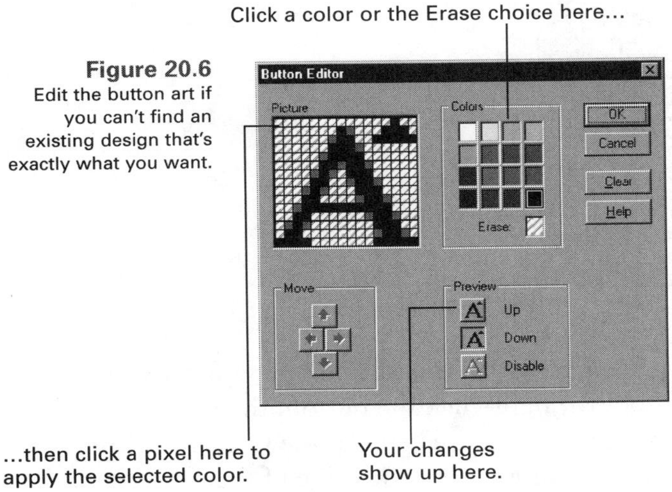

Figure 20.6
Edit the button art if you can't find an existing design that's exactly what you want.

...then click a pixel here to apply the selected color.

Your changes show up here.

Click the Command text box so that you can specify what the new toolbar button will lead to when it's clicked. To assign an existing command, macro, or custom view saved in Global.mpt, click the drop-down list arrow beside the Command text box. Scroll through the list, and click the selection you want to assign to the button.

> **NOTE:** If the command or macro you want to use doesn't appear in the Command drop-down list, you can look for it using the Browse button. See "Creating a Macro Button" in Chapter 21 for an example of browsing for a macro that you've created.

Click the Description text box and type a description for the button, which will be used to explain the button in the status bar whenever you point to the button. Then, click the ToolTip text box and type a ToolTip, which will pop up to describe the button whenever you place the mouse pointer on it. Figure 20.7 shows some sample entries. Click OK to finish creating the new toolbar button.

Figure 20.7
Here are example entries for a button in the Customize Tool dialog box.

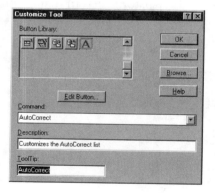

If you want to display the Customize Tool dialog box to make changes to any button on any toolbar, right-click the button, then click Customize Tool. Make any adjustments you want in the Customize Tool dialog box, using the same techniques just described for creating a custom button, then click OK. The button immediately changes to reflect your edits.

Creating a Custom Toolbar

You can create a brand new toolbar, or one that's based on an existing toolbar. To do so, right-click a toolbar, then click Toolbars. The Toolbars dialog box appears. In the Toolbars dialog box, click the New button, type a Name in the New Toolbar dialog box, and click OK. This displays a new, blank toolbar on-screen. (If you want, you can click an existing toolbar in the Toolbars list, then click Copy. In the New Toolbar dialog box, enter a toolbar Name, and click OK. Project creates a copy of the selected toolbar, and displays it on-screen.) Click Close to close the Toolbars dialog box.

Once the new toolbar appears on-screen, you can display the Customize dialog box (right-click the toolbar and then click Customize) to add or remove toolbar buttons, as described earlier. You also can right-click any individual button on the toolbar and then click Customize to modify that button.

Project does not let you delete any toolbar that comes with the program. You can, however, delete the custom toolbars you create. To delete a custom toolbar, right-click any toolbar on-screen, then click Toolbars to display the Toolbars dialog box. In the Toolbars list, click to select the name of the custom toolbar you want to delete, then click the Delete button. Project asks you to confirm that you want to delete the toolbar. Click Yes to do so, then click Close to close the dialog box.

Customizing Workgroup Message Fields

Chapter 19 explains how to send specialized messages called *workgroup messages* from Project to make resource assignments, send task updates, and request status reports from resources. In each of these messages, Project lists certain fields for each task you're communicating about, such as Task Name or Remaining work hours. You can customize the fields that appear for tasks listed in these messages by using the following steps:

1. Open the Tools menu, point to Customize, and click Workgroup. The Customize Workgroup dialog box appears, as shown in Figure 20.8.

Figure 20.8
You can control the
fields for the task
information
that appears in
workgroup
messages.

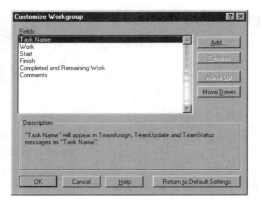

2. To add a new field, scroll through the Fields list and click the name of the field above which you'd like to insert the new field. Click the Add button. The Add Field dialog box appears (see Fig. 20.9).

Figure 20.9
Use the Add Field
dialog box to select
another field of
information to appear
in your workgroup
messages.

3. From the Field drop-down list, select the name of the field to include. In the Title text box, click the name of the column title you'd like to use for the selected field. Clear the checkmark for the Include in TeamStatus Messages option only if you want to restrict the inclusion of the new field to TeamAssign and TeamUpdate messages. If the Let Resources Change Field option is available, use it to specify whether or not you want resources to be able to change the field when replying to you. Click OK when you're done working with these options.

4. Back in the Customize Workgroup dialog box, use the Fields list to click any field you want to move to the left in the message columns, then click Move Up. Similarly, to move a field to the right, click it in the Fields list and then click Move Down.

5. To remove one of the custom Fields you've added, click it and then click Remove.

6. If at any point you're not satisfied with the Fields list, click the Return to Default Settings button.

7. When you're done specifying the custom fields for your workgroup messages, click OK.

Setting Project Options

Like most other application programs today, Project offers dozens of options that you can set for the entire program, to control how it looks and behaves. To set options for the Project program, open the Tools menu and click Options. The Options dialog box has nine tabs, each of which relates to a particular functional area of Project. Each of the tabs and its choices are described next. Click a tab to display its options, then make the changes you want on that tab. When you've finished specifying your choices for all of the tabs in the Options dialog box, click OK to close the dialog box and put your changes into effect.

View Options

The first tab in the Options dialog box, the View tab (see Fig. 20.10), specifies how Project looks on-screen when you run it. Here are the choices you have there:

- Default View—Choose a view from this drop-down list to specify the view Project will use for the current schedule when you start the program.

- Date Format—Your selection from this drop-down list specifies how dates will appear in the Task Sheet for any column holding date information.

- Show—In the Show area, you specify which of the following window features of Project should appear—Status Bar, Scroll Bar, Entry Bar, OLE Links Indicator, and Notes Indicator. Click to place a checkmark beside each feature that you want to appear.

- Currency—In the Symbol text box, specify the currency symbol, if any, that should appear to the left of columns containing cost information. The Placement drop-down list lets you control how the specified currency symbol appears in relation to the currency value. In the Decimal Digits text box, enter how many decimal places should appear after whole numbers in currency values. For example, enter 0 to see whole currency values only.

- Outline Options—If you clear the checkmark beside the Show Summary Tasks option, summary tasks won't appear in the Task Sheet, so you won't be able to use outlining features. The Project Summary Tasks option works in a similar fashion for consolidated files (see Chapter 17 to learn more about consolidated files). When the Indent Name check box is selected, any tasks you indent move to the right in the Task Name column. When the Show Outline Number check box is selected, Project displays the WBS number beside each outlined task. You can use the Show Outline Symbol check box to turn on or off the display of the outlining + (summary task) and – (subtask) symbols.

Figure 20.10
Project offers options for controlling its on-screen appearance.

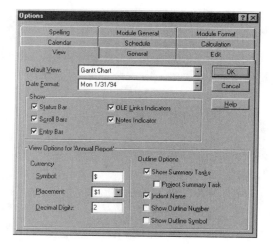

General Options

Click the General tab to display the options shown in Figure 20.11. Here's what you can do with each of these options:

- Show <u>T</u>ips At Startup—Click to place a checkmark beside this option if you want to see a Tip dialog box when you start Project.

- Show <u>W</u>elcome Dialog at Startup—When this option is checked, Project displays a special dialog box when you start the program, enabling you to view a tutorial, work on the last Project file that was open, and so on.

- Open Last <u>F</u>ile on Startup—Click to place a checkmark beside this option to tell Project to automatically reopen the last schedule file you worked in when you restart Project.

- Prompt for Project <u>I</u>nfo for New Projects—Click to place a checkmark beside this option to have Project ask you for Project schedule information when you create a new project.

- User <u>N</u>ame—Type your name in this text box.

- PlanningWizard—When no checkmark appears beside the Advice from <u>P</u>lanningWizard option, no PlanningWizard choices are available. You can click to place checkmarks to determine whether you want Project to display Advice About <u>U</u>sing Project, Advice About <u>S</u>cheduling (asks whether you want to create links where they're possible, and so on), or Advice About <u>E</u>rrors (informs you when your changes will create a scheduling conflict or other problem).

- General Options for (current file)—A checkmark beside the <u>A</u>utomatically Add New Resources option means that any name you type in the Resource Name column of the Task Sheet becomes a row entry in the Resource Sheet; otherwise, Project prompts you for resource information. If <u>A</u>utomatically Add New Resources is selected, you can specify a Default Standard <u>R</u>ate and Default <u>O</u>vertime Rate in the text boxes below.

- Set As <u>D</u>efault—If you want to make the changes on this tab the defaults for Project, click this button.

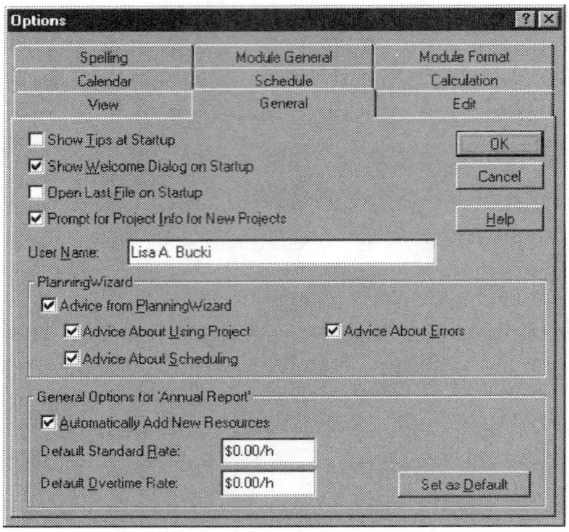

Figure 20.11
Control the most
common Project
options in this tab
of the Options
dialog box.

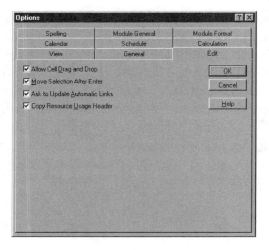

Edit Options

The Edit tab enables you to specify which editing features you want to use in Project. Click this tab to display it, as shown in Figure 20.12. When a checkmark appears in the box beside any of the options here, that option is available; otherwise, you can't use the specified editing technique.

Figure 20.12
Project offers
numerous editing
features, and here
you choose whether
or not to
use them.

The first option, Allow Cell <u>D</u>rag and Drop, controls whether you can drag to move information in the Task Sheet or Resource Sheet. <u>M</u>ove

Selection After Enter means that the cell selector will move down to the next row after you press Enter after making an entry in the Task Sheet or Resource Sheet. Ask to Update <u>A</u>utomatic Links means that Project will prompt you about links if you update a file that's linked to task or resource information in another file. The Copy Resource <u>U</u>sage Header option controls whether Project will remember column heading information when you copy information from Resource Usage view.

Calendar Options

The Calendar tab of the Options dialog box (see Fig. 20.13) enables you to specify the default base calendar for the current schedule file. Use the top two drop-down lists to specify the start of each work week and fiscal year in your calendar for the current schedule file.

Figure 20.13
Use the Calendar tab to establish the default calendar for the current schedule file.

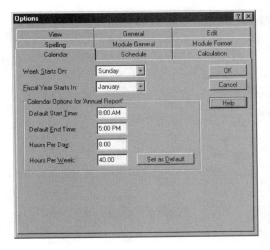

The choices in the Calendar Options area affect only the current file; they work as follows:

- Default Start <u>T</u>ime—The time you enter here is the time of day Project uses for new tasks you add to the Task Sheet, unless you specify otherwise.
- Default <u>E</u>nd Time—Sets the time of day when Project cuts off work on tasks for the day, unless you specify otherwise for a particular task or its assigned resource.

- Hours Per Day—When you enter durations in terms of days, this entry determines how many working hours each day contains.

- Hours Per Week—As with the preceding option, the number of hours you enter here is reflected in the schedule. If you enter 35 hours, each work week contains 35 hours by default.

Schedule Options

The default scheduling options, displayed by clicking the Schedule tab of the Options dialog box (see Fig. 20.14), control how Project responds when you enter information in the Task Sheet. The first option is Show Scheduling Messages. When this option is checked, Project warns you if you make a mistake that will cause a scheduling error. This tab offers numerous key settings for the current file, as well:

Figure 20.14
This tab lets you specify how Project handles scheduling choices by default.

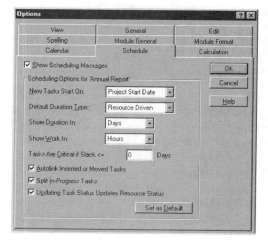

- New Tasks Start On—Choose whether the default start date Project enters for new tasks is the project start date or the current date.

- Default Duration Type—Specifies whether task durations adjust based on resource calendars (resource-driven) or are a fixed duration.

- Show Duration In—Specifies the time units (days, weeks, and so on) that Project assigns to Duration column entries if you don't specify a unit.

- Show <u>W</u>ork In—Specifies the time units (hours, minutes, and so on) that Project assigns to Work column entries if you don't specify a unit.
- Tasks Are <u>C</u>ritical if Slack <=—Enter a value here to control how many tasks are considered critical tasks (are part of the critical path). Higher values mean that fewer tasks are marked as critical.
- <u>A</u>utolink Inserted or Moved Tasks—If you insert or move tasks within a series of tasks linked by Finish-to-Start (FS) relationships and this option is checked, Project links the inserted tasks within the group of linked tasks. If you reschedule tasks, Project automatically asks whether you want to create links where they're possible.
- Split <u>I</u>n-Progress Tasks—When this option is checked and you automatically reschedule uncompleted work, uncompleted work on in-progress tasks is rescheduled, in addition to work scheduled for tasks that haven't yet begun.
- U<u>p</u>dating Task Status Updates Resource Status—Select this check box if you want information you enter into task views to be reflected in calculated fields in resource views. For example, if you enter an actual task completion amount, it's reflected in terms of actual hours worked and costs for a particular resource.

Calculation Options

Calculation options indicate whether Project automatically updates all calculated values (such as actual cost figures that equal actual hours worked multiplied by hourly rates). In the Calculation area of this tab, specify whether calculation should be <u>A</u>utomatic or <u>M</u>anual. If calculation is set to <u>M</u>anual, you can display this tab and click the Calculate A<u>l</u>l Projects button to recalculate all values in all open projects, or click the Calculate <u>P</u>roject button to simply update the values in the currently open schedule file.

Spelling Options

By default, the spelling checker in Project reviews most task and resource text information. Using the options on the Spelling tab (see Fig. 20.15), you can speed up the spelling checker by selecting which information it checks; you also can specify other options related to the spelling checker.

To tell the spelling checker not to review information in a particular task or resource field, click to select the field in the Fields to Check list, then click the drop-down list arrow and click No.

Figure 20.15
If you don't want the spelling checker to review particular fields, specify them here.

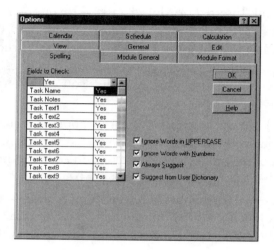

The next options on the Spelling tab are the Ignore Words in UPPER-CASE check box and the Ignore Words with Numbers check box. When these options are checked, the spelling checker does not check the spelling for words typed entirely in uppercase (such as IN) or words including numbers (such as Qtr1), respectively. Always Suggest, when checked, means that the spelling checker displays a list of suggested corrections for any unrecognized word it finds. Suggest From User Dictionary, when checked, means that the spelling checker includes corrections from your user dictionary with the suggestion list.

Module General Options

Click the Module General tab to display its options (see Fig. 20.16). These options apply when you display a macro module (see Chapter 21) or Visual Basic module.

Figure 20.16
When you're creating Visual Basic code (macros) and display a macro module, the options specified here control how the module responds.

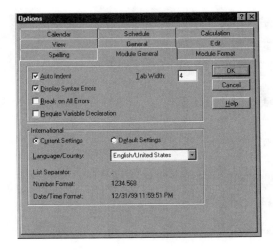

Click to place a checkmark on the Auto Indent option if you want entries to automatically indent all entries at the same level until you specify otherwise. Type a Tab Width entry here to control how many characters lines are indented by. If you're not an experienced programmer, leave the Display Syntax Errors check box selected so that Project warns you if you type a coding line that's incorrect.

Click to place a checkmark on the Break on All Errors option if you want Project to pause and give you the opportunity to debug every macro you create when you're developing and testing it. Require Variable Declaration is another programming option; when it's checked, you must enter a line of code in the macro to declare each variable it uses.

In the International area, select whether you want to use the Current Settings to control such items as list separation and the date and time formats, or use the Default Settings. You can make a selection from the Language/Country drop-down list to specify a different type of international formatting for entries.

Module Format Options

In the module for a macro or Visual Basic code you're creating, text formatting can help you make sense of the information. Use the Module Format tab (see Fig. 20.17) to specify the formatting for particular text in the module view.

Figure 20.17
These options
enable you to
control how text
appears in any
module view.

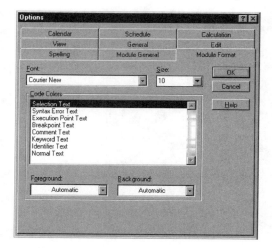

From the Font and Size drop-down lists, select the font and its size
that you want to use for all the text displayed in the module view. In
the Code Colors list, select a particular type of text, such as Comment
Text (in which you indicate notes that are not macro or VBA commands). Select a Foreground and Background color for that type of
text from the corresponding drop-down lists. Continue selecting text
types and specifying colors until you're satisfied with the color settings
for all the text types.

CHAPTER 21

CREATING AND USING MACROS

Every company's needs and projects are unique. Even seasoned temporary workers need a bit of on-site training to conform with the specific processes of a new client company. While company A might want temps to organize files and information by project name, company B might want the information to be ordered by job number. Although such differences seem to be trivial, misunderstanding the requirement or making mistakes in filing can create hours of work down the line for someone else who is searching for particular files.

Like temporary workers, Project can conform to your unique needs in building schedules. Project does so by enabling you to create *macros*, which are mini-programs that you create to perform certain tasks. This chapter introduces the following topics:

- Recording and playing back macros

- Changing macro information, such as the shortcut key

- Making changes in or removing macros

- Creating your own command or button for a macro

- Looking at a few last ideas about macros

Creating Macros

Macros store a series of commands or steps as a single entity, so that you can execute the entire series via the single step of selecting the macro. In earlier computer applications, macros had to be created manually via *scripting*, which was a "user-friendly" euphemism for *programming*. Thus, most people didn't use macros, because macros were too difficult to create.

Today's applications, including Project, enable you to record macros. You don't have to be a whiz to create a macro—all you need to know is how to start the macro recorder and how to execute the commands that you want to save as a macro. Unless you specify otherwise, a recorded and saved macro becomes available to all the files that you work with in Project.

> **NOTE:** The macros you record in Project are built from commands that resemble Microsoft's Visual Basic, Applications Edition (VBA) programming language. Each macro is stored in a VBA macro *module,* which is like a single sheet that can hold multiple macros. By default, the modules and macros are saved with the Global.mpt file, a read-only file that saves your default information for Project. Because macros are based on VBA, you can include macros with VBA programming that you create in Project module sheets. Programming with VBA is beyond the scope of this book, however, so this chapter doesn't cover it.

In two basic situations, you should record macros to automate a task:

- **When the task is lengthy and requires many steps**—Creating a macro to store such a process helps other users to work with the file, particularly if the file is stored on a network. If several users need to create and print a particular report, for example, you can create a macro for that purpose, rather than try to teach each person all the steps that are involved.

- **When the task is repetitive**—Even though formatting the text in a cell as red takes only a few steps, you might regularly need to format cells in red; if so, you'll save time with a macro that does the job for you.

Project enables you to record and work with macros by means of commands in the <u>T</u>ools menu or tools in the Visual Basic toolbar (see Fig. 21.1). To display that toolbar, right-click any toolbar on-screen and then click Visual Basic.

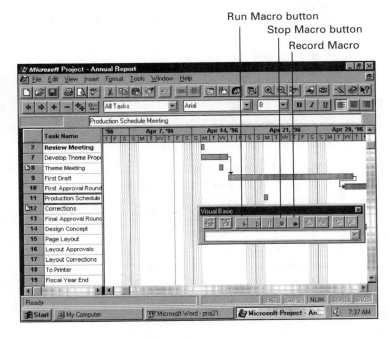

Figure 21.1
The Visual Basic toolbar, which floats in a window, has buttons that look like tape-recorder or VCR controls.

To record a macro, follow these steps:

1. Take whatever preparatory steps are necessary to bring you to the point at which you want to begin recording the macro. If you want to record a macro that formats a selected cell's text in red, for example, go ahead and select a cell in the Task Sheet.

2. Open the <u>T</u>ools menu and click <u>R</u>ecord Macro, or click the Record Macro button on the Visual Basic toolbar. The Record Macro dialog box appears, as shown in Figure 21.2.

3. In the <u>M</u>acro Name text box, enter a unique name for the macro. The name can include an underscore character but can't include spaces or punctuation. **Red_Text**, for example, is an acceptable name.

Figure 21.2
Assign a name to your macro after you start the recording process.

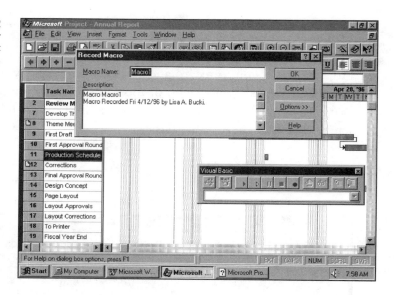

4. (Optional) If you want, edit or add more detail to the Description of the macro.

5. Click the Options button to expand the Record Macro dialog box (see Fig. 21.3).

Adds the macro, by name, to the Tools menu

Specifies how the macro will be saved

Figure 21.3
Here are more detailed options to specify for your macro.

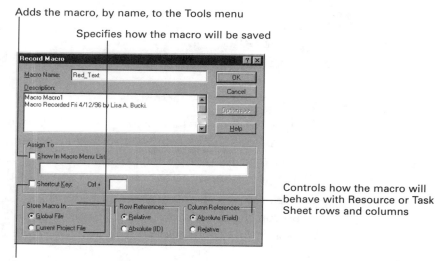

Controls how the macro will behave with Resource or Task Sheet rows and columns

Creates a shortcut-key combination for the macro

6. To list the macro as a command at the bottom of the <u>T</u>ools menu, click to select the <u>S</u>how In Macro Menu List check box. By default, the command name includes the word Run plus the macro name, as in Run Red_Text. You can edit the command name so that it reads the way you want.

7. If you want to be able to run the macro by pressing a shortcut key, click to select the Shortcut <u>K</u>ey check box, and enter the second keystroke for the combination in the Ctrl+ text box.

   You can enter any A–Z keyboard character. You can't use numbers, punctuation marks, or function keys.

NOTE: Avoid specifying a shortcut key that's already assigned to a command in Project, such as Ctrl+X (the Cu<u>t</u> command). If you attempt to specify such a key, Project later asks you to choose another shortcut key (see step 11).

TIP: You can create both a menu command and a shortcut key for the macro you're creating.

8. If you want the macro to be stored only with the currently open file (not recommended, because you might need to use the macro in future files), click to select the <u>C</u>urrent Project File option button in the Store Macro In area of the dialog box.

NOTE: You need to select the <u>C</u>urrent Project File option if you're creating a template file and want the macro to be part of that file.

9. The options in the Row References area control the way that the macro interprets row selections in Task Sheets and

Resource Sheets, and the way that it handles those selections during playback. Select one of the following options:

- Relative means that during playback, the macro selects rows based on the location of the selected cell. Suppose that you selected three rows or cells in three rows (such as rows 1–3) when you recorded the macro, and that before you played back the macro, you selected a cell in row 4. The macro selects rows 4–6, or the specified cells in those rows, during playback.

- Absolute (ID) means that during playback, the macro always selects the same rows (by row number) that were selected when the macro was recorded.

10. The options in the Column References area control the way that the macro interprets column selections in a Task Sheet or Resource Sheet, and the way that it handles those selections during playback. Select one of the following options:

- Absolute (Field) means that during playback, the macro always selects the same field (by field or column name) that was selected when the macro was recorded.

- Relative means that the macro selects columns based on the location of the selected cell. Suppose that you selected two columns or cells in two columns (such as the Start and Finish columns of the Task Sheet) when you recorded the macro, and that before you played back the macro, you selected a cell in the Predecessors column. The macro selects the Predecessors and Resources columns (or the specified cells in those rows) during playback.

11. After you make all your selections, click OK to begin recording the macro.

    If, in step 7, you specified a shortcut key that's already assigned, Project displays a warning (see Fig. 21.4). Click OK, specify another shortcut key, and click OK in the Record Macro dialog box to continue.

12. Perform the steps that you want to record in your macro.

13. When you finish performing all the steps, stop the macro recording by clicking the Stop Macro button on the Visual Basic toolbar, or by opening the Tools menu and clicking Stop Recorder.

Figure 21.4
Project warns you
when the shortcut key
you specified isn't
available.

TIP: If you're creating a macro and want to select only the range of cells in the Task Sheet or Resource Sheet that currently contains entries, select the cell in the upper-left corner of the range, then press Ctrl+Shift+End. This method is better than selecting the entire sheet. This method also is the one to use when you might end up running the macro on different sheets or filtered lists of differing lengths, to ensure that the macro highlights all the rows that contain entries, not just the number of rows that was correct during macro recording.

TIP: Project automatically saves all global macros when you exit the program. If, in step 8, you specified that the macro will be saved with the current file, make sure that you save that file immediately after you record the macro, just for safety.

Running a Macro

After you create a macro, it's immediately available for use. Running a macro is sometimes referred to as *playing back* the macro. To play back any macro, follow these steps:

1. Perform whatever preparatory tasks you need to complete before running the macro. If your macro applies red formatting to text in Task Sheet or Resource Sheet cells, for example, select the row(s), columns(s), or cell(s) to which you want to apply the formatting.

2. Use one of the following methods to execute the macro, depending on how you set up the macro when you created it:

- Press the shortcut key combination that you created for the macro.
- Open the Tools menu and click the command that you created for the macro (see Fig. 21.5).

Figure 21.5
If you added a macro to the Tools menu, simply click the macro name on that menu to run the macro.

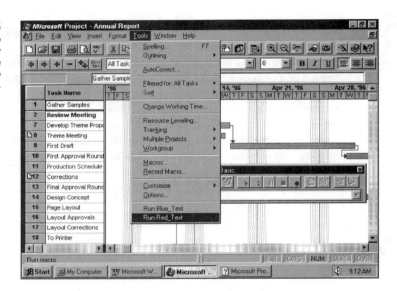

- If you didn't create a shortcut key or menu command to run the macro, click the Run Macro button on the Visual Basic toolbar, or open the Tools menu and click Macros. The Macros dialog box appears (see Fig. 21.6). Select the name of the macro in the Macro Name list, then click the Run button.

Changing Macro Options

The information and options that you specify when you create and store a macro aren't carved in stone. If you initially don't assign a shortcut key to the macro, for example, you can go back and add one. If you want to change the description of a macro, you can do so. If you want to add the macro to the Tools menu or remove the macro from that menu, you can do that, too.

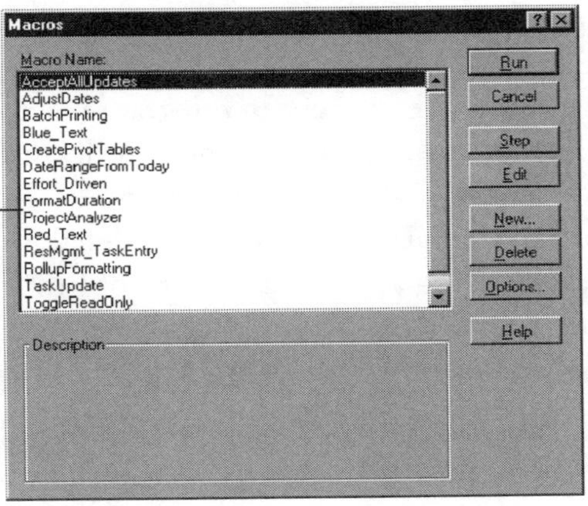

Figure 21.6
This dialog box
enables you to manage
the macros you've

Lists all available
macros, including
some samples that
come with Project

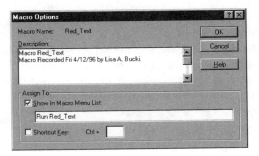

To adjust the options for a macro, follow these steps:

1. Open the <u>T</u>ools menu and click <u>M</u>acros. The Macros dialog box appears.

2. In the <u>M</u>acro Name list, select the name of the macro for which you want to change the options.

3. Click the <u>O</u>ptions button. The Macro Options dialog box appears, as shown in Figure 21.7.

Figure 21.7
Use this dialog box to
adjust the macro
description or shortcut
key.

4. Edit specific options as you want to, using the techniques described earlier in the steps for creating macros.

5. Click OK to close the Macro Options dialog box.

6. Click Close to close the Macros dialog box and activate your new macro options.

Editing Macros

Unless you have time to learn how to integrate macros with complicated VBA coding, you probably don't need to learn how to edit macros, especially if the macros are fairly complex. In such cases, the fastest way to make changes in a macro is to delete the macro (as described in the following section) and re-record it. In other cases, however, making a change or two in a relatively simply macro is much speedier than creating it again from scratch.

This section explains the basics of macro editing, so that you can experiment if you are inclined to do so. Macros and VBA coding are stored in *modules*, which are like pages in the Project Global.mpt file. Each module can store numerous macros or VBA commands. In the module, you edit the macro and VBA commands just as you would edit text. When you leave the module and return to Gantt Chart view (or whatever view you prefer to work in), your changes to the macro take effect.

CAUTION: Even if you are experienced in editing macros and VBA code, there's always a chance of introducing an error that really fouls up the macro. As a precaution, print the original macro code after you display it (and before you make any changes), so that you have a record of what the macro's contents were when the macro worked. To print macros in Project, simply click the Print icon on the Standard toolbar when the macro is displayed in the Code (Module) pane.

Suppose that you created a macro that enters a new task—named "Monthly Meeting"—in the Task Sheet and assigns the task a duration of 2h (two hours). Later, you decide that you no longer want to have a monthly meeting; you just want to prepare and distribute a monthly report. Accordingly, you want the macro to specify the task name as "Monthly Report." To make this change, follow these steps:

1. Open the <u>T</u>ools menu and click <u>M</u>acros. The Macros dialog box appears.

2. In the <u>M</u>acro Name list, select the macro that you want to edit—Month, for this example.

3. Click the <u>E</u>dit button to display the module (Code pane) for the macro.

   The Month module appears in Figure 21.8.

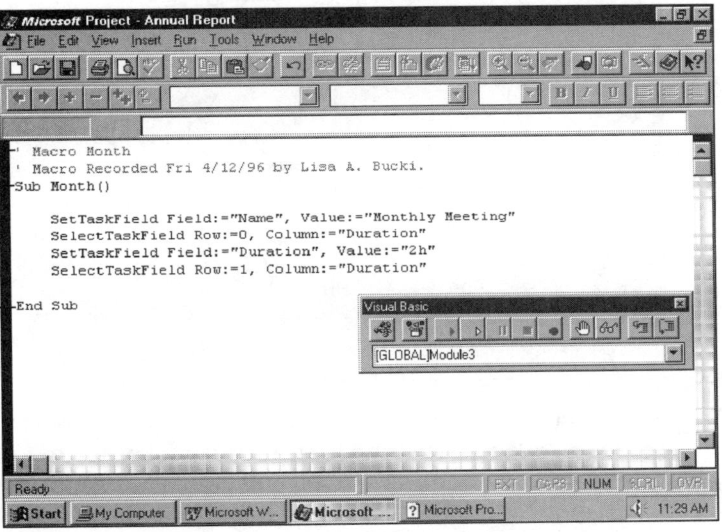

Figure 21.8
The macro looks like specially aligned text in the module.

To create a note or remark, use a single prime (single quote).

These lines start and end the macro; you usually don't want to edit them

```
' Macro Month
' Macro Recorded Fri 4/12/96 by Lisa A. Bucki.
Sub Month()

    SetTaskField Field:="Name", Value:="Monthly Meeting"
    SelectTaskField Row:=0, Column:="Duration"
    SetTaskField Field:="Duration", Value:="2h"
    SelectTaskField Row:=1, Column:="Duration"

End Sub
```

4. Make your changes in the macro's contents, using the same editing techniques that you would use in a typical word processing program such as WordPad or Microsoft Word.

   For this example, because you want to change the task name, first look for the line that defines the Name column and then look for the value assigned there, which is what you want to change. You can double-click the word Meeting to select it, as shown in Figure 21.9, being careful not to select the quotation marks. Then simply type **Report** to replace the selection.

5. When you finish making your changes, open the <u>V</u>iew menu and click the Project view you want to return to.

   For this example, to test your macro, return to <u>G</u>antt Chart view, which you use to enter tasks such as the newly retooled Monthly Report task.

6. Test the macro to ensure that your changes work correctly.

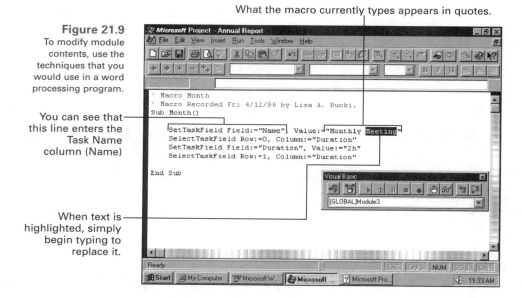

What the macro currently types appears in quotes.

Figure 21.9
To modify module
contents, use the
techniques that you
would use in a word
processing program.

You can see that
this line enters the
Task Name
column (Name)

When text is
highlighted, simply
begin typing to
replace it.

TIP: Project comes with numerous example macros, which are provided to illustrate how more complex macros and VBA coding can be structured and integrated. These macros are excellent learning tools for would-be macro gurus. If you want to see how one of these macros is written, select it in the Macros dialog box. Alternatively, if the macro module is already on-screen, use the module drop-down list in the Visual Basic toolbar to display the macro and VBA contents of other modules.

Deleting Macros

When you no longer need a macro, you can simply delete it from the Macro Name list in the Macros dialog box. If you use many macros, it's good practice to occasionally review and delete the macros you no longer need, just to keep your macro modules and Global.mpt file slim and trim.

To delete a macro, follow these steps:

1. Open the Tools menu and click Macros. The Macros dialog box appears.

2. In the Macro Name list, select the macro you want to delete.

3. Click the Delete button. Project asks you to verify that you want to remove the macro (see Fig. 21.10).

4. Click Yes to delete the macro.

5. Click Close to close the Macros dialog box.

Creating a Macro Menu

Although you can create shortcut keys for the macros you create, remembering shortcut keys can be as difficult as remembering the exact names of macros. You know that you can append the macros that you create to the bottom of the Tools menu, but this method can become unwieldy if you want menu access to more than four or five macros.

In Chapter 20, "Customizing Microsoft Project," you learned the general steps for editing Project's menus and commands. You can use that knowledge to add, to any Project menu bar, a menu that lists all your macros. This procedure not only provides quick access to your macros but also provides more room for listing macros than the Tools menu does.

To create a menu for your macros, follow these steps:

1. Display the Macro Options dialog box, and make sure that the Show In Macro Menu List check box is selected for every macro that you want to include in your menu.

2. Click to open the Tools menu, point to Customize, and click Menu Bars. The Menu Bars dialog box appears (see Fig. 21.11).

3. Select the menu bar to which you want to add the macros menu, then click the Edit button. The Menu Bar Definition dialog box for the current template file (Global.mpt, by default) appears.

Figure 21.11
You can use this dialog box to edit any menu bars that are available in Project.

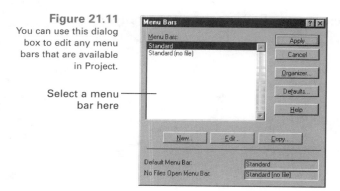

Select a menu bar here

TIP: If you have macros that enable you to open new and existing files, you should make them available in the Standard (no file) menu bar, which appears when no schedule files are open in Project. That way, you can use your macros to open files whether another file is open on-screen or not.

4. Scroll down to the last item on the Tools menu, if that menu exists in the current menu bar, which should display [Macros] (grayed-out) in the Menu Item column and (List of Macros) in the center Command/Macro column (see Fig. 21.12). Click a cell in that row, then click the Cut Rows button. This step removes the list of macros from the bottom of the Tools menu so that it won't appear twice. You can always insert a blank row and reinsert the (List of Macros) item in the center column at a later time to reinstate the macros list at the bottom of the Tools menu.

5. Scroll to the last row of the grid of menu items, which should be blank.

6. In the far-left column of that row, type **Macros** (or any other name that you want to assign to your macros menu) as shown in Figure 21.13.

7. Click the Enter button beside the text entry box. This step completes the entry and inserts a blank line after it. The cell in which you just entered the macro name should remain selected; if it isn't, click it to select it.

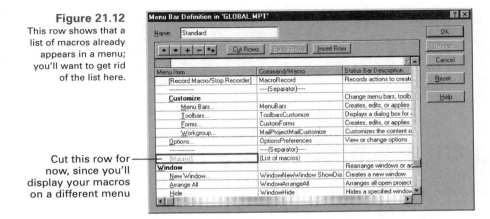

Figure 21.12
This row shows that a list of macros already appears in a menu; you'll want to get rid of the list here.

Cut this row for now, since you'll display your macros on a different menu

Figure 21.13
Enter a name for your macros menu.

Click to promote the entry to a menu name

Enter button

8. Click the promote button (the far-left button above the cells, with the left arrow) to promote the entry to a menu name.

9. Click the middle cell (Command/Macro column) of the new blank row below the menu name you've created.

10. Select List of Macros from the drop-down list next to the text entry box (see Fig. 21.14).

TIP: If you want the menu to display only the macros from a particular module, click the Browse button to select that menu.

Figure 21.14
This option lists all
your macros in a
new menu.

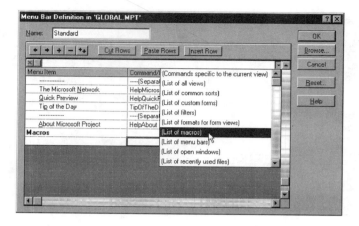

11. Click OK to close the Menu Bar Definition dialog box.
12. Click Apply to close the Menu Bars dialog box and display
    your new menu (see Fig. 21.15).

Figure 21.15
Here's a new menu
named Macros
containing a list of
macros, just as I
specified in the
Menu Bar Definition
dialog box.

Creating a Macro Button

For the ultimate in easy access to the macros that you create, add a
custom toolbar button for the macro to any on-screen toolbar. Then
you can execute your macro simply by clicking its toolbar button.

CAUTION: Although you can assign a macro to an
existing toolbar button, replacing the command that was
originally assigned to that button, this procedure is not
recommended. It would be difficult to recall what the
button's original command was, should you want to
reinstate it.

To create a toolbar button for a macro, follow these steps:

1. As you learned in Chapter 20, drag a new toolbar button onto a toolbar by right-clicking any toolbar, selecting Customize, then dragging the button you want from the Customize dialog box onto the appropriate toolbar. Ideally, the graphic on the button you choose should reflect the function of the macro. (A copy of the button you choose remains in the Customize dialog box, with its original command assignment intact.)

2. Right-click the macro button you just dragged onto the toolbar, then click Customize Tool. The Customize Tool dialog box appears (see Fig. 21.16).

Drag a button to the Formatting toolbar, right-click it, and click Customize Tool.

Figure 21.16
You can use this dialog box to change the command assigned to any toolbar button.

This command is currently assigned to the button.

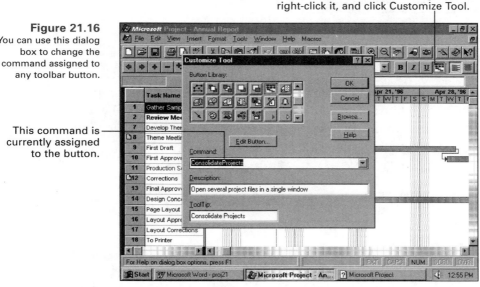

3. Click the Browse button to display the Object Browser dialog box. This dialog box enables you to select macro modules, from which you can choose a macro to attach to the button.

4. If necessary, use the Libraries/Projects drop-down list to select the location where the module you want is stored.

5. In the Classes/Modules list, click the name of the module that holds the macro you want to attach to the button. The list of

macros for that module appears at the right in the
Methods/Properties list (see Fig. 21.17).

Figure 21.17
It's easy to browse for
the macro you want.

Select a module
here...

...and a macro here.

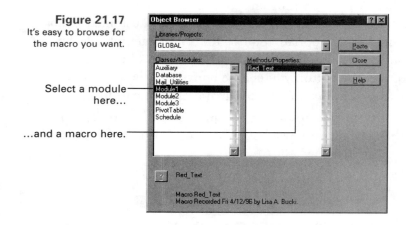

6. Click to select the macro you want, then click the
   Paste button.

7. In the Customize Tool dialog box, enter a Description for the
   button (to explain the button in the status bar) and a ToolTip
   (to describe the button when the user places the mouse
   pointer on it).

8. Click OK to finish creating the tool.

Figure 21.18 shows an example.

A Few More Macro Ideas

This chapter—the final one in the book—has shown you how to create macros to make your work in Project faster and more efficient.
Here are a few other ideas about how to use macros to get the most
out of Microsoft Project:

• Create a macro that inserts a new task, with a particular name
  and duration, that you want to use more than once. Assign a
  shortcut key to run the task.

Figure 21.18
Here's a custom macro
button with its ToolTip
displayed.

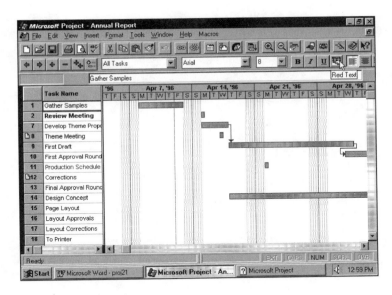

Figure 21.18
Here's a custom macro button with its ToolTip displayed.

- Create a macro to format summary commands in a way that calls even more attention to them. The macro can apply a particular font, color, or emphasis (such as italic). Add a button for the macro to the Formatting toolbar.

- Create a macro that inserts your company logo where you specify (such as in a Gantt chart), so that the logo appears on printouts you send to clients.

- Record macros that change the active view or display a particular Task Sheet table. Create a shortcut key or button for each macro.

- If you supervise a team of people and use Project to manage multiple tasks, create a macro that assigns each person (as a resource) to the currently selected task. Then you can assign a task to a particular worker with a single shortcut key, reducing the time that you spend making assignments.

- If you regularly need to print a particular form or report, create a macro that automates the process, and assign the macro to a toolbar button.

INDEX

FILL IN AND MAIL TODAY

Prima Publishing
P.O. Box 1260BK
Rocklin, CA 95677-1260

USE YOUR VISA/MC AND ORDER BY PHONE:
916-632-4400
OR, TO ORDER BOOKS ONLINE:
sales@primapub.com
YOU CAN ALSO VISIT OUR WEB SITE:
www.primapublishing.com

Please send me the following titles:

Quantity	Title	Amount
_____	_____	_____
_____	_____	_____
_____	_____	_____
_____	_____	_____
_____	_____	_____

Subtotal	$ _____
Postage & Handling ($6.00 for the first books plus $1.00 each additional books)	$ _____
Sales Tax	
7.25% Sales Tax (California only)	
8.25% Sales Tax (Tennessee only)	
5.00% Sales Tax (Maryland only)	
7.00% General Service Tax (Canada)	$ _____
TOTAL (*U.S. funds only*)	$ _____

❑ Check enclosed for $ _____ (payable to Prima Publishing)

Charge my   ❑ Master Card   ❑ Visa

Account No. _____

Exp. Date _____

Signature _____

Your Name _____

Address _____

City/State/Zip _____

Daytime Telephone _____

Satisfaction is guaranteed—or your money back!
Please allow three to four weeks for delivery.
THANK YOU FOR YOUR ORDER

Other Prima Computer Books

ISBN	Title	Release Date
0-7615-0064-2	Build a Web Site	Available Now
1-55958-744-X	The Windows 95 Book	Available Now
0-7615-0383-8	Web Advertising and Marketing	Available Now
1-55958-747-4	Introduction to Internet Security	Available Now
0-7615-0063-4	Researching on the Internet	Available Now
0-7615-0693-4	Internet Information Server	Summer 1996
0-7615-0678-0	Java Applet Powerpack, Vol. 1	Summer 1996
0-7615-0685-3	JavaScript	Summer 1996
0-7615-0684-5	VBScript	Summer 1996
0-7615-0726-4	The Webmaster's Handbook	Summer 1996
0-7615-0691-8	Netscape Fast Track Server	Summer 1996
0-7615-0733-7	Essential Netscape Navigator Gold	Summer 1996
0-7615-0759-0	Web Page Design Guide	Summer 1996